THE

INDONESIAN ECONOMY

SINCE 1966

THE
INDONESIAN ECONOMY
SINCE 1966

SOUTHEAST ASIA'S EMERGING GIANT

Hal Hill

Department of Economics
Research School of Pacific and Asian Studies
Australian National University

CAMBRIDGE
UNIVERSITY PRESS

HC
447
H55
1996

To H.W. Arndt, teacher, colleague, and friend

Published by the Press Syndicate of the University of Cambridge
The Pitt Building, Trumpington Street, Cambridge CB2 1RP, UK
40 West 20th Street, New York, NY 10011–4211, USA
10 Stamford Road, Oakleigh, Melbourne 3166, Australia

© Cambridge University Press 1996
First published 1996

Printed in Hong Kong by Colorcraft

National Library of Australia cataloguing-in-publication data

Hill, Hal.
The Indonesian economy since 1966: Southeast Asia's emerging giant.
Bibliography.
Includes index.
1. Indonesia – Economic policy. 2. Indonesia – Economic
conditions – 1945-. I. Title.
338.9598

Library of Congress cataloguing-in-publication data

Hill, Hal, 1948–
The Indonesian economy since 1966: Southeast Asia's emerging giant / Hal Hill.
p.   cm.
Includes bibliographical references and index.
1. Indonesia – Economic policy. 2. Indonesia – Economic
conditions – 1945-.   I. Title.
HC447.H55   1995
338.9598–dc20   95–17973

A catalogue record for this book is available from the British Library.

ISBN 0 521 49512 1 Hardback
ISBN 0 521 49862 7 Paperback

CONTENTS

For the units, notes and sources of the
Figures, refer to pages 321-8.

TABLES

FIGURES

The English language material on the contemporary Indonesian economy is modest in comparison with that of India, China and Asia's NIEs. Nevertheless, scholars can no longer lament, as Bruce Glassburner did one-quarter of a century ago, in the introduction to his *The Economy of Indonesia* (1971), ' . . . the minor role to which the economics profession of the world has relegated Indonesia'.

There are three journals published on the Indonesian economy, *Ekonomi dan Keuangan Indonesia, Jurnal Ekonomi Indonesia* (both published in Jakarta, and bilingual), and the *Bulletin of Indonesian Economic Studies* (Canberra). Important edited collections have been published over the past 15 years, including (Booth ed. 1992), Booth and McCawley (eds. 1981), and Papanek (1980). During the past decade, specialist books on agriculture, such as Pearson et al. (1991) and several others, have appeared, while the list on industry includes Poot et al. (1990). The World Bank publishes an annual report on the economy, for limited readership but widely circulated, as well as many other specialist reports. Then there are those books with a regional flavour, both general in nature (Hill ed., 1989) and focused (Dick, Fox and Mackie eds, 1993, on East Java). In addition, Indonesia is now regularly the focus of articles both in regional journals, such as the *ASEAN Economic Bulletin, Asian-Pacific Economic Literature*, the *Journal of Asian Business*, and in international journals.

But the literature on the Indonesian economy is still rather limited for a country which ranks as the fourth most populous in the world, as the largest Islamic nation, and as the dominant country in Southeast Asia. Moreover, as yet, there is no volume which provides an integrated treatment of the economy as a whole over the 'New Order' period, that is, from 1966 onwards. This volume is offered as an attempt to fill this lacuna. It cannot match the detailed approach of the specialized sectoral volumes, nor those which focus on a particular subperiod of the New Order. But it may be attractive to readers who want the 'big picture' of the past quarter century or more of Indonesian economic development.

Writing a book is often akin to setting off on an adventure trail, uncertain where the path will lead. So it was with this volume in some respects. It had its origins in a chapter I wrote for a volume with a group of Australian colleagues surveying the New Order's development from a variety of disciplinary perspectives, which appeared as Hill (ed., 1994). The first draft of that chapter exceeded the specified limit on length by a factor of three, and even then there was much that I had wanted to write about. More or less by accident, then, and aided by some friendly encouragement from colleagues, this book began to take shape out of this process. Like the chapter in the book, I have attempted to write this volume for a general audience, grounded thoroughly (I hope) in the basic principles of analytical economics, but accessible still to readers who do not have an understanding of—or interest in—advanced economic theory. Because the subject is a very large one I have taken care to provide a reasonably comprehensive bibliography for further reading.

In writing this book I have incurred many debts, especially in Canberra and Jakarta, and one of the most satisfying features of completing a book is the opportunity it affords to thank one's colleagues and friends.

First and foremost, I wish to record my intellectual and personal debt to H.W. Arndt. The major international scholar of the Indonesian economy since the mid-1960s, he has been an inspiration to me in the 20 years I have known him, as supervisor, colleague and friend. No-one reads drafts as carefully, promptly, or thoughtfully as Heinz does! Moreover, to the extent that Australia has established an international reputation for work on the Indonesian economy, a large part of the credit goes to him, for his foresight in establishing the ANU Indonesia Project, and for nurturing it in its infant industry stage. As a small token of my gratitude, I dedicate this book to him.

I have incurred many other debts in Canberra. The Indonesia Project, Department of Economics, Research School of Pacific and Asian Studies has provided a most congenial home on and off for some 20 years, always providing the critical mass to sustain works of scholarship on the country's economy. In 1975 I was fortunate enough to obtain a PhD scholarship which *inter alia* enabled me to wander around Indonesia as an impecunious but curious graduate student for some 16 months. Many people in Canberra then and since have assisted me in various ways, most of all in providing a stimulating research environment. Regrettably I cannot thank them all, but I do want to record my appreciation in particular to Peter McCawley and Chris Manning, together with Colin Barlow, Ross Garnaut, Jamie Mackie, and Ross McLeod.

In Indonesia it has been my privilege to have interacted with a remarkable group of economists, who have been only too willing to take time from extraordinarily busy schedules to proffer advice and wisdom. Ideally, this sort of book should have been written by one of them. One day it will be. But for the present they are all too busy doing more important things, such as offering high-level policy advice, engaging in major public debates concerning the future of economic policy in their country, as well as teaching and specialized research and publications. Over the years my closest colleague in Indonesia has been Thee Kian Wie, always generous to a fault and a model of commitment to scholarly values. I also want to place on record my thanks to—and admiration of—Iwan Azis, Boediono, Anwar Nasution, Mari Pangestu, Moh. Sadli, Sjahrir, and Hadi Soesastro for all their assistance.

Among my other international colleagues and friends, I also wish to record special thanks to Bruce Glassburner, University of California, Davis for all his assistance over the years, on this project and many others.

The Indonesia Project at the ANU has been sustained in its work by a grant from the Australian Department of Foreign Affairs and Trade, for which my colleagues and I are most grateful. In the early stages of this book, Catherina Williams and the late Sjahid Boenjamin kindly assisted with the collection of statistics. As always, Prue Phillips and the staff at the ANU's International Economic Data Bank were friendly and helpful. Carolyn Dalton, Julie Londey, Norma Hiscock, and Winnie Pradela ably assisted with the preparation of the text and tables. Marion Fahrer of Alphatex read the penultimate draft thoroughly and provided expert editorial advice.

Sections of this book were written during a period of Outside Studies which I took in 1993. For their assistance in providing a friendly and congenial environment, I particularly want to thank Sanjaya Lall and Arthur Stockwin at the University of Oxford, together with St Antony's College and the Institute of Economics and Statistics; and Jack Bresnan, Hugh Patrick and staff of the Pacific Basin Studies Program, East Asian Institute, Columbia University.

Last, but certainly not least, I want to thank my family. They have endured my absences, silences and preoccupations with good grace. Most of the time they simply shrugged in disbelief as I sat in front of my computer. This book will not be high on their reading lists, but they can now be reassured that at least there was something going on during all this time!

Hal Hill
Canberra

AFTA	ASEAN Free Trade Area
APEC	Asia-Pacific Economic Cooperation
ASEAN	Association of Southeast Asian Nations
BAPPEDA	Badan Perencanaan Pembangunan Daerah, Regional Planning Board
BAPPENAS	Badan Perencanaan Pembangunan Nasional, National Planning Board
becak	rickshaw
BIES	Bulletin of Indonesian Economic Studies
BKPM	Badan Koordinasi Penanaman Modal, Investment Coordinating Board
BPIS	Badan Pengelola Industri Strategis, Strategic Industries Board
BPS	Biro Pusat Statistik, Central Bureau of Statistics
BULOG	Badan Urusan Logistik, Food Distribution Agency
CGI	Consultative Group for Indonesia, replacing IGGI in 1992
Dati I (II)	Daerah Tingkat I (II), First (Second) Level of Regional Authority, respectively province, kabupaten/ kotamadya
daerah	region; commonly used to refer to regions outside of Jakarta, or other major urban concentrations
DIP	Daftar Isian Proyek, development budget allocation
DNEA	developing Northeast Asia, defined to include China, Hong Kong, South Korea, and Taiwan
Eastern Indonesia	a term which usually refers to all regions of Indonesia east of Bali and Kalimantan; in some cases, however, Bali and all or part of Kalimantan are also included in this region
EKI	Ekonomi dan Keuangan Indonesia, Economics and Finance of Indonesia, Indonesia's longest-established economics journal
FAO	Food and Agriculture Organization, of the United Nations
GATT	General Agreement on Tariffs and Trade
GDP	gross domestic product
GDY	gross domestic income; GDP adjusted for terms of trade movements
GRP	gross regional product
HYVs	high yielding varieties, of rice and other agricultural crops
IEDB	International Economic Data Bank, Research School of Pacific and Asian Studies, Australian National University
IGGI	Inter-Governmental Group for Indonesia, the international donor consortium, in existence until 1992
IMR	infant mortality rate
INPRES	Instruksi Presiden, Presidential Instruction

kabupaten	administrative unit below the province, excluding major urban centres (kotamadya)
KIK	kredit investasi kecil, small credits program, for fixed capital
KMKP	kredit modal kerja permanen, small credits program, for working capital
kotamadya	municipality, an administrative unit below the province
kretek	clove-flavoured cigarettes
Lampiran	(Lampiran Pidato Kenegaraan), Attachment to the President's National Address, delivered annually on 16 August
LNG	liquified natural gas
Migas	minyak dan gas, oil and gas
New Order/Orde Baru	refers to the period since the commencement of President Soeharto's rule, generally taken from March 1966, although sometimes interpreted in a constitutional sense to be from 1967
NIEs	newly industrializing economies
NODR	non-oil domestic revenue
Nota Keuangan	budget, delivered annually in early January
NTB	non-tariff barrier
Panca Sila	the five guiding principles of the Indonesian state
Pertamina	the state-owned oil and gas company
PPP	purchasing power parity
pribumi	indigenous people, as distinct from non-pribumi, mainly ethnic Chinese
pusat	literally 'centre', commonly used as a term to refer to the seat of national government, Jakarta
R&D	research and development
Repelita	Rencana Pembangunan Lima Tahun, Five Year Development Plan
Rp	rupiah
SEs	state-owned enterprises
SSI	small-scale industry
Susenas	Survey Sosial-Ekonomi Nasional, National Socio-Economic Survey, undertaken by BPS
WTO	World Trade Organization

Note: Unless otherwise specified, all $ refer to US$.

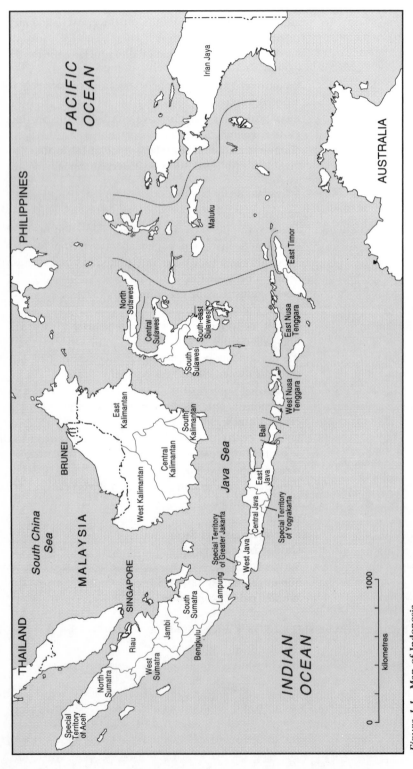

Figure 1.1 Map of Indonesia

Introduction

PRELUDE: A 1960S BASKET CASE

If the central purpose of economics is to understand why and how growth rates vary across countries and over time, Indonesia is surely one of the best laboratories. By the mid-1960s, many informed observers despaired of any prospect of significant economic advance. Benjamin Higgins, the author of the most influential book on Development Economics at that time, and one who had extensive experience of the country during the 1950s, characterized Indonesia as the "chronic dropout". He concluded that "Indonesia must surely be accounted the number one failure among the major underdeveloped countries" (Higgins, 1968, p. 678). Some years earlier, in his introduction to Geertz's classic *Agricultural Involution*, Higgins wrote: "The story of Java seems to be one of repeated nipping off of a budding entrepreneurial upsurge by a political elite essentially hostile to it" (p. ix).

Gunnar Myrdal, in his monumental *Asian Drama*, offered an equally sober assessment: "As things look at the beginning of 1966, there seems to be little prospect of rapid economic growth in Indonesia" (Myrdal, 1969, p. 489). Other social scientists were equally pessimistic, with the Demographer Nathan Keyfitz fearing that population pressure on Java was becoming so intense that the island was " ... asphyxiating for want of land" (Keyfitz, 1965, p. 503).

Indonesia in 1965 was a "basket case", its economic problems at least as serious as those of today's least developed countries in Africa and Asia. Two knowledgeable observers, one a very senior official, the other an academic, captured the flavour of the seemingly hopeless situation then:

> *Any person who entertains the idea that Indonesian society is experiencing a favourable economic situation is guilty of lack of intensive study ... If we fulfil all our [foreign debt] obligations, we have no foreign exchange left to spend for our routine needs ... In 1965 prices in general rose by more than 500 per cent ... In the 1950s the state budget sustained deficits of 10 to 30 per cent of receipts and in the 1960s it soared to more than 100 per cent. In 1965 it even reached 300 per cent. (Sultan Hamengkubuwono IX, quoted in J. Panglaykim and H.W. Arndt, 1966, pp. 3, 19)*

> *A decade of ever-increasing economic mismanagement [in Indonesia] had brought a degree of economic breakdown with few parallels in modern history. The country was literally bankrupt, unable to meet payments due to foreign debt ... Export earnings had fallen to a level where they were barely sufficient to finance half the country's minimum requirements, excluding debt service. (Arndt, 1984, p. 29)*

Nor were social conditions any better, as highlighted by the following quotation from an informed observer of Indonesia during the mid-1960s:

> *In spite of official reiteration of the goal of a just and prosperous society, the impression of many observers has been that along with a decline in per capita income, the contrast between rich and poor has actually sharpened. Real wages have fallen heavily. Yet the scale of conspicuous consumption in Djakarta seems to have grown ... the sharp increase in the number of passenger cars, at a time when public transport is deteriorating seriously, gives some indication [of the gap] ... every time there are new import–export provisions steps are taken to halt the import of luxury goods, but somehow they always get in. (Castles, 1965, pp. 38–39)*

Following the cessation of hostilities with the Dutch in 1949, Indonesia experienced modest economic progress during the early years of Independence. However, the political environment became increasingly unstable and unpredictable towards the end of the decade, especially following the regional insurrections and the expropriation of Dutch property in 1957–58. In his Independence Day speech of 17 August 1959, President Sukarno inaugurated "Guided Democracy" (*Demokrasi Terpimpin*) and its corollary "Guided Economy" (*Ekonomi Terpimpin*). The President also issued a document which was henceforth to provide the guiding framework for political philosophy and economic policy. These included a return to the 1945 Constitution, the adoption of socialism (*Socialisme à la Indonesia*, in the President's words), guided democracy and economy, and an emphasis on the development of a distinct Indonesian identity (*Kepribadian Indonesia*).[1]

In 1960 an Eight Year Plan was drawn up, symbolically comprising eight volumes, 17 chapters and 1945 paragraphs, reflecting the date of the country's Independence. According to the Plan, Indonesia was to become self-sufficient in food, clothing and basic necessities (*sandang-pangan*) within three years. In the remaining five years the country was to take-off into "self-sustained growth". The target set in the plan was annual rice and clothing availability of 115 kgs and 15 metres per capita, respectively. As the economy deteriorated, these targets were soon revised downwards, to 80 kgs and 12 metres. By 1964 the Plan was abandoned, and a new strategy was announced, emphasizing self-sufficiency and self-reliance.[2] In early 1965 Indonesia withdrew from the United Nations and established ever closer relations with China and North Korea. The political lexicon extended to include a dizzying array of new acronyms: *Necolim* (neo-colonialism), *Conefo* (Conference of New Emerging Forces, scheduled for Jakarta in the second half of 1966, but never held), *Ganyang* (crush) *Malaysia* and its counterpart Konfrontasi, *Oldefo* (old-established forces, of "colonialism and feudalism and imperialism"), and *Dekon* (*Deklarasi Ekonomi*, Economic Declaration), in addition to those mentioned above.

The poor quality of economic statistics over this period precludes a detailed assessment of economic performance. But the main picture is clear enough.[3] The economy did not expand over the 1961–64 period, the modest increase in 1965 being purely the result of a good agricultural season (Table 1.1, line 1). This stagnation resulted in declining per capita incomes for most of the period, particularly so in 1962–63 (line 2). Another consequence was the absence of any structural change in this period, or indeed over the whole of the first two decades of Independence. This was to be in marked contrast to the period after 1966. In fact the share of agriculture rose marginally over this period. Being less monetized and less reliant on the uncertain supply of

Table 1.1 **Indicators of Economic Development, 1960–65**

	1960	1961	1962	1963	1964	1965
1. NDP (Rp billion), 1960 prices	391	407	403	396	407	430
2. Per capita income, % change	−1.6	1.7	−3.0	−4.0	0.3	3.2
3. Money supply (M1): % increase	37	41	101	94	156	302
4. % increase due to budget deficit	·· 19	134	97	115	104	90
5. Budget deficit as % of expenditure	17	30	39	51	58	63
6. Inflation (CPI, % increase)	20	95	156	129	135	594

Source: Report of Bank Indonesia for the Financial Years 1960-65 (1967).

imported inputs, this sector withstood the economic ravages better than most. Production of rice, the basic staple, only just kept pace with population growth, however.

The immediate and direct causes of rising inflation were not difficult to detect. The money supply, defined in the table as narrow money (M1), began to rise quickly, from around 40 per cent in the early 1960s, to 100 per cent in 1962-63, and 300 per cent in 1965 (line 3). These increases in turn were fed directly by the galloping budget deficit, financed by the simple expedient of printing more money. From 1963 the deficit exceeded the value of revenue collections, by a factor of almost two to one (line 5). This deficit was by far the most important factor in the rapidly escalating supply of money (line 4). Many factors contributed to this downward spiral of economic decline and hyperinflation, not least the internal momentum of an eroding tax base and a flight from financial to real assets. An important additional factor was the government's "confrontation" of the newly independent country of Malaysia. The financing of this campaign absorbed about 19 per cent of total government expenditures in 1965, in addition to the claim of the regular defence budget of a further 21 per cent.

INDONESIA—THEN AND NOW

A key theme of this book is the remarkable transformation in the Indonesian economy since 1966. The Indonesia of the mid-1990s is almost unrecognizable in a comparison with that of the mid-1960s. From the despair of the earlier period, the new regime was able to engineer an amazingly rapid recovery, as manifested in sharply declining inflation and rising growth. Indeed, a little more than a decade on, Indonesia was being hailed as one of Asia's success stories. Economists cite Indonesia from 1966 to 1968 as one of the most effective instances of inflation control in the twentieth century. By the late 1980s Indonesia was being classified among the select group of developing countries destined shortly to become newly industrialized economies, following the successful path of Asia's outward-looking industrial economies. President Soeharto has received international awards in recognition of the country's success in food production and family planning. Once the world's largest importers of rice, Indonesia achieved self-sufficiency in this crop in the mid-1980s. The country was held up as a model among the OPEC group in investing its oil revenue gains effectively and in adjusting quickly to declining oil prices in the early 1980s.[4] Later in the decade, the country attracted international attention for its continuing success in poverty alleviation, even during the period of painful macroeconomic stabilization occasioned by a halving of world oil prices.

A brief comparison of economic conditions and indicators at the outset of the New Order period and more than 25 years later is a useful reminder that, immense though Indonesia's current economic challenges are, the achievements have been quite extraordinary in many respects. According to virtually every indicator, the improvements between the mid-1960s and the early 1990s have been striking (Table 1.2).

Real per capita GDP has more than trebled in just a little over one generation, and the economic decline of the first half of the 1960s has given way to strong positive growth for almost the entire period since 1966. Virtually all sectors of the economy have performed impressively. Rice yields have risen quickly, approximately doubling in the case of Java. Much of the impetus has come from various intensification programs, the coverage of which has risen from about 20 per cent to 85 per cent of area cropped. Rising output has resulted in a sharp increase—almost 50 per cent—in average daily calorie consumption. Indonesia barely possessed a modern industrial sector in 1965. Subsequently, increases in industrial output of 10-fold or more have not been uncommon, across a range of sectors. Even the per capita output of a "basic good" such as textiles has risen by more than 600 per cent. The transport infrastructure has experienced a virtual revolution in terms of both road and air capacity and the passenger fleet, with large increases in all sectors except rail. Underpinning these changes has been macroeconomic stability, as reflected in reduced inflation. External debt has of course risen enormously in absolute terms. But by and large these borrowings have been sustainable, as measured by the capacity to service them. Investment has also risen sharply; as a percentage of GDP the ratio peaked at over 30 per cent during the oil boom period, some four times the percentage of the mid-1960s.

High growth has been accompanied by equally rapid structural change. Agriculture's share of GDP is now little more than one-third of that of the mid-1960s. The share of industry has more than trebled, and manufacturing overtook agriculture in terms of value added in 1991. Manufacturing once consisted primarily of food and rubber processing, but these sectors have now shrunk to less than one-fifth of their former share. These economic changes have been mirrored by equally impressive social changes. Poverty incidence has fallen sharply, in virtually all regions of the country. The percentage of the population with no schooling is just one-third of the figure in the 1960s, while the tertiary-educated population has expanded extremely rapidly.

INDONESIA'S PERFORMANCE IN COMPARATIVE PERSPECTIVE

Comparative assessment is an important tool in evaluating a country's performance: a modest growth rate may appear impressive or mediocre depending on the international yardstick employed. Which are the appropriate comparators in Indonesia's case? Neighbouring ASEAN states, sharing proximity and some ethnic/cultural similarities, are one possibility. Others are China and India, large Asian states with per capita incomes not too far below that of Indonesia. Then there are some of the large OPEC nations, similarly affected by the oil boom and bust. All three groups are of some relevance. Equally, however, there are enough "special" features in the Indonesian record to warn against pushing a comparative assessment too far.

Table 1.2 **Indicators of Economic Development, mid-1960s to early 1990**

Indicators	mid-1960s	early 1990s
1. Real GDP per capita:		
Growth (%)	±0	±5
$1991	190	610
	(1965)	(1991)
2. Shares of GDP (%):		
Agriculture	53	19
Industry	11	40
Manufacturing	8	21
3. Employment: % in agriculture	73	50
	(1961)	(1990)
4. Industry: % of food and rubber		
products in total manufacturing	60	12
	(1963)	(1986)
5. Industrial production per capita:		
Textiles (metres)	4.1	28.0
Electricity (kWh)	17.7	218
Fertilizer (kgs)	1.1	39.1
6. Agriculture and nutrition:		
Daily calories/capita	1,816	2,605
Rice yields (tons/ha)	2.1	4.3
% rice under intensification	±20	85
7. Investment:		
Gross domestic investment as % of GDP	8	35
8. Monetary conditions:		
Inflation (% increase)	>500	5–10
Broad money/GDP (%)	7	46
9. Debt:		
Total ($ billion)	2.4	84
% of exports	524	231
10. Transport/infrastructure:		
Domestic air travel (million departures)	0.4	7.8
% of roads in 'good' condition	5	31
Registered motor vehicles ('000)		
Buses and 'colts'	20	542
Trucks	93	1,405
Motor cycles	308	6,083
11. Education: % of population with:		
No schooling	68.1	18.9
Tertiary education	0.1	1.6
	(1961)	(1990)
12. Poverty:		
Java % very poor	61	10
% 'sufficient'	8	36
Outside Java % very poor	52	7
% 'sufficient'	10	47

kWh – kilowatt hours.
kgs – kilograms.
ha – hectares.

Table 1.3 Comparative Indicators of Economic and Social Development

	Indonesia	Other ASEAN		Large Asian countries		Other OPEC		Lower middle-income countries
(1) Economic indicators		Philippines	Thailand	China	India	Mexico	Nigeria	
GNP per capita—$1992	670	770	1,840	470	310	3,470	320	1,590
—$, 1992, PPP	2,970	2,480	5,890	1,910	1,210	7,490	1,440	
growth, 1960–80 (%)	4.0	2.8	4.7	n.a.	1.4	2.6	4.1	3.8
1980–92 (%)	4.0	-1.0	6.0	7.6	3.1	-0.2	-0.4	-0.1
Inflation (%)								
1965–80	36	11	6	0	8	13	15	24
1980–92	8	14	4	7	9	62	19	41
Agricultural growth (%)								
1965–80	4.3	3.9	4.6	2.8	2.5	3.2	1.7	3.6
1980–92	3.1	1.0	4.1	5.4	3.2	0.6	3.6	2.5
Agriculture's share in GDP–1992 (%)	19	22	12	27	32	8	37	17
% decline 1965–92	63	15	63	29	27	43	33	23
Index of food production per capita 1988–90 (1969–71 = 100)	145	103	136	154	122	109	97	107
Gross domestic investment (% of GDP)								
1965	8	21	20	24	17	20	15	19
1992	35	23	40	36	23	24	18	23
Central govt expenditure (% of GNP)								
1972	15	14	17	n.a.	11	11	9	17
1992	19	19	15	n.a.	17	18	n.a.	15
Exports as % of GDP – 1992	29	29	36	20	10	13	39	28
Terms of trade, 1992 (1970 = 100)	196	48	45	n.a.	59	80	124	n.a.
Net ODA as % of GNP – 1991	1.6	2.3	0.7	0.4	1.1	0.1	0.8	1.8
Debt service as % of exports – 1992	32	28	14	10	25	44	29	18
(2) Social indicators								
Life expectancy (years), 1991	60	65	69	69	60	70	52	67
Adult illiteracy (%), 1990	23	10	7	27	52	13	49	26
Infant mortality (per 1000), 1991	74	41	27	38	90	36	85	42
% decline 1965–91	42	43	69	58	40	56	48	59
Daily calorie supply (per capita), 1989	2,750	2,375	2,316	2,639	2,229	3,052	2,312	2,768
% increase 1965–89	54	27	8	37	10	19	6	15

n.a. – not available.
In some cases data refer to one year earlier than that stated.

Source: World Bank, World Development Report, Washington, DC, various issues.

Indonesia has performed well by most comparative indicators, economic and social (Table 1.3). Its per capita GNP is less than that of most of its East Asian neighbours, at official exchange rates and in purchasing power parity (PPP) terms, although among the countries selected in the sample it exceeds that of the two Asian giants (China and India) and Nigeria. From 1965 to 1992 it grew faster than most of them, the exceptions being China, another country which enacted major reforms during this period, and Thailand (by a very small margin). Agriculture played a key role in this superior record, with Indonesia among the top performers both in the growth of output and food production, again exceeded only by the two East Asian stars. The contrast here with the two OPEC states is particularly stark, with agricultural production failing to keep up with population growth in some or all of the period under examination. Despite this rapid growth, Indonesia experienced the largest decline in the share of agriculture. The expanding oil sector explains part of the decline. Another factor was the underdeveloped state of the industrial-service sectors in 1965 and their dynamism thereafter.

Other macroeconomic and trade indicators are illuminating. Indonesia's record on inflation is moderately good, although inferior to most Asian countries in the sample. Investment levels have risen sharply since the mid 1960s, and Indonesia's record is comparable with most of the others, especially since 1992 was well past the decade of the oil-financed investment boom. Similarly, government expenditure is in the mid-range of the sample. For a large country, Indonesia has quite high exposure to international trade, although the terms of this engagement are shifting from commodity exports to manufactures. That Indonesia has profited unambiguously from its reintegration into the international economy is illustrated by its terms of trade and foreign aid receipts. Its terms of trade in 1992 were still about double the figure in 1970, even after the sharp fall in oil prices in the mid-1980s, and in marked contrast to the declining figures recorded for all other countries except Nigeria. Aid to Indonesia remains significant, in most cases at least double the share of GNP found in the Asian giants and the OPEC states. Indonesia's low income, its reform-minded government, and the constructive relationship with its donors have all played a part in this favourable outcome. However, its debt service, while manageable, is a good deal more onerous than most of the other countries.

From an international perspective Indonesia's social achievements are satisfactory, but not as impressive as its economic indicators. Relative to the other countries examined in Table 1.3, its life expectancy exceeds only that of Nigeria, while in adult illiteracy and infant mortality (and its rate of decline) Indonesia adopts an intermediate position, generally behind its East Asian neighbours. Reflecting the strong agricultural performance, per capita food production has risen significantly, although the incidence of infant malnutrition remains very high in comparative terms. The explanation for lagging social performance—relatively speaking—probably has to do with the inherited backlog in the mid 1960s and the fact that, for the first 10 to 15 years especially, the New Order government accorded a higher priority to economic sectors and physical infrastructure.

Much of the detailed comparative research on Indonesia has been with reference to the OPEC group where, faced with a common exogenous shock, it is possible to trace government responses to the windfall oil revenue. Gelb and Associates (1988) provide the most comprehensive assessment in their six-country study over the 1974–84 period. The Indonesian record compares very favourably with the other five,[5] and it would be even more impressive if the story were continued through until the 1990s. The windfall gains accruing to Indonesia were, relatively, the smallest of the six (about 17 per cent of GDP compared with a group average of 23 per cent). It had easily the most impressive economic—and particularly agricultural—performance, and it directed the highest proportion of its development spending to rural areas. Gelb concluded Indonesia was " . . . the only country in the sample to implement a determined policy of expenditure reduction and exchange rate realignment before the fading of the second oil boom" (p. 91). Moreover, "only Indonesia and possibly Ecuador managed to strengthen and diversify the non-hydrocarbon traded sectors during the windfall decade" (p. 136).

The differences were further illuminated in the Indonesia–Nigeria case by Pinto (1987). Although inflation and money supply growth were similar in the two countries, Indonesia's fiscal discipline was much tighter. Its exchange rate policy had restored competitiveness to the non-oil tradeables sector by the mid-1980s, while its public expenditure mix was more "balanced" between physical infrastructure, education, agriculture and industry. Moreover, Indonesian agriculture performed well throughout the period, in contrast to the rapid increase in Nigeria's food imports.

Other comparative studies have drawn favourable attention to Indonesia's strong economic and equity performance. A study sponsored by the OECD Development Centre examined the effects of macroeconomic adjustment policies on poverty and income distribution in six developing countries, of which Indonesia was one. The findings, published in a special issue of *World Development* (19(11), 1991), emphasized Indonesia's credible record: "Indonesia not only achieved stabilization but also carried out structural reforms that helped to increase the credibility of its adjustment program" (p. 1500). Moreover, Indonesia and Malaysia were the only countries in the sample which " . . . managed to adjust without any apparent adverse impact on the poor, despite some cuts in social expenditures in Indonesia" (p. 1505).

A massive 17-country comparative assessment of macroeconomic adjustment and stabilization over the 1973–89 period (Little et al., 1993), sponsored by the World Bank and covering most major regions in the developing world, also included Indonesia. The study makes numerous, extensive, and generally positive references to the latter's experience (for example, pp. 91-5, 165-6, 205-9). Grouping Indonesia with Korea and Thailand as among the best performers, it comments favourably on Indonesia's generally cautious fiscal policy and its effective exchange rate management. It also praises the regime's capacity to respond quickly to adverse external circumstances, such as over the 1982-86 period, and draws attention to its close relationship with the international donor community, and international capital markets more generally.

OUTLINE OF THIS BOOK

This book examines Indonesia's economic development and policy since 1966 both in terms of processes and outcomes. The most obvious outcomes have been generally high economic growth, rapid structural and technological change, and improved indicators of human welfare. The processes trace the formulation of policy at both a macro and a sectoral level, and the government's response to the many large and unanticipated exogenous shocks experienced since 1966. Wherever possible, the story is a continuous one since 1966. However, data limitations preclude such an approach in some instances. There is something of a discontinuity in the late 1960s, in the sense that many long-run, consistent data series released by the government begin only in 1969, when the first Five Year Plan (*Repelita*) was launched.

Chapter 2 provides an overview of Indonesian economic development over the whole period. An attempt is made to sketch the major parameters—growth, structural change, productivity increases, the impact of international trade, and so on, and also to delineate key sub-phases. The next two chapters assess the basic 'building blocks' of the New Order's macroeconomic developments, focusing on monetary and fiscal policy respectively. Chapter 5 investigates international dimensions of the record, including patterns of trade, foreign investment and aid. Particular attention is given to the successful reforms of the 1980s. Chapter 6 examines the nature and framework of government intervention and planning efforts. There is an attempt to identify shifts in the ideological climate over this period, and their manifestation in terms of policy directions.

The next three chapters analyze developments at the sectoral level, considering agriculture, industry and services, in turn. In Chapter 10 the attention turns to indicators of social progress, in particular, trends in poverty alleviation, inequality, health and education. Being such a spatially diverse nation, a separate Chapter (11) is devoted to regional dimensions of Indonesian development. Finally, Chapter 12 summarizes the record, emphasizes key lessons from the country's development experience since 1966, and identifies some of the factors which are likely to shape the course of future development.

Two further observations on the approach adopted in this book are pertinent. I am concerned basically with the record of economic development, of what policies were adopted, and how, and what their outcomes have been. I stray into the realm of political economy on occasions, as is inevitable in such a book. But essentially I am leaving it to political scientists to explain the 'whys'—why certain policies were adopted, and in what form and sequence.[6] Many of the answers to these questions are fairly straightforward: conservative macroeconomic policies in response to the traumas of the 1960s; open trade and investment policies from the late 1960s, as an essential prerequisite for rejoining the international community and receiving large volumes of development assistance; an increasingly interventionist policy regime during the oil boom period to ameliorate nationalist sentiment; and a strong commitment to regional development, in view of the regional insurrections in 1957-58. But to understand why certain policies were implemented in many areas, particularly at the micro level, a good deal of the work has to be left to political scientists, hopefully those of the economically literate variety.

Much of the Indonesian record since 1966 is a confirmation of the principles of orthodoxy. The characterization of that record as a "miracle" may serve to attract attention to significant economic developments (cf, World Bank, 1993), but the recipe of success is no great secret. A new, orthodox and pragmatic regime of economic management after 1966 signalled a decisive change in direction. The government provided a stable economic and political environment, property rights were respected, Indonesia re-entered the international community, prices—especially the exchange rate—reflected conditions of demand and supply, and the provision of public goods such as physical and social infrastructure began to increase substantially.

Viewed in this light, Indonesia's dramatic transformation after 1966 is not so difficult to explain. As one leading economic historian remarks, in the broad sweep of development:

> *The propensity for growth will assert and reassert itself,* ceteris paribus, *and the question becomes, what were the constraints lurking in the* cet. par. *clause? . . . [W]e need to construct a new explanation of how growth starts, and here the most fruitful approach seems to be to consider the removal of impediments, not to search for laser-beam miracles. (Jones, 1988, pp. 186, 193-4)*

The implication of this assertion is that, except in abnormal periods of turbulence, growth is a natural state of affairs. For growth to occur there must be a conducive economic environment, and a government neither overbearing nor incapacitated. The Indonesian regime since 1966 broadly fits this description. It is easy to document all manner of mistakes, scandals and inappropriate interventions—hence the description of the record as a 'qualified success story'. But public administration and economic management of a poor, ethnically diverse archipelagic state such as Indonesia is a daunting task. The essential recipe is one in which the government has got its policies 'right' more often than it has not, and has usually displayed political will to take tough and unpopular decisions when necessary.

The second observation, perhaps equally obvious, is that Indonesia's record over this period provides no grounds for complacency. Viewed from a 1965 perspective Indonesia's performance has been better than most observers would have dared to hope for. But conditions were so disastrous in 1965 that any return to normalcy would have resulted in significant improvements. And, although domestic policies have been the critical ingredient, the international environment has been especially conducive to growth. Indonesia experienced a huge increase in its terms of trade from the early 1970s. It was so large that even after the decline in oil prices in 1985–86 the ratio remained well above the 1970 figure. The country has enjoyed continued access to foreign aid, particularly when it needed it, in the second half of the 1960s and in the mid-1980s. Exogenous technical change in the form of the new rice varieties assisted in transforming Indonesia's once gloomy agricultural prospects. The country has been rather cavalier in the exploitation of its natural resources, both renewable and non-renewable. Moreover, even recognizing this record, in the political arena the revolution of rising expectations heavily discounts such achievements. For a new generation of Indonesians entering the workforce, the universities and the political processes, a comparison with the 1960s is irrelevant. Their future options are defined by what is on offer in the booming East Asian economies, not the stagnation which was present in Indonesia before 1966 and is still evident in so many other parts of the Third World. Thus, while economic circumstances are no longer as desperate as they were in the 1960s, the challenges to policy-makers in the 1990s are, in many respects, just as formidable. It is therefore appropriate to conclude this book with an attempt in Chapter 12 to identify some of these major challenges—maintaining the reform momentum, inculcating a liberal economic ideology, adjusting to the exhaustion of the oil surplus, managing a large external debt, enhancing the efficient provision of supply-side capacities, and responding to the special challenges of equity and distribution.

An Overview of Economic Development Since 1966

This chapter provides an overview of the Indonesian economy since 1966. In the broad sweep of economic development, it examines, in turn, the dimensions of rapid economic growth, episodes in economic policy and development, the issue of investment and efficiency, and the nature and extent of structural and technological change. A final section considers some of the major criticisms of the development record. The exposition in this chapter is necessarily brief. The purpose is to set the scene for the more detailed analyses to follow in subsequent chapters.

RAPID GROWTH

The economy recovered surprisingly quickly from the dislocation of the first half of the 1960s, recording double-digit growth for the first time in 1968.[1] Thereafter, rapid annual growth, of at least 5 per cent, was maintained until 1982, when softening international oil markets induced a sharp slowdown (Figure 2.1). This subdued expansion continued until 1986 (except for 1984, as massive oil and gas investments came on stream, boosting industrial expansion to 10 per cent), when policy reforms which commenced in the mid–1980s began to take effect. By the end of the decade, the economy had recovered and growth rates in the 6-7 per cent range were again being recorded, not too far short of those of the high-growth oil boom period.

Figure 2.2 charts the course of expanding per capita GDP over this period, as measured in constant price rupiah and dollars. Both series show an increase of around 150 per cent from 1969 to 1992, or equivalent to a rise of some 200 per cent over the full life of the New Order. But, importantly, the series diverge for much of this period. The increases in the dollar series are compressed almost entirely into the oil boom era, according to which per capita incomes in 1982 were 230 per cent higher as compared to 1969. Then there was a steep decline during the 1980s, such that the figure for 1989 was just two-thirds that of the peak year 1982. From the late 1980s the figure began to rise again, but by 1992 it was still below that of 1976. By contrast, the conventional GDP series, measured in constant price rupiah, shows a more gradual expansion, with a minor decline occurring only once, in 1982. The principal explanation for these diverging trends is of course the oil boom and bust of the 1970s and 1980s (see Chapter 5). During much of the 1970s there was a marked real appreciation of the rupiah, resulting from a constant nominal exchange rate against the US dollar but inflation rates higher than those of major trading partners. The opposite phenomenon was observed in the 1980s, with two large devaluations, which

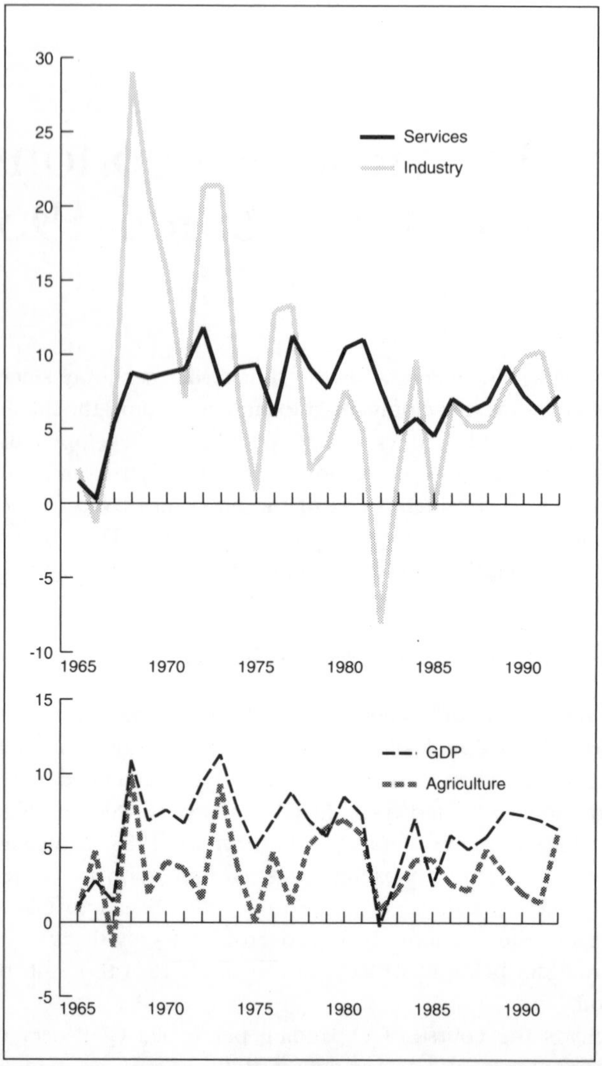

Figure 2.1   Economic growth, 1965–92

translated into a sharp real depreciation for the decade and, in turn, a decline in the US dollar per capita income series. These series explain why, for example, Indonesia was elevated, with considerable official jubilation, into the lower ranks of the World Bank's "middle-income countries" group in 1980. However, under the impact of the 1980s devaluations, appropriately, it slid back to the top of the low-income group in 1987.

The broad sectoral aggregates mirror the trends in the (rupiah denominated) national accounts, with some exceptions. Industrial expansion has been the most uneven of all the major sectors (see Chapter 8), with spectacular increases recorded in some years prior to 1980. All but one of the eight cases of super (double-digit) growth occurred in the decade from 1968 to 1977. They reflect a combination of factors: dramatic increases in manufacturing capacity as the backlog in consumer

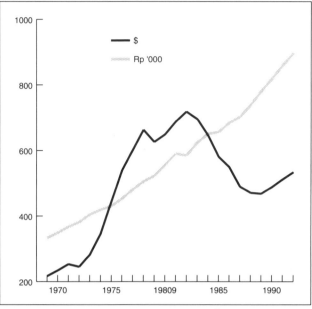

Figure 2.2   Estimates of GNP per capita, 1969-92

demand was overcome, a more effective exploitation of mineral resources,[2] and the impact of the construction boom. Conversely, industrial growth has been slow in some years, especially in the late 1970s and early 1980s when Indonesia adhered to OPEC production quotas. Manufacturing growth was also very sluggish in 1982 and 1983. Thus industry could hardly be described as a "leading sector" throughout this period. It was the fastest growing sector for much of the oil boom period, and non-oil manufacturing spurred the recovery of the late 1980s. But until this recent period of broad-based, export-oriented industrial growth, the sector has tended to swing between periods of boom and bust.

Agricultural expansion has, not surprisingly, been slower and less erratic. Growth has exceeded the historically high figure of 5 per cent on only a few occasions. These figures were recorded in years of recovery from severe droughts, for example 1968, 1973, and 1992. But perhaps the most significant period in the New Order's agricultural history was 1978 to 1981, when high growth laid the foundations of the much-vaunted achievement of rice self-sufficiency in 1985. Such a record was in marked contrast to the sluggish performance of much of the 1960s and 1970s, when an indifferent policy environment, combined with problems of climate and pest attacks, resulted in periodic rice crises. These were particularly serious when, as in 1972, they coincided with poor harvests in other major producing nations. More generally, agricultural performance reflects the interplay between policy regimes and climatic conditions, as we shall see in Chapter 7.

Of the three major sectors, the services sector has most closely followed the economy's growth rate. Rebounding quickly from the mid-1960s stagnation, services grew by at least 8 per cent in most years between 1968 and 1981. The rate of expansion then slowed down, as did the economy as a whole, before picking up in the late 1980s. Consistent with the theory of economic development, services output has grown more rapidly than GDP, and the sector is now almost unrecognizable compared with that in the 1960s (Chapter 9). But one hesitates to characterize it, too, as an engine of growth, since for much of the oil boom period its fortunes were closely tied to the government budget. More recently, however, rapid services growth has been achieved independent of government expenditure, especially with the expansion of tourism and an increasingly diverse array of business services.

Export performance has been a crucial factor in Indonesian economic development since 1966, as discussed in more detail in Chapter 5. Exports as a share of GDP began rising in the early 1970s, in response to the rehabilitation of traditional export sectors, the strong commodity performance (most notably timber), and the adoption of realistic foreign exchange pricing, which induced exporters to sell through legal channels (Figure 2.3). The first round of oil price increases had a dramatic effect, resulting in a doubling of the exports/GDP ratio from 1971 to 1974. The ratio then declined slightly, before jumping again between 1978 and 1980. Conversely, it began to fall during the early 1980s, initially at a slow rate partly due to the large devaluation in 1983 (recall that the export series is dollar denominated, whereas GDP is in rupiah). In the mid–1980s the ratio fell further, and in the trough of 1986 it was actually below that of 1973, immediately prior to the first oil boom. Thereafter, it rose again mainly due to the strong performance of non-oil exports over this period. By 1992 the ratio was not far short of the peak periods in 1974 and 1979–81. The non-oil series show the underlying trends more clearly.[3] This series increased gradually during the 1970s compared with the sharp increase in the oil series ratio. The non-oil ratio then fell sharply in the early 1980s, owing to low agricultural commodity prices (which then dominated these exports) but recovered quickly during the 1980s, stimulated by the rapid expansion in manufactured exports (see Chapter 5). For the 10 years to 1992, non-oil exports relative to GDP rose a remarkable 300 per cent, far outpacing the rise in oil GDP at any period, and underlining the significance of the Indonesian economy's growing internationalization.

Despite its creditable export performance, Indonesian economic development since 1966 has not really been "export-led" in the way it has in some of the smaller East Asian neighbouring economies. Reflecting its size, exports have never been more than 31 per cent of GDP, or more than 21 per cent in the non-mining series. These figures are far below those of East Asia's small, highly export-oriented economies, where ratios in excess of 50 per cent are not uncommon. Conversely, the export series do underline the dynamics of Indonesian economic development since 1966, and the important role played by exports, particularly oil in the 1970s and manufactures in the 1980s.[4,5]

EPISODES IN ECONOMIC POLICY AND DEVELOPMENT

The year 1966 was a watershed in Indonesia's economic history, marking a decisive change in policy direction and economic fortunes. The next 25 years witnessed rapid development and structural change. But the growth path, and the policy directions underpinning this expansion, were hardly smooth and uniform. Indonesia experienced significant exogenous shocks over this period, principally from fluctuating international oil prices. These shocks demanded, and generally resulted in,

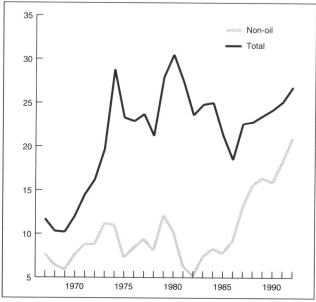

Figure 2.3   Exports and GDP, 1967–92

a flexible policy response. Consequently, the pace and sources of economic growth, and the dominant issues of economic policy, have changed frequently over the past 28 years. It is not possible to neatly divide these events, and the related trends in economic indicators, into clearly identifiable subperiods. Rather they tend to merge into one another, with the policy response generally lagging changing economic circumstances by a year or more. Nevertheless, at the risk of oversimplification, it is useful to demarcate a number of subperiods since 1966, each identifiable in terms of the major economic trends and policy emphases. What is of primary interest is major swings in policy and performance. The chronology at the end of the book documents the dominant events and policy initiatives in more detail.

(a) *Rehabilitation and recovery, 1966 to 1970:* Over this period, the government was concerned to control inflation above all else, to re-establish ties with the international donor community, and to rehabilitate physical infrastructure. The introduction of orthodox monetary and fiscal policies brought inflation down surprisingly quickly. The government's clear commitment to economic orthodoxy and its close relationship with the international donor consortium resulted in a strong response from both domestic and foreign investors. The economy grew at an annual average rate of 6.6 per cent; 1968 marked the beginning of the recovery phase, with growth of 10.9 per cent. H.W. Arndt captured the rising tide of optimism over this period in a series of *BIES* Surveys:

The Indonesian economy has turned a corner. The first objective of the Suharto government, stabilisation, has been achieved. (July 1969, p.1)

Priming the pump of economic development after years of stagnation is proving a slow and difficult business. But there has been progress in recent months. Earlier talk of recession has stopped. Budgetary development expenditure, though still lagging, has picked up substantially. Bank credit expansion has proceeded apace. (November 1969, p. 1)

The four months covered by this Survey, February to May 1970, have been as relatively trouble free a period for the Indonesian economy as any since 1966, and perhaps since 1957 ... [T]here has been progress on many fronts, in economic activity, in output and investment, and in institutional reform. (July 1970, p. 1)

(b) *Rapid growth, 1971 to 1981:* This was a period of sustained economic growth. Real GDP increased at an annual average rate of 7.7 per cent and in all years grew by at least 5 per cent. It was also a period of extraordinary economic turbulence. Some of the difficulties were self-inflicted but many were exogenous (external) in nature. A poor rice harvest domestically and abroad resulted in serious shortages in late 1972 and a doubling of rice prices. In the second half of 1973 international petroleum prices quadrupled, conferring massive windfall revenue gains on Indonesia. These two events, combined with the government's limited policy response, triggered significant inflationary pressures. Ironically, part of the increase in international reserves was sterilized by Pertamina's profligate expenditure programs, the bitter lessons from which dominated economic management in 1976. High international oil prices also resulted in the resurgence of a nationalist economic agenda. Over this period, official policy strongly favoured *pribumi* business interests. Trade and foreign investment policy became more restrictive, and new plans for an expanded state enterprise sector were announced. Towards the end of the decade policy-makers became increasingly concerned at the prospect of declining oil prices. Consequently, a large devaluation occurred in November 1978, not for the usual balance of payments reasons, but to restore the competitiveness of non-oil tradeable sectors in preparation for an anticipated softening in world oil markets. In the event, this softening did not occur for another four years. In 1979 the Iran–Iraq war precipitated another round of large price increases, thus rendering the devaluation largely irrelevant.

(c) *Adjustment to lower oil prices, 1982 to 1986:* Falling oil prices, rising external indebtedness and a sudden decline in economic growth in 1982 signalled an end to the decade of oil-financed growth and abundance. For the first time in the regime's history, seemingly automatic increments to revenue from oil and aid evaporated. Moreover, much of the debt from the past 15 years was now maturing, and a sharp increase in principal repayments lay ahead. Owing partly to a good agricultural performance, and partly to the one-off effect of huge oil-related investments, the economy continued to grow over this period, at a respectable annual average rate of 4 per cent. Nevertheless, gross domestic income, adjusting for the falling terms of trade, grew much more slowly. In the August 1984 *BIES* Survey, a little over one year before the really sharp oil price declines, I offered the following summary picture:

The Indonesian economy in mid-1984 is something of a puzzle. The macro indicators are encouraging ... Yet investment is sluggish, the deep-seated problems of protection and regulation and of indifferent performance of the large state enterprise sector remain, and some of the government's recent industrial policy initiatives appear to be very costly ... The paradox is resolved partly when it is remembered that rice and oil are still crucial. A good performance in these two sectors can gloss over problems elsewhere.

The policy response was ambivalent during this phase. The macroeconomic adjustments were generally prompt and effective, as the government quickly cut back on expenditure, deferred, then cancelled, a number of large projects, and devalued the rupiah in April 1983. Tax, customs, and banking reforms were also introduced. On the other side of the ledger, however, much of the strategy of industrial deepening, developed in the early 1980s in an era of abundance, continued to receive high priority. Non-tariff barriers proliferated, exacerbating the problems faced by a high-cost and inefficient industrial sector. It was only in 1986, when oil prices fell very sharply, that this interventionist trend was arrested.

(d) *Liberalization and recovery, 1987 to the present:* Continued fiscal austerity, effective exchange rate management, and decisive microeconomic reform together resulted in a strong recovery beginning in 1987. As Jamie Mackie and Sjahrir observed in the December 1989 *BIES* Survey (p. 1):

> *The Indonesian economy has been experiencing something near boom conditions in most sectors throughout 1989 ... Anticipated benefits from the various deregulation packages of 1986–88 ... are now obvious ... Exports of manufactured goods are continuing to rise to unprecedented levels, the banking system is awash with liquidity, the 1989 rice harvests have been exceptionally good, while the construction industry is now operating at near-capacity levels ...*

Annual growth from 1987 to 1992 averaged 6.7 per cent, approaching that of the 1971–81 period, but on this occasion was achieved without buoyant oil revenues. For the first time in its history, Indonesia became a significant industrial exporter, following the well-travelled route of its East Asian neighbours. Another novel feature of this period was the growing commercial strength and independence of the private sector. The share of state enterprises in the economy began to shrink, *dirigisme* took a back seat, and government subsidies and protection became a less significant feature of some—but by no means all—firms' commercial calculus. The regime had demonstrated its capacity to engineer growth in adverse economic circumstances. By the early 1990s Indonesia appeared to have weathered the debt crisis of the 1980s effectively. However, the resumption of strong growth produced new policy challenges, occasioned by the waning authority of the technocrats, the seemingly inexorable rise of the "technologs" headed by Minister Habibie, and widespread public suspicion of the huge, politically well-connected conglomerates.

INVESTMENT AND EFFICIENCY

High rates of investment have facilitated rapid technological change and provided the base for sustained economic growth. Investment picked up quickly during the rehabilitation phase of the late 1960s (Figure 2.4). Gross domestic investment as a share of GDP almost doubled in 1966–67 and again between 1967 and 1971. The share continued to rise to historically unprecedented levels under the impetus of the oil boom and the government's massive public investment programs. In the second half of the 1970s it remained at about 24 per cent, rising still higher in the early 1980s. A surprising feature of the 1980s is that, notwithstanding the reduction in the government's development budget (see Chapter 4), investment levels held up strongly. There was a small decline in the mid-1980s, but a strong recovery to a new peak of over 35 per cent at the end of the decade. Rising external debt in the mid-1980s and, later in the decade, the strong private sector response to the liberalization reforms, appear to be the main explanations of this buoyancy.[6]

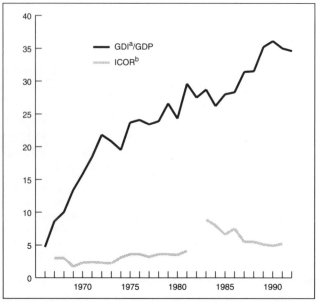

Figure 2.4   Investment and efficiency, 1966–92

How productively have these funds been invested? A crude indicator of investment efficiency is the incremental capital output ratio (ICOR). As would be expected, the ICORs were very low during the rehabilitation phase. Investment opportunities were plentiful and quick-yielding, while output was expanding rapidly in response to the more liberal economic environment (Figure 2.4). The ICORs began to rise in the mid-1970s as the government embarked on many ambitious, capital-intensive projects. Some, such as those involving physical infrastructure, had a long gestation period, while others, such as investments by Pertamina and other state enterprises, were of doubtful economic viability. Slower economic growth but continuing high investment resulted in a sharp rise in the ICOR during the early 1980s. Indonesia's high ICOR over this period became a matter of concern among economists, and was one of the factors triggering debate over the "high-cost economy" in the mid-1980s.[7] The resumption of rapid growth in the late 1980s, more efficient and labour-intensive than before, saw the ICOR fall to something closer to internationally accepted norms.

Thus the ICORs do provide a useful, though partial, indicator of trends in investment efficiency: the ratio was low in the catch-up period from 1967 to 1973 and fell again in the reform era of the late 1980s. Nevertheless, the ratio for Indonesia does appear to be consistently higher than that of most of its high growth neighbours. It is possible that the investment series are inflated, for the reasons discussed in Note 6. But, equally plausible, the higher ratio for Indonesia lends further circumstantial support to the notion that serious problems of inefficiency remain, which can be resolved only through further policy reform.

RAPID STRUCTURAL CHANGE

Reflecting these patterns of growth, Indonesia's structural transformation has been remarkably rapid. As noted earlier, agriculture's share of GDP has more than halved

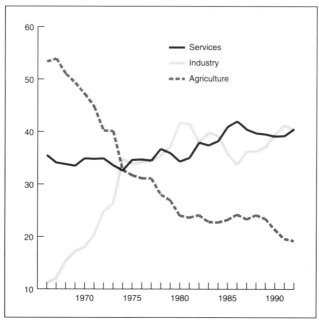

Figure 2.5   Structural change, 1966–92

since 1966, and by 1992 it was just 36 per cent of that of its share at the outset of the New Order (Figure 2.5). There has been a commensurate increase in the share of industry (broadly defined to include mining, manufacturing, utilities and construction), which is now 350 per cent above what it was in the mid-1960s. There has been no clear trend in the share of services, both for the period as a whole or for any major subperiod. Agriculture's share declined particularly quickly in the early 1970s, hastened by the oil boom and the indifferent performance of food and cash crops during some of these years. Indeed, most of the decline in agriculture was recorded over the period from 1966 to 1980. During the 1980s there was no significant change in its share, reflecting its stronger performance especially in the early part of the decade. Correspondingly, most of the increase in industry's share occurred over the decade ending in 1976, in which a 300 per cent rise was recorded. Thereafter, its share rose only slowly, fluctuating with high and low oil prices (around 1980 and the mid-1980s, respectively), and rising in the late 1980s in response to the strong growth of non-oil manufacturing.[8]

What effect has the oil boom and bust had on the recorded path of structural change? The oil price increases greatly magnified the rising share of industry and hastened the decline of agriculture (Figure 2.6). Excluding the mining sector, agriculture's decline was slower: for example, including mining, its 1980 share was 45 per cent of that of 1966, but was 57 per cent excluding mining. The rise of industry during this period was also much slower: its share was 275 per cent and 150 per cent higher including and excluding mining, respectively. Conversely, during the 1980s both the decline of agriculture and the rise of industry were faster excluding mining, as would be expected. The share of services also displays a consistent upward trend through to the mid-1980s in the latter series. Its strong growth over the 1970–85 period underlines the importance of aid and oil-financed infrastructure in

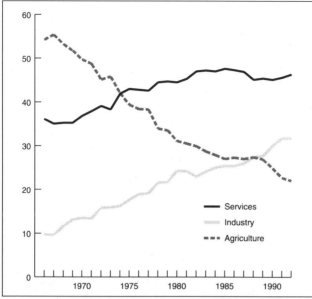

Figure 2.6   Structural change, excluding mining, 1966–92

underpinning the expansion of services. There is a clear and positive correlation between the growth of real government expenditure and the rise in the share of services; the growth rate of both tapered off in the late 1980s. In aggregate, therefore, the oil boom and bust obscured, but did not fundamentally alter, the dimensions of structural change in the economy.

The dimensions of this process of growth and structural change are illustrated further by examining the sectoral contributions to growth over the period, focusing in particular on the development phases identified above (Table 2.1). The incremental contributions reflect both the size of a sector and its rate of growth. Therefore, in the early period, it is not surprising that the two largest sectors, agriculture and trade, also made the largest contribution to growth; both also benefited from the return to more normal economic conditions. During the recovery phase, those sectors dependent on the growth of government expenditure, such as transport and construction, made a relatively modest contribution. During the oil boom period, by contrast, there were major changes in these sectoral shares. Rapid manufacturing growth, behind rising import barriers, became the single largest source of expansion. The contribution of the government sector rose more than three-fold, while that of construction and transport also jumped. The oil boom financed much of this expansion. But the direct contribution of mining to output growth was very small since the major increase in this sector was in prices, not in the physical quantity of output. Agriculture's absolute contribution was still large, but falling quickly, owing to faster growth elsewhere.

During the recession and readjustment phase these broad trends were maintained. The government adopted a tighter fiscal strategy, but many of the large public sector investments, in heavy industry and infrastructure, were coming on stream. Thus the share of public administration actually rose still further, as did those of manufacturing, transport, and utilities. Agriculture's contribution also rose, reflecting both slower

Table 2.1   **Sectoral Contribution to GDP Growth, 1967–92**
(% of increment to real GDP)

Sector	Recovery, 1967-73	Oil boom, 1973-81	Recession, 1982-86	Export growth, 1987-92
Agriculture	28.2	16.4	23.2	10.4
Mining	12.8	4.9	−5.0	7.4
Manufacturing	10.0	22.9	28.9	29.2
Utilities	0.6	1.1	2.5	1.2
Construction	7.3	8.8	2.0	9.3
Trade	25.4	17.2	12.5	18.3
Transport	4.2	8.0	10.2	7.3
Finance	4.3	2.8	4.7	7.1
Housing	1.6	4.3	3.2	1.6
Public administration	3.8	12.6	15.5	5.4
Other services	1.6	1.1	2.2	2.8
Total	100	100	100	100
(Annual average GDP growth, %)	(7.90)	(7.51)	(4.01)	(6.73)

Sources: 1967-73 and 1973-81: Sundrum (1986, p. 58). 1982-86: Sundrum (1988, p. 46). 1987-92: author's estimates, from BPS, *National Accounts.*

GDP growth in aggregate and strong food crop performance over part of this period. Mining output contracted in absolute terms. The final period represents the most decisive change in the determinants of growth. The impact of both a contracting government share and strong non-oil export growth is clearly evident. Manufacturing was again the major contributor (through export growth rather than the expansion of heavy industry capacity, as in the previous period), whereas the share of the government sector in the increase was just a little over one-third of that in the 1982-86 period. The strong construction recovery had a significant impact on growth, almost as large as that of agriculture. Trade was again the second largest contributor, while financial liberalization boosted the role of the finance sector, its incremental share being almost as large as that of mining.

Thus this sectoral disaggregation further illuminates the pattern of economic growth since the mid-1960s. Agriculture's contribution to growth has declined during the period as a whole, while manufacturing has emerged as the leading sector for much of the period (albeit for different reasons in different subperiods). The government sector, and those activities relying directly on public sector investments, prospered during the oil boom period and its aftermath, but their shares generally fell in the late 1980s. The contribution of mining is obscured by the fact that the data measure the growth at constant prices, and the impact of rising revenues was felt elsewhere in the economy.

Changing employment patterns further illuminate the dimensions of structural change.[9] Sectoral employment shares typically change less rapidly than those of output, since labour is slow to move out of low productivity sectors, especially agriculture. Moreover, employment data often obscure these shifts owing to multiple job-holdings across sectors, particularly in the process of the shift out of agriculture. Nevertheless, the Indonesian labour force data show very clear trends over the period covered by the four population censuses conducted since Independence (Table 2.2).

Table 2.2 **Employment by Sector, 1961–90**

	Shares (%)				Increment (%)		
	1961	*1971*	*1980*	*1990*	*1961–71*	*1971–80*	*1980–90*
I. Indonesia							
Agriculture	73.0	65.8	56.1	50.1	28.2	24.4	34.1
Industry	8.1	10.1	13.3	17.0	20.6	23.7	26.7
Manufacturing	5.9	7.8	9.2	11.6	18.2	13.6	18.1
Construction	1.8	1.9	3.2	4.1	2.6	7.5	6.5
Services	18.9	24.1	30.6	32.9	51.2	51.8	39.2
Trade	6.9	11.0	13.1	15.0	32.4	20.1	20.0
Transport	2.2	2.4	2.9	3.7	3.8	4.4	5.9
Finance and other	9.8	10.7	14.6	14.2	15.0	27.4	13.2
Total	100	100	100	100	100	100	100
('000)	32,911	39,163	51,196	70,608	6,252	6,810	19,412
II. Java							
Agriculture	68.8	60.9	50.6	42.5	19.4	13.9	17.8
Industry	9.4	11.6	15.2	20.3	23.0	28.2	35.8
Manufacturing	7.1	9.3	10.9	14.3	20.9	16.7	24.9
Construction	2.0	2.0	3.6	4.8	2.1	9.0	8.6
Services	21.8	27.5	34.2	37.2	57.6	58.0	46.4
Trade	8.0	13.3	15.3	17.6	41.2	22.5	24.7
Transport	2.3	2.6	3.1	4.2	3.8	5.0	7.6
Finance and other	11.5	11.7	15.8	15.4	12.6	30.4	14.1
Total	100	100	100	100	100	100	100
('000)	21,658	25,757	33,026	43,798	4,099	7,269	10,772

Source: BPS, *Sensus Penduduk*, 1961, 1971, 1980, 1990. I am indebted to Chris Manning and Abrar Yusuf for supplying these data.

The share of the agricultural labour force has fallen steadily, from almost three-quarters of the total in 1961 to one-half in 1990. That of industry has doubled over the same period, while the share of services has risen by about 75 per cent. These general trends and directions are consistent with expectations. But in addition there have been some interesting variations both over time and across regions. Agriculture's share of incremental employment expansion was close to one-quarter in both the 1960s and 1970s, and appeared to confirm expectations that its role as a source of employment generation was rapidly coming to an end. However, its share actually rose in the 1980s, to over one-third of the increase. This unexpected result is explained by several factors. The pace of technological progress was probably more rapid in the 1970s, at least in terms of the adoption of high-yielding food crop varieties and in the rehabilitation of plantations (see Table 2.4 and Figure 7.5, pp. 27,133). By the 1980s, a more labour-intensive trajectory was resumed, aided especially by the expansion of the smallholder sector.

The share of manufacturing in Indonesia's total employment has risen steadily, but its incremental contribution has fluctuated. It reached a low point in the 1970s, generating little more than one-eighth of the new jobs, a trend which was the source of much official consternation and academic debate at the time. However, during the

1980s its share rose to a level comparable with that of the 1960s, spurred on by export-oriented, labour-intensive growth. The 1970s was thus an aberration, essentially the result of two factors—the backwash from the displacement of traditional technologies, to be discussed shortly, and the capital-intensive course of industrialization induced by state investment in heavy industry, together with protection, an anti-export bias, and capital-cheapening fiscal incentives.

The services sector has consistently provided the largest percentage of new jobs, even during the 1960s when its share of aggregate employment was less than one-quarter. However, while its share of employment has been rising, consistent with the theory of economic development, its incremental share actually declined in the 1980s. Both these trends require brief elaboration. First, on the large increments in the 1960s and 1970s: in the former period, which embraces both phases of stagnation and recovery, it is probable that services acted to some extent as a source of "last resort" employment, most notably in the dominant subsector of trade, which provided one-third of the new jobs in the 1960s, and was later stimulated by the revival of economic activity in construction, transport, and the government sector; during the 1970s, the public sector spending effects of the oil boom are clearly evident. The direct effects of the boom were minuscule but the contribution of finance and other services (which includes the public sector) rose sharply, and was larger even than agriculture. Construction also increased very quickly, its contribution being over half that of the much larger manufacturing sector during the 1970s.[10] During the 1980s, by contrast, the share of services in employment expansion fell markedly, for two reasons— growth in both agriculture and manufacturing was more labour-intensive than in the previous decade, and public sector spending fell in real terms and with it the share of government and related activities.

Employment patterns and trends in Java confirm these general trends, but also underline differences in economic structure between this island and the rest of the country. Reflecting its comparative advantage, agriculture's share of employment is smaller, and its decline has been more rapid. As for the country as a whole, however, there was an increase in agriculture's incremental employment share during the 1980s, albeit of smaller proportion. Conversely, the share of employment in manufacturing is higher and its incremental contribution always greater. During the 1980s, one-quarter of the new jobs on Java were in manufacturing, the largest of all the subsectors (including trade, by a very small margin). The employment intensity of industrialization on Java over this decade is clearly illustrated by the comparison with the previous decade. Services, too, were a more important source of both total and incremental employment on Java as compared with the rest of the country. Trends within these subsectors, and construction, are explained mainly by the national factors adumbrated above.

Thus the pace of structural change is consistent with both the theory of economic development and Indonesia's rapid economic development since 1966. The structure of the Indonesian economy changed little over the period of low growth and disruption from 1939 to 1966. But by contrast, over the past quarter of a century or so, agriculture's share of output and, to a lesser extent, employment, has fallen markedly, and that of industry and services has risen. In the early 1990s, Indonesia passed three milestones in the long sweep of economic development and structural transformation: manufacturing output overtook that of agriculture, the share of the labour force in agriculture dipped below 50 per cent (although absolute numbers engaged in agriculture continue to rise), and manufactures constituted more than one-half of total merchandise exports. The 1990s is likely to witness a continuation of these trends, with the possibility of the agricultural labour force beginning to decline, on Java at least, early next century. Both manufacturing and services are likely to constitute the source of increasingly large increments to output and employment growth.[11]

RAPID TECHNOLOGICAL CHANGE

Accompanying these high rates of economic growth and structural change has been equally rapid technological change within most sectors. In the mid-1960s Indonesia's economy was so riddled with distortions, its international commercial channels so disrupted, and its commercial environment so uncertain that investment had virtually collapsed.[12] As a result, Indonesia's technological base was extremely weak. Industrial techniques—and indeed machinery—introduced in the country's first spurt of industrial growth during the 1930s, were still in use. Transport and communications stock was seriously run down. Both the food and cash crops sectors of agriculture had failed to innovate and introduce new technologies.

The liberal environment after 1966 and rapidly rising investment rates had a profound effect on the pace of technological development. Extremely labour-intensive technologies in agriculture, industry and services, whose use had been prolonged by the chaotic business environment of the late 1950s and early 1960s, now began to disappear very quickly. In effect, changes which in normal circumstances might have occurred over a generation were compressed into less than a decade. Many observers were concerned at the implications for employment and income distribution of the rapid demise of these traditional technologies. Factor price distortions, particularly interest rate subsidies, were widely criticized as exacerbating the problem of underemployment. Others saw in the weakening of village institutions and traditional obligations the removal of constraints on the adoption of new more capital-intensive technologies.

These concerns were voiced by one of Indonesia's foremost economists, and Minister of Manpower at the time of writing. Reflecting on the rapid changes in rice milling technologies, he remarked:

> Nowadays, villages are humming with small, Japanese-made engines, milling paddy; they are called rice hullers. These innovations profit the landowners or the owners of the paddy. The rice is better polished, less broken, and hence fetches a better price. It can also be stored a little longer than the hand-pounded rice. Yet as a result many female working hours at hand-pounding are foregone with adverse distributional effects. These shifts in employment and income distribution will probably never be registered in a census on account of definitions of employment, but they can shake the foundations of village life. (Sadli, 1973, p. 154)

Several other studies pointed to the far-reaching technological changes occurring in a diverse range of activities. Timmer (1973) also studied changes in rice-milling technologies. His conclusion, that an intermediate technology (in terms of its capital intensity) was both socially and privately optimal, triggered a spirited debate with a team of researchers (see Collier et al. [1974], and Timmer [1974] for a reply). Sinaga (1978) examined trends and implications of agricultural mechanization, particularly the introduction of mini-tractors. Collier et al. (1973) initiated a long-running debate over the effects of the introduction of sickles in place of the traditional knife (*ani-ani*) in rice harvesting. Dick (1981) pointed to the major changes occurring in urban public transport, particularly the introduction of mini-buses (colts), in place of the traditional *becak*. Nelson (1986) studied the changing technology of cassava starch manufacture, finding that an intermediate mechanized technology was superior, on both a social and a private calculus, to the traditional labour-intensive technology it was rapidly replacing. In the weaving industry, hand loom technologies began to disappear quickly in the late 1960s, unable to compete with the mechanical looms except in certain niche markets (Hill, 1983).

As the quote above from Professor Sadli highlights, the social implications of these changes should not be underestimated. Technological innovation is, inherently, a disruptive process. Many of the groups and individuals adversely affected—the unskilled, especially women—are also the most vulnerable, particularly since social support networks tend to weaken as the forces of commercialization become more powerful. Nevertheless, the process of rapid technological change is inevitable, and an essential prerequisite for broad-based increases in living standards. Consumers wanted cheaper textiles, rice and public transport. Indonesian firms have to compete in international markets. Capital subsidies (essentially confined to the 1970s and the first half of the 1980s, it should be stressed) may have induced the adoption of excessively capital-intensive technologies in some instances. But the process of technological change was driven primarily by the need to recover lost ground, by the dictates of consumer preferences, and by considerations of international competitiveness. The appropriate strategy for the poor in these circumstances is to ease the costs of transition, facilitate the expansion of alternative employment opportunities, and enhance the supply of public goods in the areas of education, health, and sanitation.

Tables 2.3 and 2.4 provide sectoral estimates of the levels and growth of labour productivity, and thus constitute an additional insight into the dimensions of technological progress, albeit at an aggregated level. Labour productivity in industry has always been the highest, inflated by the extremely capital-intensive mining sector (series A, Table 2.3). The exclusion of mining (the B series in the table) thus provides a more accurate picture of levels and trends. For all three periods, agricultural productivity is below the economy-wide average, while the industrial and service sectors are above it. There does not appear to be any "evening out" process at work, in that some sectoral labour productivities have moved closer to the national average, while others have diverged. Agriculture has become steadily more labour-intensive relative to the other sectors, its decline being particularly evident in the country's "capital-intensive" growth phase of the 1970s. Agriculture's declining relative labour productivity is of course a key factor in inducing continuing labour flows into non-agricultural activities. Manufacturing has become steadily more capital-intensive compared with the other sectors, and by 1990 it was more than double the non-mining average. Most of the increase occurred in the 1970s. By contrast, services have become steadily more labour-intensive, reflecting the fact that capital accumulation and technological progress appear to have been faster elsewhere, most notably in industry.

Real labour productivity growth was twice as fast in the 1970s as compared with the 1980s, but this reflected mainly the impact of the mining boom. Excluding mining,

Table 2.3   **Indices of Labour Productivity, 1971, 1980, 1990**
(indices, or Rp '000)

	1971 A	1971 B	1980 A	1980 B	1990 A	1990 B
Agriculture	65	70	43	55	39	44
Industry	206	223	314	404	243	277
Excluding mining	130	141	149	192	174	199
Manufacturing	117	127	141	182	183	209
Services	152	164	112	145	120	137
GDP/worker (Rp '000)						
All sectors	99.0		955.4		3,217.2	
Excluding mining		91.3		741.5		2,816.0

Notes: The data refer to labour productivity, expressed as an index with the ratio for all sectors, and all sectors excluding mining, equal to 100 (columns A and B respectively). Value added, measured at current prices, is from the national accounts, labour force from the 1971, 1980 and 1990 population censuses.

the growth rates in the two decades were broadly similar, with some acceleration of growth apparent in the latter decade. However, productivity grew more slowly in both agriculture and manufacturing in the 1980s, and it made a smaller contribution to output growth. Both these conclusions confirm *a priori* expectations. The major impetus to agricultural growth from the introduction of high-yielding seed varieties occurred in the 1970s (see Figure 7.5, p.133). In manufacturing, also, the faster rate of productivity growth in the 1970s reflected both the shedding of extremely labour-intensive, traditional technologies, together with the push towards oil-financed heavy industry over this decade. The latter process continued into the early 1980s, but for the decade as a whole the dominant feature was the adoption of a labour-intensive, export-oriented industrialization strategy; as a result, the share of these low productivity sectors in manufacturing rose. Nevertheless, labour productivity growth was still respectable, averaging almost 6 per cent per annum. Productivity in services grew more slowly than the non-mining average in both decades. It accelerated during the 1980s, despite the government's fiscal austerity, presumably owing in large measure to the advances in finance, telecommunications, tourism, and the retail trade. In both decades, however, the largest contribution to output growth came from employment expansion.[13]

SOME QUALIFICATIONS

Indonesia's impressive economic performance over this period is undeniable. However, the record is not without its critics. Some countries, not many, have grown faster still (see Table 1.3, p.6). A range of other criticisms have been levelled at the regime's economic performance since 1966. It is appropriate in this overview chapter to conclude with a brief review highlighting some of the major criticisms. These issues are examined in more detail in subsequent chapters, and are revisited in the concluding chapter.

Table 2.4 **The Growth of Labour Productivity, 1971–90**
(%)

| | 1971–80 | 1980–90 | 1971–90 | Contribution to output | | |
				1971–80	1980–90	1971–90
Agriculture	3.1	1.0	2.0	72	33	54
Industry	3.6	−0.3	1.5	37	−5	22
Excluding mining	1.2	5.3	3.3	18	48	38
Manufacturing	10.0	5.7	7.7	66	50	57
Services	1.3	3.0	2.2	19	43	33
GDP	4.1	2.2	3.1	57	41	50
Excluding mining	3.0	3.5	3.3	51	52	51

Notes: See notes to Table 2.3 for explanation. The value added data are in constant 1987 prices. The figures refer to annual average growth rates. The 'contribution to output' columns show the percentage increase in real value added attributable to the increase in labour productivity.

At least four major criticisms have been directed at Indonesia's development record, all suggesting that the actual performance has in some respects been inferior to that suggested in the official statistics. These arguments include the following. First, that high growth has been achieved mainly by a favourable movement in the terms of trade. Secondly, that the growth is largely the result of the exploitation of non-renewable natural resources. Thirdly, that rising external indebtedness underpinned and sustained the expansion of the 1980s, after the impetus from oil disappeared. Fourthly, there are arguments in relation to distributional considerations, and concern that the wealthy (or more accurately the "non-poor") have been the primary beneficiaries of economic growth. These are complex issues which in some cases cannot be resolved easily. However, it is important to emphasize that, while some are significant caveats, none of these criticisms invalidates the fundamental proposition that Indonesia's economic performance since 1966 has been very good.

On the first criticism, while it is undeniable that rising oil prices contributed to high rates of economic growth in the 1970s, growth was rapid even after adjusting for the terms of trade effect. This is illustrated in Figure 2.7, which compares growth in the conventionally defined gross domestic product (GDP) and gross domestic income (GDY). The latter incorporates the impact of movements in the terms of trade. In effect, it measures the effective "purchasing power" of GDP. As would be expected, the GDY series fluctuates more than that of GDP, especially over the 1972–86 period when there was much movement in the terms of trade. Very high rates of growth in GDY were recorded in the peak oil boom years of 1974 and 1979–81; in 1974, GDY growth was almost three times that of GDP. Conversely, as oil prices declined in the 1980s the GDY series grew more slowly, notably so in 1986 when international oil prices collapsed. Nevertheless, the data clearly illustrate that oil price movements have not been the fundamental determinant of growth. Whichever series is used, growth has been reasonably rapid. Moreover, as the economy continues to diversify quickly away from its heavy reliance on oil and gas—their share of government revenue and exports have more than halved since 1982—the two series will increasingly converge.[14]

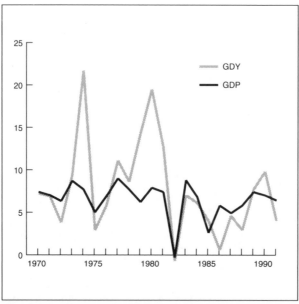

Figure 2.7 The growth of GDP and GDY, 1970-91

The preceding argument has important implications for the second caveat, that growth has been "purchased" at the expense of the rapid depletion of non-renewable natural resources. By the late 1980s it was clear that non-oil sectors were the primary engine of growth, particularly as labour-intensive manufactured exports and tourism began to grow very quickly. This is not to deny that the exploitation of natural resources has been an important factor in Indonesia's economic growth, particularly during the oil boom decade, nor that the country's record of environmental management has been a rather poor one. As discussed in Chapter 7 (see Natural Resource Management), there have been some attempts by researchers to calculate the effects of the depletion of non-renewable natural resources using a "natural resource accounting" framework. The best-known work is that of Repetto et al. (1989), who estimated net natural resource depletion for petroleum, timber, and soils on Java. Their alternative series diverged considerably from GDP, with an estimated growth rate of 4 per cent over the 1971–84 period, as compared with the GDP series of 7.1 per cent. The heroic estimates underlying this research are examined in more detail in Chapter 7. Important as the work is, the numbers are extremely approximate and the assumptions questionable in some cases. In any case, the divergence between the series would have narrowed by the late 1980s, given the declining importance of the natural resource sector.

The third qualification relates to Indonesia's external debt. This rose sharply in the 1980s as the government attempted to cushion the effects of the deteriorating terms of trade (see the section in Chapter 5, External Debt). Such debt constitutes a claim on future income streams in Indonesia and, since most of it is with the public sector, will result in lower national incomes than would otherwise be the case. In addition, there are grounds for concern that some of the external borrowings have been ill-advised, being undertaken at the behest of politically powerful cronies or for uneconomic state-funded projects. Nevertheless, on both political and social grounds a strategy of external borrowing to ease the painful process of structural adjustment during the 1980s was justified. By 1990, also, the most difficult period of adjustment to rising debt service payments had passed, although new challenges in the form of rapidly rising private external debt began to surface. Moreover, to the extent that at least some of the borrowed funds have been used judiciously, they will generate future income flows to service the debt.

The fourth concern, that of deteriorating equity, is the source of much public comment and debate. But, as discussed in Chapter 10, it appears to have little empirical basis. All available evidence suggests that there was no observable deterioration in inequality during the 1970s and 1980s, and that the benefits of growth were therefore distributed reasonably widely. Most social indicators have also improved considerably. The New Order's outstanding social policy agenda is a large one. Poverty remains a serious problem, and arguably much more could have been done in this area. In the political domain, the perception remains in many quarters that the elite—non-*pribumi*, the bureaucracy, the army—has benefited disproportionately. But the record to date in achieving a broad-based rise in living standards needs to be emphasized.[15]

Money and Finance

AN OVERVIEW

The distinction between the Old and New Order is nowhere more pronounced than in monetary and financial developments. As noted in Chapter 1, mounting budget deficits resulted in accelerating inflation in the first half of the 1960s, and there was a total lack of political will to address the problem.[1] As a former Governor of Bank Indonesia over the period from 1974 to 1983 aptly observed, prior to 1966 "[A] perfect condition for McKinnon's financial repression was found in Indonesia".[2] The Soeharto government tackled inflation surprisingly quickly and effectively. Indeed, one of the hallmarks of the regime since 1966 has been its commitment to control inflation. There have been inflationary episodes, especially during the peak of the oil booms. There has been a good deal of "financial repression". Until recently monetary policy instruments have been blunt and underdeveloped. But the regime has established a credible reputation for basically sound macroeconomic management: each burst of inflation has been followed by corrective intervention. Unquestionably, one of the positive legacies of the bitter experience of the 1960s has been an aversion to high inflation. Indeed, as soon as inflation has approached the threshold of double-digit levels, alarm bells have sounded in the central bank and the Department of Finance and the response has generally been prompt.

The macroeconomic management and reform story is an important one, comprising a number of distinct though interrelated analytical issues: the restoration of internal balance in the late 1960s; the adjustment to large exogenous shocks in the oil boom decade; the particular mix of monetary policy instruments throughout the post–1966 period; the slow pace of policy reform until 1983, followed by significant progress; and the gradual process of financial deepening and maturity.

In the conduct and outcome of monetary policy and financial development since 1966 at least five important features stand out:

☐ An open international capital account since 1970. In consequence, exogenous shocks such as the oil price fluctuations have been transmitted quickly to the domestic economy, posing particular challenges for the short-run management of the money supply. In this respect, Indonesia has, superficially at least, enacted its policy reforms in reverse order to that suggested in the (primarily Latin American) sequencing literature, with little adverse effect.

☐ A fixed exchange rate (with the US dollar, rather than a bundle of currencies) for lengthy periods, including the first five years of the oil boom period. Thus the

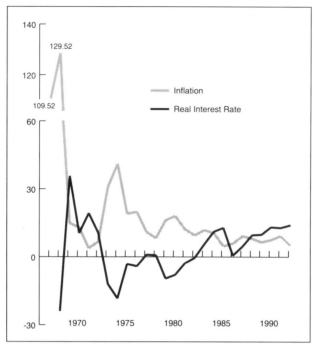

Figure 3.1   Inflation and interest rates, 1967–92

government was without one of the standard economic policy instruments, and adjustment to the large terms of trade increase over the period took other forms, principally rising inflation and blunt quantitative controls.

☐ The balanced budget principle. Introduced for commendable political reasons (see Chapter 4), in some respects it has hampered the government's fiscal flexibility. Nevertheless, in practice this constraint has been less serious since the authorities effectively ran 'economic' deficits and (occasional) surpluses. In fiscal years 1991/92 and 1992/93 the government explicitly departed from this principle by establishing additional fiscal reserves.

☐ In the conduct of monetary and financial policy there has been a continual tension: (a) between regulation and direct controls, which broadly characterized the system in the 1970s, and indirect market-based interventions, which become increasingly important in the 1980s; and (b) over the extent to which social and equity objectives (such as small enterprise development) can be pursued alongside the usual macroeconomic objective of internal balance, principally the control of inflation.

☐ The transformation of monetary and financial institutions has been quite dramatic. Monetary 'restocking' has occurred, initially in response to lower inflation and a renewed confidence in the currency, and later as the menu of financial assets widened. New financial institutions have evolved. However, fiscal and monetary instruments still remain quite underdeveloped. There is no government bond market, and open market monetary operations are still evolving. In the absence of

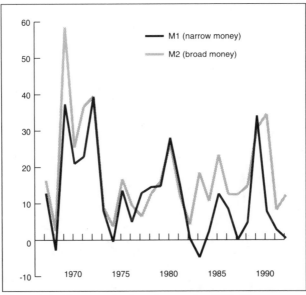

Figure 3.2 The growth of money supply, 1967–92

a private bond market, and therefore private borrowings by the government, budget deficits have to be financed directly or indirectly via the banking system. Hence there is not the sharp distinction between fiscal and monetary policy that is the case in countries with a better developed bond market.

INFLATION AND MONEY SUPPLY[3]

Figures 3.1–3.3 provide a summary picture of monetary developments over this period. In the late 1960s, the government was able to control inflation much more quickly than most observers expected. The budget deficit, which prior to 1966 had been the direct and major cause of money supply growth, was quickly brought under control. Hence inflation, which had peaked at an annual rate of almost 1,500 per cent in mid 1966, fell sharply and, at an annual rate of just 15 per cent, was effectively under control by 1969 (Figure 3.1). The very low inflation of 1971 and 1972 was, however, shortlived. Real money supply (that is, nominal money supply deflated by the inflation rate) continued to grow very rapidly through to 1972 (Figure 3.2), much higher than that of GDP or at a rate consistent with single-digit inflation. That inflation was not higher still, according to the prediction of the Quantity Theory of Money in its simplest, static formulation, may be attributed to the restoration of real money balances as the public's confidence in the stability of the currency rose. Such monetary restocking is revealed in the growth of monetary aggregates in relation to GDP. From 1967 to 1972 the M1/GDP and M2/GDP ratios rose 70 per cent and 140 per cent respectively (Figure 3.3).

To return to the inflation story, the 1972 rice crisis saw retail rice prices double over the period from August to December, and was viewed by some as the proximate cause of the sharply rising inflation in 1973. However, an accommodating monetary

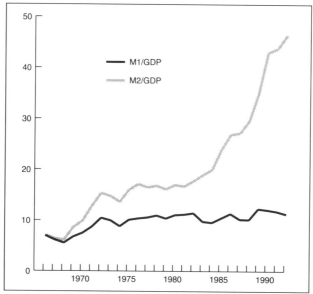

Figure 3.3   Money supply as a percentage of GDP, 1967–92

policy and rising international inflation—combined with the fixed exchange rate—
were the underlying causes. Inflation accelerated further in 1973 in response to the
quadrupling of oil prices, which led to an enormous increase in government revenue
and exports. The observations of H.W. Arndt, in the July 1974 *BIES* Survey (p. 31),
were prophetic:

> *Indonesia in 1974 is like a man who has won first prize in a lottery. The*
> *opportunities are immense, almost unimaginable. But so are the pressures and*
> *temptations to spend too much too fast, and the difficulties in making wise and*
> *effective use of the windfall.*

Inflation soared to 41 per cent in 1974, threatening the regime's hard-won
reputation for credible economic management. Drastic measures were necessary.
There was tremendous political pressure on the government to spend the windfall
gains domestically, but deflationary measures were urgently required. A range of
'*pribumi* first' promotional packages was introduced in the wake of the 1974 *Malari*
disturbances accompanying the visit of the Japanese Prime Minister. However, in
other respects the government's macroeconomic response was prompt, if blunt. The
rupiah remained pegged to the (weakening) US dollar; a revaluation might have been
appropriate, but this was still the era of fixed exchange rates, and the government
was anxious to preserve the symbols, if not the substance, of stability. Instead, the
government chose to fight inflation by, in effect, running a budget surplus with the
monetary authorities (see below), and by introducing an anti-inflationary package in
April 1974. Interest rates were increased, the banks' reserve requirements were raised
to 30 per cent, and ceilings were placed on commercial credit expansion. The latter
in particular became one of the principal instruments for controlling money supply
and growth over the next few years. The Pertamina debacle in the following year
ironically facilitated the process of monetary restraint. In the process of meeting the

state oil company's debts, large volumes of liquidity were drained from the system. Both inflation and money supply growth slowed as these measures took effect, although for most of the second half of the 1970s inflation remained stubbornly high, hovering between 10 and 20 per cent.

Trends in interest rates over this period reflected the government's ambivalent response to pressures of macroeconomic management, and the interplay of monetary conditions and government policy priorities. The very high real interest rates of the late 1960s, introduced to control inflation and stimulate saving, began to decline (Figure 3.1).[4] By 1973 they were large and negative; they remained negative throughout the oil boom period, with the minor exception of 1977-78 when they were approximately zero. Part of the explanation for these trends was conditions in international capital markets, where for a number of years negative rates became the norm. But it was also the result of deliberate government policy. At this stage, the government dominated the formal financial sector, both directly through the large market share of the state banks, and indirectly through the central bank's pervasive regulatory regime. There was a reluctance to adjust nominal rates in the face of accelerating inflation, particularly after the *Malari* incident when the government was under political pressure to support *pribumi* business. In effect, negative real rates enabled the government to subsidize priority sectors, while rationing excess demand for loan funds by administrative edict rather than through the price mechanism.[5] One consequence of this strategy was that the process of financial development and deepening was retarded. For example, negative interest rates rendered unattractive the holding of quasi-money such as time deposits. As a result, the M2/GDP ratio, hitherto rising rapidly, remained virtually constant throughout the oil boom period.

Negative real interest rates were in fact part of a deliberate government strategy of selective business promotion. Such a strategy also resulted in a heavily segmented capital market over this period. Interest rates from the state banks were far below those on offer from the non-subsidized private banks, even allowing for routine and significant corruption, and a good deal of arbitrage. The political disturbances of 1974 further increased pressure on the government to maintain these subsidized programs, and to channel more funds to *pribumi* and small-scale borrowers. In 1969 the government had introduced a program of medium- to long-term investment finance known as *Kredit Investasi Biasa* (KIB). Following the protests, KIB was supposedly to be restricted to *pribumi* borrowers. In addition, specially focused small-scale credit programs, known as KIK/KMKP, were introduced. These grew to be very large: by mid 1981 credits under these programs were equivalent to 12 per cent of total deposit money bank credit outstanding, and they served over half a million clients.[6]

To return again to the inflation story, there was another acceleration in prices in 1979. In November 1978 the rupiah was devalued by 50 per cent against the US dollar.[7] With inflation on the decline in 1977 and 1978, both domestically and internationally, it was hoped that the resulting price increases would be modest. A determined but largely ineffective program of domestic price controls was employed to make the devaluation "stick". However, less than a year later, and quite unforeseen in international markets, oil prices began to rise steeply. The government's nominal oil revenues rose almost two-fold in 1980-81, and international reserves increased by more than 50 per cent. Writing in the November 1979 *BIES* Survey, Ross Garnaut (p. 1) observed:

Like its predecessor, the Soeharto Government's third five-year plan, Repelita III, has been overtaken in its early months by a huge increase in fiscal receipts and export earnings from oil. This windfall, carrying potential for disruption of economic stability similar to that of 1974, becomes available while the economy is still recuperating from the trauma of devaluation and adjusting to large increases in world market prices for non-oil exports.

Once more, the government had great difficulty sterilizing the monetary impact of the oil boom. Money supply growth accelerated in 1980 (Figure 3.2), even though the government again ran an effective surplus with the monetary authorities. As we shall see shortly, rising international reserves were the main source of money supply growth over this period, and their impact far outweighed the government's contractionary fiscal efforts. As in the first oil boom, even with a fixed exchange rate, the government could have sterilized the monetary impact by investing abroad, settling international debts or spending in particularly import-intensive areas. The first and third options were employed to a limited extent, in the latter case exemplified by ambitious industrial sector projects and large fertilizer imports. But international aid and borrowing continued apace, because the concessional terms were generally very favourable, because of the important technology imports embodied in these transactions, and because the government wished to maintain access to international capital markets and the aid community more generally.

In other respects, however, the experience of the first and second oil boom differed. The second oil boom was smaller (that is, in terms of the percentage oil price increases) and of shorter duration. By 1982 oil prices were tapering off. Moreover, the government had learned some lessons from the first boom, and it had its (albeit still clumsy) monetary control instruments firmly in place.

THE 1980s REFORMS

Developments after 1982 differed from those of the 1970s in three important respects. First, oil prices fell and remained low. Hence the previous trigger to inflation—the monetary impact of rising terms of trade—disappeared, and in some years exerted a negative impact. In the 1982–84 period and in 1987 real M1 (but not M2) growth was either negative or close to zero. Secondly, the government slowly began to develop a more sophisticated approach to monetary policy management, in particular through increased resort to indirect intervention rather than direct regulatory controls. Thirdly, largely due to indirect intervention inflation remained low, and for most of the 1980s was less than 10 per cent. This rate was achieved in spite of two large nominal devaluations (in 1983 and 1986), and virtually continuous 'crawling peg' depreciations in other years.

The first set of monetary and financial reforms was enacted in June 1983. The state banks were now permitted to set some deposit and lending rates, except in the case of the still extensive priority programs. Credit ceilings were partially removed, and the availability of subsidized credit trimmed back. There was also the first shift to open market operations, with the development of new monetary policy instruments.[8] Implementation of these reforms remained patchy and spasmodic, however, and the government still lacked the instruments to deal with the consequences of an open international capital market. Thus, in September 1984, fears of a devaluation prompted massive capital flight and drained domestic liquidity to such an extent that overnight rates on the interbank market reached 90 per cent. Similar problems arose in the first half of 1987, culminating in decisive though heavy-handed intervention by the Acting Finance Minister, who in June ordered four large state enterprises to withdraw deposits of some Rp 900 billion from state banks and to purchase SBIs from Bank Indonesia. The intervention, which quickly saw interbank rates rise to 45 per cent and reversed the capital flight, achieved its immediate objectives. But it set back the longer-term goal of shifting towards indirect monetary management.[9]

The next major reforms, introduced in October 1988, proved to be the most decisive financial policy initiative of the decade. All domestic banks, provided they were sound, were now free to open new offices, and new private banks were permitted. Foreign banks were allowed to operate outside Jakarta subject to certain conditions. Non-bank state enterprises were permitted to deposit up to 50 per cent of their funds with private (national) banks. Reserve requirements for commercial banks were cut from 15 per cent to 2 per cent of their liabilities. A 15 per cent tax on bank deposits was introduced, primarily to stimulate the stock market. Finally, monetary policy instruments and the swap on foreign borrowings were fine tuned.

These reforms had a dramatic impact, as discussed in Chapter 9.[10] The long-dormant stock market suddenly sprang into life and for a short period registered the most spectacular increases in value and volume of turnover in the world. Indonesia for the first time experienced a genuine private banking sector boom, as these institutions began to compete aggressively for customers and market share. The state banks, long accustomed to operating as administrative arms of the central bank, were slow to adjust to these new commercial opportunities, and the decline in their market share accelerated. Private banks began to offer a wide selection of financial portfolios, including very attractive term deposit rates. The response in terms of money aggregates was quite predictable (Figure 3.3). The ratio of narrow money (M1) to GDP barely rose, since cash holdings were by then fully replenished. However, competition among the banks for customers greatly extended the financial menu, especially in the available range of term deposits. In consequence, the M2/GDP ratio began to rise very quickly, by 70 per cent over the 1987-92 period; the biggest increase occurred in 1989-90, in the immediate aftermath of the reforms.

These reforms unleashed a more competitive private banking sector. But macroeconomic management faced new challenges, particularly as both the banks and the regulatory authorities attempted to adjust to the very different financial landscape. The sharp fall in deposit requirements arguably increased the money multiplier. The particular institutional arrangements associated with the swap facility on foreign borrowings rendered more difficult the control of money supply aggregates.[11] Bank Indonesia had also shifted more to reliance on reserve money targets, rather than on interest rates as it did some years earlier.[12] A period of loose monetary policy in the immediate aftermath of the reforms created additional problems. Money supply growth was exceptionally high in 1989: real M1 grew by over 34 per cent, a figure exceeded only twice in the history of the New Order, in 1969 and 1972, both in the period of monetary restocking (Figure 3.2). As inflation jumped in response, Bank Indonesia was forced to control these monetary aggregates, by quickly pushing up interest rates. In contrast to the oil boom period, real interest rates had become positive again from 1983, partly in response to the partial banking reforms of that year, but also because, in the face of declining inflation, administered (and therefore 'sticky') nominal rates translated into higher real rates. Real rates jumped appreciably in the late 1980s, to the levels prevailing in the early stabilization period (Figure 3.1). If interest rates were 'too low' in the 1970s, a decade later many believed they were now 'too high'.

In the event, this strategy had an immediate effect on money supply: M1 growth dropped sharply, although M2 more slowly, partly because of the effects of liberalization, and an increased array of financial services on offer. Inflation began to approach 10 per cent—and according to some yardsticks probably exceeded this figure—but then subsided in the early 1990s as the tighter monetary policy took hold.

This combination of monetary looseness and financial liberalization placed great pressure on the banking system. The private banks began to seek expanded market share aggressively, by offering attractive term deposit rates. They also sought new lending opportunities, which were proliferating in the boom conditions which had developed in the late 1980s. In the process, the underlying fragility of these institutions was exposed. Breaking out of the straitjacket of heavy central bank control, few banks had much experience of project appraisal and loan assessments. There was an acute shortage of qualified staff, leading to very high salaries and frequent 'hijackings' of personnel. Accounting and auditing standards continued to be very poor. The closed nature of many of the major business conglomerates, and the fact that in many instances they were really lending back to themselves, put further strain on the system. Finally, Bank Indonesia's monitoring and supervisory capacity was still rudimentary. Over this period, there were frequent allegations that sizeable proportions of outstanding loans were either in arrears or in outright default. Yet the central bank appeared not to have accurate data on the extent of these problems. The liquidity squeeze was exacerbated at the time by the introduction of new prudential requirements designed to meet standards set by the Bank for International Settlements.

The result of all these factors has been that the banking system has a somewhat tarnished reputation, and financial scandals have diminished public and investor confidence in the reforms and in Bank Indonesia's regulatory capacity. In September 1990 it was announced that Bank Duta, a large nominally private bank which possessed impeccable political connections, had incurred foreign exchange losses of $420 million. A rescue operation was quickly mounted and several *yayasan* contributed large sums to the bank. In December 1992 another crisis emerged with the collapse of Bank Summa, an offshoot of the country's second largest conglomerate, the Astra Group. Bank Summa was the first bank to be liquidated by the central bank, when it was announced that it had non-performing loans of some Rp1.5 trillion, equivalent to about $720 million and therefore much larger than the Bank Duta case.[13] In early 1994, new problems surfaced, in this case in the form of arrests in connection with an amount of some $650 million owing to the state development bank, Bapindo. The very public airing of the case held out the prospect that the government was intent on enacting major reforms to clean up the state banking system. Also, throughout the 1990-93 mismanagement, manipulation and fraud began to tarnish the image of the Jakarta Stock Exchange. For a period, foreign and domestic investors began to withdraw from the exchange and the pace of new listings slackened off; most of the much-vaunted state enterprise offerings failed to materialize.

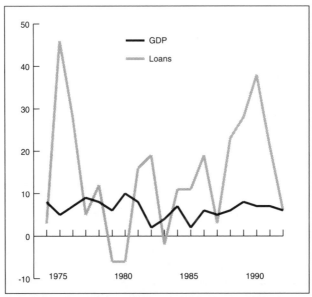

Figure 3.4 The growth of commercial loans and GDP,
1974-92

A STOCK TAKE

What are the general conclusions and implications of the Indonesian story post-1966? Looking at the long sweep of monetary and financial development over this quarter century, at least six interrelated features stand out.

First, Indonesia has never been able to match its neighbours, Singapore, Malaysia and Thailand, in providing a consistently low-inflation environment. Especially during periods of economic boom, such as the mid and late 1970s and late 1980s, serious inflationary pressures have emerged. Its record is nonetheless commendable, in stark contrast to the period up to 1966, and better than most developing countries (Little et al., 1993). When inflationary pressures have surfaced, the monetary authorities have quickly reasserted control. After 1980, inflation was held below 10 per cent. Indonesia has credibility as a macroeconomic manager, an accolade which would have been unthinkable in the 1960s. Moreover, the government is now able to control inflation in a more sophisticated fashion. During the 1970s, its policy arsenal was extremely limited. In effect, it had limited its degrees of freedom by adherence to a fixed exchange rate. It therefore had great difficulty sterilizing the monetary effects of the windfall oil gains. Similarly, the adoption of the balanced budget principle obstructed macroeconomic policy over this period to some extent, even though in practice the principle was rarely adhered to. The key to inflation control over the 1974-83 period was heavy-handed regulation of the banks, particularly their commercial credit expansion. Since the early 1980s there has been a gradual shift away from controls and towards a range of indirect levers. While the process has some way to go, Indonesia is now much better prepared to cope with sudden exogenous shocks and to maintain a predictable, low-inflation environment.

Secondly, at the risk of stating the obvious, Indonesia could hardly be characterized as a staunchly "monetarist" regime. This pejorative label has sometimes been applied by critics of the New Order government, who have viewed it as one committed to the control of inflation regardless of the economic and social consequences. While inflation control was, understandably, a high priority in the late 1960s, and there was considerable dislocation over this period, the record thereafter provides little support for such a criticism. Growth resumed quickly, and thus the social costs of dislocation were endured for only a short period. Moreover, in important respects the regime was not monetarist enough. As illustrated earlier in Figures 3.1 and 3.2, financial repression was practised, inflation was frequently at double-digit levels until the early 1980s, and money supply growth was erratic.[14]

Commercial credit expansion was also very uneven. There has, in fact, been a very weak association between the rate of growth of lending and economic activity (Figure 3.4). The growth of lending in real terms has displayed tremendous volatility since the mid-1970s, in contrast to the comparatively even pace of GDP. The impact of the government's periodic attempts to control inflation is clearly evident, in the mid-1970s, in 1979–80 (both at the height of international oil prices), 1983, 1987 (the latter two in the wake of large devaluations), and 1992. The extremely rapid growth in lending following the 1988 financial liberalization is also very clear. Again, this picture is hardly one of a devout "monetarist" regime.

A third general feature, which links directly to one of the principal themes of this book, that of rapid structural transformation, has been the growing depth and sophistication of the financial system. Indonesia had a particularly underdeveloped financial structure in the mid-1960s, in terms of the relative size of conventional monetary aggregates and the array of financial services available. The control of inflation by the late 1960s resulted in a return of confidence in the currency and in a process of monetary restocking. Monetary aggregates, relative to GDP, rose rapidly from the late 1960s, levelled off during the 1970s financial repression, and then began to rise again in response to the 1980s reforms. A much wider menu of financial services became available, particularly as a result of the 1988 reforms. Indonesia's financial sector remains underdeveloped compared with its sophisticated neighbours, Malaysia and Singapore, and also Thailand (Table 3.1). Its stock market capitalization is just a tiny fraction of these countries (and is lower also than the Philippines), while its broad money base is less well developed. But it is catching up, and will most likely continue to do so in the 1990s.

Fourthly, and related to these three points, in financial policy-making there has been a continuous tension between regulation and controls on the one hand, and liberalization and open market operations on the other. In the 1970s, as already noted, the former approach was dominant. The government had to respond quickly to the exogenous oil shock. Possessing few monetary instruments, and little experience of their practical application, the government perhaps understandably chose the regulatory route.[15] But there was also a second motive for regulation. While clamping down on monetary expansion, there was a desire to recycle at least some of the new found oil wealth through the banking sector to favoured clients, particularly rice farmers, state enterprises, and *pribumi* businesses. Throughout this period, as Grenville (1981, p. 106) observed:

> *The twin goals of a banking system which is both market-oriented and at the same time carries out a 'development' role (fostering small indigenous enterprises and financing those whose collateral or credit rating is inadequate) have sometimes proved irreconcilable.*

Table 3.1   **Indicators of Financial Development in ASEAN**
(as % of GDP)

	Stock market capitalization	Narrow money (M1)		Broad money (M2)	
	1992	*1970*	*1992*	*1970*	*1992*
Indonesia	7	8	11	10	46
Malaysia	153	17	22[a]	34	70[a]
Philippines	36	10	9	21	36
Singapore	109	28	25	66	101
Thailand	59	14	9[a]	31	77[a]

[a] Indicates refers to 1991.

Notes: Stock market capitalization data refer to end-1992 and are from *Asia Week*. M1, M2 and GDP data are from IMF, *International Financial Statistics*, various issues.

In the 1980s, the policy focus changed. The government was unable to sustain huge credit subsidies and there was growing concern that the subsidies were often misdirected and did not have the intended developmental effects.[16] In addition to scaling back the subsidies, the authorities began to reduce controls and place more reliance on indirect, market-oriented policy instruments. Notwithstanding the difficulties created by a sharp deterioration in the terms of trade during the mid-1980s, the reform process moved slowly. The two major reform packages of the decade were over five years apart. The process was set back by the two *Gebrakan Sumarlin*, heavy-handed interventions which, while successfully abating capital flight, ran counter to the government's expressed philosophy of financial deregulation. In sum, the path to financial liberalization has been a very rocky one.

In examining the record of inflation, it is instructive to examine the determinants of changes in base money. We follow here the analysis developed by McLeod (1993b), as reported in Figure 3.5. These determinants are decomposed into changes owing to three factors: fiscal transactions by the government, balance of payments transactions by the central bank, and other transactions by the central bank, much of the latter being with the private sector and selected government agencies. There is considerable volatility in all three series, and the data for 1975 are not presented because of the confusion caused by the Pertamina debacle. However, a number of observations are pertinent. First, the balance of payments has been the largest contributor on average to the expansion in base money, accounting for an average 25 per cent increase in the 1969 to 1991 period. This factor was especially important throughout the 1972–80 oil boom period and again more recently as the capital account strengthened. Secondly, the budget, by contrast, generally played an offsetting, contractionary role, with an average −12 per cent impact. Again this was evident during the oil boom period, whereas the budget had a stimulating effect during the 1980s recession. The government's practice of a balanced budget, in an accounting sense, largely contributed to the appearance of a counter-cyclical policy although, as we shall see in the next chapter, in reality this was not always the case. Thirdly, other transactions usually exerted a positive influence on base money, with an average 10 per cent increase, and without such a clear pattern of fluctuations.[17]

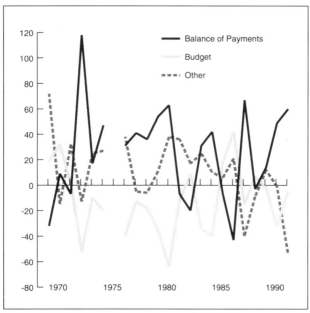

Figure 3.5 Sources of changes in base money, 1969-91

This picture therefore supports the earlier analysis concerning the proximate determinants of inflation over the New Order period. For much of the period, the key factor has been the balance of payments, and the inability of the government to sterilize its monetary impact. Fiscal policy, by contrast, has been much less significant.

Finally, Indonesia is sometimes cited as an exception to the propositions advanced in the 'sequencing' literature. According to this school of thought (see, for example, McKinnon, 1991), in the liberalization process the capital account should be opened last, after the restoration of financial stability and the opening of the current account (that is, trade liberalization). Indonesia is sometimes used as a counterexample because its international capital account was opened in 1970, while trade reform was pursued more than a decade later.

In fact, however, Indonesia's experience does not invalidate the main tenets of the sequencing literature. By 1970, inflation was broadly under control and fiscal deficits were modest. With few exceptions they have remained so ever since. The trade regime was also fairly open by the late 1960s, and quantitative restrictions quite limited. Indeed import protection was lower than the official estimates suggest, given the immediate proximity of free-trade Singapore. Smuggling, both technical and physical, was (and still is) widespread. It was only during the 1970s and early 1980s that protection proliferated.

It might be argued that the opening of the capital account was premature, in the sense that it occurred too quickly after the control of inflation, when the newly won stabilization was still fragile. However, policy-makers knew from bitter experience before 1966 that an open capital account had to be a central plank of policy:[18] Controls bred corruption and disaffection, particularly among distant exporters in the Outer Islands. International borders are as porous for goods as they are for capital, with Singapore again being a key consideration. Perhaps most important of all, these officials knew that an open capital account would impose a discipline on government and, in particular, a check on populist demands for a more adventurous monetary and fiscal policy. In all these respects they have been entirely vindicated by history. Indonesia's success in this regard has apparently continued to confound some international observers who may not comprehend fully the country's historical experience or its political economy equations.[19]

CHAPTER 4

Fiscal Policy

AN OVERVIEW

There are two fundamental differences between fiscal policy in the pre- and post-1966 eras in Indonesia. The first is that the government has ceased to be the major and direct contributor to inflation. As pointed out in Chapter 1, mounting budget deficits in the first half of the 1960s were immediately monetized by the simple expedient of printing more money. Early in the life of the New Order regime, the government adopted the "balanced budget" principle. Although in a conventional economic sense the government has continued to run budget deficits, the balanced budget rule has been firmly adhered to ever since. It is one of the basic tenets of the regime, and it helps to explain why macroeconomic stability has been broadly maintained since the late 1960s.

The second major difference concerns the size of government. Relative to the rest of the economy, the size of the government sector has risen sharply. As a share of GDP, government revenue and expenditure more than doubled over the decade to 1975. The increases have been essentially revenue-driven, as initially aid flows then rapidly rising oil prices swelled the government's coffers. In the second half of the 1980s, non-oil domestic revenues began to rise significantly. The size and funding of this expenditure has had two immediate and important political implications: the central government has had hitherto unimaginable resources at its disposal, thus reinforcing its political authority. And, until the early 1980s, most of the government's revenue was raised painlessly, financed abroad by taxpayers and oil consumers.

The government's fiscal policy objectives have been essentially three-fold:[1] to ensure macroeconomic stability, to reduce the dependence on foreign aid, and to improve income distribution. With a few exceptions, it has been successful in its first goal. Inflation was brought down surprisingly quickly in the late 1960s, and control was reasserted after each of the inflationary episodes corresponding to the peaks of international oil prices. The government was also able to reduce its dependence on foreign aid during the oil boom period, but aid became increasingly important again in the mid 1980s. The evidence with regard to income distribution is mixed, with some notable achievements on the expenditure side but much less progress on revenue.

The size of the government sector has risen dramatically since the mid-1960s. Real government expenditure (that is nominal expenditure deflated by the CPI) has risen approximately 24 times over the 1966-92 period, from about Rp 1.4 trillion to Rp 35.5 trillion, measured in 1985 prices (Figure 4.1). The increase was particularly sharp

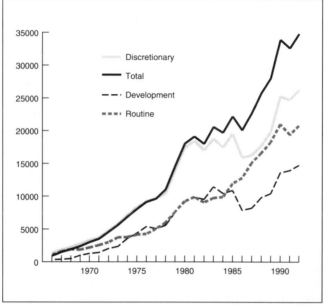

Figure 4.1   Real government expenditures, 1966–92

during the rehabilitation phase and the first oil boom. Real expenditures doubled in the 1966–69 period and more than doubled in the 1971–75 period.[2] A further sharp increase occurred around 1980, with real expenditures rising some 60 per cent from 1978 to 1980. Expenditure levels then remained flat for much of the 1980s, with a succession of austere budgets in the wake of declining international oil prices. But a strong increase occurred at the end of the decade as the economy recovered, with real expenditure increasing more than 50 per cent from 1987 to 1992.

As noted above, until 1980 government expenditure rose much more rapidly than GDP, resulting in a substantial rise in the fiscal importance of government (Figure 4.2). The share of government expenditure in GDP approximately doubled from 1966 to 1974, and almost trebled over the 1966–80 period. The sharpest increase occurred during the first oil boom period: from 14.9 per cent in 1971 to 21.6 per cent in 1975. Thereafter, the share plateaued until a further modest increase occurred in 1979–80. The share then declined during the early 1980s. There was little change during the vigorous economic growth of the late 1980s, which again underlines the major difference between this period of growth, mainly led by the private sector, and the 1970s, when the power of the state was strengthened immeasurably. Notwithstanding the decline after 1980, the government's share of GDP in 1992 was still more than double that of 1967.

These figures vastly understate the significance of the government's economic role in Indonesia. As discussed in the next Chapter, the government has a powerful regulatory presence in the economy, and it operates a large state enterprise sector. Moreover, the data in Figures 4.1 and 4.2 understate even its fiscal impact because, especially during the oil boom period, a large though unknown volume of government expenditure occurred off-budget. The most famous example of this was the state oil company Pertamina. Oil tax revenues owed to the government were simply

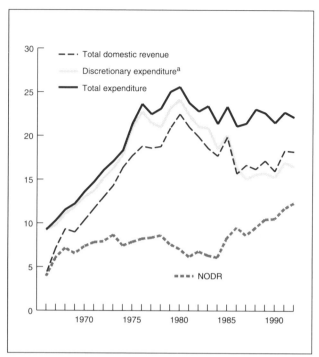

30 ┌   - - - · Total domestic revenue

         Discretionary expenditure[a]

25 ├   ─── Total expenditure

20

15

10

5   ▪ ▪ ▪ · NODR

0 └

1970   1975   1980   1985   1990

Figure 4.2   The government budget as a percentage of GDP,
1969–92

appropriated for Pertamina's grandiose projects. A good deal of defence expenditure is also known to occur off-budget, as has been the case with many of the large industrial projects of Minister Habibie since the late 1970s. The large government banking sector was the conduit for much of this off-budget expenditure. It is significant here that while the government instituted a policy of fiscal austerity from the late 1970s, bank credit continued to rise quickly (see Table 4.7, p. 61). Following the banking reforms of 1983 and 1988 the scope for off-budget expenditure via "command loans" through the state banking sector has diminished, and these banks now constitute a much smaller share of the formal banking system. But the budget still understates the government's fiscal impact on the economy.

Two points concerning the presentation of the government's fiscal statements need to be emphasized at the outset. Both cause confusion for the unwary, and both tend to obscure the economic impact of the budget. First, aggregate revenues and expenditures are always presented in official documents as being identical in an ex ante and ex post sense. This arises because the government tailors its expenditure policies to the availability of revenue from oil, other domestic sources, and aid, and because aid (including international borrowings) is included on the revenue side of the budget. Secondly, since 1969 the government has employed a distinction between "development" and "routine" expenditures. Much of the routine budget comprises civil service salaries and (from the 1980s) debt service repayments. The notional distinction that the routine budget encompasses mainly regular operating expenses and the development budget capital works does not always hold, however. For example, income supplements to civil servants are frequently paid through the

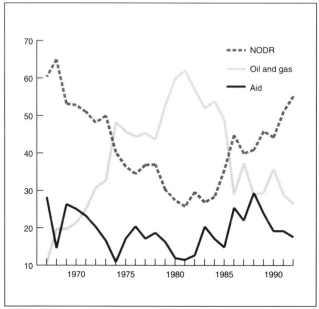

Figure 4.3   The composition of government revenue, 1967–92

development budget. Grants to the regions appear in both sections of the budget. Aid receipts are placed in the development budget, whereas their repayment is an item of the routine budget. Sectoral expenditure appears in both sections, and it is therefore difficult to obtain accurate estimates of the total in these cases. This is a frustrating presentational technique. It means, for example, that it is not possible to determine the government's total education expenditure from the official budget documents.

The following section examines trends in and the composition of revenues, placing particular emphasis on the 1980s tax reforms. Expenditures are then analysed in the following section. In a later section, the Balanced Budget Rule, the economic implications of the budget are investigated, especially the likely magnitudes of fiscal deficits, concealed as they are in the official budget figures. This is followed by a summary assessment of fiscal policy.

REVENUE

The revenue picture is dominated by the changing relative importance of the three main aggregates, oil and gas revenue, other domestic revenue (usually referred to as non-oil domestic revenue, NODR, in Indonesia), and foreign aid. In the late 1960s aid played a major role, providing 25 to 30 per cent of government revenue (Figure 4.3). Before oil prices began to rise steeply, oil and gas contributed 10 to 20 per cent of the total, with the remaining 50 to 60 per cent coming from NODR. Increasing oil prices in the 1970s resulted in significant changes in these shares. That of oil almost doubled from 1971 (25 per cent of the total) to 1974 (48 per cent), rising still further to its peak share of 62 per cent in 1981.

THE KEY ROLE OF AID

Over this period, the share of aid fell to less than 20 per cent, and during the early 1980s it was as low as 12 to 13 per cent. However, just as the government could, in deference to nationalist sentiment, credibly point to a reduced dependence on foreign aid, declining oil prices produced another major change in revenue composition. By 1986, the low point in international prices, oil's share in revenue had fallen to 29 per cent, less than one-half of that of its maximum in 1981. Even nominal oil revenues fell sharply, from Rp 11.1 trillion in 1985 to just Rp 6.3 trillion in 1986. The importance of the flexible and prompt international donor response was underlined during this difficult adjustment period. Aid revenues rose sharply, from Rp 3.6 trillion in 1985 to Rp 5.8 trillion in 1986 and Rp 10 trillion in 1988. As a share of government revenue the increases were sharper still, from 15.7 per cent to 26.3 per cent and 30.3 per cent respectively.

During the oil boom period, aid funded an increasingly small percentage of the development budget: 70 to 75 per cent of the total around 1970, declining to as little as 25 per cent in 1974 and again in 1980–82 (Figure 4.4). However, by the late 1980s its share had risen to about 70 per cent (with a high of 81.6 per cent in 1988), before falling again to less than 50 per cent in the early 1990s following half a decade of strong growth. As significant as the increased volume of aid was the flexible manner of its delivery, including a shift back to program aid and some financing of local "rupiah" items. The responsiveness of the international donor community is illustrated in part in the fluctuating share of program aid in the total (Figure 4.5). Before the oil boom, when Indonesia's financial and implementation capacity was weak, program aid made up over 50 per cent of the total. This fell sharply from the mid-1970s, and by the early 1980s was minuscule. However, its share rose quickly during the mid-1980s crisis, from 1 per cent to 34 per cent in the 1983–86 period. In 1989 aid was as important a source of revenue to the Indonesian government as it was in 1972, immediately before the first oil boom. In spite of the successful program of adjustment in the late 1980s, and notwithstanding the gradual decline in the importance of aid after 1988, Indonesia has not yet achieved one of its major fiscal objectives, that of reduced dependence on foreign aid. The annual "IGGI [since 1992 CGI] fix", to quote Benedict Anderson (1983, p. 489), remains important.

NODR AND TAXATION REFORM IN THE 1980S

Large volumes of aid, not to mention oil revenues, arguably had an adverse effect on NODR, which was overshadowed by these items from the late 1960s until the mid-1980s. The share of NODR in total revenue halved over the 1968–79 period (from 64.9 per cent to 30.2 per cent), and it fell still further during the second oil boom, to as low as 25.8 per cent in 1981. Despite the opportunities for rapid increases in NODR during the high growth 1970s, the oil boom induced a lazy fiscal regime. There was no serious attempt to overhaul ramshackle administrative structures, some inherited from the Dutch colonial era, and to ensure tax compliance. Collection processes were inefficient and corrupt. Non-oil tax revenue, as a percentage of GDP, was well below its potential, or that of comparable countries. Consequently, real NODR rose quite slowly over this period, doubling from 1969 to 1975 and rising a

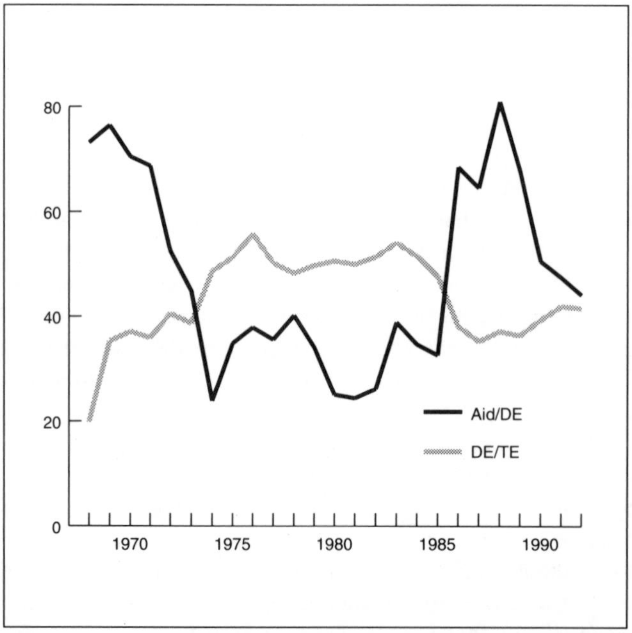

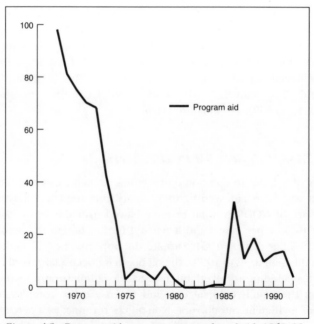

Figure 4.4 Indicators of development expenditure, 1968–92

Figure 4.5 Program aid as a percentage of total aid, 1968–92

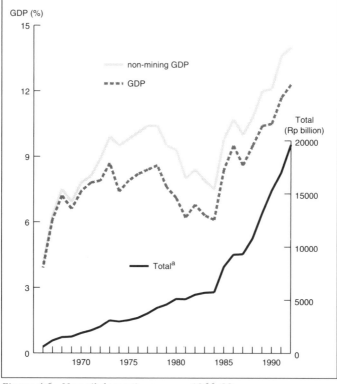

Figure 4.6   Non-oil domestic revenue, 1966-92

further 60 per cent from 1975 to 1981 (Figure 4.6). From 1969 to 1981 real GDP rose some 2.4 times, while real NODR rose by a factor of 3.3. Admittedly the "tax buoyancy" (the elasticity of increased NODR with respect to increased GDP) exceeded unity, but it should have been much higher given the extremely low initial base. Part of the problem was that the New Order inherited a "typical" developing country tax regime in which taxes on international trade were the major non-oil component. These totalled almost 37 per cent in 1969, while all indirect taxes contributed about 74 per cent of the total (Table 4.1).

It took the prospect of a significant decline in oil revenue to provide the initial stimulus for tax reform, and a decade of continuing low oil prices to ensure that these reforms were implemented with vigour. Gillis (1985, p. 224; see also Lerche, 1980) aptly summarized the situation in the early 1980s thus:

> *Perhaps the only redeeming feature of the tax regime in force in the early eighties was that enforcement of the income tax on oil companies was reasonably effective. Otherwise, the system was unproductive of revenue, ineffective in redistributing income, highly vulnerable to manipulation in compliance and administration, and was replete with incentives for inefficiency and waste.*

The reforms introduced in 1984-85, the background to which is described in detail by Gillis (1985), constituted the first serious attempt in Indonesia's independent history to produce a more efficient, buoyant, and "clean" tax system. Income and company taxation rates were unified into three marginal rates, rising from 15 per cent

Table 4.1   **The Composition of Non-oil Domestic Revenues, 1969–92**
(% of total)

Year[a]	Income tax	Indirect tax				Non-tax receipts
		Total	VA[b]	Trade	Others	
1969	24.2	74.1	17.4	36.6	20.1	1.7
1970	21.5	73.2	16.5	39.0	17.7	5.4
1971	23.7	66.8	16.2	33.9	16.7	9.6
1972	24.4	66.0	17.3	29.4	19.3	9.6
1973	24.0	67.5	18.0	33.6	15.9	8.5
1974	28.4	63.2	19.3	29.0	15.0	8.4
1975	30.8	58.1	19.3	23.7	15.1	11.1
1976	30.1	60.6	20.8	25.1	14.7	9.3
1977	31.8	59.2	20.0	23.2	16.0	9.1
1978	31.5	58.7	17.7	23.6	17.4	9.8
1979	32.5	59.8	13.5	29.0	17.3	7.7
1980	34.7	55.5	14.4	23.5	17.6	9.8
1981	38.1	52.5	14.9	18.5	19.0	9.4
1982	40.2	49.6	16.7	14.2	18.7	10.3
1983	39.3	50.1	16.9	13.5	19.7	10.6
1984	38.7	48.7	16.0	11.3	21.3	12.6
1985	28.5	53.1	28.7	8.1	16.3	18.4
1986	23.2	54.8	29.6	10.6	14.7	22.0
1987	24.8	56.9	31.5	10.4	14.9	18.4
1988	29.3	59.1	33.4	10.0	15.6	11.6
1989	31.4	56.8	33.4	10.1	13.4	11.8
1990	30.9	59.4	34.2	11.6	13.6	9.7
1991	36.1	54.5	33.6	8.1	12.8	9.4
1992	37.1	53.6	33.4	8.3	11.9	9.3

[a] Financial year (1969 refers to 1969/70, etc.).
[b] Value added tax, formerly sales tax

Source: *Nota Keuangan*, various issues.

to 35 per cent, broadly comparable with the rates being charged throughout East Asia (see Shome, 1993, Table 1 for comprehensive comparative data on tax rates). They replaced an unworkable system which previously featured as many as 17 rates for personal income tax. Investment incentives were largely abolished. Capital gains were taxed as from 1990, as was interest on bank deposits from late 1988 (the latter contributing to the stock market boom in 1989-90). The sales tax system was discarded in favour of a value added tax, introduced progressively from 1985 and self-enforcing in nature. A new more comprehensive land and buildings tax was also introduced from 1986, replacing the seven complex and unworkable land tax ordinances in existence (Kelly, 1989, 1993). In addition, since the mid-1980s there have been various attempts at inculcating civic fiscal obligations. In a society known previously for its extraordinary secrecy on tax matters, lists of major corporate and individual tax payers—including the President—are now released. This trend towards commercial openness has been hastened in some measure by the "regularization" of commercial reporting practices, as more and more companies have sought to go public. The identity of the prominent taxpayers so revealed, both confirmed *pribumi* suspicions regarding the extent of non-*pribumi* control over the economy, and ameliorated this dissatisfaction to the extent that the latter were now seen to be contributing to public revenue.

The results of these reforms have been impressive. Real NODR rose appreciably after 1984: over the 1973–84 period they increased by some 86 per cent, whereas the increase from 1984 to 1992 was over 200 per cent (Figure 4.6). Particularly sharp increases occurred in the mid-1980s, with the introduction of the VAT, and from the late 1980s, with further reforms and much more vigorous implementation. All budgets in the early 1990s have foreshadowed additional large increases, and there now appears to be both the political will and the institutional capacity to carry out these ambitious targets.[3] These trends resulted in an appreciable rise in the share of NODR in GDP, and implied a significant rise in tax buoyancy. For the 1966–92 period the share rose over three-fold, and slightly faster as a percentage of non-mining GDP. But almost all the increases were concentrated in the periods from 1966 to 1973 and after 1984. For both series the NODR share actually declined over the oil boom decade from 1973 to 1983 (Figure 4.6).

Important compositional shifts have also occurred within the NODR category (Table 4.1). Some of these predate the 1980s tax reform. For example, the relative importance of trade taxes shrunk continuously from the late 1960s, reaching a low of just 8 per cent in 1985. The decline was explained by the removal or reduction of most export taxes, especially in the April 1976 reform package, and by the shift from tariffs to non-tariff barriers, which was particularly pronounced in the early 1980s. By far the most successful item in the tax reforms has been the VAT, which more than doubled its share of NODR from 1984 to 1991 (from 16 per cent to 33.6 per cent), and which until 1991 exceeded direct tax as the primary source of revenue in this group. The introduction of the tax was relatively painless, and its self-policing nature reduced the scope for evasion. Over time its coverage has been extended, and it has become more progressive through the introduction of higher rates for luxury items such as automobiles. Thus the record on VAT is an impressive achievement, given the complexity of the changes and the time required to educate both officials and taxpayers.

The record on other taxes has been mixed. The system of property tax was reformed following the introduction of a new land and building tax (PBB, *pajak bumi dan bangunan*), which replaced the old land tax, *Ipeda* (Kelly, 1989, 1993). PBB revenues began to rise quickly, more than trebling from 1986 to 1992. However, the amounts involved are still quite modest, and collection is hampered by the pervasive corruption that exists in the land market. Attempts to increase income and corporate tax returns have also met with mixed success. The contribution of direct taxes, on individuals and corporations (but excluding oil taxes, which appear as a separate budget item), has risen significantly since the 1960s. But most of the increase occurred in the 1970s. Its proportion of NODR actually fell sharply during the first half of the 1980s, during the period of slower economic growth, and following the introduction of new tax scales in 1984 and the vigorous indirect tax effort (Table 4.1). With the introduction of more realistic schedules, during the 1980s there was an effort to collect more direct tax, and receipts more than doubled in real terms from 1984 to 1991. This has now become a major government priority, as evidenced in the steep rises in the early 1990s, and a determination to extend coverage to the country's newly emerging middle class. If implementation is comprehensive, there is much scope for continuing large increases, especially as standards of accounting and

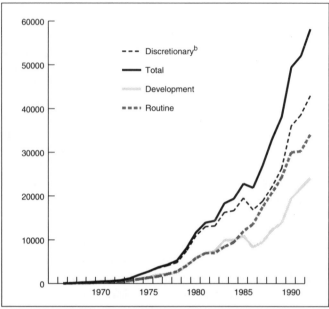

Figure 4.7   Government expenditure, 1966-92

auditing improve and because the number of taxpayers is still very small.[4] Nevertheless, tax bargaining and evasion are still widespread, and attempts to meet ever more ambitious targets are likely to encounter stiff opposition from powerful vested interests.

EXPENDITURE

MAJOR TRENDS

The trends in expenditures mirror those of the revenues in important respects. Real government expenditure rose very sharply in the 1970s, in direct response to the oil revenue and aid inflows (Figures 4.1 and 4.7). The government quickly began to allocate an increasing proportion of its budget to "development" expenditures, the latter's share rising from 20 per cent in 1968 to 56 per cent at the height of the oil boom in 1976 (Figure 4.8). The rising proportion of funds spent on development projects over this period corresponded to the declining importance of aid as a source of development expenditure (Figure 4.4), and for similar reasons.

The seemingly inexorable growth in government expenditure came to a sudden halt in 1984 when, for the first time in the regime's history, real expenditure actually declined. After a modest increase in 1985, real expenditure declined further in 1986, when the government faced its most serious fiscal problems since 1966. These difficulties were compounded by the fact that, just as the oil revenue began to decline, debt servicing (DS) obligations rose sharply. DS, which is classified as part of the routine budget, absorbed less than 10 per cent of expenditure throughout the 1970s; in the mid-1970s it was less than 5 per cent (Figure 4.8). However, it rose sharply in the 1980s, from 8.4 per cent in 1982 to 14.5 per cent in 1985 and 30.3 per cent in 1987.

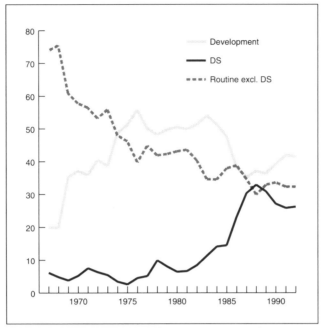

Figure 4.8   The composition of government expenditures,
1967–92

The government thus faced a "scissor problem", hemmed in by declining revenue and rising DS payments. Since practically all the debt was (and is) external, the counterpart in the balance of payments over this period was net outward resource flows (Table 5.1, p. 67). Consequently, the government's "discretionary expenditure" (that is, total expenditure less DS payments) fell more sharply still (Figures 4.1 and 4.7). Real discretionary expenditures (measured in 1985 prices) peaked at Rp 19.5 trillion in 1985, but fell by almost one-fifth to Rp 15.9 trillion in 1986. They recovered in the late 1980s, but even by 1989 they were only 7 per cent higher than those of 1981, equivalent to a fall of about 10 per cent in per capita terms over the decade. The government was able to insulate the community—and particularly civil servants— from some of the austerity by focusing most of the cuts in the development budget.[5] However, real routine expenditures had risen very little from 1980 to 1984, and so the scope for major reductions in this component of the budget was limited.

The adjustment process was facilitated by sharp reductions in a range of government subsidies (Table 4.2). Food (mainly rice) subsidies were phased out in 1981 as domestic supplies began to increase quickly. Indeed rice consumers began to be taxed in the 1980s, as domestic prices exceeded those in the international market. The oil price subsidy also fell quickly after 1981. In the early 1980s this was achieved through a series of large increases in domestic petroleum prices, while from 1984 to 1986 it resulted from a constant nominal domestic price in the face of falling international prices. The sharp jump in 1990 reflected the short-lived price rise as a consequence of the Middle East dispute. The government finally abolished the subsidy altogether in the 1994 budget, and given low international price levels over this period began to actually tax consumers for the first time. The fertilizer subsidy has proved

Table 4.2 **Government Subsidies, 1973–92**
(Rp billion)

Year	Food	Oil	Fertilizer
1973	0	0	33
1974	154	0	227
1975	50	0	135
1976	39	35	107
1977	0	65	32
1978	44	197	83
1979	125	535	125
1980	282	1,022	284
1981	224	1,316	371
1982	1	962	420
1983	0	928	324
1984	0	507	732
1985	0	374	477
1986	0	0	467
1987	0	402	756
1988	0	133	200
1989	0	706	278
1990	0	3,301	265
1991	0	1,030	301
1992	0	692	175

Source: As for Figure 4.1.

more resistant to change. It increased substantially in the first half of the 1980s and by 1987 constituted some 15 per cent of the total development budget. By this time, any economic rationale for the subsidy—such as the need to induce farmers to "commercialize" their inputs—had disappeared. In effect it had become a subsidy to vested producer interests (Tabor, 1992, pp. 180-3).[6] In response to mounting criticism on both economic and environmental grounds, the subsidy was scaled back from 1988, but by the early 1990s it was still sizeable.

Notwithstanding the strong recovery from the late 1980s, these fiscal data underline the diminished economic authority of the central government. By the late 1980s, the discretionary and development budgets were smaller in real per capita terms than they were almost a decade ago. The most difficult fiscal and balance of payments challenges of 1985-86 had been negotiated successfully. By 1992 debt payments had fallen back to one-quarter of total expenditures, the share of development expenditures had risen, and real discretionary expenditures were on the increase. But maturing debt obligations and soft international oil markets meant that the period of politically painless revenue increases was over. The old adage "no taxation without representation" began to assume particular significance in the late 1980s.[7] These fiscal challenges set the agenda for the microeconomic reform program, for the measures to enhance NODR, and for continuing financial austerity.

MAJOR COMPONENTS

As argued above, the presentation of budgetary data in Indonesia does not facilitate easy analysis of fiscal policy and its components. It is regrettable, in particular, that no estimates of the overall fiscal impact of the budget are available, and that integrated sectoral expenditures are not presented. Nevertheless, a number of observations may be made on both the routine and development components of expenditure.

First, the analysis of trends in the composition of the routine budget is relatively straightforward (Table 4.3). In the early years of the New Order, civil servants' salaries dominated the picture, accounting for almost half the total. Regional subsidies and categories termed "material" and "other" expenses, not disaggregated, absorbed most of the remainder of the routine budget. Debt payments, curiously located in this section of the budget, were minor, and as a percentage of the total budget they actually declined through the early 1970s (Figure 4.8). There were no major changes in the rankings of these four items during the 1970s, with salaries continuing to be the most important among them. However, important compositional changes were evident during the fiscal austerity of the 1980s. Debt payments began to rise sharply from the late 1970s, quadrupling in nominal terms from 1977 to 1981, and again from 1982 to 1986. Since the overall budget was now increasing very slowly, these increases translated into a dramatic rise in shares, from 10.6 per cent in 1977 to 52.8 per cent in 1988. These payments overtook salaries in 1986, and have remained much larger ever since. Total expenditure on salaries increased slowly through this period. On several occasions (including the three election years, 1982, 1987, and 1992) substantive rates were frozen, resulting in considerable real declines, exacerbated further in the middle year by savage cuts in the development budget, from which civil servants typically receive salary supplementation.[8] Regional subsidies were also affected by the fiscal austerity, although in deference to the importance of regional sentiment the cutbacks were less than those of salaries. Material and other expenditures were cut the most severely and, for a period, allocations of both building programs and routine office expenses were virtually frozen.

By contrast, the development budget has displayed much more fluctuation (Table 4.4). It grew extremely rapidly during the oil boom period, by some 15 times in nominal terms from 1973 to 1981. But then it was subject to much sharper cutbacks in the mid-1980s: with salaries and debt absorbing more than three-quarters of the routine budget in some years, the government had much less flexibility in this area, and so had little choice but to concentrate the austerity in the development budget. Thus the total was slashed by about 23 per cent in nominal terms in 1986. Since project aid commitments could not easily be trimmed (and in some cases donors assisted by providing some rupiah funding), other items bore the brunt of the cuts. Departments' development budgets were reduced extremely sharply and in 1987 they were less than one-third of the 1985 total in nominal terms. The "other" item, mainly subsidies and state enterprise investments at this time, was also cut, though not as sharply. Similarly, regional expenditures were pruned, but as with the routine budget this item was insulated from the austerity to some degree. As the economic recovery gathered pace, real expenditures began to increase, consistent with the government's target that the development budget comprise over half the total, as it did in the late 1970s and early 1980s.

How have the government's sectoral priorities changed over time? The New Order has issued six Five Year Plans (*Repelita*), and we now have data for realized development expenditure for five of them. To examine the changing patterns, it is useful to look at the first year of each plan, together with the most recent year for which data are available (Table 4.5). At the beginning of *Repelita* I, in 1969, the

Table 4.3   **Major Components of Routine Expenditure, 1969–92**
(Rp billion)

Year[a]	Personnel		Regional subsidies	Debt	Materials & other	Total
	Total	Salaries & pensions				
1969	103.8	56.4	44.1	14.4	54.2	216.5
1970	131.4	70.6	56.2	25.6	75.0	288.2
1971	163.4	99.7	66.8	46.6	72.3	349.1
1972	200.4	131.6	83.9	53.4	100.4	438.1
1973	268.9	173.9	108.6	70.7	265.1	713.3
1974	420.1	301.7	201.9	73.7	320.4	1,016.1
1975	593.9	400.0	284.5	78.5	375.7	1,332.6
1976	636.6	424.8	313.0	189.5	490.7	1,629.8
1977	893.2	672.9	478.4	228.3	549.0	2,148.9
1978	1,001.6	760.3	522.3	534.5	685.3	2,743.7
1979	1,419.9	1,053.9	669.9	684.1	1,287.9	4,061.8
1980	2,023.3	1,482.9	976.1	784.8	2,015.8	5,800.0
1981	2,277.1	1,660.4	1,209.1	931.1	2,560.3	6,977.6
1982	2,418.1	1,749.0	1,315.4	1,224.5	2,038.3	6,996.3
1983	2,757.0	1,996.0	1,547.0	2,102.6	2,005.2	8,411.8
1984	3,046.8	2,206.6	1,883.3	2,776.5	1,722.4	9,429.0
1985	4,018.3	3,072.6	2,489.0	3,323.1	2,121.1	11,951.5
1986	4,310.6	3,330.0	2,649.7	5,058.1	1,540.9	13,559.3
1987	4,616.9	3,561.0	2,815.6	8,204.6	1,844.4	17,481.5
1988	4,998.2	3,832.7	3,037.7	10,940.2	1,762.9	20,739.0
1989	6,201.5	4,826.0	3,566.4	11,938.7	2,624.5	24,331.1
1990	7,053.5	5,570.5	4,236.6	13,394.6	5,313.0	29,997.7
1991	8,102.5	6,299.3	4,834.2	13,433.8	3,857.1	30,227.6
1992	9,465.7	7,532.8	5,283.2	15,217.1	4,065.2	34,031.2

[a] Financial years (that is, 1969 refers to 1969/70, etc.).

Source: Nota Keuangan, various issues

emphasis was very much on basic infrastructure and sectoral development. These three items (that is, agriculture, industry/mining, and communications) dominated the budget, absorbing over 70 per cent of the total. At the outset of Repelita II, changing priorities were in evidence. Agriculture was by far the most important sector, receiving over 30 per cent of the total. This was shortly after the 1972–73 rice crisis, and the period when the foundations for the rapid growth in rice production were laid. Regional development expenditure and state enterprise investments also began to figure prominently; the regions have retained their high priority ever since. Together with the three large items of Repelita I, the regions and state enterprises received 84 per cent of the allocated funds in that year.

Further changes of emphasis are evident in 1979, six years into the oil boom. These five sectors retained their importance (industry and mining and energy were now subdivided), but new priorities emerged. The most important of these were defence, education, and labour and transmigration. Part of the increase in defence expenditure was probably due to the "regularization" of funding for the armed forces, as more of the expenditures appeared in the budget. Education received higher priority at all levels, but particularly with the drive to achieve universal primary school enrolments. The ambitious transmigration scheme, designed to shift large numbers of people from Java–Bali to more remote regions of the country, was also getting under way over

Table 4.4   **Major Components of Development Expenditure, 1969–92**
(Rp billion)

Year[a]	Departments	Regional[b]	Other[c]	Project aid	Total
1969	79.8	5.5	7.6	25.3	118.2
1970	83.0	32.7	12.4	48.7	176.8
1971	102.6	37.3	11.0	63.5	214.4
1972	150.0	57.8	28.1	74.4	310.3
1973	167.3	85.7	83.8	121.5	458.3
1974	221.6	158.3	386.0	203.7	969.6
1975	384.9	234.2	307.2	474.6	1,400.9
1976	590.9	285.0	405.0	779.1	2,060.0
1977	744.5	366.3	308.4	740.7	2,159.9
1978	851.0	431.1	286.2	989.6	2,557.9
1979	1,480.3	548.9	668.7	1,318.2	4,016.1
1980	2,533.2	807.6	1,145.6	1,434.4	5,920.8
1981	2,724.6	1,134.0	1,417.6	1,667.8	6,944.0
1982	3,260.9	1,090.4	1,083.4	1,927.3	7,362.0
1983	3,219.6	1,447.5	1,364.6	3,871.6	9,903.3
1984	3,474.4	1,526.2	1,542.6	3,411.3	9,954.5
1985	4,466.5	1,502.6	1,400.6	3,504.2	10,873.9
1986	2,003.5	1,466.5	1,067.3	3,796.2	8,333.5
1987	1,384.6	1,334.3	1,328.3	5,432.6	9,479.8
1988	1,855.3	1,491.7	953.7	7,955.3	12,256.0
1989	2,508.8	1,720.1	1,183.3	8,425.8	13,838.0
1990	4,853.7	2,997.7	3,092.8	8,509.1	19,453.3
1991	5,971.4	3,953.2	2,993.8	8,847.9	21,766.3
1992	7,858.0	5,040.3	1,032.5	10,206.2	24,137.0

[a] Financial years (that is, 1969 refers to 1969/70, etc.)
[b] Includes grants to regions and *Inpres* schemes.
[c] Includes the fertilizer subsidy, government equity investments, and other expenditures. In 1990 and 1991, it also includes special fiscal reserves, of Rp 2 trillion and Rp 1.5 trillion, respectively.

Source: Nota Keuangan, various issues.

this period. Five years later, in 1984, agriculture and communications still retained their highest rankings, but education had moved into third place. In the latter two years identified in Table 4.5, the emphasis was clearly on physical and social infrastructure. Communications was the largest recipient, having overtaken agriculture. Mining and energy, the regions, and education all received a high priority. The shares of defence and state enterprise investments declined. The environment began to receive significant funding by the late 1980s.

Among these items the special case of defence requires further explanation. The New Order is an unusual regime in this respect—an army-dominated government, albeit with an increasingly civilian flavour by the late 1980s, which has nevertheless starved the armed forces of funding. As shown in Table 4.5, defence has never ranked highly in the development budget. Moreover, by any international yardstick, defence spending has been relatively small. Among its ASEAN neighbours, for example, apart from the special case of the Philippines, until recently under the US military umbrella, Indonesia has consistently recorded the lowest military expenditure as a proportion of GDP (Figure 4.9). Indeed, in most years it has been less than half the Malaysian and Singaporean ratios. Moreover, Indonesia's figure declined consistently through the 1980s.

Table 4.5 **Development Expenditure by Sector, 1969–92**
(Rp billion)

Sector	1969	1974	1979	1984	1989	1992[c]
Agriculture[b]	29.8	301.8	508.2	1,699.1	2,049.4	3,240.2
Industry	} 21.3	} 149.7	356.3	602.9	399.8	570.2
Mining and energy			376.4	1,147.7	1,417.3	3,332.9
Communications[c]	33.3	123.5	465.8	1,428.3	3,006.0	4,537.2
Trade and cooperatives	a	4.2	30.5	342.5	414.5	338.4
Labour and transmigration	0.2	4.5	162.2	421.6	281.2	897.3
Regions	5.9	135.9	335.8	790.8	1,369.4	2,920.1
Religion	1.2	3.0	19.0	59.8	24.9	69.3
Education	8.1	47.2	361.4	1,231.0	1,506.6	3,146.7
Health, social[d]	} 5.4	25.3	142.4	320.0	469.9	957.2
Housing		6.5	117.3	224.2	494.6	1,053.1
Law	a	1.9	30.8	60.5	25.1	74.9
Defence	4.6	22.7	330.2	702.3	720.1	1,203.7
Information	a	2.7	22.4	45.5	59.7	81.9
Science and technology	a	11.2	58.0	190.0	333.5	585.8
State apparatus	a	23.9	111.5	164.3	163.8	326.2
Commercial investments	0	97.8	465.6	291.7	624.9	408.9
Environment	0	0	120.4	229.7	473.6	390.8
Total	118.2	961.8	4,014.2	9,951.9	13,834.3	24,134.8

[a] Included in Other, totalling Rp 8.4 billion.
[b] Includes irrigation.
[c] Includes tourism.
[d] Includes also women's affairs and family planning.
[e] All years are financial years (1969 refers to 1969/70, etc.).

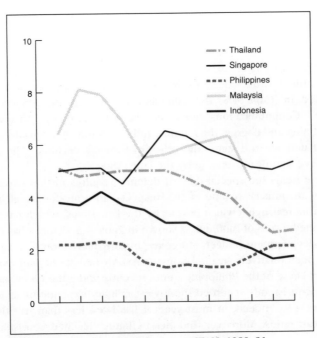

Figure 4.9 Defence expenditure in ASEAN, 1980-91

These figures require qualification in a number of respects. In international comparisons, there needs to be adjustment for the fact that large countries do not have to allocate such a high proportion of resources to achieve a defence force of the same size. In the ASEAN comparison, much higher wage levels in Singapore and Malaysia partly explain these countries' higher ratios. In addition, there is much off-budget military expenditure in Indonesia, through various government concessions and facilities (the timber industry has always featured heavy military involvement, for example), and through a host of informal exactions. Nevertheless, it is likely that, as a proportion of the total military budget, the latter are declining. There has been much less scope for largesse through informal channels following the decline in oil prices; the termination of most subsidized interest programs removed a major source of funding for the military; and Indonesia's budgetary procedures are a good deal more "regular" than they were in the early years of the New Order.[9]

A final feature of the development budget worthy of note concerns the components of the regional development expenditures (Table 4.6). As noted above, these have become increasingly important over the course of the New Order, even though a coherent funding rationale for them has not yet emerged (see Chapter 11). In the first *Repelita*, the small sums involved were allocated to Irian Jaya, as part of special funding arrangements in the wake of that province's incorporation into Indonesia, and to village development. During the oil boom period, these grants were extended as part of the *Inpres* (*Instruksi Presiden*, Presidential Instruction) scheme. They have been viewed as a means of promoting rural development and of recycling the sudden windfall revenue gains relatively quickly, and somewhat free of the usual bureaucratic constraints on such expenditure programs. Primary schools and first and second tier regional governments were initially the major beneficiaries. These three sectors have continued to be important throughout the New Order period. Over time the central government has begun to strengthen administrative capacity below the subprovincial level, enabling it to direct increasing proportions of funds directly to second tier (*kabupaten* and *kotamadya*) and village governments. Expenditure on roads has risen sharply since the early 1980s, and is now the single largest grant item. Special grants to the provinces of East Timor and Irian Jaya have been phased out, although these provinces continue to be treated relatively generously in other respects. The land and building tax (PBB) has been returned to subnational governments, although it is collected by the national government. Health, regreening and markets have also been funded.

THE BALANCED BUDGET RULE

No slogan has been more central in the New Order's economic philosophy than that of the balanced budget (BB). The regime correctly points to the financial profligacy and recklessness of the Sukarno era as the principal explanation for accelerating inflation and economic decline. Early in its life the Soeharto regime initiated the balanced budget principle, from which it has rarely deviated. Each year the government introduces a budget in which, ex post, realized expenditures equal realized revenues, and in which planned aggregates for the coming year are equal.

In an economic sense the BB is, of course, a fiction. The budget is "balanced" only because the items financing the deficit (aid and external borrowings) are counted as

Table 4.6 **Regional Development Expenditures, 1969–92**
(Rp billion)

	1969	1974	1979	1984	1989	1992
Villages	2.6	11.4	31.0	92.8	112.0	326.5
Kabupaten and municipalities	0	42.5	87.1	194.6	270.0	825.1
Provinces	0	47.4	100.8	253.0	324.0	701.2
Primary schools	0	19.7	155.8	572.0	100.0	654.5
Health	0	5.3	30.0	64.6	122.2	320.0
Markets	0	0	12.4	25.5	3.0	1.5
Regreening	0	0	40.8	61.2	16.2	95.0
Roads and bridges	0	0	13.0	101.1	294.5	1,225.0
East Timor and Irian Jaya	2.9	4.0	6.6	4.2	0	0
Land & building tax	0	28.0	71.4	157.2	478.2	891.5
Total	5.5	158.3	548.9	1,526.2	1,720.1	5,040.3

Note: Data refer to financial years (1969 to 1969/70, etc.).

"revenue". If they were excluded, the budget would not be in balance and in most years the government would be revealed as running a deficit. The BB rule therefore raises interesting economic and political questions. Why was it instituted, and what is the real economic impact of the budget?

The answer to the first part of the question is straightforward. It was introduced as a clever and effective political tactic to guard against a recurrence of the financial excesses of the early 1960s. By ensuring that expenditure is determined by revenue—the latter albeit elastically defined—the government has been able to control political pressures demanding economically unsustainable expenditure levels. As one senior government official has put it:

> *The strongest case for the balanced budget principle rests on the politico-economic argument. Balanced budget is a simple rule, and while certainly not optimal, makes life easier for everybody including the Minister of Finance and the Minister for Development Planning who have to be constantly on guard against excessive demands for funds by other agencies in the government. (Boediono, 1990, p. 13)*

The budget's economic impact is far less clear. The government has consistently run a deficit, and an increasingly large one in the late 1980s, if the measure adopted is total domestic revenue (oil and non-oil) less all expenditure (see Table 4.7, column 2). Yet such a measure does not capture accurately the domestic economic impact of the budget, since there are large "leakages" (abroad) on both sides of the ledger. Almost all debt service payments are to creditors abroad; the import-intensive oil sector includes significant payments to factors abroad; and a substantial, though probably declining, proportion of the development budget consists of material and capital imports.

A number of alternative estimates of the budgetary impact have been proposed. One approach is to calculate the effect of advances to the government on the increase in money supply (Table 4.7, column 3). This series suggests that the government has adopted a conservative fiscal strategy. In most years these advances have been negative, indicating that the government was in surplus with the monetary system. The surpluses were generally larger at the height of the oil booms (1974 was an

Table 4.7   **Estimates of the Budget Impact, 1969–92**
(Rp billion)

	IMF	E-R[a]	Monetary impact[b]	
			Govt.	Govt. +SEs
1969	−76	−91	4	−22
1970	−101	−113	19	−5
1971	−91	−117	−16	−29
1972	−117	−146	20	−23
1973	−163	−197	24	−9
1974	−168	−224	−25	−334
1975	−468	−488	410	−518
1976	−693	−778	387	−37
1977	−393	−770	293	230
1978	−754	−1,033	291	−683
1979	−764	−1,379	1,140	890
1980	−1,102	−1,489	1,876	1,336
1981	−1,172	−1,705	131	−552
1982	−1,191	−1,938	−581	−963
1983	−1,862	−3,878	2,220	1,942
1984	−1,219	−3,475	2,878	2,740
1985	−948	−3,572	−1,199	−1,376
1986	−3,621	−5,751	1,503	863
1987	−1,028	−6,156	−1,822	−2,355
1988	−4,179	−9,985	102	−1,113
1989	−3,362	−9,426	62	−1,046
1990	−798	−9,903	4,819	6,323
1991	—	−10,407	2,407	895
1992	—	−10,714	62	9

[a] Refers to total expenditure less total domestic revenue
[b] Refers to expansion in the money supply due to (i) advances to the government, and
(ii) advances to the government plus bank credit to state enterprises and public
entities.

Note: Minus sign indicates a deficit or borrowings.
Sources: IMF, *Government Finance Statistics,* various issues; and *Nota Keuangan,* various issues.

exception) and during the more recently instituted tight money policy, 1990–91 (see also Figure 3.5). Conversely, during the difficult adjustment period of 1985-87 the government was a net borrower from the monetary system. However, the data in column 3 understate the impact of the government since, as noted above, some of its activities have occurred off-budget, including those projects funded through the banking system. Accordingly, if "government" is extended to include bank credit to public enterprises and entities, a deficit is recorded in most years (see column 4). Most of the surpluses (employing the narrow government definition) of the oil boom period are transformed into deficits according to this wider definition. The difference reflects the growth in bank credit for the state enterprise sector, ranging from the major claimants such as Pertamina, Bulog, and Minister Habibie's projects, through to the 200 or so non-bank commercial enterprises under government control.

A third estimate of the budget's economic impact is that prepared by the International Monetary Fund according to the procedure employed in its *Government Finance Statistics Yearbook* (Table 4.7, column 1, and Figure 4.10). This series

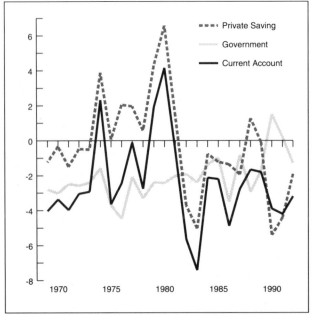

Figure 4.10 Macroeconomic balances, 1969–92

suggests that, except for 1990 and 1991, the government has run a deficit in every year since 1969, though on a significantly smaller scale than that suggested by a simple comparison of total expenditure and domestic revenue (column 2). As a proportion of GDP, according to this definition, the deficit has been with the 2 to 3 per cent range, somewhat lower (less than 2 per cent) in 1974, 1982, 1984–85, and 1987, and considerably higher (above 3.5 per cent) in 1975, 1976 and 1986 (Figure 4.10). *Prima facie*, this series suggests that the government has not attempted to run a countercyclical fiscal policy, since small and large deficits have both been recorded in years of boom and recession. Part of the explanation for the historically high deficits in 1975 and 1976 was undoubtedly the debt payments in the wake of the Pertamina crisis.[10]

Is there now a case for rethinking in the BB rule? Fiscal policy has been less flexible as a result of the rule. In the peak oil boom period the government might have run a surplus to dampen inflation, while in the mid-1980s a carefully targeted and modest fiscal stimulus might have been appropriate. Adherence to the BB rule, and the absence of a market for government securities, have meant that fiscal fine-tuning, not to mention countercyclical strategies, have rarely been a feature of economic policy since 1966. Consequently, monetary policy and quantitative restrictions on bank credit (up to 1983) have been the primary instruments of short-run macroeconomic stabilization.

Conversely, one would hesitate to recommend tampering with a system which has assisted in delivering reasonably good outcomes in terms of macroeconomic stability, and which may still be politically the most effective mechanism for delivering expenditure restraint. Moreover, the system is not as rigid as it might appear to be (Boediono, 1990). The government was able to sterilize some of the windfall oil revenues in the 1970s, and later to stimulate the economy in the mid-1980s, through its transactions with the monetary sector (Table 4.7, columns 3 and 4). In budget years 1990 and 1991, the government deliberately adopted a cautious fiscal stance, for a number of reasons,[11] and established special fiscal reserves of Rp 2 trillion and Rp 1.5 trillion respectively. These reserves coincide with, and largely explain, the New Order's two real budget surpluses since 1966. They also demonstrate that there is more flexibility in the system than is commonly appreciated.

A SUMMING UP

What of the New Order's fiscal record, on balance? The regime has assigned itself three principal, and widely accepted, targets. It is useful to evaluate its performance in light of these objectives.

First, macroeconomic stability. Here the record is an unambiguous success. Fiscal policy has lacked flexibility owing both to the rigidities inherent in the balanced budget rule, and to the absence of a well-developed government bonds market. In periods of boom, such as the mid-1970s, late 1970s and late 1980s, inflation has emerged as a serious problem. Nevertheless, the fiscal regime has contributed to impressive outcomes in terms of macroeconomic stability. Each time inflationary pressures have developed, there has been a firm response. The record was especially exemplary during the 1980s, when a series of austere budgets was introduced in response to declining oil prices. Few countries can match Indonesia in its stabilization policies, as emphasized in the large comparative World Bank research project on the subject (Little et al., 1993).

The government's second objective, that of reducing its dependence on foreign aid, remains as elusive as ever.[12] During the oil boom period the relative importance of aid flows fell sharply, but in the mid-1980s they rose again, to a level approaching that of the early 1970s. The mid-1980s witnessed the first serious attempt to tackle the regime's poor record of (non-oil) tax collection. There have been notable achievements in the past decade, particularly in the case of the VAT and, more recently, income tax. But the agenda of unfinished business is a lengthy one. The tax structure is at best only weakly progressive. Tax evasion and straight-out corruption are still formidable problems. Regional finance arrangements are in need of major reform (Chapter 11). Perhaps most serious of all is the huge undercollection of rents in the timber industry, discussed in Chapter 7.

Finally, there has been little serious research on the equity implications of the fiscal regime. At best the tax regime is only mildly progressive and, given non-compliance among the politically powerful and rich, it may even be regressive. On the expenditure side, the picture is more positive. The evidence suggests that Indonesia's relatively good equity and poverty alleviation record during the adjustment period 1984–87 is at least partly due to the targeted nature of the government's expenditure programs. Two pieces of recent empirical research support such a conclusion.

First, van de Walle (1992) analyzed the distributional implications of public expenditure on health and education, using the 1978 and 1987 Susenas (national socioeconomic survey) data. Besides finding considerable progress in both areas, and a general narrowing of differentials by gender, socioeconomic status, and region (see Chapters 10 and 11), she also concluded that public expenditure was well targeted. In explaining improved education attainment, her results indicate

> ... *rising living standards played a part* ... *but that other factors* ... *contributed substantially more to overall shifts, and in particular to those in female enrolments. Public policy aimed at increasing the number of primary schools and teachers, as well as lowering the costs of having children attend elementary school, is likely to have been crucial to these effects* ... *Government subsidies for education are quite well targeted and this is particularly so for primary education. (van de Walle, 1992, pp. 40-1)*

By contrast, health subsidies were found to be less well targeted, and to be only mildly progressive at best.

The second piece of research was conducted by Thorbecke (1992), who focused on the impact of the mid-1980s period of stabilization and structural adjustment. Constructing a CGE model of the Indonesian economy, he conducted a series of five counterfactual policy experiments,[13] and assessed their impact on a range of outcomes. His conclusions were instructive: The adopted reform package was found to be:

> ... *superior to practically all other alternatives in its impact on growth, income distribution and the restoration of internal and external equilibrium, in both the short run and medium to long run. (p. 106)*

CHAPTER 5

International Dimensions

AN OVERVIEW

Trade policy is another area where a marked shift in economic policies and priorities occurred after 1966. During the first half of the 1960s Indonesia had been disengaging steadily from the international economy. Moreover, its declining trade, investment and aid relationships, such as they were, were oriented increasingly towards the then USSR, eastern Europe, and China. By 1965 the government was unable to service its hard currency debt of some $2.5 billion. In December of that year, for the first time, the central bank was unable to honour letters of credit. In 1966, debt repayments were estimated to be about $530 million, exceeding the projected official foreign exchange earnings of $430 million. Businesses were closing down because necessary raw materials and spare parts could not be imported. The public was exhorted to eat maize and other rice substitutes to reduce the nation's rice import bill. Multiple exchange rates and a proliferation of trade restrictions produced a flourishing and uncontrollable illegal trade, mainly across the Straits of Malacca. Cash crop exporters in Sumatra were unwilling to surrender their foreign exchange earnings at a ridiculously low exchange rate to an uncaring Jakarta government.[1]

The reopening of international commercial channels after 1966, and the impact of the global economy on Indonesian development, are of great interest for a number of reasons. The government began to dismantle the maze of trade regulations quite quickly, introducing a series of major liberalizing reforms over the 1966–69 period. By 1970 a unified exchange rate had been restored and the international capital account was virtually completely open. As noted in the previous chapter, this has been one of the cornerstones of macroeconomic policy over the New Order period, and has acted as a brake on the government's fiscal and monetary excesses. With these reforms Indonesia was at last adopting the outward-looking economic policies which have contributed so much to the whole of East Asia's economic success. Nevertheless, merchandise trade flows were heavily regulated from the mid-1970s until the late 1980s. Despite its open international capital account, in its trade policies Indonesia remained an inward-looking economy over this period.

Paradoxically, for all the lingering reservations in Indonesia towards international markets, the country has benefited immensely from its openness to the world economy.[2] Indonesia has enjoyed a very close relationship with the international aid community, both bilateral donors and multinational organizations. Aid played a critical role in the early years of the regime. Meetings were arranged with non-communist creditors in 1966, culminating in the formal establishment of the Inter-Governmental

Group on Indonesia (IGGI) in 1967, which has met annually thereafter.[3] Debts were quickly rescheduled, and the consortium's confidence in the regime facilitated the resumption of private capital inflows. During the period of balance of payments difficulties some 20 years later, when petroleum prices halved, the donor community was again responsive and supportive.

In other respects, too, the international economic environment has been benign. Indonesia's terms of trade rose steeply during the 1970s in the wake of the OPEC initiatives, and remained at historically high levels even after declining significantly from 1982 to 1986. Merchandise exports have faced comparatively few international market restrictions, apart from some primary commodity cartels (now largely moribund) and quotas on textile and garment sales which became binding (but subject to loopholes) by the late 1980s. In addition, Indonesia has been favoured by geography. Its proximity to the high-growth East Asian economies has propelled its own development in a number of ways.

An examination of the structure and impact of international trade and payments since 1966 is important for a number of other reasons. First, there are interesting analytical issues associated with Indonesia's adjustment to the large exogenous oil shocks. These include adaptation to the changing relative prices induced by large fluctuations in the terms of trade, the management of exchange rate, monetary and fiscal policy during this period, and adjustment to rising external indebtedness after 1985. Indonesia has performed much better than most petroleum-dependent economies in these areas since 1970, and there are significant general lessons from its experience.

Secondly, as noted above, the order of Indonesia's major policy reforms does not conform to the postulates of the sequencing literature. According to this view, the international capital account should be opened "last", that is, *after* fiscal and monetary reforms have been introduced and the current account opened.[4] Owing to historically specific factors (the proximity of Singapore with its completely open capital account, and the evident futility of controls before 1966), and to the speed of monetary and fiscal stabilization after 1966, the opening of the capital account caused very little dislocation. It has continued to discipline economic policy-making ever since.

Thirdly, trade patterns are indicative of important shifts in economic structure and regional orientation over the past quarter-century. Since the 1980s two such shifts have been especially pronounced. These are Indonesia's increasing economic integration within the dynamic East Asian region and the rapid growth of manufactured exports. International commercial diplomacy has also become a more important policy issue, through Indonesia's membership of ASEAN and its participation in the Asia Pacific Economic Conference forum.

THE BALANCE OF PAYMENTS[5]

Table 5.1 provides a summary picture of Indonesia's balance of payments since 1969. There are both continuities and discontinuities in this picture. The former include oil and gas exports "financing" most of the other current account transactions, a current account deficit in almost every year, and large official capital inflows. Equally there are some sharp discontinuities, notably during the period of the oil boom, and in the late 1980s when heavy debt amortization became a feature as non-oil exports began to increase significantly.

Table 5.1   **Summary Balance of Payments, 1969–92[a]**
($ million)

	1969	1970	1971	1972	1973	1974	1975	1976
1. Net oil/LNG exports[b]	92	135	204	399	641	2,638	3,138	3,710
2. Net non-oil/LNG exports	−593	−523	−652	−956	−1,397	−2,776	−3,992	−4,512
—merchandise trade	−349	−247	−332	−518	−708	−1,789	−2,606	−2,557
—services trade	−244	−276	−320	−438	−689	−987	−1,386	−1,955
3. Current account (=1+2)	−501	−388	−448	−557	−756	−138	−854	−802
4. Official capital movements	371	369	400	481	643	660	1,995	1,823
5. Debt amortization	−31	−47	−78	−66	−81	−89	−77	−166
6. Other capital movements[c]	62	143	220	480	+549	−131	−1,075	+38
7. Total (=3+4+5+6)	−99	+77	+94	+338	+355	+302	−11	+893
8. Errors and omissions	+56	−95	+6	+87	+5	−311	−353	+108
9. Monetary movements [= −(7+8)][d]	+43	+18	−100	−425	−360	+9	+364	−1,001

	1977	1978	1979	1980	1981	1982	1983	1984
1. Net oil/LNG exports[b]	4,445	4,010	6,975	10,601	9,761	7,166	7,371	7,816
2. Net non-oil/LNG exports	−5,135	−5,165	−4,777	−8,470	−12,551	−14,205	−11,522	−9,784
—merchandise trade	−2,869	−2,753	−1,879	−4,974	−8,825	−10,203	−7,448	−5,723
—services trade	−2,266	−2,412	−2,898	−3,496	−3,726	−4,002	−4,074	−4,061
3. Current account (=1+2)	−690	−1,155	+2,198	+2,131	−2,790	−7,039	−4,151	−1,968
4. Official capital movements	2,106	2,208	+2,690	+2,684	+3,521	5,011	5,793	3,519
5. Debt amortization	−761	−632	−692	−615	−809	−926	−1,010	−1,292
6. Other capital movements[c]	+176	456	−1,253	−299	1,140	+1,795	1,191	499
7. Total (=3+4+5+6)	+831	877	2,943	+3,901	+1,062	−1,159	+1,823	758
8. Errors and omissions	−180	−169	−1,253	−1,165	−2,050	−2,121	+247	−91
9. Monetary movements [= −(7+8)][d]	−651	−708	−1,690	−2,736	+988	+3,280	−2,070	−667

	1985	1986	1987	1988	1989	1990	1991	1992
1. Net oil/LNG exports[b]	6,123	2,584	3,760	3,060	3,911	6,010	4,562	3,515
2. Net non-oil/LNG exports	−7,955	−6,635	−5,467	−4,919	−5,510	−9,751	−8,914	−6,077
—merchandise trade	−3,903	−2,625	−1,095	−55	−352	−4,068	−2,652	1,072
—services trade	−4,052	−4,010	−4,372	−4,864	−5,158	−5,683	−6,262	−7,148
3. Current account (=1+2)	−1,832	−4,051	−1,707	−1,859	−1,599	−3,741	−4,352	−2,561
4. Official capital movements	3,432	5,472	4,575	6,588	5,516	5,006	5,600	5,755
5. Debt amortization	−1,644	−2,129	−3,049	−3,763	−3,686	−4,082	−4,182	−4,840
6. Other capital movements[c]	572	+1,232	+1,709	−211	+575	+5,856	+4,133	+4,284
7. Total (=3+4+5+6)	528	524	1,528	755	806	3,039	1,199	+2,638
8. Errors and omissions	−498	−1,262	+57	−1,432	−558	+263	−218	−1,199
9. Monetary movements [= −(7+8)][d]	−30	+738	−1,585	+677	−248	−3,302	−981	−1,439

[a] Refers to fiscal years (that is, 1969 refers to 1969/70, and similarly for following years).
[b] Includes services for oil and gas.
[c] Includes SDRs 1969-71, 1978-80.
[d] A negative amount refers to the accumulation of assets.

Source: Nota Keuangan, various issues.

Exports began to rise quickly from the late 1960s, quadrupling over the 1969-72 period in response to the adoption of a realistic foreign exchange regime and buoyed especially by the timber boom (Manning, 1971). The most dramatic increase then occurred in 1974, when the nominal value of net oil exports rose more than four-fold. These values were sustained in the next few years, followed by a further massive

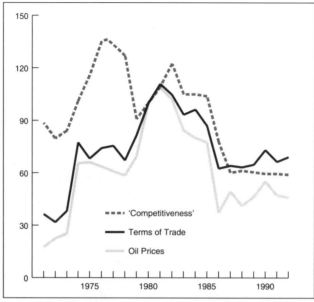

Figure 5.1   The terms of trade, oil prices, and competitiveness,
1971–92

increase from 1978 to 1980. The value of oil exports fell quickly from the 1980 peak, plateauing for three years from 1982 to 1984. It then plunged precipitously in 1986 to less than one-quarter of the nominal value in 1980 and lower even than that of 1974. The decline would have been sharper still but for the commencement in 1977 of LNG exports, the value of which by 1990 equalled that of oil and oil products. The value of oil and gas exports recovered somewhat from the trough of 1986, but remained flat apart from a temporary increase in 1990 following the short-lived Middle East dispute. Throughout this period price variations have been the major factor determining the fluctuations in the value of oil exports.[6] Indonesia has usually observed OPEC output quotas, and output expansion has generally been inhibited by financial considerations. Exploration has been less attractive during periods of low prices, such as after 1985, while Indonesia's tough fiscal regime deterred companies during peak oil price periods.

The magnitude of these external shocks is illustrated clearly in Figure 5.1. Over the 1971–75 period the real international oil price almost quadrupled, followed by a further 90 per cent rise from 1978 to 1981. The slide was almost as severe, with the real price declining by over 25 per cent from 1981 to 1984 and more than 100 per cent in 1986. Because oil has until recently dominated Indonesia's balance of payments, the terms of trade have mirrored these fluctuations closely. Non-oil commodity exports were significant prior to 1970 while manufactures grew rapidly after 1985. But over the 1971–87 period Indonesia was very much a petroleum-dependent economy, with all the potential for instability that this status implied. Figure 5.1 also draws attention to one of the key instruments in Indonesia's post-oil adjustments, its exchange rate management. We return to this issue shortly.

Non-oil current account transactions essentially adjusted, with a lag, to movements in oil exports up to the mid-1980s. Net non-oil imports rose steeply in the mid 1970s—

quadrupling from 1972 to 1975—and again from the late 1970s, but declined sharply after 1982. By 1986, for example, the nominal value of non-oil and total merchandise imports had fallen to approximately two-thirds that of the peak year 1982. That they fell consistently and quickly over this period is testimony to the government's prompt and effective response to declining oil prices. Absorption, especially including the cancellation or scaling down of many large, import-intensive government projects, and expenditure switching (notably the 1983 and 1986 devaluations), were the key to this successful restraint.

The major autonomous movements in the current account, independent of oil price fluctuations, have been the growth of non-oil exports and rising interest payments on external debt during the 1980s. Although overshadowed by oil, non-oil exports grew quite strongly for some periods of the 1970s in response to favourable international commodity prices.[7] However, most commodity prices remained depressed in the 1980s,[8] with the result that non-oil exports declined from 1979 to 1983. Growth has however been sustained and rapid in the decade since the manufacturing export boom took hold. Interest payments on external debt became a significant factor in the increased service "imports" recorded from the late 1970s.

Indonesia entered the first oil boom period with a comparatively high though sustainable current account deficit which, over the 1969–72 period, was some 30 to 50 per cent of merchandise exports. This inherited feature, plus the surge in non-oil imports, explains why current account deficits continued to be recorded during the first oil boom. The sudden increase in oil prices in 1979, the devaluation of late 1978, and fiscal caution in the wake of the Pertamina crisis of 1975–76 all combined to produce the regime's first current account surpluses in 1979 and 1980. However, the delayed effect of the import response to the second oil boom, together with a sudden softening in international oil markets, resulted in an alarmingly large current account deficit in 1982. The deficit was quickly reduced as the government took prompt remedial action. However, it increased sharply again in 1986 as oil prices collapsed. Once more, the deficit was brought down quickly. It is the management of the current account, together with control of inflation, that have established the regime as an effective and credible macroeconomic manager. On each occasion when serious macroeconomic imbalances have emerged—sometimes, though not always, in response to government excesses—the response has been prompt and decisive.

This tight balance of payments management is illustrated further in Figure 4.10.[9] As a percentage of GDP, the current account deficit was comparatively large from 1969 to 1971. A surplus was recorded in 1974, and again in 1979–80. The sharp deterioration of 1982 and 1983 is clearly evident, the latter year registering the highest percentage deficit of the entire period, greater even than the figure for 1986. It was the signal for the change in policy direction in the 1980s, because it strengthened the technocrats' arguments for macroeconomic caution and microeconomic reform. The deficit also rose sharply in the early 1990s in response to the return of high economic growth, but was again controlled quite quickly.

Because so much of the capital transactions have, until recently, been in the government sector, the capital account has generally responded to and accommodated developments in the current account, rather than the reverse. Official capital inflows record the very large aid receipts over the entire period. These rose steeply after the first oil boom, when large inflows were not needed for balance of payments support. However, the government actively sought aid because it embodied urgently required technical inputs. Donors, too, were eager to be involved, for commercial–strategic reasons and to indicate their approval of the regime's effective economic management. For example, writing in the March 1972 *BIES* Survey, Benjamin Higgins observed that " ... the Indonesian Government comes close to being able to write its own foreign aid ticket". A similarly sharp and lagged increase in aid occurred after the second round of oil price increases.

During the 1970s, debt amortization was relatively trivial. The debt from the Sukarno era was rescheduled, many of the new loans contained a significant grace period before repayment commenced, and the economy was growing so quickly that even rising absolute debt repayments were a shrinking percentage of GDP and exports. The first significant increase in debt amortization occurred in 1977, but payments plateaued over the next four years. Repayment obligations began to rise quickly only after 1983, which coincided with declining oil prices. Indonesia, like other oil exporters, then faced its most severe problem of external indebtedness. As we shall see, it was rescued by effective macro and microeconomic reform, the fruits of productive investments (especially in food crops and infrastructure) during the oil boom period, and a flexible response from the international donor community.

As would be expected, other capital flows have fluctuated much more. At the beginning of the period, SDRs (special drawing rights) were sizeable, being more than half the "other" total in 1969. Thereafter, as Indonesia's balance of payments strengthened, SDRs became quite unimportant. Except for 1974, foreign direct investment was positive in all years. Most of the fluctuation within this category is explained by the volatility of the oil sector (especially, paradoxically, in the peak oil boom years of 1979–80) and the repayment of short-term Pertamina debt in 1975. Private sector flows became more important in the late 1980s. Most of the capital flight, which was particularly pronounced in 1984 and 1987, is not registered in these capital movements, owing to their short-term nature and to weaknesses in the statistical recording system. Reflecting these weaknesses, the errors and omissions item is very large in some years.

Owing to its open international capital account, estimates of private sector external indebtedness are necessarily very crude. However, until the late 1980s public sector debt probably accounted for well over 80 per cent of the total. Private sector external debt began to rise quickly at this time, for a number of reasons. Indonesia's major business conglomerates were forging new international connections, and for the first time obtained an established reputation in international capital markets. Very high domestic interest rates, even allowing for inflation rate differentials and exchange risk, made offshore borrowing attractive. Rising private sector external debt did, however, become an issue of heated public debate from around 1990. Some of the debt appeared to have been undertaken by politically powerful individuals with the possibility of state guarantees and support. It was for this reason that the technocrats, seemingly helpless to control such borrowings, in September 1991 resorted to the second-best expedient which involved a modest departure from the fundamental axiom of an open capital account. Under the new policy, all foreign borrowings undertaken by, or involving, state entities (including the banks) would have to receive the permission of a coordinating team of senior officials. By early 1994, the team was still in existence. Its longevity now threatens the viability of this fundamental tenet of the New Order regime.

Indonesia's response to the sizeable exogenous shocks of the 1970s and 1980s is central to an understanding of the country's good economic performance over the past quarter-century. Many factors contributed to these good outcomes, and it is useful to examine them separately, under the following five headings: external debt management, exchange rate policy, the foreign investment regime, the relationship with the donor community, and the supply response to the microeconomic reforms which began in 1985. These sections constitute the major part of the remainder of this chapter. In the final section, the interrelated issues of shifts in the regional patterns of Indonesia's trade, investment and aid relationships are examined.

It is important to emphasize that the components of the adjustment program were interrelated, and that their combined effect was greater than the sum of the individual initiatives. The far-reaching policy reforms during the 1980s took a number of forms (the summary chronology shows the main components and their sequence): in fiscal policy, large government projects were cancelled or scaled down in 1983 and again in 1991, while a regime of austerity was maintained continuously after 1983. Two large devaluations occurred in 1983 and 1986 and, combined with low inflation and a continuing downward "float", exchange rates constituted an important spur to competitiveness. Trade policy reforms enabled exporters to compete without significant domestic cost handicaps. A more liberal foreign investment code, combined with the above reforms, attracted a flood of new investment.

EXTERNAL DEBT

How did Indonesia manage to avoid the debt crisis in the 1980s, a crisis which afflicted so many developing countries, particularly the oil exporters? Indonesia's debt was already sizeable at the peak of the second oil boom, at $21 billion, equivalent to 28 per cent of GDP (Table 5.2). However, buoyant exports at this time resulted in a low debt-service ratio, of some 14 per cent. Declining oil prices in the first half of the 1980s resulted in the rapid accumulation of debt. Both total debt and its proportion of GDP approximately doubled between 1980 and 1986. The debt service ratio increased faster still, almost trebling. As noted above the maturity profile of the debt placed further strains on the balance of payments: while net resource flows continued to be large and positive, net transfers remained negative.[10] Perhaps the most difficult period of debt management was in 1986–87, when a large current account deficit, rapid appreciation of the yen (in which some 40 per cent of Indonesia's debt was denominated) following the G-7 Plaza Accord, and negative net transfers resulted in a sharp escalation of debt. Indonesia's dollar-denominated debt rose by $9.7 billion in that year, and was now equivalent to 69 per cent of GDP. If Indonesia was ever going to have to reschedule or default, it would have been at this time.

Thereafter, debt management became a good deal more comfortable. The debt service ratio rose still further in 1988, but then declined as rapid export growth took hold. Total debt continued to rise sharply from 1989 to 1992, owing largely to a substantial increase in private sector borrowing, again pushing up the debt/GDP ratio. However, the management of the current account deficit remained tight, debt service ratios were well below those of the difficult years from 1986 to 1988, and net transfers were once again positive.

Despite the more comfortable position in the 1990s, external indebtedness and the

Table 5.2   **Indicators of Indonesia's External Debt, 1980–92**

	Total[a]	Private non-guaranteed	Net resource flows[a]	Net transfers[a]	Total debt, % of GDP	Debt service as % of exports	Debt as % of exports	% of Total	
								Short-term	Concess-ional
1980	20,944	3,142	1,902	−2,514	28.0	13.9	94.2	13.2	36.4
1982	26,305	3,200	2,785	−2,676	29.2	18.1	116.3	13.0	32.2
1983	29,978	3,400	4,285	−952	37.0	20.1	150.8	10.5	29.0
1984	31,861	3,800	3,009	−1,662	38.7	21.3	143.5	12.0	26.9
1985	34,265	3,837	1,583	−2,603	40.9	28.8	169.6	10.6	27.1
1986	40,071	3,778	1,953	−1,888	52.2	37.3	249.8	9.0	27.3
1987	49,738	4,571	3,371	−625	68.8	37.0	262.9	7.3	29.1
1988	51,415	5,545	3,727	−545	64.1	40.2	239.5	7.9	29.3
1989	53,494	6,556	4,143	−722	59.5	35.4	209.1	9.9	29.7
1990	67,011	10,343	6,120	781	66.4	31.0	224.3	16.7	27.8
1991	76,110	12,943	6,409	625	69.0	32.6	230.7	18.9	27.9
1992	84,385	16,891	7,711	1,764	67.4	32.1	231.2	21.6	26.6

[a] $ million.

Source: World Bank, *World Debt Tables, 1993–94*, and earlier issues.

current account deficits continued to preoccupy policy-makers and public commentators. There are very few accurate data on private debt, especially that with a short-term maturity. The figures in Table 5.2 are almost certainly a considerable underestimate.[11] Informed estimates suggest that Indonesia's total debt may actually exceed $100 billion, although no official confirmation of this figure has been forthcoming. There has perhaps been excessive public attention on the magnitude of this debt, and much less analysis of its composition. In the absence of distortions in factor and goods markets, and putting aside concerns of sovereign risk, it makes sense for Indonesia to borrow abroad for projects where the rate of return exceeds the costs of borrowed funds. The real issue is whether these funds are being used productively. On the latter, there has been insufficient analysis, apart from the focus on the "megaprojects" which surfaced in the 1990–92 period and some of the "high-tech" investment projects of Minister Habibie. No accurate and detailed compilation of the external debt holdings has ever been released.

Two additional aspects of this debt management record warrant comment. The first is that the debt structure has eased the process of adjustment. The "short-term" (less than one-year maturity) component of the total remained small throughout the 1980s, rarely exceeding 12 per cent, and rising sharply only in the 1990s.[12] Indonesia was therefore less vulnerable to sudden swings in creditors' perceptions of the country's economic prospects, a factor of some importance from 1983 to 1986 in the more exposed Philippines' debt structure. A second significant feature has been the concessional component of the debt. Reflecting Indonesia's close relationship with the international donor community, the share of this debt has remained in the 25 to 30 per cent range since 1984, even with the resumption of rapid growth from 1988.

Indonesia's debt management performance also compared favourably in international perspective over this period (Table 5.3). The country started the 1980s in a position roughly similar to that of other large oil exporters, and the "moderately

Table 5.3   Indonesia's External Debt in Comparative Perspective

	Indonesia	Mexico	Nigeria	Moderately indebted countries	
				Low-income	Middle-income
Total debt ($ million)					
1980	20,944	57,378	8,934		
1986	40,071	100,881	23,403		
1992	84,385	113,378	30,998		
Debt/GDP (%)					
1980	28.0	30.5	10.1	20.6	38.2
1986	52.2	82.9	60.5	33.4	27.2
1992	67.4	35.2	110.7	47.6	34.3
Debt service/Exports (%)					
1980	13.9	49.5	4.2	12.4	13.7
1986	37.3	54.2	32.7	32.2	25.0
1992	32.1	44.4	30.6	25.4	21.1
Total debt/Exports (%)					
1980	94.2	259.2	32.2	126.6	85.0
1986	249.8	422.7	370.4	274.5	163.7
1992	231.2	243.2	251.3	248.3	182.4
Concessional/Total debt (%)					
1980	36.4	0.9	6.1	59.6	9.0
1986	27.3	0.4	2.1	46.1	7.5
1992	26.6	1.1	3.9	42.3	8.1

Source: World Bank. *World Debt Tables, 1993-94,* and earlier issues.

indebted" group in which it is classified by the World Bank. Its various debt ratios were appreciably higher than those of Nigeria, while its debt service was much lower than Mexico. But in other respects the initial conditions were approximately comparable. Its record through the decade was similar to that of the moderately indebted group (Indonesia dropped from "middle-" to "low-income" in 1987, owing primarily to its successive devaluations), which as a whole did not experience such a steep decline in their terms of trade. Mexico arguably adjusted more quickly over the period as a whole. All its ratios declined between 1986 and 1992, but at a cost of much slower growth. Nigeria not only experienced slower growth, but its debt rose to unmanageable proportions and in 1992 exceeded its GDP by 11 per cent.[13] A striking difference has been in the proportion of Indonesia's debt on concessional terms, which has consistently remained far higher than that of either the other two oil exporters or the middle income group, underlining again the value of its close ties with the international aid community. Indonesia was also able to avoid the painful debt restructuring which Nigeria, Mexico and many other countries had to endure.

EXCHANGE RATE MANAGEMENT

Exchange rate management has been one of the regime's most obvious success stories, in which minor qualifications and shortcomings should not be allowed to obscure the big picture of notable achievement. The realignment and liberalization of the exchange rate in the early years of the New Order regime was swift and effective. By 1970 all vestiges of the old multiple exchange rate system had been removed entirely and a "market-consistent" rate had been established. Combined with tight fiscal policy and the sharp reduction in inflation, this was arguably the major achievement in economic policy-making during the first four years of the regime. Following a further devaluation in August 1971 the rupiah was then pegged to the US dollar for over seven years, ushering in a period of unprecedented exchange rate stability.

In fact, there was probably too much "stability". The massive inflows of funds from oil and aid for the first time in Indonesia's independent history transformed the balance of payments. If the rupiah had been allowed to float freely, it almost certainly would have *appreciated*, as most writers of this period emphasize.[14] The reluctance of the government to employ exchange rate policy as a means of macroeconomic stabilization was perhaps understandable. A predictable and stable macroeconomic environment had just been achieved. This was also still the era when fixed exchange rates were the norm. But the cost was accelerating inflation, indeed the only serious inflationary episode over the period since 1968. Money supply grew rapidly, fuelled by the accumulation of international reserves (see Chapter 3), and inflation peaked at 40 per cent in 1974.

The next major phase in exchange rate policy was the surprising and ill-fated 50 per cent devaluation of November 1978: surprising because of the strength of the balance of payments at the time of the devaluation. Ill-fated because less than 12 months later the Iran–Iraq dispute led to a second round of very large oil price increases. The devaluation was motivated by a concern to increase non-oil exports, which had been squeezed by the effective appreciation of the rupiah after 1973. Both balance of payments and income distribution motives were important. The former were bolstered by the view that international oil prices were tapering off, while the latter consideration focused on the cash-crop producing regions off-Java and on the importance of stimulating manufactured exports. The devaluation was preceded by a period of low inflation, and accompanied by tight fiscal and monetary policy. There were various and unsuccessful attempts to freeze and otherwise regulate prices after the devaluation.[15] However, the beneficial effects of the devaluation began to be eroded fairly quickly during the second round of oil price increases, which again led to rapid monetary expansion.

This brings us to the post-oil boom period of the 1980s when exchange rate management was particularly effective. There were large devaluations in March 1983 and September 1986, and a gradual nominal depreciation for much of the period since then. Both devaluations had little inflationary impact. They "stuck" because money supply growth was very low, the latter in part the result of the sharp decline in oil prices. Fiscal policy was also austere over this period, including a freeze on civil service wages for three years from 1986 to 1988, and deficits exceeded 4 per cent of GDP on only one occasion (Figure 4.10). There is little doubt that exchange rate management, together with the trade reforms (particularly the very liberal import procedures for exporters introduced in May 1986) to be discussed in the next chapter, were the major determinants of the surge of labour-intensive manufacturing exports which, in turn, averted a balance of payments crisis after 1986.

After the 1986 devaluation, the central bank adopted a "managed float" policy. The three large devaluations were viewed as excessively destabilizing, in that they created much business uncertainty. Thereafter the objective was to maintain a constant real

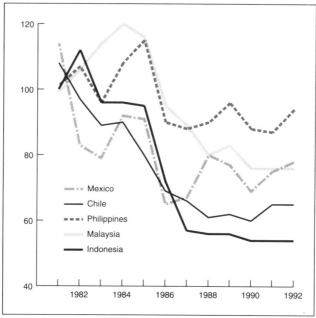

Figure 5.2   Indonesia's exchange rate management in
comparative perspective, 1981-92

effective exchange rate which, given Indonesia's slightly higher inflation rates as
compared with its major trading partners, translated into something approximating a
5 per cent depreciation against the dollar. In the early 1990s this strategy was modified
to incorporate movements against a basket of currencies. The rate continued to be
administratively set, and in no sense was a genuine float in which market forces
determined day-to-day movements. Despite this "stability" and the country's
comfortable level of international reserves since 1987, on occasions the capital market
has been apprehensive, anticipating yet another large devaluation. To stem large
capital outflows expecting such a devaluation, the government has twice intervened
to push up interest rates by the simple yet overbearing strategy of compelling state
enterprises to rearrange their banking deposits (see Chapter 3, The 1980s Reforms).

  While the overall impact of exchange rate movements is clear enough, the precise
magnitude of these changes is not. The issue here is whether the devaluations should
be measured by means of a "competitiveness" index—a "real effective" rate,
adjusting nominal exchange rate movements for relative inflation rates in Indonesia
and its major trading partners—or by means of a relative price index of tradeables to
non-tradeables.[16] The former approach has the virtue that international comparative
data are readily available. These data, published by Morgan Guaranty and employed
in Figure 5.1, indicate that from 1983 onwards Indonesia recorded a very sharp real
effective depreciation, or at least a major increase in competitiveness. Indeed, using
1980–82 as a base period, Indonesia had easily the lowest rate by 1992 (and
throughout the 1986–92 period) among a representative sample of ASEAN and Latin
American countries (Figure 5.2). This conclusion holds not only for these five
countries but for the larger sample of countries included in the Morgan series.[17,18]

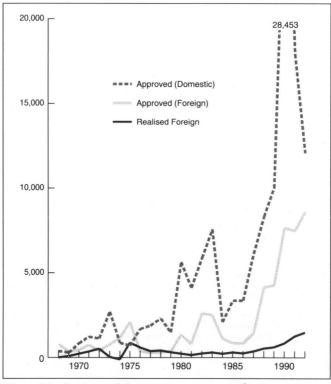

Figure 5.3   Foreign and domestic investment, 1968–92

FOREIGN INVESTMENT

Foreign investment made a significant contribution to economic recovery and export growth in the late 1960s and 1980s. Absolute amounts of foreign investment rose rapidly in both periods. In the 1980s, unlike the earlier period, foreign firms began to engage in efficient, export-oriented projects, mainly in manufacturing but also in services. Over the whole New Order period, foreign investment flows have fluctuated considerably (Figure 5.3) in response to domestic economic conditions and the regulatory regime.[19] These investments grew rapidly from the late 1960s spurred on by the new liberal fiscal and regulatory regime, the prospects of lucrative import substitution projects, and rising oil prices. The actual figure, as distinct from the approvals, was then negative in 1974, the only year of net outflow since 1967, as more restrictive regulations affecting both the oil and non-oil sectors were introduced. A sharp jump was recorded in 1975 as investor confidence returned and the huge Asahan project (arguably still the largest single investment in the nation's history) commenced.

In the next few years rapid growth made Indonesia an attractive destination for foreign firms, but they were deterred by an increasingly restrictive regulatory regime. After 1974 foreign firms were excluded from a number of sectors, there was mounting pressure for localization (of both equity shares and senior personnel), and bureaucratic procedures were time-consuming and complex. In the wake of the second oil boom the government announced an ambitious heavy industry program, and invited the participation of foreign firms. However, many of these projects were

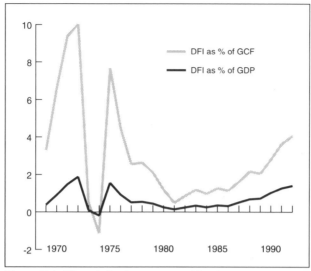

Figure 5.4   The relative importance of foreign investment,
1969-92

never implemented, as indicated by the large gap between the realized and approved foreign totals in 1982 and 1983. There was also an increase in 1983, a year of low economic growth, as investors sought to take advantage of fiscal incentives which were withdrawn as part of the 1984 tax package. All three series revealed subdued investor interest from 1984 to 1986. In 1987 and 1988 sweeping changes to the investment regulatory regime were announced which, combined with the other reform measures and accelerating economic growth, generated strong investor interest, for the first time primarily export-oriented in nature (Pangestu, 1991b; Thee, 1991). In 1992, 100 per cent foreign ownership was again permitted, with conditions, returning the regime to its liberal orientation of the late 1960s.

Three additional observations are relevant concerning trends in foreign investment. First, domestic approvals have exceeded those of foreign firms in all but four of the 25 years from 1968 to 1992, and in every year after 1975 (Figure 5.3). Moreover, the gap between the two widened during the reform period of the late 1980s as the domestic conglomerates became a significant commercial force.[20] The data provide a convincing refutation of any notion of "denationalization" which is sometimes advanced in the Latin American literature on foreign investment.

Secondly, both groups of investors have responded in like fashion to the same commercial environment and policy emphases. At an aggregate level, this is revealed in the fact that the sectoral compositions of foreign and domestic investment in BKPM sectors (that is, excluding oil, LNG, and finance) have been quite similar (Table 5.4). Non-oil industry, broadly defined, has been easily the largest recipient of investment, with over 80 per cent of the totals through to 1980 and 69 per cent to 1992. In both cases, too, manufacturing has dominated this sector; the higher share of foreign firms in mining reflects a number of very large projects in the 1960s and 1970s, and these companies' special expertise in this area. Investment in services by both groups rose strongly in the 1980s, with foreign firms' involvement in hotels, real estate, and commercial services leading the way. Agriculture has never been a large recipient of

Table 5.4 **Foreign and Domestic Investment by Sector, 1980 and 1992**
(% of total)

	Foreign		Domestic	
	1980	1992	1980	1992
Industry	82.8	68.5	80.4	69.0
Manufacturing	67.2	61.4	78.0	67.3
Mining	14.7	6.1	2.0	1.1
Construction	0.9	1.0	0.4	0.6
Services	7.3	28.0	8.0	16.6
Trade, hotels	2.7	11.6	1.6	7.2
Real estate, business services	2.6	11.8	2.8	4.6
Transport and communications	1.7	2.6	3.3	2.6
Other	0.3	2.0	0.3	2.2
Agriculture	9.8	3.4	11.6	14.4
Total	100	100	100	100
	(9.0)	(59.2)	(6.8)	(211.0)

Notes: Data refer to investment projects approved by the Investment Coordinating Board, excluding oil, gas, and financial services.
The figures are cumulative totals up to 1980 and 1992, commencing in 1967 and 1968 for foreign and domestic investments respectively. Figures in parentheses refer to totals, in $ billion and Rp trillion.
Source: BPS, *Indikator Ekonomi*, various issues.

BKPM investments. An important reason for its larger share of domestic investments is the difficulty foreigners have in obtaining secure access to land.

The third observation is that, despite Indonesia's openness to foreign investment since 1967, and especially the periods from 1967 to 1974 and after 1986, these inflows have never loomed large in the aggregate picture. For example, their share of GDP has been rising since the mid 1980s, but over the 24 years from 1969 to 1992 they have only exceeded 1 per cent on six years, three in the years from 1990 to 1992. As a share of gross capital formation, also, the numbers are quite small, in most years less than 4 per cent (Figure 5.4). Neither, in comparative international perspective, has Indonesia been a large recipient of foreign investment. Among the developing market economies of East Asia, for example, only Korea and the Philippines have received less as a percentage of various macroeconomic aggregates, the former by choice, the latter the result of political uncertainty and slow growth.[21]

FOREIGN AID

In 1966 Indonesia moved to quickly establish a close and supportive relationship with international donors. This relationship was of critical importance in the difficult initial period from 1966 to 1968, when much of the assistance was emergency in nature, primarily in the form of program aid, and channelled through the so-called BE (Export Bonus) scheme.[22] In 1969, for the first time, the development budget was financed partly by internal resources. The full story of the highly successful aid program over this crucial period has yet to be written. Posthumus (1971) provides an informative though early account, and its exposition in any case is somewhat constrained by the volume's semi-official status. Both donors and the government had to move cautiously. Quite recently, exploiting popular nationalist sentiment, Sukarno had told the West to "go to hell with your aid". Both parties sought constructive re-engagement in a manner which avoided any suggestion that donors were dictating the pace or nature of Indonesia's economic reform. Pragmatism and the personalities on the two sides quickly laid the basis for a close and durable relationship, which has continued ever since. The observations of one Indonesian "insider" are particularly apt:

> [The] relationship with the IMF and the World Bank had been friendly from the beginning in 1967 ... The relationship between the IMF and World Bank at one hand, and the "economic technocrats" on the other hand, was also based on a sympathetic understanding and trust between the Widjojo group at the Indonesian end, and personalities such as Bernie Bell (World Bank) at the other ... There was something unique in the chemistry between the different personalities in the game that is difficult to explain and rationalize ... These remarkable relations with the Bank and Fund remain even today. (Sadli, 1989, pp. 6–7)[23]

During the oil boom period, official aid flows remained sizeable (Table 5.1, line 4). But aid became much less important as a source of government revenues (Figure 4.3), and a higher proportion of the government's development budget began to be financed by its own resources (Figure 4.4). There was also a marked shift in the proportion of development assistance received in the form of program aid, which fell from 83 per cent in 1969 to just 1 per cent in the early 1980s (Figure 4.5). The shift from quick-disbursing program aid, which was dominant until 1972, to project aid reflected Indonesia's more comfortable balance of payments position and the improved capacity of its bureaucracy to initiate, implement and evaluate development projects. However, by the mid-1980s aid suddenly became more significant again, and for a brief period the situation again resembled that of the early 1970s. Thus aid funded most of the development budget in 1988, while its share of government revenue jumped from 15.7 per cent in 1985 to 30.3 per cent in 1988. Donors responded flexibly by quickly shifting resources back into program aid—the latter's share of total aid rising from 2 per cent of the total in 1985 to 34 per cent in the following year, before declining again. Domestic counterpart funding requirements were waived, and some of the aid flows virtually took the form of direct budgetary grants. The large Japanese aid program was particularly significant in this respect.

An assessment of the broader development impact of these aid flows is beyond the scope of this chapter, but a number of general observations are pertinent. First, aid has supported the policy reform environment and facilitated continuing access to international capital markets in a number of ways. There was its crucial contribution to the stabilization program from 1966 to 1968, when the regime's political support and attempts to revive a shattered economy were extremely fragile. Foreign investors showed little interest until official flows had assisted in laying this important foundation, and international agencies provided positive assessments of the new government's economic management and prospects. The stability of foreign aid flows, in contrast to the volatility of private flows, illustrated in Figure 5.5, has been a recurring feature of the New Order.[24] In the early 1970s and 1980s, as boom conditions developed, private flows overtook the official figures, in some years exceeding them by a large margin. But in the late 1970s, and in the crucial period following the mid-1980s collapse in oil prices, private flows dried up. Indeed, by the early 1990s, they were still less than the official flows. This stability of official flows underlines a crucial contribution of foreign aid, and one often neglected in the literature (an important exception is McCawley, 1990). In a close relationship with

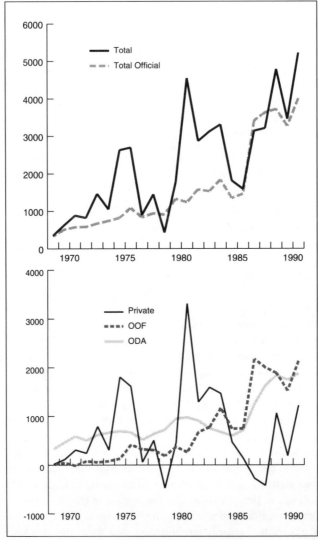

Figure 5.5   Resource flows by source, 1969–91

donors, aid flows are more consistent, they provide a basis on which governments may plan longer-term investment projects and they enable nations to endure difficult economic periods and to enact policy reforms less painfully than would be the case in their absence.[25]

In addition to its balance of payments and budget support, aid has facilitated large technological transfers, primarily within the public sector. To the extent that these projects have yielded net social returns in excess of the (concessional) interest charges, which appears generally to have been the case, Indonesia has benefited from the aid relationship. There have of course been costs associated with the programs. Much of the aid has been tied, either implicitly or explicitly, to the donor country, thus reducing its effective value. High level bureaucratic resources have been diverted to the intricacies of aid project negotiation and implementation. The oil and aid boom of the 1970s also contributed to a lazy fiscal regime, as indicated for example in Indonesia's poor record of non-oil domestic revenue collection. Indonesia may have even suffered from a surfeit of expatriate policy advisers and a seemingly endless flow of consultancy reports. It is surprising, however, that there has been no serious academic study of one of the world's largest and most successful aid programs over the past quarter-century, examining in detail the impact of the various aid programs and projects, and assessing the importance of expatriate economic policy advice from the World Bank, the Harvard group, and other organizations. It is clear that Indonesia has strenuously resisted falling into the trap of the "aid-dependent" syndrome,[26] and that the government has always set the major economic policy parameters. But much of the story concerning detailed policy and implementation remain unexplored research territory.

Structural Adjustment and the Export Boom, 1985 to the Present

A number of factors explain why a quite sudden shift towards liberalism after 1985 produced an effective supply-side response, particularly in manufacturing, by the end of the decade. These factors are discussed in detail elsewhere in this book. There was credible macroeconomic management and a political predisposition towards moderately low inflation (Chapters 3 and 4), thus facilitating the large effective devaluation of the 1980s. Savings and investment rates were high, with much of the oil and aid revenues of the 1970s being recycled into physical infrastructure (Chapter 9), education (Chapter 10), and food crops (Chapter 7). Liberal trade reforms were introduced from the mid-1980s (Chapter 6). Finally, a range of other microeconomic, efficiency-promoting reforms began to have an important effect.

The manufacturing export boom generated by the policy changes surprised even the proponents of reform. Indonesia, for half a century the home of dualism, supply-side rigidities and export pessimism, began to emulate the record of its outward-looking neighbours in their dramatic export success and extremely rapid change in export composition. This structural change is revealed in the rising share of manufactures in exports, from less than 3 per cent in 1980 and 7 per cent in 1983 to almost 50 per cent in 1992 (Figure 5.6). By 1987 the value of manufactured exports exceeded that of the once-dominant agricultural commodities, while in 1992 they overtook the fuels, minerals and metals group. Manufactured exports continued to grow strongly right through the decade, in 1991 and 1992 at rates comparable to those in the early stages of the industrial boom (Figure 5.7), although there was a sharp slowdown in 1993. The shift to manufactured exports has also facilitated smoother macroeconomic management, since Indonesia's more diversified export structure is less vulnerable to sudden exogenous shocks. As noted above, its heavy dependence on commodity exports until the late 1980s resulted in sharp swings in its terms of trade. The real values of both agricultural and fuel exports have fluctuated sharply, mainly in response to international commodity prices (Figure 5.7). While manufactured exports grew at an uneven pace during the early outward thrust when volumes were small, from the mid-1980s the rate of expansion has been a good deal more smooth.

Further evidence of the pace of structural change is illustrated by indices of revealed

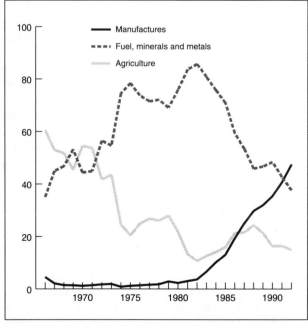

Figure 5.6 Commodity composition of exports, 1966-92

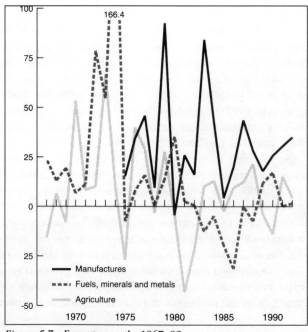

Figure 5.7 Export growth, 1967-92

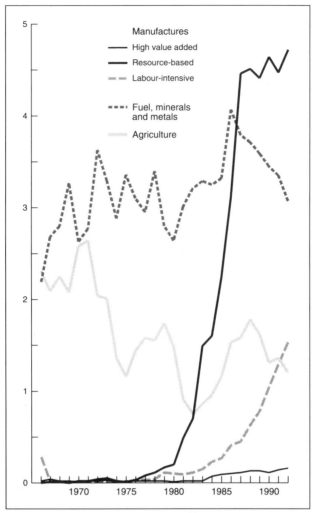

Figure 5.8   RCA indices, exports, 1966–92

comparative advantage (RCAs), which essentially measure a country's export specialization. Reflecting its relative factor endowments, Indonesia has always exhibited a strong specialization in natural resource-based goods. Since the 1960s the indices for the fuels group have always exceeded two, while in most years that for agricultural commodities has exceeded unity (Figure 5.8). The major changes have occurred within the manufactures group. The RCAs for resource-based manufactures began to rise steeply in the early 1980s, mainly in response to the log export ban. As the growth of manufactured exports gathered momentum and diversified, the RCAs for labour-intensive manufactures also rose quickly, and for the first time exceeded unity in 1990. Significantly, the figure for high value added manufactures remained very low. These indices are therefore particularly illuminating. They provide clear evidence that Indonesia is following the well-trodden path of labour-intensive, outward orientation of the East Asian economies, albeit a good deal later than most, and embodying a much stronger specialization in natural resources.

As noted in Chapter 8, these figures do exaggerate the real economic significance of the manufactured export boom for a number of reasons. Part of the increased share is explained by declining commodity prices, especially oil but also traditional cash crops such as rubber, in the 1980s. Enforced export substitution, notably the log export ban, accounted for much of the early increase, when plywood alone generated 40 to 50 per cent of the manufacturing total. Moreover, domestic value added in manufactured exports is generally a good deal less than that of most other sectors. Nevertheless, the importance of the rise in manufactures should not be understated. It represents a watershed in Indonesia's modern economic development. Rapid growth was sustained through the 1980s and the early 1990s, and diversification away from a small number of items has proceeded quickly.

SHIFTING REGIONAL PATTERNS OF INTERNATIONAL COMMERCE

The final major feature of Indonesia's international economic relationship since 1966 has been the shift from the traditionally dominant northern hemisphere centres of commerce, the US and Europe, and towards the Western Pacific region, particularly Japan and the Asian NIEs. This reorientation, particularly evident from the mid-1980s, has not been the result of a conscious commercial strategy, but rather is primarily due to fundamental economic forces. Three factors have been especially important: the rapid growth of the East Asian region; the ever stronger economic complementarities between a low-wage but resource-rich Indonesia alongside the resource-poor, high-wage economies of Japan and the NIEs; and political-institutional changes which have gradually weakened old ties to Europe in particular, in place of strongly growing networks based on ASEAN and other regional initiatives. These changes are evident in Indonesia's trade patterns once adjustment is made for the impact of oil prices. But they are much clearer in investment, aid and services transactions where the effect of geographic proximity is very powerful.

In the case of trade, Japan and the developing economies of East Asia have been significant throughout the period since 1966, with a share of total trade generally fluctuating in the 50 to 60 per cent range, well in excess of the combined US–EC total of 25 to 40 per cent (Figure 5.9). The Japan–East Asia group has been more important still in Indonesia's exports, at the peak of the oil boom absorbing some 70 per cent of the total, in contrast to the 20–35 per cent range for the US and EC (Figure 5.10). Country and regional shares have fluctuated considerably. Japan's share of both total trade and exports peaked during the oil boom period, when for a short period it actually purchased over one-half of Indonesia's merchandise exports. Thereafter its share began to decline slowly, although it retains its position as the most important trading partner. The share of the Developing East Asia group (DEA— the NIEs, ASEAN, and China) has risen commensurately, and by the early 1990s had overtaken the combined US–EC export share. The US was a major trading partner through to the mid-1980s, but since then its share has declined steadily, to about 12 per cent of both total trade and exports. The EC shares fell away in the 1970s and early 1980s, but have since recovered quite strongly and they now exceed those of the US.

These fluctuations in country and regional shares are partly attributable to the

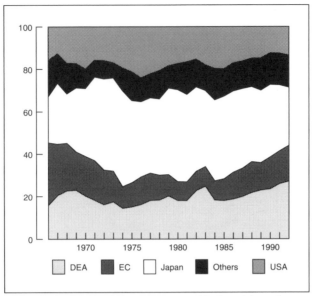

Figure 5.9   The regional composition of Indonesia's trade,
1966-92

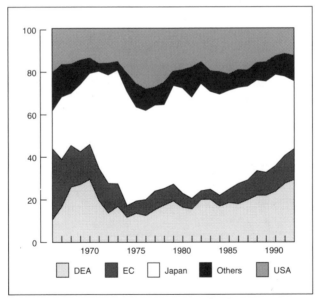

Figure 5.10   The regional composition of Indonesia's exports,
1966-92

changing commodity composition of Indonesia's exports (Figures 5.11-5.13).
Reflecting relative resource endowments and (in the case of LNG) proximity,
Indonesia's exports of fuels, metals, and minerals have always been directed strongly
towards Japan and the East Asian group. The US, the major investor in these industries,
was a significant buyer in the 1970s but more recently its share has declined. Japan

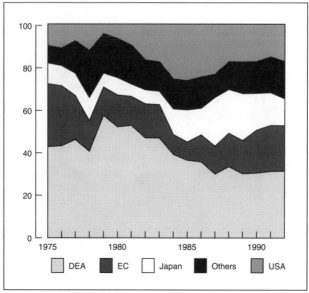

Figure 5.11   The regional composition of Indonesia's
manufactured exports, 1975–92

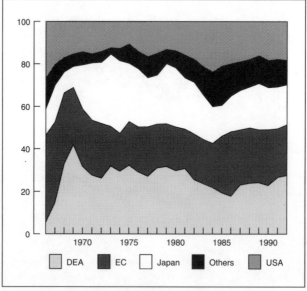

Figure 5.12   The regional composition of Indonesia's
agricultural exports, 1966–92

has consistently been the major buyer, in some years accounting for almost 70 per
cent of the total, and underlining the extraordinarily close commercial ties between
the two countries. More recently the Developing Northeast Asia (DNEA) group have
become major buyers, particularly with Korean and Taiwanese purchases of LNG and
coal. Since 1966 the EC share of these exports has always been less than 5 per cent,
because these nations purchase primarily from the Middle East.

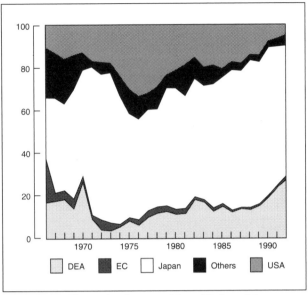

Figure 5.13   The regional composition of Indonesia's energy
and metals exports, 1966–92

Manufactured and agricultural exports are more evenly distributed. Here the developing DNEA group has been the major market throughout the 1980s, with Japan, the US and the EC of roughly similar importance over the decade (Figure 5.11). A good deal of the DNEA total is, in fact, trade with and through Singapore, for further processing, to supply tourist demands and, most importantly, as an *entrepôt* base for re-export.[27] Here also there is something of a division among markets. Resource-based manufactures such as plywood are relatively more important in exports to Japan,[28] while labour-intensive manufactures occupy a larger share of exports to the US and the EC. Garments, the largest item in the latter group, displayed a heavy orientation towards the US, which purchased as much as 60 per cent of the total until the late 1980s, when MFA export quotas induced firms to shift towards non-MFA markets. In the case of agricultural exports there are no clear trends, with average shares being distributed fairly evenly across major markets. The EC has actually been the largest market in several years, with its share being much higher than is the case for manufactures and fuels.

These regional specializations in turn explain much of the fluctuations observed in aggregate trade shares (Figures 5.9 and 5.10). In particular, the declining Japanese share in the 1980s was primarily the result of compositional shifts in Indonesia's exports, notably the shrinking value of resource-based products. The same phenomenon explains the small decline in the DNEA share in the early 1980s. Conversely, the very low EC share in the 1970s, and its subsequent recovery, are also partly attributable to these factors. Nevertheless, these fluctuations should not obscure the fundamental trend over this period, which has been unambiguously towards stronger commercial ties with the Western Pacific region, and most particularly Japan, the NIEs and very recently China.

Trade intensity indices further underline these strong regional connections (Table 5.5). These indices adjust for countries' and regions' shares of international trade.

Table 5.5   **Trade Intensity Indices, 1970–90**

	1970	1980	1990
(1) Trade intensity			
Japan	6.3	6.7	5.9
DNEA	1.0	0.9	1.8
Singapore	18.3	8.8	4.1
ASEAN excl.			
Singapore	4.5	0.9	0.9
USA	1.1	1.4	0.9
EC	0.4	0.2	0.3
Other	0.2	0.3	0.4
(2) Complementarity			
Japan	2.5	2.5	2.3
DNEA	1.0	0.9	1.0
Singapore	3.3	1.6	1.1
ASEAN excl.			
Singapore	0.8	0.7	0.6
USA	0.9	1.3	1.0
EC	1.0	1.0	0.8
Other	0.7	0.6	0.8
(3) Country bias			
Japan	2.6	2.7	2.6
DNEA	1.0	1.1	1.9
Singapore	5.6	5.6	3.8
ASEAN excl.			
Singapore	5.8	1.2	1.5
USA	1.2	1.1	0.9
EC	0.4	0.2	0.4
Other	0.3	0.5	0.5

Notes: The data refer to three-year averages (1970 to 1969–71, etc.). They are based on Indonesia's exports. DNEA, developing Northeast Asia, includes China, Hong Kong, South Korea, and Taiwan. EC, European Community, includes the 1992 membership of 12.

The indices are defined as follows:

Intensity Index, $Iij = \dfrac{Xij}{Xi} \Big/ \dfrac{Mj}{Mw-Mi}$

Complementarity Index, $Cij = \sum_{k} \left(\dfrac{Xi^k}{Xi} \cdot \dfrac{Mw-Mi}{Mu^k-Mi^k} \cdot \dfrac{Mj^k}{Mj} \right)$

Country Bias Index, $Bij = \sum_{k} \left(Bij^k \cdot \dfrac{\overline{Xij^k}}{\overline{Xij}} \right)$

where:
Xij = exports of country i to country j
Xi = total exports of country i
Mj = total imports of country j
M^w = world imports
Mi = total imports of country i
Xi^k = country i's exports of commodity k
Mj^k = country j's imports of commodity k
Mu^k = world imports of commodity k
Xij^k = country i's exports of commodity k to country j

For further elaboration of these terms, see Drysdale and Garnaut (1982).
Source: International Economic Data Bank, based on United Nations trade data tapes.

A ratio of unity indicates that a trading partner's share of trade with a given country is similar to that of its global trade. A figure of two indicates its share is twice that of its international trade shares. As section 1 of the table demonstrates, Indonesia trades intensely with East Asia, and most particularly with Japan and Singapore, for which the figures are extraordinarily high. The figure for the DNEA group rose strongly in the 1980s, while by 1990 those for other non-Asian countries and regions (including the rest of ASEAN it should be noted) were below unity. The EC figure was particularly low, revealing that this group's importance to Indonesia is the result primarily of its (EC's) significance as a global trader, rather than a close bilateral relationship.

These figures may be decomposed further into indices of complementarity and country bias. The former captures the extent to which the composition of exports and imports between trading partners "match", while the latter measures the importance of such residual factors as proximity, membership of commercial blocs and agreements, and associated flows of investment, technology and aid. Here also Japan stands out as the only major trading partner to record consistently high indices of both complementarity and country bias. Apart from Singapore in the early period, in no other case are Indonesia's trade patterns strongly complementary. As would be expected, the country bias indices are always at least unity for all East Asian groups. They rose strongly for the DNEA in the 1980s, as a result of rapidly increasing investment, growing commercial links with China, and several other factors.[29]

As noted, the reorientation towards Japan and developing East Asia is more pronounced in the case of investment, aid and services. Japan has been the dominant investor in the "BKPM" sectors, providing over 30 per cent of the realized total for the period from 1967 to 1992 (Table 5.6).[30] Up to 1980 its share was higher still, at 45 per cent, and there were periods where it reached up to 60 per cent. Combined with NIE investment, East Asia has dominated these sectors of the economy, consistently supplying over 60 per cent of the total, and in some years a good deal more. As Japanese investment tapered off somewhat in the 1980s, the NIEs quickly became a major force, and from the late 1980s their combined total actually exceeded that of Japan. Hong Kong has always been a significant investor in Indonesia, but until 1980 the other three were of minor significance. In the 1980s firms from these countries have shifted their labour-intensive manufacturing capacity into newly competitive low-wage countries such as Indonesia on a massive scale (Thee, 1991). As with Japan two decades earlier, there emerged a strong complementarity between Indonesia and the NIEs in their policy regimes and economic conditions. The NIEs were quickly losing comparative advantage in low-wage activities and liberalizing their policies towards outward capital flows (at least Korea and Taiwan; Hong Kong and Singapore were always liberal in this respect), just as Indonesia began to introduce its liberalizing reforms, which included a return to a more open foreign investment regime.[31]

Among the other investors, the US figure requires particular elaboration. The US has never been an important investor in the BKPM sectors, either during the import-substituting or export-oriented industrialization phases. By 1992, its cumulative totals were very small, less than any of the NIEs. It has, however, been the major investor in oil and LNG, which through to the mid-1980s received much more foreign equity capital than the BKPM sectors. Consequently the shares in Table 5.6 vastly understate the importance of the US.[32] Conversely, the declining proportion of oil in total foreign investments after 1985 has resulted in a diminished US presence in recent years. Unlike the US, European investment flows have held up quite strongly, and by 1992 were still over one-fifth of cumulative totals.[33]

Regional aid and service flows further underline this growing East Asian prominence. As discussed later, in Chapter 9, there are no reliable and comprehensive estimates of services trade by region, but what limited evidence is available reveals a

Table 5.6 **Major Foreign Investors, 1980 and 1992**
(% of total)

	1980	1992
Japan	44.4	31.8
NIEs	16.2	35.2
Hong Kong	11.5	13.0
Taiwan	1.3	9.9
Korea	0.9	7.2
Singapore	2.5	5.1
Australia	3.1	3.1
Other Western Pacific	6.9	1.5
Europe	17.1	21.7
Netherlands	3.7	5.6
United Kingdom	5.6	5.5
Germany	2.9	4.7
Other	4.9	5.9
USA	10.5	4.8
Other	1.8	1.8
Total	100	100
	(9.0)	(59.2)

Notes: Data refer to investment projects approved by the Investment Coordinating Board, excluding oil, gas, and financial services. The figures are cumulative totals from 1967. The figures in parentheses refer to totals, in $ billion. The large multicountry group has been allocated across countries and regions according to single-country shares.
Source: BPS, Indikator Ekonomi, various issues.

picture of expanding Western Pacific ties. In the case of aid the trends are quite unambiguous. Japan has emerged as Indonesia's largest aid donor in the 1980s by a very large margin, eclipsing the once dominant US and EC programs (Figure 5.14).[34] Such a reorientation is hardly surprising. Japan is now the world's largest donor country, and its aid program still retains a strong regional (East Asian) focus. The US aid budget has been declining steadily in real terms, and the countries of the Middle East and Latin America (and the Philippines until very recently) have occupied a higher profile in American strategic thinking. In the EC, countries nearer to home, notably in Africa and South Asia, have received more largesse. Nevertheless, the changing orders of magnitude are quite astonishing. In 1969, for example, the US was easily the largest donor, contributing 46 per cent of total bilateral and multilateral flows, followed by the EC (27 per cent) and Japan (20 per cent). By contrast, 22 years later the US was a very minor contributor (just 1 per cent of the total), while Japan supplied 57 per cent. The EC share held up over the period, an interesting commentary on the political economy of aid in Western Europe as compared to the US. The share of multilateral institutions rose strongly in the 1970s but was declining in the late 1980s, partly as Indonesia "graduated" to less concessional forms of finance.[35]

This trend towards greater economic integration within East Asia is likely to continue, hastened by global shifts in economic activity and by the mutuality of interests across a wide range of commercial policy issues. As Mangkusuwondo et al. (1988) point out, by the late 1980s Indonesia was engaging seriously in such processes

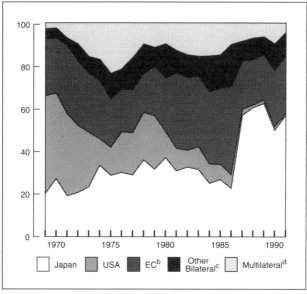

Figure 5.14 Major aid donors, 1969–91

and exchanges for the first time in its history. The growing appreciation of their importance and the potential for national benefit gradually overcame earlier suspicion and mistrust of international agreements and institutions. Indonesia has participated actively in the Asia Pacific Economic Cooperation (APEC) forum, and hosted the leaders' summit in November 1994. Its increasingly diverse range of manufactured exports dictates that, to ensure continuing international market access, it must engage in ever more vigorous and sophisticated international commercial diplomacy.

Indonesia is also regarded as the natural—albeit low-profile—leader of the ASEAN group, in which economic cooperation measures are being strongly promoted. Indonesia has always been a strong supporter of the Association, while displaying ambivalence towards its more detailed trade initiatives. In the first round of intraregional trade liberalization, following the 1976 Bali summit, it made very minor concessions, as did the other members. It was a party to the second round, formalized as the ASEAN Free Trade Area (AFTA) proposal following the 1992 summit.[36] Nevertheless, it insisted that its highly protected sectors, such as capital goods and consumer durables industries, be exempt from the scheme, along with agriculture, mining and services. Prior to the summit it also proposed that small-scale industry be exempt, although this was later dropped on the grounds of administrative impracticality. ASEAN's share of Indonesia's trade has not changed markedly over the course of the New Order, apart from the increase which occurred during the oil boom period, a consequence of Indonesia's intense trade of this commodity with and through Singapore.

Singapore dominates Indonesia's ASEAN trade, consistently accounting for 70 to 80 per cent of the total (and a similar proportion of inward ASEAN investment). The two economies are of course highly complementary, with Singapore an efficient supplier of high value added manufacturing, trade and commercial services.[37] The increasing spillover of labour-intensive manufacturing and service activities, best exemplified in the growth triangle concept (Lee ed., 1992), will further intensify commercial relations.[38] ASEAN political, commercial and cultural networks will hasten the development of ties with the other states too, but these will develop more slowly because their economies are essentially competitive rather than complementary. The most rapidly developing relationship will most likely be with Malaysia. Underpinned by proximity and cultural affinity, the latter's extremely rapid economic development is strengthening complementarities between the two nations. Very large numbers of Indonesian workers—some estimates suggest up to one million, many on an illegal basis—are employed in labour-intensive manufacturing, plantation, and construction activities in both the East and West of the country. As Malaysia continues to lose comparative advantage in labour-intensive activities, this process of inward labour migration (that is, into Malaysia) will likely accelerate. As discussed below in Chapter 7, Indonesia is benefiting from the transfers of Malaysia's more advanced cash crop technology. An economic zone embracing northern West Malaysia, northern Sumatra, and southern Thailand is under active discussion, although its scale will be much more modest than that of the growth triangle to the south.

Indonesia's economic ties with Japan will continue to be the most important and arguably the most complex. It is puzzling that there has been so little serious academic attention devoted to this large and many-faceted relationship.[39] There are fears in many Indonesian quarters, voiced for example by the influential former Minister of Industry, that Japan attempts to impose unreasonable conditions in its commercial dealings:

> *People are fearful of the Japanese because of their relentless ways of pursuing their interests . . . Japan . . . has to be aware of its prominent position now in the world, a prominence which brings with it responsibilities . . . [I]n the private sector, a lot of adjustment still has to be made before the advantages of cooperation are really shared by all concerned. (Soehoed, 1988, p. 55)*

There are also reservations concerning the closeness of the economic embrace, among the older generation, and on the part of those who believe Indonesia is becoming too reliant on Japan for its aid and investment.

Yet relations are much more cordial and relaxed than they were in the mid-1970s, when strong nationalist sentiment spilled over into the streets of Jakarta during the visit of the then Prime Minister Tanaka. There is admiration at Japan's remarkable economic record, its superior commercial organization and its technological prowess. There is appreciation, too, of the fact that Japan has acted as a flexible and faithful donor, especially in times of need such as the 1985–87 period. Along with China, ASEAN continues to be the major recipient of Japan's aid, and within the grouping "Indonesia remains the focus of Japan's Southeast Asian aid priorities . . . " (Rix, 1993, p. 20).[40] Issues of national security, including the shipping lifelines of the Straits of Malacca and Lombok, strong trade and investment ties, and Indonesia's role as a reliable supplier of natural resources are likely to result in a continuation of these close aid ties. Also frequently overlooked is the fact that Japanese aid is generally delivered free of the pontifications on human rights and economic reforms which often accompanies aid from other donors.[41]

The State and Public Policy:
Ideology and Intervention

AN OVERVIEW

Much of this book emphasizes the discontinuities in Indonesian economic development before and after 1966. The late 1960s was indeed a watershed in the country's history: macroeconomic stability, rapid growth, and greater reliance on the price mechanism replaced accelerating inflation, economic stagnation, and a chaotic system of price incentives. But how far-reaching have the changes been after 1966? Has there been an equally profound transformation in national ideology, economic policy-making processes, and the system and structure of public administration? The purpose of this chapter is to address these questions. In the process, and unlike other chapters, it maintains that significant continuities remain between the two eras. It argues that the changes in structures and ideologies have been a good deal less pronounced than that of economic performance.

It is therefore a mistake to view the change in regime in 1966 as a switch from a "socialist" to a "capitalist" or "free market" regime. There remains a deep-seated mistrust of market forces, economic liberalism, and private (especially Chinese) ownership in many influential quarters in Indonesia. Such sentiment has been subdued during the most decisive periods of liberal economic reform—1967–72 and 1985–92. But since 1966 the policy pendulum has swung back and forth, between periods of more and less economic intervention. Indonesia in the mid-1960s may have been "the most laissez-faire socialist economy in the world", a remark attributed to a prominent economist and businessman, the late Dr J. Panglaykim. But as Professor Sadli observes, in perhaps the best and frankest exposition of New Order economic ideology, the embrace of a liberal economic order after 1966 has been half-hearted and ambivalent:

> *When the New Order government came in it abolished the extensive price controls of the old regime because it wanted to rely on the price mechanism for the allocation of resources. Such is still the ruling policy, but old habits die hard. One of the economic doctrines of the New Order is that it is against "free fight competition", because the latter is too much identified with "capitalism", which even the New Order cannot embrace. (Sadli, 1988, p. 364)*

Traditionally, there was a strong strand of socialist thinking among Indonesian officials and intellectuals, inspired especially by the ideals of the Independence struggle (see for example Arndt, 1980; Robison, 1986; Sadli, 1988). But, among most economists at least, a strategy of extensive nationalization was never espoused. Rather the emphasis was on alternatives to both private and public ownership. Symptomatic of this search for a "middle way" (*jalan tengah*) was former Vice President Hatta's advocacy of cooperatives as a desirable form of ownership and organization (see Higgins, 1958), and debate concerning interpretation of the 1945 Constitution. As Rice (1983, p. 60 ff) observes, there was extensive discussion in the 1950s over the meaning of the word *menguasai* in Paragraph 33 of the Constitution. While most economists argued that the intention was for the state to "control"—in the sense of regulate—major sectors of the economy, there were some who invoked the phrase as justification for state ownership. And, as Soesastro et al. (1988, p. 33) point out, "[f]orty years after the adoption of the constitution different interpretations of Article 33 continue to exist".

Despite the change of regime in 1966, it is not easy to identify a coherent philosophy, much less a precise set of economic and social objectives, over the last quarter-century.[1] The *Garis-Garis Besar Haluan Negara* (or Broad Outline of Government Policy) and the five-year development plans (*Repelita, Rencana Pembangunan Lima Tahun*) enunciate economic objectives at the broadest level. A non-exhaustive list would include the following: economic growth; economic stability (that is, low inflation); reduced dependence on foreign aid (and by implication a "manageable" foreign debt); and equity (between individuals, regions, but most of all ethnic groups) and poverty alleviation. There are then what may be termed a second tier of more specific objectives, some of which are an elaboration of the main goals. These include the maintenance of environmental quality; the development of technological capacity; the enhanced role of women; the promotion of indigenous (especially *pribumi*) enterprise; employment generation; and food self-sufficiency.

These objectives are generally couched in a vague and all-embracing manner. In their interpretation three fundamental considerations need to be emphasized. First, there is much less discussion in official documents of options and trade-offs: between growth and environmental quality, between *laissez-faire* and positive discrimination in favour of *pribumi* entrepreneurs, and so on. Secondly, the emphasis accorded to these objectives has fluctuated considerably since 1966, as we shall see shortly, and as was demonstrated in the development budget allocations (Chapter 4). In the late 1960s stabilization and rehabilitation of basic infrastructure understandably received the highest priority, and all other social and equity objectives were subordinated to the overriding imperatives of economic recovery. The economic successes of these early years, combined with the massive windfall oil revenues after 1973, transformed key parameters. Economic nationalism re-emerged as a potent political force, and a range of economic policies became more restrictive. Subsequently, the difficult circumstances of the 1980s forced another major reappraisal, and a shift back towards liberalism. The much-cited and accurate adage in Indonesia that "bad times make for good policies", seems at least in some measure to apply in reverse.

A final feature warranting emphasis is that, as in most countries, the regime rarely speaks with one voice on matters of detail. On industrial policy, for example, there has been a long-running debate between those advocating a "guided" industrial policy and groups proposing a less interventionist strategy.[2] These differences were also illustrated sharply following the November 1978 devaluation. The initiative sought to induce structural change—the growth of non-oil tradeable sectors—through the market mechanism (that is, by devaluing the rupiah), but a plethora of administrative (especially price) controls was introduced in an attempt to suppress price signals.[3] The seemingly inexorable rise of the Minister for Research and Technology, Professor Habibie, is another example.

For all the discussion of "planning" in Indonesia—the Five Year Plans, the 25-year long-term plans, the pivotal role of the National Planning Agency (*Bappenas*) and the regional planning boards (the *Bappeda*), the prominent position of the Planning Agencies (*Biro Perencanaan*) in many government departments—there is surprisingly little detailed planning effort. The *Repelita* indicate the government's broad priorities in the coming five years, they contain estimates of trends in a wide range of macroeconomic, sectoral, demographic and social indicators, and they attempt to place these estimates within a consistent macroeconomic analytical framework. The plans also attempt to inject financial content into these projections by indicating likely trends in the magnitude and structure of public sector investments. In some cases a measure of planning is both feasible and desirable. Public authorities can and should be able to make informed estimates of the demand for education and health services, for urban infrastructure, for telecommunication services, and for many other variables, into the next decade.

But economic forecasting, developed on the basis of macroeconomic models, is an inherently uncertain exercise subject to wide margins of error. This was especially the case for Indonesia during the 1972–85 period when one price, that of oil, so dominated the economy's fortunes that even the most carefully constructed forecast could—and did—prove to be quite unreliable. Indeed, a number of *Repelita* became dated and virtually irrelevant shortly after their publication. *Repelita* II (1 April 1974–31 March 1979) and *Repelita* III (to 31 March 1984) were both essentially formulated before large oil price increases rendered their basic assumptions obsolete. *Repelita* IV (to 31 March 1989) was developed when oil prices were softening but still buoyant, and accordingly it incorporated the government's ambitious thinking about industrial deepening and import substitution. Yet a little over a year after its formal introduction, oil prices plummeted, leading to a major reappraisal of trade and industry strategy.

Table 6.1 illustrates some of these diverging estimates. In *Repelita* II, for example, actual receipts from oil were almost double the forecast figures in some years. Even in the first year of the plan they were 42 per cent higher. During *Repelita* III the discrepancies were greater still, peaking in 1981 when the forecast figure was 214 per cent higher. In *Repelita* IV the opposite problem emerged when, apart from the first year, the actual figures were consistently below the forecasts; at the low-point of oil prices, 1986, they were only 43 per cent of the forecast figure. Even in *Repelita* V the forecasts were generally wide of the mark. Except for the final year, they were consistently conservative, in the years 1990 to 1991 owing in part to the effects of the short-lived Middle East dispute.

Forecasts of economic growth have been similarly approximate (Table 6.2). Only in *Repelita* II has the official forecast been within 10 per cent of the actual figure. In *Repelita* III and IV, both affected by an unanticipated softening in oil prices, the government was too optimistic, while the cautious estimates of *Repelita* V indicate that the authorities did not anticipate such a strong recovery in the wake of the liberalizing policy reforms. Forecasts at the sectoral level reveal a mixed picture. Apart from *Repelita* II, when growth was pulled down by the poor performance of the rice sector, agricultural forecasts have been reasonably accurate. In manufacturing, too, the divergence is not great. The largest differences are evident in mining, for reasons mentioned above, and in some of the services, particularly transport and communication.[4] The record therefore strongly suggests that *Repelita* and other official documents should be viewed not as predictions of likely economic trends, but more as statements of broad economic philosophy: of what the government would

Table 6.1   **Forecast and Actual Receipts from Oil,**
1974–93
(Rp billion)

Repelita	Year[a]	Forecast	Actual
II	1974	673	957
	1975	820	1,248
	1976	889	1,635
	1977	994	1,949
	1978	1,228	2,309
III	1979	3,345	4,260
	1980	3,579	7,020
	1981	3,897	8,628
	1982	4,244	8,170
	1983	4,703	9,520
IV	1984	10,367	10,430
	1985	13,001	11,144
	1986	14,625	6,338
	1987	16,611	10,047
	1988	18,505	9,527
V	1989	7,900	11,252
	1990	9,149	17,712
	1991	9,706	15,039
	1992	10,950	15,330
	1993	11,779	—

[a] Data refer to financial years, 1974 to 1974/75, etc.

like to occur, if (in the unlikely event) it was a prescient authority and one able to impose its will on the pattern of economic development. Conversely, as the economy becomes more diversified in its structure, and therefore less vulnerable to exogenous shocks, and as techniques of quantitative forecasting become more sophisticated, it is likely that the quality and accuracy of these forecasts will improve.[5]

Finally in this overview section it needs to be stressed that there is as yet no comprehensive study of the structures and mechanics of economic policy-making in Indonesia since 1966. There has been some detailed sectoral work, referred to elsewhere in this book, for example on tax reform (Chapter 4), industry policy (Chapter 8), food policy (Chapter 7), and regional development (Chapter 11). The following sections of this chapter examine the sensitive areas of foreign investment, state enterprises, and trade policy. It is also clearly the case that the general parameters of economic policy-making are well understood. There has been an extremely cohesive group of technocrats in power since 1967 (although that cohesion is probably weaker now than at any time in the New Order). The system of governance is both authoritarian and highly centralized, so decisions can be enacted quickly and effectively. The power of the state apparatus has always been considerable, both in a financial and a military sense. It peaked in the early years of the New Order, with the influx of oil and aid funds, and when the private sector was recovering from the ravages of the Sukarno era; by the early 1990s the private sector was immeasurably more powerful and independent, and the state weaker, though still maintaining considerable fiscal authority, direct ownership, and regulatory reach.[6]

Yet in spite of these important contributions, the political economy of economic policy making in the New Order has yet to be written. Such an exercise is beyond

Table 6.2   **A Comparison of Growth Forecasts and Outcomes, *Repelita* II–V**
(annual real growth, %)

	Repelita *II* 1974/75–78/79		Repelita *III* 1979/80–83/84		Repelita *IV* 1984/85–88/89		Repelita *V* 1989/90–93/94	
	F	*A*	*F*	*A*	*F*	*A*	*F*	*A*
GDP	7.5	6.9	6.5	4.6	6.5	4.8	5.0	6.9
Agriculture	4.6	2.8	3.5	3.6	3.5	3.5	3.6	2.8
Mining	9.0	5.1	4.0	−3.5	4.0	−1.8	0.4	4.1
Manufacturing	13.0	11.7	11.0	8.4	11.0	10.8	8.5	10.0
Construction	9.2	13.3	9.0	8.9	9.1	4.6	6.0	11.6
Trade	n.a.	n.a.	n.a.	n.a.	n.a.	n.a.	6.0	7.5
Transport and comm.	10.0	14.2	10.0	10.5	10.1	4.1	6.4	9.7
Other services	7.6	2.4	8.1	3.8	8.1	3.5	6.1	6.4

n.a.–not available.
F = forecast   A = actual

Notes: Repelita forecasts are provided on a financial-year basis, whereas the national accounts refer to calendar years. The actual
estimates for *Repelita* V are based on very preliminary 1993 data.
Sources: Repelita II, III, IV and V; and BPS, National Accounts.

the scope of this book. But the issues are too important to ignore altogether. Therefore, to provide at least something of a sketch of the nature of the policy regime and policy-making processes since 1966, it is useful to investigate several facets of government intervention. These include ownership issues, embracing foreign investment, state enterprises, and the rise of domestic private business conglomerates, and the trade and regulatory regimes. These areas are all sensitive barometers of the government's economic philosophy and objectives. In each case, policies reflect the interplay of the economic imperative (the need for efficiency and growth) and the political agenda (responding to popular objectives, such as equity, *pribumi* participation), and the vested interests which exploit the latter for personal or ideological purposes. In each case, too, policy shifts illustrate clearly how exogenous shocks, mainly in the form of changes in the terms of trade, impinge on policy processes and outcomes. This chapter rounds out the discussion by concluding with a brief look at the issues of public administration and corruption.

INTERVENTION I: OWNERSHIP ISSUES

There are no accurate and comprehensive estimates of ownership shares in Indonesia, either at a point of time or longitudinally. However, the broad picture is clear enough. According to one set of approximate estimates for the late 1980s, prepared by the author in consultation with colleagues, the (domestic) private sector is the largest of the three main groups (Table 6.3). As would be expected, it dominates food crops and most of the other agricultural sectors. It also plays a key role in non-oil manufacturing, construction, trade and tourism, and other services. Nevertheless, state enterprises occupy a prominent position in the economy, much larger than that in most developing countries. In the late 1980s government entities contributed about 30 per cent of GDP, and almost 40 per cent of non-agricultural GDP. Apart from

Table 6.3 **Estimates of Ownership Shares in Indonesia, late 1980s**
(% of each sector's value added)

	Domestic sector	Foreign	Government	Share (1988)[a]
Agriculture				
Food crops, smallholders,				
Livestock	100	0	0	18
Fisheries, forestry, plantation	80	5	15	3
Mining				
Oil and gas	0	50	50	15
Other	30	30	40	1
Manufacturing				
Oil and gas	0	0	100	4
Other	59	17	24	14
Construction	90	5	5	5
Utilities	0	0	100	1
Transport and communications	50	0	50	5
Trade and tourism	90	5	5	16
Banking and finance	30	5	65	4
Government	0	0	100	8
Accommodation	90	0	10	3
Other services	100	0	0	4
Total (excluding oil and gas)	57	12	31	
	71	5	25	

[a] Refers to share of GDP at current prices. These shares are used as weights to compute the ownership shares in the last two rows.

Source: Hill (1990c, p. 55).

public administration and utilities, government corporations are the key actors in transport and communication, mining, and parts of manufacturing and agriculture; historically they have dominated the financial sector, although their presence here has receded quickly since the 1988 banking reforms. By contrast, the role of foreign firms is a relatively modest one. The greatest concentration occurs in the mining sector, in addition to sizeable investments in non-oil manufacturing. Elsewhere their role is marginal, and in sectors other than oil and gas they probably contribute little more than 5 per cent of GDP. The foreign presence may be visible in Jakarta and in several mining enclaves. But in aggregate, this presence is a very modest one—a point frequently overlooked both inside and outside the country.

Ownership is an inherently slippery concept in Indonesia, as in most countries, and the distinction between the three ownership categories in Table 6.3 is often blurred. A number of large industrial projects, such as the Krakatau Steel complex, have investors from all three groups. As discussed shortly, many large, nominally "private" firms have achieved commercial success through various forms of state patronage, demonstrated vividly most recently in the business success of the President's children. Some private firms have found it expedient to convert state bank debt into state equity when the commercial environment is less profitable (such as the Indocement case in 1985). It is common practice for senior officials, right up to

Ministerial level, to retire and assume senior positions in the private sector, often including those parts of it which they formerly regulated. There are a vast number of *yayasan* (foundations) and military enterprises which are nominally private but in reality might be regarded as extensions of the state apparatus. The bail-out in late 1990 of the "private" bank, Bank Duta, by several *yayasan* closely connected to the government, underlines the sometimes academic distinction between "state" and "private" ownership. Many foreign firms have little or no equity in their local operations, but they dominate by virtue of licensing, technology or franchise agreements and restrictions. The distinction is particularly blurred in the case of non-*pribumi* investments, where Sino-Indonesians may have ethnic Chinese partners from neighbouring countries. In the past, it has not been uncommon for these firms to be registered as either domestic (PMDN) or foreign (PMA) firms, depending on the perceived commercial or regulatory advantage.

THE FOREIGN INVESTMENT REGIME

Of the four major areas of policy-making under examination in this chapter, the analysis of foreign investment policy is the most straightforward. Nowhere has the policy pendulum swung more directly in response to external circumstances and domestic political sentiment than here. Nor have the changing policy emphases been more marked than in this area. By the mid-1960s, inflows of foreign equity capital had practically dried up. Foreign involvement was restricted to a small residual presence in the oil sector, and production-sharing joint ventures with the socialist bloc (Gibson, 1966), a good deal of which was thought to be politically inspired (Sadli, 1972). The new regime, in urgent need of foreign capital and technology, but inheriting a tarnished reputation among foreign investors, had little choice but to institute a radical change in direction. As the principal architect of the new foreign investment regime put it:

> When we started out attracting foreign investment in 1967 everything and everyone was welcome. We did not dare to refuse; we did not even dare to ask for bonafidity of credentials. We needed a list of names and dollar figures of intended investments, to give credence to our drive. The first mining company virtually wrote its own ticket. Since we had no conception about a mining contract we accepted the draft written by the company as a basis for negotiation and only common sense and the desire to bag the first contract were our guidelines. (Moh. Sadli, quoted in Palmer, 1978, p. 100)

The 1967 Law, and similar changes in the separately administered petroleum sector, ushered in an era of unprecedented foreign investor interest in Indonesia, as reflected in the sharply increased investment flows (Figure 5.3). This very open posture continued for about six years. By about 1973 the government began to introduce restrictions on foreign investment. These restrictions were intensified in early 1974 in response to the Malari disturbances: a local partner was henceforth required in all cases, regulations relating to employment of expatriate personnel were tightened, and more sectors were closed to new joint ventures. Moreover, the government initiated several ambitious state enterprise projects, some as part of the ill-fated Pertamina investment program, but many also occurred through either the technical departments or the Department of Finance. These had the effect of crowding out potential foreign investors, although some still entered as joint venture partners.

This increasingly restrictive environment explains both the reasons why foreign investment remained rather subdued in the decade to 1984, apart from the "Asahan bulge" in 1974-75, and the rash of foreign investments in 1983 to gain approval before most of the tax incentives were abolished in 1984. Some attempts were made to simplify bureaucratic procedures in 1977, when the priority list DSP (*Daftar Skala Prioritas*) was published for the first time.[7] Fiscal regulations governing the petroleum sector were also liberalized in that year. But for most of the oil boom decade, entry procedures for foreign firms remained opaque, complex, time-consuming and costly. As one knowledgeable official observed, perhaps with unintended understatement:

> The [Foreign Investment] Law is brief and simple, though one should not look at [it] only, but at the 328 kinds of related legislation as well. (Sumantoro, 1984, pp. 28-9)

The second oil boom period further accentuated the resurgence in economic nationalism. More large-scale state commercial investments were planned, and foreign investment regulations were further tightened.

During the 1980s, however, the policy pendulum swung back towards a more liberal regime. As economic growth declined, so too did investor interest. Intent on diversification away from the oil sector, the government saw the need to provide a more attractive investment environment. Some administrative simplifications were introduced in April 1985, while in the following year the 6 May package extended this process considerably. In 1988 a major reform was the introduction of the Negative List (*Daftar Negatif*), which clarified regulatory provisions still further. For the first time, the regulations merely specified which sectors were closed to foreign investment; any sector not so mentioned was automatically open to investors. In subsequent reforms, this negative list has been further shortened. Then in a major reform introduced in March 1992, fully foreign-owned enterprises were again permitted, subject to some restrictions.[8]

Thus by the early 1990s Indonesia's foreign investment regime had come full circle. Though still more restrictive than that of neighbouring Malaysia and Singapore, or of Indonesia 25 years earlier, in its key elements the code is now a liberal one. Regulatory impediments remain, of course. Smaller foreign firms are apprehensive of the predatory activities of the newly emerging conglomerates owned by the children of the politically powerful. Pressures remain for localization of equity and senior staff, and these pressures sometimes manifest themselves in unpredictable bureaucratic behaviour. Security of land tenure, implementation at the regional level, and the paucity of competent local partners all constitute significant barriers. Nevertheless, barring a major change in the political landscape, it is not unreasonable to expect that this more liberal posture will become a more or less permanent feature of Indonesia's commercial environment. Domestic firms are immeasurably more powerful (see below) and so there is not the same pressure on the government from this group for protection from foreign entrants. Indeed, some of these firms are going international on a modest scale, and therefore appreciate the importance of an open regulatory regime. The government itself is more confident of its capacity to regulate, and extract the benefits from, foreign investors. General community attitudes are—with some notable exceptions—less xenophobic. Other countries in the region, in particular China and Vietnam, are bidding aggressively for foreign capital by offering very liberal regimes, thus placing further pressure on Indonesia to maintain the liberal momentum.

Thus, the nature of the policy regime in the early 1990s, as compared with that of 10 to 15 years earlier, offers the prospect of greater durability. There were inherent tensions in the heavily regulated regime of the late 1970s and early 1980s, which rendered it unsustainable as soon as oil prices fell. Foreign firms paid high entry costs into a heavily regulated environment, but benefited from the import protection they received. The country as a whole lost from the ensuing inefficiency, in which foreign firms generated low or even negative value added at international prices. Trade reform and export orientation attracted very different types of foreign investors from the mid-1980s onwards. These firms received less assistance from the government in the form of protection or subsidized credit, and they contributed significantly to the export thrust. Their reduced dependence on government largesse therefore rendered them less of a target of public criticism.[9]

STATE ENTERPRISES

The picture is more complex in the case of state enterprise policy. In some respects the government's policy towards state enterprises has been a mirror image of its foreign investment regime, again reflecting the interplay of ideology and fiscal restraints. But the pendulum has swung far less, and the opposition to liberal reforms is much more deeply entrenched. In the late 1980s Indonesia was at the forefront of reform in trade, tax and finance policy. But it was a conspicuous exception to the worldwide trend towards privatization. Indeed by early 1994, and despite much public discussion, not a single major state-owned entity had been privatized.

A large state enterprise sector is an act of faith for many in Indonesia, inspired by socialist ideals, a mistrust of capital markets, and a desire to promote *pribumi* business development. The New Order regime inherited a large, ramshackle state enterprise sector, including the Dutch and other foreign firms nationalized over the 1958-64 period, and mostly run by the military. Levels of performance and efficiency were generally abysmal, and these firms were major claimants on the state budget.[10] State enterprise reform was thus essential—to control the budget deficit, to improve efficiency, and to restore Indonesia's commercial credibility abroad. The new government began to reform the state enterprise sector quite quickly. In 1967, a number of enterprises were handed back to their former owners, and a measure of commercial autonomy was granted to those firms remaining in state hands. A major reorganization occurred in 1969, when most state enterprises were established as limited liability corporations, subject to the commercial law in the same manner as private corporations. Government equity investment in these firms remained tightly controlled, although aid programs were used to rehabilitate capital equipment in some instances.

Despite major progress with commercial "regularization", there remained many formidable obstacles to reform. Technical departments were reluctant to surrender authority to the Department of Finance, negotiations with former owners over such matters as the value of assets were often protracted, and a range of government enterprises—notably the oil company Pertamina and the rice procurement agency Bulog—remained outside the formal control system. The activities of these "states within states" began to attract critical public attention in the late 1960s. The report of the "Commission of Four", appointed by President Soeharto in January 1970 to examine corruption, was particularly critical of Pertamina, pointing to its failure to

Table 6.4   **Government Investments in State Enterprises, 1969–92**
(Rp billion)

1969	*1970*	*1971*	*1972*	*1973*	*1974*	*1975*	*1976*
8	1	7	23	41	91	109	218

1977	*1978*	*1979*	*1980*	*1981*	*1982*	*1983*	*1984*
167	129	253	477	481	337	592	336

1985	*1986*	*1987*	*1988*	*1989*	*1990*	*1991*	*1992*
412	86	57	125	141	323	470	150

Source: Nota Keuangan, various issues.

pay taxes, to its inefficiency in many areas, and to its lack of accountability (Mackie, 1970, pp. 90–6). The first oil boom pushed reform—and certainly privatization—off the public agenda. There was now scope for the government to shape the pattern of industrial development by investing directly in such priority areas as steel (including revival of the languishing Krakatau plant, see Arndt, 1975), fertilizer, aluminium, petroleum refining, and cement. Consequently, government equity investment in state enterprises began to rise sharply, with a lag, by almost 10-fold in nominal terms over the 1972–76 period (Table 6.4).[11]

This process of expansion came to a sudden halt in 1975–76, when the full details of the Pertamina scandal shook the nation.[12] The origins of the problem lay in a government requirement, introduced in 1972, that all state enterprises were to obtain official approval for overseas borrowings of between one and 15 years' maturity. To circumvent this, Pertamina's President Director, Dr Ibnu Sutowo, embarked on an ambitious program of short-term external borrowing. Initially international banks were eager to lend to Pertamina. But as world economic growth began to slow in 1974 problems arose, and in March 1975 the company was unable to meet its debt commitments. The Indonesian government assumed responsibility for Pertamina's external obligations, which initially appeared to be quite modest in total.

However, in the President's budget speech of January 1976 it was revealed that the problem was far more serious. According to the first complete public report, by Professor Sadli, then Minister of Mining, Pertamina's external debts exceeded $10 billion, equivalent to almost 30 per cent of Indonesia's GDP at that time. Approximately one-half of the debts had been incurred in the purchase and charter of tankers ($3.3 billion) and on P.T. Krakatau Steel contracts ($2.1 billion). The government moved quickly to reassert its control over Pertamina, "dismissing with honour" Dr Sutowo,[13] divesting Pertamina of most of its non-oil enterprises, and renegotiating its debts. The core Pertamina debt was finally reduced to about one-half of the original public estimate.

The general repercussions of the Pertamina debacle for the state enterprise sector were surprisingly limited. Undoubtedly, the hands of the technocrats for the remaining eight years of the oil boom period were strengthened, at least in the area of macroeconomic policy, and probably also in their capacity to block large and uneconomic investment projects.[14] There was no major overhaul of administrative procedures, nor a re-evaluation of these enterprises' role in the economy. New equity injections fell in 1977–78, but then rose steeply again in 1979 under the impact of the second oil boom (Table 6.4). Investment levels remained buoyant through the first half of the 1980s, as the government embarked on a second round of ambitious "industrial deepening" projects. Indeed these investments remained high well after the government had instituted a program of fiscal austerity, including the cancellation of many large projects in 1983, owing to the long lead times involved in executing such projects.

By late 1986, however, a change in direction was evident. The President instructed the Coordinating Economics Minister, then Professor Ali Wardhana, to undertake a comprehensive review of the state enterprise sector. In March the following year a high-level team was established to evaluate the reports from the technical ministries. Over the next 18 months, public debate concerning the performance and role of state enterprises intensified. Departments defended those enterprises under their jurisdiction, and pointed to the numerous commercial handicaps which contributed to their poor performance. In October 1988 the Department of Finance delivered a report to the President classifying the commercial status of state enterprises, and including policy options ranging from improved efficiency, to partial or full privatization. In the following year further progress was apparent. It was revealed that 129 of the 189 state enterprises which had been reviewed were either "not healthy" or "less healthy". In August of that year an interdepartmental team was established to pursue the objectives of improved efficiency, including disposal to the private sector. Over this time, also, the state enterprise sector grew slowly. Faced with a precarious financial situation, government capital injections declined (Table 6.4). Moreover, while in absolute terms it is probable that the size of the state enterprise sector did not contract, it was overshadowed by the faster growing private sector. Nevertheless, despite the momentum for change, and many official statements emphasizing the importance of the issue, the reform process has moved very slowly, much more so than in the case of foreign investment or trade policy. There have undoubtedly been instances of increased efficiency, and the government has introduced measures to improve incentives systems and allow at least a measure of autonomy. But implementation of the various edicts has been patchy, and no major case of privatization has occurred (Habir, 1990, pp. 100–4).

Before looking at the reasons for the absence of significant reform, it is useful to underline just how poor state enterprise performance has been. The database here also is rather weak, but the general picture from a range of secondary and primary data is consistent and clear.

The secondary data on state enterprises collected by the Department of Finance indicate that their performance in aggregate has been very poor. Throughout the 1980s, the rate of return on assets was in the 2 to 4 per cent range, somewhat higher in the boom years from 1979 to 1981 and with the resumption of economic growth in 1988, but lower in the recession period of the mid-1980s (Table 6.5). Such low rates of return, which are well below interest rates over this period, would be unacceptable to private investors. Moreover, the overall picture is worse than that depicted in the table for at least three reasons. First, the aggregate figures are pulled up by the higher returns of the state banking sector. The return on non-banking

Table 6.5   **The State Enterprise Sector, 1979–92**
(Rp billion, or %)

Year	Assets	Sales	Profit	Dividend	Rate of return	Sales as % of GDP
1979	26,316	6,522	1,179	38.0	4.5	20.4
1980	34,514	9,796	1,422	69.6	4.1	21.6
1981	40,409	11,404	1,628	96.5	4.0	19.6
1982	48,268	14,533	1,329	153.5	2.8	23.3
1983	70,185	20,891	2,296	171.2	3.3	26.9
1984	87,368	25,920	2,200	266.0	2.5	28.8
1985	98,715	29,539	2,525	625.0	2.6	30.5
1986	118,966	28,269	1,811	583.7	1.5	27.5
1987	140,100	37,293	3,036	932.9	2.2	29.9
1988	124,013	40,065	5,170	636.4	4.2	28.2
1989	144,455	47,687	6,613	958.0	4.6	28.5
1990	179,153	60,990	8,300	1,096.0	4.6	31.2
1991	201,068	62,113	6,844	1,311.2	3.4	27.6
1992	231,232	68,446[a]	6,290	1,053.2	2.7	26.2

[a] This figure compares with 1993 turnover of the country's leading private conglomerates (see Table 6.7) as follows: Salim group Rp 18 trillion; 10 largest conglomerates Rp 51.2 trillion; 20 largest conglomerates Rp 70.6 trillion

Notes: The profit data are pre-tax. 1992 data are preliminary. The rate of return refers to profits as a percentage of assets, the latter measured at book value. Some series are presented on a calendar-year basis, while others are financial years. Beginning 1989, state enterprises in which the government has a minority shareholding are excluded. No data are published before 1979. The data are approximate: coverage is incomplete, and there are occasionally large revisions in the series.
Sources: *Lampiran Pidato Kenegaraan*, various issues; and BPS, *National Accounts*.

commercial enterprises is therefore even more dismal, often as little as 1 per cent. Public utilities invariably run at a loss, and offer indifferent standards of service. Secondly, assets are valued conservatively. They are measured at book value, and are therefore well below market value. If the rate of return were calculated on the basis of the latter, the return would be lower still. Thirdly, even the low official estimates of profitability overstate the real figures owing to the presence of many implicit and explicit subsidies, such as free land, preferential access to government procurements, occasional direct subventions, and access to concessional and publicly guaranteed credit.

The data also reveal that there has been very little change in the aggregate importance of the state enterprise sector since 1979. Both assets and sales continued to expand over this period. Sales as a percentage of GDP rose strongly in the first half of the 1980s as investments from the oil boom period came on stream. The share then remained broadly constant from 1985 to 1991.

Almost every micro-level study of these enterprises has also pointed to their poor commercial performance. This is not the place to summarize these studies in detail, but the main picture is clear enough. Dick's (1987) study of inter-island shipping included a section on the state shipping company, Pelni, which has a consistently poor record of profitability. Funkhouser and MacAvoy (1979) undertook a comparison of 150 public and private firms based on data from the early 1970s, finding that the state firms compared unfavourably in most respects. Gillis (1982) compared mining companies in Bolivia and Indonesia, finding a consistent record of poor performance in both countries. Hill (1982) examined state and private weaving companies in the late 1970s, and showed that the former were unable to compete without subsidy. McCawley (1971, 1978) undertook detailed studies of two very large state enterprise monopolies, the state electricity company (PLN) and the state oil company (Pertamina) respectively. The PLN recorded consistently low levels of profitability, while the rampant mismanagement in Pertamina has already been referred to. McKendrick (1989, 1992) included a detailed study of the controversial state aircraft company IPTN, finding, as would be expected, extremely low levels of profitability. Soesastro et al. (1988) assessed state enterprise performance as part of a broader study of fiscal policy, which included the first detailed inspection of some state enterprises' financial statements. Here also the picture was one of poor performance. Mardjana (1993) compared the performance and efficiency of private and public bus companies, finding the private entities to be superior in both respects.[15]

The foregoing does not demonstrate that state enterprise performance is inherently inferior to that of private firms. The problem in Indonesia, as elsewhere, is that the government imposes a multiplicity of objectives on its enterprises. Many are non-commercial in nature. Moreover, the commercial autonomy of senior management is so severely restricted that the plants often operate merely as production units subject to the priorities of sometimes distant bureaucratic masters. Numerous illustrations of these propositions are provided in the studies referred to in the preceding paragraph: for example, an aircraft factory having an explicit "technological mission"; utility companies unable to raise their prices to cover even operating expenses; senior management having to obtain approval from Jakarta for appointment (not to mention dismissal) of relatively junior staff and being encumbered with a wide array of sometimes inappropriate, aid-financed machinery; and the imposition of other social responsibilities such as assistance for small-scale enterprise including those under the *bapak angkat* ("foster parent") scheme.

Why has there been so little progress in the area of state enterprise reform? The contrasts, with Indonesia's bold reforms elsewhere and with other countries' overhaul of the state enterprise sector, are particularly striking. The absence of reform is testimony to the presence of powerful vested interests opposing such measures. Several factors appear to have been important.

First, the technical departments have generally resisted the process, except in the case of obviously unprofitable ventures of no strategic value. State enterprises under their control constitute a valuable source of additional funding. It is common practice for senior bureaucrats to sit on the board of such companies, the fees from which often exceed their official government salary. These enterprises frequently provide additional perquisites for departmental staff, ranging from housing to international travel. State enterprises are also viewed by the departments as a vehicle for their development objectives, in areas such as small enterprise development and the promotion of subcontracting networks.[16] In addition, particular Ministers have regarded state enterprises as personal fiefdoms, immune from public inspection and accountability. The most obvious example since the early 1980s has been the powerful Minister for Research and Technology, Professor Habibie. He has been able to circumvent the reforms and protect his extensive commercial interests through his direct and close contact with the President. To further protect and extend his empire the Strategic Industry Board (BPIS, *Badan Pengelola Industri Strategis*) was established, in August 1989. Under this arrangement, 10 of the largest state enterprises were placed under his direct control. These include not just the companies already operating under his agency, but in addition such major plants as the Krakatau Steel complex.

A second major source of concern, and an explanation of the limited reform thus far, relates to disposal procedures and the likely buyers of privatized enterprises. The buyers would almost certainly be either foreign investors or the major domestic conglomerates which, as we shall see shortly, consist almost entirely of non-*pribumi* or politically powerful owners. It is impossible to overstate the sensitivity of the ethnic issue in Indonesia. While the New Order has managed ethnic relations rather well, deep-seated *pribumi* reservations—and in some quarters hostility—persist over the extent of non-*pribumi* wealth and commercial dominance. These tensions remain just as powerful now as they were in the mid-1960s. Indeed they may have been intensifying since the late 1980s. As Indonesia has become unambiguously more "capitalist", and as large Sino-Indonesian conglomerates become ever more visible, there is a perception that the latter are the primary beneficiaries of liberalization. In 1991 *Tempo*, then Indonesia's most influential weekly magazine, and a publication known for its ethnic tolerance, aired such sentiments as follows:

> The gap between pribumi *and non-*pribumi *looks more transparent because the Indonesian economic cake has not been distributed proportionally. According to a businessman, three million non-*pribumi *control 60 per cent of the Indonesian economy . . . If the* pribumi *are allowed to remain weak, later, by the year 2000, the* pribumi *may have no power at all. (Tempo, 20 July 1991, as quoted in Mardjana, 1993, p. 263)*

Faced with this sort of public sentiment, it is not surprising that the government has been reluctant to initiate bold reforms. In effect, many senior officials regard a large state enterprise sector as a necessary political condition for the introduction of liberal reforms elsewhere in the economy. But, in addition, opposition has come from those groups who might have been expected to support privatization measures. The principal concern in this case has focused on the transparency and accountability of disposal procedures. There is a very real fear that state enterprises may be handed over to the politically powerful without independent verification of the firms' financial value, and without proper tendering or other disposal mechanisms. A popular phrase in the late 1980s reflecting such a sentiment was that privatization might end up being "familization".[17] An additional concern of this liberal-oriented group has been that there is little point in transforming public monopolies into private monopolies, and that privatization without reform in the fields of trade and competition policies would produce little benefit.

The process of reform was retarded also by two events in the early 1990s. The stock market might have been an attractive means of disposing of state enterprises either partially or fully, especially as there would have been a better prospect of a more diversified ownership structure (including *pribumi* participation) than in the case of sale to one of the country's conglomerates. However, in 1991–92 the stock market slumped. There were few new listings, and the value of most existing stocks declined. This channel for divesting parcels of state enterprise equity therefore lost its appeal, at least temporarily. Secondly, the difficulties experienced by some of the aggressive new business entrants during the period of tight monetary policy in the early 1990s had an impact on public sentiment towards state enterprises. Particularly in the wake of the Bank Summa debacle (see Chapter 3), many began to question the assumption that private firms are inherently more efficient. The fact that the cosseted state banks also experienced difficulty over this period suggests that this argument is not very persuasive. But it does appear to have had an impact on policy in this area.

Thus the New Order has faced, but never effectively resolved, the fundamental dilemma in state enterprise policy: these firms occupy such a large part of the economy that the country's growth and international competitiveness will be retarded as long as levels of efficiency remain low. But there is a continuing political imperative for a commanding state enterprise sector, as a demonstration of the government's *pribumi* credentials, and as a counterweight to foreign and non-*pribumi* ownership. Indeed, as the conglomerates rose to prominence in the late 1980s (see next section), that imperative became even more powerful. The government's ambivalent attitude towards state enterprises is illustrated also in its reluctance to enunciate a clear set of policy objectives for them: are they strictly commercial entities, or do they have wider social obligations? If they do have such obligations, what precisely are they, and can they be fulfilled without jeopardizing overall commercial performance? Can or should a financial value associated with performing such functions be assigned explicitly in their budgets? Writing in the aftermath of the Pertamina affair, McCawley (1978, p. 24) observed, appropriately, that:

> *Ever since Independence, successive Indonesian governments have been experimenting with different methods of regulation [of state enterprises] in an effort to find a successful way of balancing accountability against autonomy, unfortunately with only a little success.*

In important respects, this conclusion remains as broadly accurate a characterization of the early 1990s as it was of the late 1970s. Nevertheless, there have been some modest achievements, and even if major reform is not possible, at least some progress has been made. First, trade reform has exposed those enterprises in tradeable markets to greater competition. Secondly, even where new entrants to an industry, previously a state enterprise monopoly, have been political "cronies", at least they have introduced some competitive pressures, if only in the area of non-price service delivery. Notable examples include domestic airlines, television service and electric power. Thirdly, financial reporting and public accountability is now much better than it was two decades ago with the result that, while the system is still insufficiently transparent, it is much more open than it was in the past. Finally, the government has been putting much greater pressure on these firms to perform. Salaries are now more closely linked to financial performance, for example. Consequently, while reform has proceeded very slowly, within sharply constrained political boundaries, there has at least been some progress, and the institutional framework established in the late 1980s should generate improved performance and accountability in the 1990s and beyond.

CONGLOMERATES AND THE GROWTH OF THE PRIVATE SECTOR

The emergence of a large and dynamic (domestic) private sector is a recent phenomenon in Indonesia. Given the country's colonial history, its small middle class and low per capita income through until the 1980s, and its large and paternalistic government, it is not surprising that the commanding heights of the economy were dominated by other business groups—foreign interests in the colonial era, and the state after the 1957–58 nationalizations. Especially during the early years of the New

Table 6.6   **Projected *Repelita* Funding Sources**
(% of total)

Repelita	Domestic				Foreign	Total
	Public	*Private*	*Total*	*(Private as % of public)*		
II	36.7	35.0	71.7	95.4	28.3	100
III	29.4	49.6	79.0	168.7	21.0	100
IV	33.3	47.6	80.9	142.9	19.1	100
V	37.1	56.8	93.9	153.1	6.1	100
VI	25.7	68.8	94.5	267.7	5.5	100

Source: *Repelita* II, III, IV, V, VI.

Order, state power was in the ascendancy owing to the weak position of private capital following the ravages of the Sukarno era,[18] and to the influx of oil and aid funds. "The rise of capital", to paraphrase the influential work of Robison (1986), is part of the process of capitalist evolution and maturity in Indonesia. It would have occurred anyway in the course of the country's economic development. But for two reasons the process has attracted particular comment. First, owing to the abrupt decline in oil prices, the period encompassing the retreat of the state and the transition to private-sector-led economic development has been greatly compressed. Secondly, the nature of the new private sector actors has attracted much critical comment, as noted above. "Conglomerates" and "monopolies" are terms which have often been employed as means of thinly veiled criticism of prominent Sino-Indonesian business families, or the business operations of the President's family, or both these groups.

The shift to the private sector is revealed both in the government's *Repelita* documents and in actual investment shares. Each plan from *Repelita* II onwards has envisaged a larger role for the private sector in resource mobilization (Table 6.6). The increase was particularly pronounced from *Repelita* II to III, and from V to VI. In *Repelita* V, for the first time, it was envisaged that the private sector would provide over 50 per cent of the total funding, a share rising to over two-thirds in *Repelita* VI. Through until *Repelita* V, most of the increased private sector share was at the expense of foreign funding, with the result that the state share has not altered greatly; in the current plan, however, the state share has fallen to just one-quarter. As noted above, the *Repelita* forecasts have not always been particularly accurate. But they are indicative of government thinking and priorities. As for investment shares, the data are at best approximate, but they do show clearly that the public share rose during the first half of the 1980s, peaked in 1985, then fell quite sharply during the reform phase of the late 1980s (Figure 6.1). By 1990, public investment was just 69 per cent of that in the private sector. The decline of the public sector during the 1980s was of course a worldwide phenomenon, and in this perspective the Indonesian story is not so special. In neighbouring Malaysia, the decline was just as rapid over this period, and for similar reasons. In Mexico, afflicted by the debt crisis and a painful period of structural adjustment, the decline in the

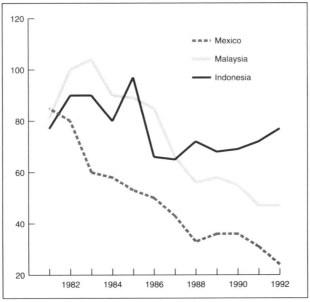

120

∎∎∎∎ Mexico

Malaysia

—— Indonesia

Figure 6.1   Public investment shares, 1981–92

public sector share was faster still. But compared with countries which did not experience a sharp decline in their terms of trade, Indonesia's compositional changes were quite rapid.

The major Indonesian conglomerates are listed in Table 6.7, which includes information on their principal owner(s), estimated turnover, and number of companies in the group.[19] Several features of these groups stand out. First, the list underscores the non-*pribumi* dominance of the economy. The top seven are all in the hands of Sino-Indonesian individuals or families. Only four *pribumi* firms make it into the top 25 conglomerates; two of the three largest are owned by the President's sons, and another two are in the very bottom ranking.[20] It is not surprising therefore that the conglomerates are subject to criticism, especially among the ''outsider'' *pribumi* community groups. A second feature is that the Salim group is in a class of its own, particularly since late 1992, when the resources of the Astra group were diluted by the bail-out of Bank Summa, owned by the son of the Astra founder, William Soeryadjaya. Salim is the only conglomerate of real international significance, and regional presence, although others—notably the Lippo group—are beginning to make a mark. Thirdly, virtually all the groups are ''new money'', in Mackie's (1990) terminology. Some of the owners became adults only during the New Order, the most obvious examples being the President's sons. Several of the leading players had not been heard of until as recently as the mid-1980s, a notable case being timber tycoon Prajogo Pangestu. Most of the companies were established in some form before 1966, but generally on a small scale, often in trading and with a long history of military ties. Starting as highly personalistic companies, centred around the owner and immediate family, they have gradually become more professional in orientation. The second-generation owners usually possess international education, in marked contrast to most of the founders, who had little formal education. Finally, many are highly diversified operations, with investment in finance, manufacturing, plantations, real estate, and other fields.[21] Their skill lies in being able to identify commercial opportunities, to understand the Indonesian bureaucracy and the system of patronage, and to be able to marshal packages of finance, management, and technical inputs. Their role in, and access to, regional ethnic Chinese trading and business networks has obviously facilitated their growth.

It is useful to look more closely at the Salim group.[22] Salim is the clear and undisputed leader among the conglomerates. It is also prominent in regional terms, its turnover being greater than that of any other conglomerate in ASEAN, Taiwan, and Hong Kong, though well below that of the largest Korean group. Liem Sioe Liong's commercial connections with the military date from the 1940s Independence struggle. They were strengthened further by his ties with Soeharto in the 1950s when the latter headed Central Java's Diponegoro Division, a relationship which appears to have been crucial to the growth of the group in the late 1960s. Liem was able to diversify quickly from his trading operations into import-substituting manufacturing, beginning in about 1968, and to banking and cement in the 1970s. In the 1980s it diversified even more rapidly, and was an early entrant into export-oriented activities. The group also proved adept at shedding loss-making activities, often to the state banks as in the 1985 debt-for-equity conversion of Indocement, and in securing government-sanctioned monopolies in fields as diverse as clove imports, flour milling, steel, and cement. From the mid-1980s the group began to internationalize rapidly, becoming a leading actor in Southeast Asian commerce, so much so that by the early 1990s about 35 per cent of its revenues came from abroad. Such a process introduced an entirely new element into the political economy of the relationship between conglomerates and the state. The conglomerates have begun to mature beyond their earlier intense dependence on state patronage and support, in the process becoming more powerful independent actors. Internationalization in this respect, as in several others, is weakening the power of the state in Indonesian society.

While the Salim group dominates the picture, the lessons from its experience have general applicability. The success of the other leading conglomerates owes much to this powerful combination of commercial acumen and government patronage. A number are becoming more international in their investment and sales strategies. Ironically, the most prominent group to falter during the early 1990s credit squeeze was Astra, the second largest conglomerate until recently, and viewed by most observers as less "political" and more professional than any other in the top dozen or so.

INTERVENTION II: TRADE AND REGULATORY POLICIES

THE TRADE REGIME

There is a popular saying in Indonesia something like: "with its thousands of kilometres of coastline, Indonesia was made by God for free trade". Yet there is a remarkable contrast between the regime's open international capital account and freely convertible currency, and its increasingly restrictive trade policy, especially over the 1980–85 period. During the early 1960s there were extensive, if widely flouted, barriers to international trade. By 1970 many of these barriers had been removed.

Table 6.7 **Major Business Conglomerates in Indonesia**

Conglomerate	Principal owner[a]	Principal activities	Turn-over Rp[b]	Ranking 1993	Ranking 1987[b]	No. of com-panies 1993
Salim	Liem Sioe Liong	Cement, finance, autos, agro-industry	18,000	1	1	450
Astra	Prasetia Mulya group, and public	Autos, estates	5,890	2	2	205
Lippo	Mochtar Riady	Finance	4,750	3	4	78
Sinar Mas	Eka Tjipta Widjaya	Agro-industry, pulp and paper, finance	4,200	4	3	150
Gudang Garam	Rachman Halim	Kretek cigarettes	3,600	5	5	6
Bob Hasan	Bob Hasan, Sigit Harjojudanto	Timber, estates	3,400	6	12	92
Barito Pacific	Prajogo Pangestu	Timber	3,050	7	26	92
Bimantara	Bambang Trihatmodjo[P]	Trade, real estate, chemicals	3,000	8	13	134
Argo Manunggal	The Ning King	Textiles	2,940	9	15	54
Dharmala	Soehargo Gondokusumo	Agro-industry, real estate	2,530	10	14	151
Djarum	Budi and Michael Hartono	Kretek cigarettes	2,360	11	6	25
Ongko	Kaharuddin Ongko	Real estate, finance	2,100	12	11	59
Panin	Mu'min Ali Gunawan	Finance	2,080	13	10	43
Rodamas	Tan Siong Kie	Chemicals	2,000	14	18	41
Surya Raya	Soeryadjaya	Property, estates, trade	1,980	15	n.a.	242
Jan Darmadi	Jan Darmadi	Real estate	1,940	16	9	60
CCM/Berca	Murdaya Widya-wimarta Poo	Electronics, electricity	1,800	17	n.a.	32
Humpus	Hutomo Mandala Putra[P]	Oil, trade, chemicals	1,750	18	23	11
Gadjah Tunggal	Sjamsul Nursalim	Tyres, finance, real estate	1,650	19	24	49
Raja Garuda Mas	Sukanto Tanoto	Pulp and rayon, finance	1,590	20	34	66
Gemala	Wanandi	Chemicals, autos	1,550	21	7	78
Pembangunan Jaya	several	Real estate	1,390	22	n.a.	57
Metropolitan	several	Real estate	1,200	23	n.a.	57
Soedarpo	Soedarpo Sastrosatomo[P]	Shipping, trade, pharmaceuticals	1,200	23	16	35
Tahija	Julius Tahija[P]	Finance	1,200	23	n.a.	39

[a] In some cases owned by the family of this individual. 'P' denotes *pribumi* ownership; otherwise the conglomerate is majority or solely non-*pribumi* owned.
[b] n.a. indicates the conglomerate was not ranked in the top 40 in 1987.

Source: Warta Ekonomi, 24 April 1994, and earlier listings in this magazine. I am most grateful to Dr Thee Kian Wie for assistance with this table.

Table 6.8 **Estimates of Effective Rates of Protection**
(%)

	Pitt	World Bank	Pangestu & Boediono		Parker	Fane & Phillips	Wymenga
	1971	1975	1975	1980	1984	1987	1989
	(1)	(2)	(3)	(4)	(5)	(6)	(7)
All tradeables	33	30	115	56	133	19	15
Exportables	−11	−2	91	32	−4	−2	−6
Importables:	66	58	n.a.	n.a.	224	n.a.	n.a.
import competing	n.a.	61	121	60	n.a.	47	44
non-import competing	15	9	21	9	n.a.	n.a.	n.a.
Subsectors:							
cigarettes	556	4	246	105	n.a.	600	600
sugar refining	154	−9	−8	0	141	600	247
weaving	NVA	192	135	127	589	195	217
motor vehicles	526	718	28	33	2,948	499	600

NVA indicates negative value added at international prices; 'n.a.' indicates there were no estimates presented for this category.

Note: These series are generally not directly comparable, except where the same author (Pitt/World Bank, Pangestu & Boediono) or methodology (Fane & Phillips/Wymenga) is involved. Qualifications apply to many of the estimates. See the original publications for full details.
Sources: Pitt (1981, pp.208-9); World Bank (1981, pp. 10-17); Pangestu and Boediono (1986, pp. 25-6); Parker (1985, pp. 12-17); Fane & Phillips (1991, pp. 118, 123-5); Wymenga (1991, pp. 138, 150-3).

Apart from the unified and realistic exchange rate, the government had moved decisively to dismantle the battery of controls in a series of packages introduced between 1966 and 1971. Most export taxes were reduced though not abolished (this was to occur later in the 1970s), tariffs again became the primary instrument of import protection, and the tariff structure was simplified.[23]

Three broad indicators of the evolution of trade policy are the various estimates of effective protection, the incidence of non-tariff barriers, and revenue from trade taxes. The protection estimates, summarized in Table 6.8, provide a bewildering array of figures with no obvious trends discernible. Indeed, differences in coverage, methodology, concepts and data render these series broadly non-comparable. But several consistent features do emerge from the data: all studies except Pangestu-Boediono (who did not include all NTBs, non-tariff barriers) found negative protection for exportables. In all studies the interindustry variations in protection are extremely large, ranging from negative rates to several hundred per cent. It is therefore clear that, even in the more liberal policy eras, embracing especially the first and last sets of estimates, the trade regime has had a marked impact on the distribution of resources among industries. It has also tended to penalize efficient export activities, although with some compensating mechanisms to be discussed shortly. Manufacturing has, on average, received positive effective protection, with most of the assistance for agricultural activities, at least in the food crop sector, coming directly from the budget in the form of subsidized inputs.

As noted in Chapter 4, taxes on trade have contributed a diminishing proportion of non-oil domestic revenue (NODR), itself a declining proportion of total government revenue until the mid-1980s. Export taxes and import duties constituted some 37 per cent of NODR around 1970, but this share declined more or less continuously during the 1970s. By the early 1980s the contribution was less than 20 per cent, hastened by the sharp fall in the nominal value of export taxes. Revenue from import duties remained flat as more and more NTBs—most yielding little or no government revenues—were imposed. Following the customs reform of 1985, and the economic recovery after 1987, the government began to collect more import duties, but other non-oil tax receipts rose faster. Thus by the end of the decade the share of trade taxes was just 10 per cent of NODR, a little over one-quarter of that 20 years earlier.

Just as the late 1960s represented one of the high points of economic liberalism with respect to foreign investment and state enterprises, so too was it the case with trade policy. Import bans began to reappear in the early 1970s, notably in the case of automobiles and textiles. The trend towards regulation gathered pace in 1974, in the wake of the Malari protests and in response to demands for protection of "national" firms and industries. As the intersectoral implications of the oil boom became increasingly evident, these pressures intensified. As pointed out in Chapter 5, the November 1978 devaluation was motivated more by a desire to protect non-oil tradeable activities than for balance of payments reasons (at least the short-run payments position).

The second round of oil price increases provided a further fillip to a rapidly increasing array of trade restrictions: in 1980 the ban on log exports was announced, and a *"pribumi* first" policy for government procurements (including aid projects) was introduced. The mandatory deletion program in the automotive industry, affecting the sourcing of components, was enforced more vigorously. In late 1982 and 1983 NTBs proliferated still further.

Three features of the protection regime over this period became quickly evident. First, not only was there greater resort to NTBs, but the nature of these NTBs became increasingly complex. Pangestu and Boediono (1986, pp. 9–22), writing at the time when these devices were most commonly employed, identified some 22 separate instruments. Apart from the outright prohibitions, the "approved importer" system (TNI, *Tata Niaga Impor*), introduced in November 1982, began to have pernicious protective effects. This was especially so for the controversial cases where import licences were discretionary and firm-specific in nature. Secondly, trade policy became a much more explicit instrument of industrial policy over this period. Large projects, many of them joint ventures between state and foreign firms, such as those in the Krakatau Steel complex, were granted not just import protection but complete authority over their industry's imports. The ostensible justification for these so-called "Sole Importer" provisions was to provide an implicit cross-subsidy to infant industry activities. There was, in fact, an informal but quite explicit contract with the government: private interests invested in "pioneering" activities, in exchange for which they could (within limits) control price levels by regulating the flow of imports. Such an approach contributed to a third major feature of trade policy in the first half of the 1980s, namely its politicization. As the coverage of NTBs extended to more industries—plastics, glass, steel, dairy and meat products, electronics, to name just a few—it became increasingly obvious that powerful political business interests were the prime beneficiaries.

As a result of these trends, the 1982–85 period lacked economic policy coherence.

The government's macroeconomic response to the declining terms of trade was swift and effective, taking the form of a devaluation, banking reform, and fiscal adjustments of 1983, and the 1984 tax reform. Conversely, industrial planners had embarked on many major projects with long gestation periods in the early 1980s. These began to come on-stream just as the government's capacity to underwrite uneconomic projects was shrinking rapidly.

The counterattack, to arrest and reverse the drift towards regulation, began in 1985 as oil prices continued to decline. Economists at the University of Indonesia attempted to shape the political agenda by initiating debate on the "high-cost" economy. They pointed to the uncompetitive nature of many of Indonesia's industries, and to the link between high costs and government regulation. In April of that year, sweeping reforms were introduced into the customs service, which was riddled with corruption and inefficiency. Henceforth, the Swiss surveillance company SGS was to assume responsibility for verification at point of export of all imports valued at more than $5,000. Shipping was also partially deregulated as part of this package, known as Inpres 4. This was one of the government's boldest political acts, since customs was a highly sought-after posting and a key source of military fund-raising and patronage. The move signalled the government's intention to act decisively on microeconomic reform. The effect of Inpres 4 was to greatly expedite the flow of goods through Indonesia's airports and harbours, and to increase government tariff revenues.

The next major step was the introduction of effective import liberalization measures for exporters in May 1986. On Indonesia's accession to the GATT treaty, the previous means of export promotion, the *Sertifikat Ekspor* (SE, Export Certificate) scheme, was abolished as it was deemed to be a subsidy. The SE scheme was, in any case, a costly, blunt and much-abused instrument. Exporters received direct payments up to a specified amount on presentation of relevant documentation. But these payments, after allowing for extensive unofficial levies, often bore little relation to actual export performance. The new scheme, known by its Indonesian acronyms P4BM and subsequently Bapeksta, proved remarkably effective. Supervised in its initial years by a most able senior official from the Department of Finance, exporters were able to either import duty-free or seek reimbursement for such duties. Initially there were some teething problems, and exporters were not always fully compensated for indirect imports or for prices of non-traded inputs which were above international levels. Nevertheless, the scheme has had a powerful demonstration effect in its efficient and corruption-free implementation. It has also provided an element of "overcompensation" for exporters to the extent that they are usually allowed a small quota of surplus imports, which can be used for sale in the still protected domestic market. The scheme has undoubtedly been one of the major contributing factors in the growth of non-oil exports, particularly so for footloose manufactures.[24]

The dismantling of quantitative restrictions and the shift to tariffs commenced effectively in October 1986 when the first of the reform packages was introduced.[25] Further trade packages were introduced in 1987 (January and December), 1988 (November), 1990 (May) and 1991 (June), in addition to the many other reforms enacted over this period. They were often accompanied by intense discussion and debate in the media: which influential parties were affected adversely by the reforms? Did this package signal the end of the reform process, as only the most politically difficult sectors now remained unaffected? Would these reforms be subverted by other, "backtracking" measures? In any event, the results of the reforms were

Table 6.9 **The Coverage of Non-tariff Barriers, 1986–93**[a]

	1986	*1987*	*1988*	*1989*	*1990*	*1991*	*1992*	*1993*
Production	41	38	29	28	25	22	22	22
Manufacturing	68	58	45	38	33	32	31	31
Agriculture	54	53	41	40	38	30	30	30
Imports	43	25	21	17	15	13	13	13

[a] Data refer to coverage after the reform packages of each year. Weights are based on 1985 production for 1986, and 1987 subsequently.

Source: Pangestu (1994), based on World Bank estimates.

impressive. The coverage of NTBs began to decline significantly, from 43 per cent of imports by value in mid-1986 to some 13 per cent just five years later (Table 6.9). The declining coverage in terms of numbers of manufacturing production was also impressive, the share of output more than halving over the same period. In practice the achievements were not as comprehensive as suggested in Table 6.9, since no account is taken of the "intensity" of NTBs. Moreover, the absence of further reforms over the years from 1990 to 1993 is clearly illustrated by these data. The high point of trade reform was the 1986–89 period, when the trend towards growing protection was halted and reversed decisively.

As Soesastro (1989) points out, in a most sophisticated analysis of the reform process, the packages were introduced in a pragmatic non-ideological fashion. Indeed, the government carefully chose *not* to engage in grander ideological and philosophical debates:

> To [have done] so would result in a political polarization even within the government itself that would be of a much greater intensity than the clashes of interests and development ideas that have characterized the opposing camps on the issue of deregulation in its initial years. Thus it appears that the best strategy to keep the deregulation policy going is to keep the debate at the level of "low politics". (Soesastro, 1989, pp. 866–7)

There can be little doubt that the packages have transformed Indonesian industry from a protected, inward-looking sector to one which is increasingly outward-looking and internationally competitive. The very success of the packages added to the momentum for reform, and to "winning over a new constituency for further reform".[26] For the first time in the country's history an export lobby emerged in manufacturing industry, a group for which an internationally efficient economy was of more concern than the dispensation of licences and other bureaucratic largesse. The reorientation of thinking over this period within the Department of Industry, extending up to the Minister, from protection and control to promotion and export, was clearly evident. There has been regress in some cases—such as the imposition of export controls on some resource-based manufactures in the late 1980s—and other areas still remain largely untouched (notably the automotive industry and much of agriculture), but the net gains have been significant. By the early 1990s, seemingly, a more liberal ideology was in the ascendancy, and officials and economists were better able to turn their attention to overcoming the many pressing supply-side constraints to enhanced performance.

THE SYSTEM OF REGULATION AND LICENSING

This is an area of reform in which the New Order has promised much but so far delivered comparatively little. Indonesia has an international reputation for a corrupt, unpredictable and complex commercial environment. In the late 1960s there were high hopes that, as part of the liberal economic reforms being introduced, the system of licensing and regulation would be simplified. Frequent official statements critical of the Sukarno regime in this respect buoyed such expectations. Strong statements such as the following, contained in the first *Repelita*, were not uncommon:

> ... *many industrial enterprises were taken over from their original owners, thus causing an exodus of managers and foreign skilled labor. The Government began to interfere increasingly in various economic activities. Industrial enterprises were dependent on Government rationing of foreign exchange to meet their demands for raw materials, spare parts, and equipment. Freedom to make managerial decisions became more restricted ... Manpower could not be utilized in accordance with economic criteria and politics dominated industry. (Repelita I, 1969, ch. 5, pp. 1-2)*

Yet little substantive progress has been made since the late 1960s. Indonesia's legal infrastructure and licensing system are ill-defined, antiquated and opaque. Despite recent attempts at reform, enforcement is often haphazard and unpredictable. The operation of the licensing regime is sometimes quite different from official objectives and intentions. And the costs to the business sector are not insubstantial, in compliance, uncertainty and illegal exactions.

Many of these features of the licensing regime were examined in a report prepared for the World Bank by Peter McCawley,[27] unpublished but widely reported in the press at the time. The report, still the most comprehensive document of its kind for Indonesia, emphasized several key aspects of the licensing system. Many of the provisions of the industrial and legal code are still based essentially on that which the Dutch colonial regime introduced in the 1930s. There is a wide range of decrees emanating from the bureaucracy, from different departments, from different tiers within departments, and from both central and regional offices. It is not uncommon for these decrees to be inconsistent, either in the letter of the law or in the spirit of its implementation. There are lengthy delays in granting permits, which in turn have to be renewed frequently. Moreover, and ironically, there is an essential "lawlessness" in the system, in spite of official attempts to achieve an ordered and regulated commercial system.

The McCawley report observed (p. 42) that, far from attempting a major overhaul of the system, minor reforms and efforts to clarify the system seemed to create further uncertainty:

> *Each regulation seems to generate more "elucidating" regulations so that in the end minor officials in regional offices and harbors feel at liberty—indeed feel obliged—to "define" certain vague matters by issuing their own regulations ... This generally unsatisfactory situation is not infrequently compounded by the tendency of senior officials to attempt to cut through all of the red tape and delays by granting exemptions to the rules or by making general pronouncements as to "desirable" measures. When this happens it is often unclear as to whether they are expressing their own opinion or actually laying down government policy.*

Recent research on Indonesia's legal system points to similar concerns. In an era when the development economics literature is emphasizing the importance of a stable, open and "fair" system of property rights, Indonesia's legal system combines elements of the old Dutch legal code (without an official Indonesian translation it should be mentioned), the system of *adat* (laws based on tradition), and some limited attempts at reform. The ambiguity of the legal code results in frequent disputes which are reported in great detail in the Indonesian press. A case in point are the laws relating to the transfer, zoning, and acquisition of land. It is estimated, for example, that there are over 300 separate decrees, administered at the provincial level by the *Kantor Agraria* (Agrarian Office). To this already complex situation must be added the fact that several other government departments and agencies—including Forestry, Mining, Environment, the BKPM, Agriculture and Home Affairs—are also involved in implementation. Press reports highlight the operation of a "Land Mafia" (*Mafia Tanah*) controlling the land market in Jakarta and other major cities. Disputes between farmers and companies undertaking rural development projects (such as golf construction and agro-business) are frequent. In the absence of major reform this unsatisfactory situation is likely to persist. For, as Gray (1991, p. 772) aptly remarks:

> ... *the Indonesian legal system tends to be characterized by a lack of clear, consistent, and binding standards. Laws may be contradicted by lower-level decrees and regulations, and both may be contradicted by the day-to-day actions of administrators.*

A striking feature of the 1980s reform process was the speed of change in foreign investment and trade policy, and the lack of progress in the area of legal and regulatory reform. Changes in the latter field lagged behind even those in state enterprise reform. Admittedly, there have been some improvements. There has been some simplification of the licensing system operated by the BKPM discussed above, notably the adoption of a "negative list", and the streamlining of approval and implementation procedures. Regulatory aspects of the trade reform packages have had important implications for the overall regulatory framework. These include especially the 1985 Customs reform, which revolutionized trade through the ports, the export facilitation scheme, implemented cleanly and efficiently, and the shift from non-tariff to tariff protection. Yet these reforms, admirable though they are, address only the tip of the iceberg. In most fields—labour, industry, mining, agriculture, transport (with the notable exception of shipping)—there have been few significant reforms. A modern new commercial code has been under active consideration for almost a decade, yet is still to be released for public discussion, let alone formally enacted. As with state enterprise reform, the slow pace of change in this area reflects the interplay of a set of delicate political and administrative factors. The sheer complexity of the task has undoubtedly been a factor, particularly in the drafting of a whole new legal and commercial code. This is also an area beyond the immediate jurisdiction of the technocrats, who are the major proponents of change. The strength of bureaucratic opposition to reform has been another important factor. The technical departments have been reluctant to surrender regulatory powers, both because it would diminish their administrative power (including their capacity to extract rents), and because of deep-seated notions of paternalism and a lingering mistrust of liberalism and markets.[28]

PUBLIC ADMINISTRATION AND CORRUPTION

Corruption is a perennial topic of debate and discussion in Indonesia. Hardly a month passes without press reports of a new set of corruption allegations, or judicial proceedings at home or abroad which reveal illegal payments. Some of the major cases are referred to elsewhere in this book—the Pertamina affair of 1975-76, numerous scandals in the finance sector, and the failure of the government to appropriate a reasonable portion of the rents from the forestry industry. These and many other major revelations of course represent just a tiny portion of the problem. Illegal payments and exactions are an everyday occurrence for all manner of government services: to expedite the installation of a telephone, to extend an expatriate's work permit, to reclassify a land zoning, for minor immigration services, in the process of "tax bargaining", to secure government contracts large and small, and so on. The focus of discussion and public perceptions may have altered, but the importance of the topic has not diminished.[29]

Corruption in Indonesia of course is not just a phenomenon of the New Order. As Mackie (1970, pp. 87-8) pointed out: corruption

> ... *was becoming almost endemic under the Sukarno regime, when his disastrously inflationary budgets eroded civil service salaries to the point where people simply could not live on them and where financial accountability virtually collapsed because of administrative deterioration.*

Mackie was writing shortly after the release of the report to the President of the "Commission of Four" distinguished public figures in mid-1970. Since the report there have been numerous government campaigns and pronouncements directed at controlling corruption. In the 1970s the focus was on *komersialasi jabatan* (the "commercialisation" of public sector offices). Later in the decade, the acronym *pungli* (*pungutan liar*, illegal payments) was used widely. Initially the latter arose out of efforts to control bribes which transport operators carrying loads in excess of their prescribed limits paid to officials; later the term gained wider currency. During the 1980s, other initiatives were launched.

Despite endless discussion of the topic, there have been very few careful studies of the incidence of corruption.[30] Perhaps inevitably, most analyses are journalistic and anecdotal in nature (but see Note 19). Similarly, the economic costs are virtually unquantifiable. In the final analysis, the political implications of widespread corruption may be more serious still, as manifested in the disaffection of non-favoured business groups, the erosion of the ethical bases of governance, and widespread community discontent with networks of patronage and nepotism.

Corruption is present in virtually all societies. But it is a particularly serious problem in countries like Indonesia characterized by an authoritarian political system, a controlled press, a poorly paid civil service, and a complex commercial regulatory regime. Nevertheless, there have been some positive trends, especially since the early 1980s, and there is the prospect of further reform. As noted, the blatantly corrupt Customs Service was tackled decisively in April 1985. The export incentive scheme has been a model of efficiency. The banking reforms of 1983 and 1988 removed most credit subsidies and reduced the incidence of "command loans"—both sources of significant corruption. Many NTBs have been removed, and with it the revenues accruing to the licence-holder. The taxation system has been overhauled, and tax regulations more vigorously enforced. State enterprises have begun to report in a more orderly and detailed manner. The State Audit Office has become more active, as have various Parliamentary Committees, and the financial press is now much more intrusive and sophisticated. And with the growing internationalization of the Indonesian economy there have been stronger demands for commercial regularity—extending to better accounting practices and firmer regulation of the stock exchange. Moreover, it needs to be remembered that Indonesia's open international capital account and freely convertible currency have removed a source of corruption endemic in so many other developing countries. In sum, corruption in Indonesia is serious, widespread, and inherently non-quantifiable in its incidence and consequences. But at least there have been some notable achievements in the struggle to contain it.

What are the implications of corruption, particularly for public policy and standards of public administration? At least two deserve mention: the case for administrative simplicity and reform, and for an overhaul of civil service conditions of employment.

In formulating public policy, there is a strong case for devising simple schemes which minimize the scope for discretionary authority on the part of implementing officials. Writing in early 1978, at the height of widespread anti-corruption allegations, H.W. Arndt observed, somewhat gloomily:

> *There is hardly an economic policy—whether for the levying of income tax or an urban real estate tax, or for tariff protection of domestic industry, or for subsidies to depressed industries, or for minimal regulation of foreign investment or of road traffic, or for conservation of forests or for provision of rural credit to farmers or for priorities in investment credit by state banks, or for social welfare services or development projects of every kind—which, whatever its economic or technical merits, does not now need to be weighed—and often ruled out—almost wholly on grounds of its administrative impracticability in the face of corruption. (BIES Survey, March 1978, p. 28)*

While administrative capacity and surveillance are undoubtedly a good deal stronger now, these observations remain pertinent. They are relevant especially in the context of widespread calls for Indonesia to adopt an interventionist, "guided" industrial policy, following the alleged path of some Northeast Asian countries, notably Japan and Korea. Whatever the merits of this approach, the case for an interventionist strategy is weakened significantly by a bureaucracy vulnerable to capture by vested interests and characterized by widespread administrative malpractice.[31]

THE CIVIL SERVICE

The second element concerns reform of public sector employment conditions and practices. Public servants are immeasurably better off than they were in the mid-1960s, owing mainly to sharp real increases in salaries through to the early 1980s.[32] In many other respects, too, the civil service has undergone rapid transformation during the New Order period (Table 6.10). Since 1975, when systematic data were first released, it has grown rapidly, at about twice the rate of growth of the labour force as a whole. Interestingly, for all the 1980s austerity, the pace of expansion was not markedly slower during the 1983-92 period as compared with the 1975-83 period. The civil service is still overwhelming male, though becoming less so; male dominance is particularly striking at the senior echelons, and declining much

Table 6.10   **The Indonesian Civil Service, 1975, 1983, 1992**[a]

		1975	1983	1992
Total ('000)		1,674.9	2,628.5	4,009.3
(annual growth, %)			(5.8)	(4.8)
% male:	total	81.9	73.5	66.7
	in rank IV[b]	91.0[c]	91.2	89.0[g]
% in rank:	I	52.7	27.4	15.4
	IV[b]	0.4	0.6	0.9
% of education:[d]	up to primary	38.7	22.5	13.7
		(90.7)	(80.2)	(73.6)
	tertiary[e]	7.2	10.2	13.1
		(1.2)	(0.9)	(1.7)
% located in:	Jakarta	10.9[f]	10.6	9.4[g]
	Java	62.6	58.3	53.4

[a] Excludes the armed forces.
[b] Rank IV is the most senior classification.
[c] Refers to 1980.
[d] Numbers in parentheses refer to the relevant percentage for the whole population aged 15 years and above, for 1976, 1985 and 1990 respectively.
[e] Includes graduates of academies.
[f] Refers to 1978.
[g] Refers to 1991.

Sources: Lampiran Pidato Kenegaraan; and BPS, *Statistik Indonesia*, various issues. Education data for the whole population from Jones (1994, Table 3.14) and Hugo et al. (1987, p. 282), based on population census and labour force surveys data.

more slowly. There has been a general progression of employees out of the very lowest classification, though the numbers in the highest of the four echelons still constitute less than 1 per cent of the total. Education levels are rising quite rapidly. The proportion with only primary education in 1992 is a little over one-third of the 1975 figure, while the proportion of tertiary graduates has almost doubled. These improvements reflect, in part, the general rise in education standards. But the improvement in the civil service has been faster, and the standards are far higher than the general workforce. In 1990–91, for example, the proportion of the civil service with completed tertiary education was eight times that of the general workforce. Almost 10 per cent of the civil service is located in Jakarta, and over one-half on Java. But it is becoming less Jakarta and Java-centric over time, as a consequence of demographic shifts and very limited attempts at decentralization.

However, notwithstanding this progress, the present system has at least three principal deficiencies. One is that the structure of salaries is extraordinarily complex. Partly in deference to strong egalitarian sentiment, official *base* salaries are very low, even for the most senior officials. But there are, in addition, a wide range of supplementary payments, as noted by one observer who conducted a detailed study in the late 1970s:

> *An outsider ... will wonder how Indonesian civil servants survive, and how the government attracts any talent to its service, if ... the respondent confines himself to the nominal salary plus automatic cash supplements ... Upon closer questioning, a bewildering variety of supplements both in cash and kind comes to*

light, and the comparison between civil service and private sector compensation begins to make more sense. (Gray, 1979, p. 85)

Fifteen years after this observation, there has yet to be a major overhaul of the structure of civil service salaries, a structure which remains inefficient, administratively complex, and conducive to nepotism.

Another deficiency is that for all the various forms of supplementation, salaries for skilled labour are generally not competitive with compensation in the private sector. Thus the government has difficulty recruiting skills as diverse as accountants, computer analysts, engineers, economists and high-quality secretaries. These difficulties are particularly evident in the academic labour market, where salaries are tied to the civil service structure. According to one survey in the late 1980s, academics stated that their official salary provided only one-fifth to one-third of their (quite modest) "desired" income (Clark and Oey-Gardiner, 1991). In consequence, the authors found that "moonlighting" was extensive and that often only a small fraction of the academics' time was devoted to official teaching, research and administrative duties. The efficiency implications of low wages here and elsewhere are therefore obvious: accompanied by other reforms, higher wages would very likely lead to increased productivity.

There has been some attempt to redress this problem, prompted by a recognition that talented staff have been leaving to take up more lucrative positions in the private sector. The official base salary of Ministers through until 1992 was just Rp 2 million (approximately $1,000) per month, a figure which was doubled as part of the January 1993 increases. Even though a plethora of allowances pushes this figure up many times, it still places a cap on civil service salaries, especially since sizeable supplementary allowances are generally confined to senior staff. And even with these allowances, official salaries are far behind those of top private sector officials.[33] Not surprisingly, as one senior academic at the University of Indonesia is reported to have observed in 1992:

> ... *we face the reality that more of the best and brightest graduates do not want to be lecturers and, tragically, do not want to be civil servants ... The best only want to go to the private sector.*[34]

In the 1992–94 budgets the government attempted to alleviate this problem. In January 1993 base salaries were raised substantially, by around 15 to 30 per cent in nominal terms, sufficient to compensate for the erosion in real levels since the mid-1980s. In addition, structural allowances were increased, in some cases very significantly, and an attempt was made to target skills in particularly short supply.[35] As a result of these increases, conditions for middle and junior civil servants are probably broadly competitive with those in the private sector, and in some instances may be superior. However, at senior levels and for marketable skills, the disparity still remains. In addition the systems of promotion and performance-based incentives are unattractive as compared with the private sector.

A final deficiency of the civil service system, and one frequently highlighted by the recent Ministers for Reform of the State Apparatus, is its rigidity. Civil servants rarely move between Departments, inhibiting the scope for introducing new ideas and structures. Senior positions within the bureaucracy are not advertized, and so promotion invariably occurs from within the ranks. Dismissal is virtually unheard of. There is almost no cross-fertilization between the public and private sectors, except for the cases of senior civil servants' retirements, noted above. Here also the academic labour market illustrates these weaknesses. Within the state system, academics rarely transfer between universities, and senior posts are not filled through open and competitive advertisement.[36]

Agricultural Modernization

AN OVERVIEW

Agriculture has consistently been a central focus of the New Order's development strategies and priorities. Although this sector suffered less from the ravages of the Sukarno era than other, more monetized and urban-based components of the economy, agricultural performance in the period before 1966 was hardly impressive. Indonesia had been slow to exploit the then emerging opportunities from the new high-yielding varieties known as the green revolution, partly because modern sector commercial inputs were not readily available. Its once dynamic and efficient cash crop sector was stagnating in the face of neglect and a totally unrealistic exchange rate regime. More generally, rural markets were unable to function effectively owing to the deteriorating state of infrastructure and a plethora of unrealistic government pricing and output regulations. Reflecting the collapse of exports and indifferent food crop performance, moreover, nutritional standards were stagnant at best, and probably declining, in the early 1960s.

In important respects, the rice sector became the barometer of the new regime's success, at least in the first decade after 1966. Rice loomed large in the traditionally dominant Javanese heartland. In the late 1960s, when the government's grip on power was still rather precarious, the price and availability of rice had an important bearing on political stability. Even as late as 1972–73, when President Soeharto was immeasurably more powerful, a rice crisis in the form of sharply escalating prices shook the regime. In an era when agricultural taxation and extracting an agricultural surplus were still in vogue, and governments were being criticized for adopting strategies of "urban bias", Indonesia's achievement of rapid growth in the food sector is an important story, both in itself and for its more general implications and lessons. This chapter focuses primarily on how such a strategy was implemented. There is some speculation on, though no attempt to provide a complete answer to, the complex political economy question of why the New Order has been consistently "pro-food", especially during the oil boom decade when agriculture languished in so many other OPEC countries.

The overall record of Indonesian agricultural development since 1966 is a mixed one. The highlight has been the dramatic success of rice, especially over the period from 1978 to 1983. From its status as the world's largest rice importer in the late 1970s, at the peak purchasing some 30 per cent of the world's traded rice, the cherished and hitherto elusive goal of self-sufficiency was achieved in 1985 and has been maintained broadly since then. Indonesia capitalized on the opportunities presented by the technological advances in food crop production in the 1960s and 1970s. In this respect, its performance has been in stark contrast to that of many other OPEC countries, whose food sectors either stagnated or declined.

But, on the other side of the ledger, the strong rice performance was a costly achievement, owing to very high input subsidies. Moreover, non-food agricultural development has been much less impressive. With a few notable exceptions—most importantly palm oil—the cash crop sector has not displayed the dynamism evident in some neighbouring countries. This is especially the case in the smallholder sector, where a combination of neglect, discrimination in favour of plantations, and inappropriate policies has resulted in slow output growth and virtually stagnant yields. The record in forestry, fisheries and livestock could also have been much better.[1]

Food crop agriculture, as noted, had been less affected by the economic decline before 1966, being more subsistence-oriented and less dependent on imported inputs than industry and some services. Nevertheless, for a generation of Indonesian scholars raised on Clifford Geertz's influential *Agricultural Involution*, few observers saw any prospect of rapid agricultural development in the early years of the New Order. Geertz (1963, p. 146) himself argued that:

> *[i]n the absence of any genuine reconstruction of Indonesian civilization ... pouring fertilizer onto Java's Lilliputian fields is likely, as modern irrigation, labor-intensive cultivation and crop diversification before it, to make only one thing grow: paralysis.*

David Penny (1969, p. 263), another foreign researcher with extensive experience of rural Indonesia, agreed with this diagnosis. Writing a few years later, he argued:

> *[T]he reluctance of farmers to buy fertiliser, modern tools, etc., is still so great that it is unlikely that any substantial modernisation of Indonesian peasant agriculture will take place in the next decade or two.[2]*

Why was agricultural growth so much better than anticipated by these and other knowledgeable observers? Two sets of factors have been critical. First, there has been a strong government commitment, particularly to rice and the plantations. Rice production has been boosted by realistic output pricing and large input subsidies (fertilizer, pesticides, irrigation). The plantations, especially those which are state-owned, have received subsidized credit, equity capital injections, and assistance under the foreign aid program. Agriculture, like the rest of the economy, has benefited from the government's large infrastructure investments.

The second general factor has been a favourable external environment. Rapid technological advances have pushed out production frontiers for rice, other food crops, and certain cash crops. Also, though less important, Indonesia's proximity to arguably the two most efficient and dynamic tropical cash crop producing countries, Malaysia and Thailand, has resulted in some favourable spin-offs among the private estates and acted as a demonstration effect for the more slowly expanding government estates. Indonesia has thus been able to build effectively on its comparative advantage, in the case of rice concentrated mainly on Java–Bali, South Sulawesi and West Sumatra, and in cash crops located primarily in Sulawesi, Sumatra, and Kalimantan.

Figures 7.1a,b and Table 7.1 provide an overview of agricultural output growth from the late 1960s to the early 1990s. From 1966 to 1992 agricultural output grew at an annual average rate of almost 4 per cent per annum, by any comparative

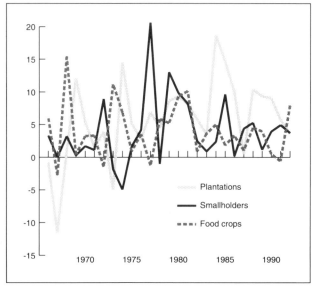

Figure 7.1a   The growth of agricultural output: plantations,
smallholders and food crops, 1966–92

indicator (see for example Table 1.3, p. 6) an impressive performance. Food crops have always dominated the sector, generating consistently about 60 per cent of agricultural value added. The relative size of the other sub-sectors has also changed very little over this period—smallholders (about 13 per cent of the total), plantations (2 to 3 per cent), livestock (a little over 10 per cent), fisheries (7 to 8 per cent), and forestry (about 5 per cent). Output growth has been more uneven among those sectors directly dependent on international markets and prices. This is particularly evident, for example, in the fluctuations in smallholder, plantations and fisheries output, all more export-oriented than food crops and livestock (Figures 7.1a,b).

The major subsector, food crops, has grown quite steadily since 1970. Dominated by rice, output has fallen in only three years: 1972 and 1991 when particularly severe droughts occurred, and in 1977 when pests caused major disruption. The strong output growth from 1978 to 1981, which laid the base for self-sufficiency a few years later, is also evident. With the exception of palm oil, easily the most dynamic cash crop of the New Order, and cocoa, sharp increases in smallholder and estate production can generally be attributed to rising international prices. Examples include coffee smallholder output in the late 1970s, and estate rubber production in the mid-1970s and mid-1980s. The extent of crop specialization between smallholders and estates is illustrated by the fact that these sectors' output growth is not highly correlated. In the case of forestry, the subsector subject to the most intensive government regulation, the prohibition on the export of unprocessed timber and the removal of easily accessible stands both explain the sharp fall in production throughout most of the 1980s.

Two general observations on Indonesian agricultural development are pertinent at this stage. First, as discussed in more detail in Chapter 11, there is tremendous regional

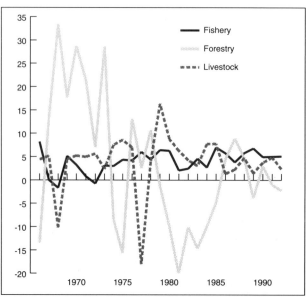

Figure 7.1b The growth of agricultural output: fishery, forestry and livestock, 1966–92

variation in agricultural structure and performance, reflecting ecology, consumer preferences, regional comparative advantage, and government policy. This regional mosaic is crucial to an understanding of Indonesian agricultural development. Thus, rice dominates much of agriculture in what is still sometimes referred to as "Inner Indonesia", Java and Bali. It is also significant in a number of traditional "surplus" provinces outside, such as South Sulawesi and West Sumatra. In the case of cash crops Sumatra is the largest producer, and has been for many decades. These crops are also significant elsewhere, in parts of West Kalimantan, East Java (where they are still a surprisingly sizeable share of agriculture—see Mackie, 1993), Sulawesi, and East Timor. Much of the forestry industry is located on Kalimantan, and to a lesser extent Maluku. In the dry regions of Nusa Tenggara, the livestock industry has traditionally been important, as have roots and tubers. Most high value, consumer-oriented agriculture, such as poultry and vegetables, tends to be located in proximity to major urban markets.

The second observation is that Indonesia's agricultural record compares favourably with that of most other developing countries. Summary comparative statistics were provided in Table 1.3. Figure 7.2 provides a more detailed picture for agricultural production as a whole, together with food and all crops. In each case the comparison is with developing Asian countries and all developing countries. In all three comparisons, Indonesia is above average. Using 1979–81 as a base year, by 1991 the country was at least 7 per cent and 17 per cent ahead of the Asian and developing country groups respectively. A similar conclusion holds for the pre-1980 period. The fact that Indonesia emerges favourably in all three comparisons, and for both time periods, points to the consistency and durability of its agricultural record. For all the problems encountered, to be discussed shortly, it is important not to lose sight of this creditable performance.

Table 7.1 **Agricultural Production and Yields, 1970–90**
(three-year averages)

		1970	1980	1990
Food crops				
Rice: Total	P	19,180	29,570	44,864
	Y	23.5	32.6	43.0
	A[a]	8,162	9,071	10,433
Rice: Java	P	11,686	18,218	26,860
	Y	26.9	37.7	50.2
	A[a]	4,344	4,832	5,351
Rice: off-Java	P	7,494	11,352	18,004
	Y	19.6	26.7	35.4
	A[a]	3,823	4,252	5,086
Maize	P	2,574	4,036	6,394
	Y	9.6	14.6	21.3
	A	2,681	2,764	3,002
Cassava	P	10,695	13,609	16,300
	Y	75	97	121
	A	1,426	1,403	1,347
Cash crops: Estates				
Rubber	P	233	285	324
	Y	479	646	631
	A	486	441	513
Palm Oil	P	218	681	1,934
	Y	1,796	2,963	2,780
	A	121	230	696
Tea	P	43	78	125
	Y	679	1,146	1,455
	A	63	68	86
Cash crops: Smallholders				
Rubber	P	557	668	895
	Y	308	342	342
	A	1,808	1,953	2,616
Coconuts	P	1,212	1,664	2,274
	Y	n.a.	632	695
	A	n.a.	2,633	3,272
Coffee	P	164	274	384
	Y	457	416	382
	A	359	659	1,005
Tea	P	22	21	29
	Y	379	519	577
	A	58	40	50
Tobacco	P	71	103	129
	Y	489	562	658
	A	145	183	196
Cloves	P	12	27	66
	Y	127	66	103
	A	94	409	641

[a] The Java and off-Java areas do not always add exactly to the total owing to
rounding errors.
P–production, in '000 tons.
Y–yields, in '00 kilograms/hectare for food crops, and kg/ha for cash crops.
A–area, in '000 ha.
n.a.–not available.

Source: BPS, *Statistik Indonesia*, various issues.

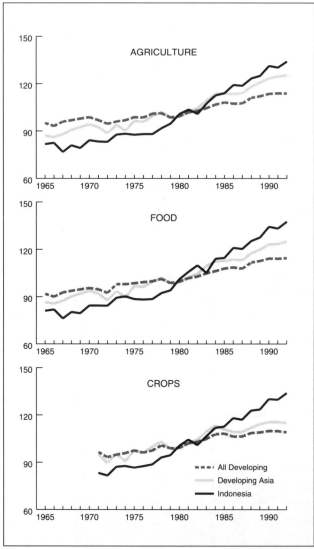

Figure 7.2 Indices of per capita agricultural production,
1965–92

FOOD CROPS

RICE

Rice has been the success story, dominated by the growth of *sawah* (wet rice): *Sawah* output rose by more than 250 per cent from 1966 to 1992, while apparent per capita consumption jumped by almost 80 per cent. Yields more than doubled over this period, and contributed almost 70 per cent of the increased production; the contrast with the minimal yield increases before 1966 is a stark one. Rice dominates the Indonesia diet, except in a few of the eastern provinces, and in the late 1960s had a weight of 31 per cent in the Jakarta 62-commodity CPI. It is therefore not surprising that rice became a major preoccupation of the government after the macroeconomic stabilization phase (1966–68) was completed. "Indeed food policy *was* rice policy" during *Repelita* I, according to Mears and Moeljono (1981, p. 23), although a decade later the government began to place more emphasis on food crop diversification.

Developments in rice reflect the interplay between longer-term policy and institutional factors, and shorter-term influences such as climatic conditions and pest attacks. The longer-term development strategy comprised principally the introduction of high yielding varieties (HYVs), rising input (fertilizer and pesticide) subsidies, output price stabilization and (at least in the 1980s) support, and the rehabilitation and development of irrigation and extension networks. It is the latter factors which explain Indonesia's dramatic rice success, while the shorter-term influences explain annual fluctuations around an improving trend line.[3]

The regime inherited the agricultural extension efforts developed in the early 1960s, known as *Bimas*[4] (Penny, 1969). *Bimas* and several subsequent rice intensification efforts, together with the food procurement agency *Bulog*,[5] have been the institutional pillars of the government's rice promotion efforts. By the late 1960s an operational framework, first expounded systematically by Mears and Afiff (1969), involved the establishment by *Bulog* of floor and ceiling prices for paddy, with margins providing sufficient incentive for private traders to enter the market. The *Bimas* program, operating through village cooperative units,[6] provided a package of seed and other inputs, together with credit from the government bank specializing in agriculture, Bank Rakyat Indonesia. *Inmas*, an intensification program without credit subsidies, was also introduced.[7]

The first decade after 1966 saw mixed results, in terms of both output and yields (Figures 7.3 and 7.4). In some years output rose significantly, notably 1968 owing to increased fertilizer availability (from imports), and 1970 under the impetus of *Bimas* organizational reforms and good rainfall. But for much of the 1970s the record was indifferent. In 1972 a prolonged dry season resulted in falling output. *Bulog* was slow to act, and eventually was unable to defend its ceiling. It was later to enter international markets which in any case were characterized by shortages and rising prices. As a result, domestic rice prices doubled in the last four months of that year. Problems emerged again a few years later. Arrears under the *Bimas* credit program escalated. There was a prolonged drought in 1976. Outbreaks of the *wereng* (brown plant hopper) pest, which first appeared on a wide scale in the 1974/5 season, were particularly serious in 1977. From 1974 to 1977 output barely increased. It appeared then that Indonesia would never be able to achieve significant output expansion, much less the goal of self-sufficiency. By the late 1970s it was importing up to one-third of the world's traded rice, becoming something of a price-maker on thin and then volatile international markets. Mears and Moeljono (1981, p. 49) reflected authoritative thinking at the time, stating that ' . . . it seems that the goal of self-sufficiency in rice by 1985 (or any reasonable time thereafter) will be very hard to achieve'.

Unlike the situation a decade earlier, by the mid-1970s Indonesia had ample foreign exchange reserves with which to purchase rice. But policy-makers were concerned about the sluggish growth in rice production for at least two reasons: first, as real oil prices began to taper off, the prospect of continuing large imports in a thin international market was viewed with concern. The arguments invoked at that time to promote rice were in some respects similar to the justification for the November

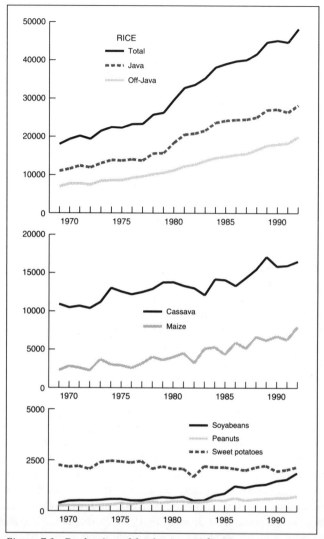

Figure 7.3   Production of food crops, 1969–92

1978 devaluation. That is, there needed to be exchange rate protection, or at least compensation, for the intersectoral effects of the Dutch disease.

Secondly, there was a political motive for intervention, to avoid a repetition of the damaging 1972 crisis and to ensure that the benefits of the oil boom were recycled into rural areas, especially the Javanese heartland. In this respect, Indonesia's political economy equations were and are quite unlike those of other OPEC countries, and indeed of much of the third world in general. The issue of why the country adopted a strong rural development strategy in the 1970s has been a question attracting much speculation but limited systematic analysis by political scientists. A fashionable explanation, invoking Soeharto's rural origins, does appear to be quite convincing. Consider, for example, the following quote recorded in his semi-official biography: 'It's natural that I pay greater attention to the problem of rural development. What's

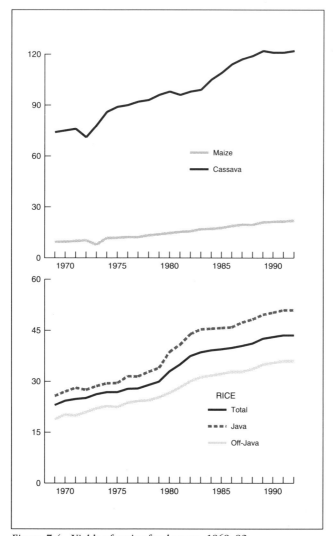

Figure 7.4   Yields of major food crops, 1969–92

more, I am myself the son of a peasant' (Roeder, 1976, p. 218).[8] It may be misleading to invoke essentially anecdotal and highly personalized remarks as the basis for understanding the political economy of rice in the New Order. But there does seem to be little doubt that the President's strong support for the rice program has been a major factor in its success.

Alternative explanations for Indonesia's pro-rural strategies might focus on the bases of the regime's political and military support, especially its Javanese power base, and the belief that security in this arena would ensure the New Order's popularity. The fact that rice has been heavily supported, in marked contrast to the poorly performing smallholder cash crop sector, located mainly off-Java, lends superficial support to the notion that the regime has been more 'pro-Java' than 'pro-rural' in general. But this is an issue on which more research by political scientists is required.[9]

The mid-1970s was therefore something of a watershed in rice policy, the effects of which were to become evident by the end of the decade. A number of measures, to be discussed shortly, had a dramatic impact on rice production. These initiatives had a delayed but relatively swift impact on production from the late 1970s. In 1977–78, rice production began to grow rapidly, from 23.3 million tons in 1977 to 29.7 million tons in 1980 and 38.1 million tons in 1984 (Figure 7.3). Good rainfall and the absence of pest problems facilitated the expansion, but the primary explanation was the concerted and comprehensive policy measures discussed above.[10] In 1980, serious storage capacity problems emerged, indicative of the fact that the supply response caught even officials by surprise. The country weathered the 1982–83 drought, the most serious in a decade. Output growth resumed quickly in 1984 and 1985, once again leading to storage problems for *Bulog*, which was left with large quantities of deteriorating, low quality rice. In November 1985 President Soeharto announced that rice self-sufficiency had been achieved, on the occasion of an invited address to the 40th anniversary conference of the FAO.

Indonesia engaged in very little international trade from 1985 to 1990. The President's declaration of self-sufficiency was an absolute one at the time, involving as it did the maintenance of huge rice stockpiles. No public or policy debate on the topic was permitted for a number of years, and rice policy became so sensitive in senior policy circles as to jeopardize the goal of efficient agricultural development.[11] Rice was offered on an exchange basis to neighbouring countries such as Vietnam and the Philippines, and the effects of both renewed pest attacks in 1986–87 and drought in 1987–88 were overcome without deviating from the 'no-imports' policy. However, a prolonged dry season in 1991 hastened a shift away from the rigid and politically motivated strategy. The fact that a general election was on the horizon may also have contributed to the policy reappraisal. The official policy was then eased somewhat to become one of 'trend' self-sufficiency, allowing for imports and exports on a minor scale as seasonal conditions dictated.

Figures 7.5 and 7.6 document the key policy instruments used to increase production over this period, all funded by the government's newly found oil wealth. First, there was a concerted effort to accelerate the spread of HYVs. The percentage of the rice area covered by various intensification programs is a reasonable proxy for the coverage of HYVs. The latter's share of rice crop plantings over the 1970–80 decade more than doubled, from about 26 per cent to 61 per cent (Figure 7.5). The percentage continued to rise strongly in the first half of the 1980s, before tapering off around 1987. Over this period, also, the extent of subsidy implicit in the intensification program began to diminish, especially as farmers began to pay interest rates approximating market levels.[12]

A second instrument, and a key ingredient of the intensification program, was fertilizer. The new varieties are particularly responsive to fertilizer usage, and in the 1960s Indonesia's consumption of commercial fertilizer varieties was low. However, fertilizer application began to rise rapidly during the 1970s, by some five-fold over the 1970–80 decade, doubling again in the following decade (Figure 7.5). Given that the area under food crop cultivation expanded very slowly, these increases translated into greatly intensified fertilizer usage per hectare, rising by more than 12-fold from 1969 to 1992.[13] Expanding supplies were facilitated by the growth of the domestic industry (see Table 8.1, p. 154), but most important, initially, by the availability of foreign exchange to finance imports. Increased usage was unquestionably desirable

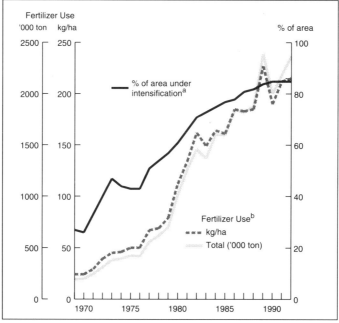

Figure 7.5   Rice: intensification and fertilizer use, 1969–92

in the 1970s, and it made a major contribution to rising yields. However, fertilizer became a topic of intense economic and ecological debate in the late 1980s. The former concern was on the grounds of budgetary expense and the belief that application may have exceeded optimum rates.[14] The ecological concern centred on the fact that low official prices were encouraging indiscriminate application, possibly leading to pollution of waterways and fisheries, and soil degradation.

The sharp increase in the fertilizer subsidy is documented in Table 4.2 (p. 54). It rose from Rp 32 billion in 1977 to Rp 756 billion in 1987 before tapering off. But even in 1991, retail prices were, on average, 42 per cent below world prices and, in the important case of urea fertilizer, 50 per cent below (World Bank, 1992, p. 62). The pesticide subsidy also increased significantly, peaking at Rp 175 billion in 1987. However, in a major victory for both economic rationality and environmental management, it was abolished in the following year, and replaced with a program of integrated pest management.[15] The impact of the fertilizer subsidy is clearly evident in the rice-fertilizer price ratios (Figure 7.6). After being constant during the first Five Year Plan (1969–73), they began to rise appreciably in the mid-1970s, coinciding more or less exactly with the growth in the government's oil revenue. The sharp increase from 1978 to 1982, the critical period in terms of achieving rice self-sufficiency, is particularly noticeable. The ratio began to fall after the mid-1980s as the value of the subsidy declined marginally. But even by 1990 it was higher than that of any year over the 1969–78 period.

The third component of rice strategy was price support. Indonesia has largely avoided the extremes of excessive rice protection or taxation. But especially in the 1970s, the government did attempt to insulate the domestic rice market from international fluctuations. During most of the 1970s, the world price exceeded the

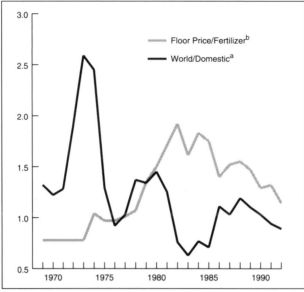

Figure 7.6 Rice: price ratios, 1969–92

domestic price by a significant margin, peaking at a differential of more than two to one in 1973–74, when international prices were historically high (Figure 7.6). Already grappling with its first serious inflation problem since the restoration of price stability in 1968–69, the government sought to restrain domestic rice prices for fear that a significant increase would further fuel inflationary pressures. An additional factor was that this was also a period of domestic political uncertainty, following the January 1974 *Malari* riots, and so any sharp rise in the price of such a basic staple would have been unpopular with vocal urban opinion.

Thereafter, however, relative prices moved in favour of rice producers. After the traumatic experience of 1972–73, *Bulog* began to build up its storage and stock capacity, which enabled it to influence domestic prices significantly. During the 1980s, domestic rice prices did not deviate significantly from world prices. Between 1982 and 1990 the ratio ranged from 0.63 to 1.19, and over this period world prices were, on average, some 91 per cent of domestic prices. Thus in a number of years rice producers received assistance both in the form of input subsidies and output protection.

There were other important components of the rice program which contributed to output growth. The irrigation infrastructure, mainly on Java, had been run down badly over the 1940–66 period (Booth, 1977). Major rehabilitation projects were initiated, many as part of foreign aid programs. Water rates incorporated significant public subsidy. The government stepped up its R&D efforts, building on the work of the International Rice Research Institute in the Philippines, particularly in the development of varieties which were resistant to local pest attacks. Finally, of course, very large subsidies flowed to the rice sector in the form of credit subsidies, both through below-market interest rates, and arrears on repayment, including outright default. These subsidies were channelled directly from the Central Bank to the two key implementing agencies, *Bulog* and Bank Rakyat Indonesia.

Table 7.2   Contribution of Yields to Agricultural Production Growth, 1970–90

	1970-80	*1980-90*	*1970-90*
Food crops			
Rice—total	75	66	68
Java	76	74	74
off-Java	74	61	67
Maize	93	82	87
Cassava	95	123	113
Cash crops: Estates			
Rubber	149	−18	83
Palm Oil	44	−7	23
Tea	87	51	68
Cash crops: Smallholders			
Rubber	58	0	22
Coconuts	n.a.	30	n.a.
Coffee	−19	−26	−23
Tea	−8	(positive)	160
Tobacco	37	70	50

n.a.-not available

Note: These calculations are based on the decomposition formula which attributes output growth to changes in area and yields, as follows:

let O_o, O_t be output in periods o and t
Y_o, Y_t be yields in periods o and t
A_o, A_t be area in periods o and t

The area contribution is given by:

$$(A_t - A_o)\ (Y_t + Y_o)/2$$

while that for yields is:

$$(Y_t - Y_o)\ (A_t + A_o)/2$$

Data are derived from those presented in Table 7.1.

What was the magnitude in aggregate of these various forms of assistance? Quantification of the impact of all forms of intervention is virtually impossible. But it is useful to cite the results of one innovative study, by Morrisson and Thorbecke (1990), who provided a fresh perspective on these subsidies, by calculating the domestic agricultural surplus for Indonesia using a 1980 Social Accounting Matrix. Not surprisingly, though unusually for developing countries, they found that the surplus was negative, meaning that 'the non-agricultural sector provided a net excess of goods and factors to agriculture . . . of Rp 74 billion' (p. 1086). Significantly, they estimated the net positive public transfer from the government to agriculture to be some Rp 175 billion.

Decomposing rice production growth into its principal components provides further insights into the bases of this sector's dynamics. First, rising yields have consistently been the most important factor in the expansion. Rice yields almost doubled from 1969 to 1992, from 2.25 tons per hectare to 4.35. Consequently, they account for most of the increased output, some 68 per cent over the 1970-90 period. The contribution was somewhat less in the 1980s, owing to considerable area expansion off-Java, but higher in the 1970s (Table 7.2).

Secondly, contrary to widely held expectations that Java has already hit the limits of food production expansion, the shares of Java and off-Java have not changed appreciably. Indeed, there has been a remarkable overall consistency in the two regions' performance. From 1969 to 1992, rice production rose 156 per cent and 186 per cent on Java and off-Java respectively, while the yield increases were 98 per cent and 91 per cent. Off-Java's share of rice output has been within the 37 to 41 per cent range throughout the period. Only in very recent years has its share displayed the upward trend that many observers had been anticipating for some time as the signal that Java may be losing its comparative advantage in food crop production. But the rise is still very small, and hardly constitutes a decisive turning point in the country's agricultural development. As would be expected, yields have played a larger role in output growth on Java, especially in the 1980s when several large rice estate projects were initiated off-Java.[16]

OTHER FOOD CROPS[17]

The rice success story has overshadowed the rest of the food sector. In the last days of the Sukarno regime, when even the resilient rice sector was in decline, the population was exhorted to 'eat maize' (*makan jagung*), to conserve dwindling foreign exchange. Rice is the preferred staple in all but a few eastern regions of the country, and it received almost all the new government's attention in its early years. In consequence, *palawija* (that is, non-rice food) crops were largely neglected until the late 1970s. Some intensification programs for maize, peanuts and soybeans were initiated during *Repelita* II, out of concern at the indifferent rice performance and the need to diversify diets. This nutritional diversification extended to wheat imports, then seen as a cheaper means of purchasing calories, an initiative encouraged by wheat's larger and less volatile international market. There was also some stimulus to output in 1972–74 when rice prices peaked, as consumers switched to cassava and maize, but the effects were short-lived.

Over the decade of the first two Five Year Plans, *palawija* output was largely static. Maize output in 1976, for example, was only marginally higher than that of 1969. Cassava output expanded erratically and very slowly, and from the mid-1970s until the mid-1980s showed no overall increase. There was little dynamism evident in any of the other crops (Figure 7.3). Yield growth was also unimpressive (Figure 7.4). These results were in stark contrast to the record in rice, which was seen as the 'glamour' crop over this period. Promotional efforts and research and extension support were very limited. Yields remained low by international standards.

It was only during *Repelita* III that *palawija* crops received anything like the same attention as rice (Mears, 1978). Maize yields proved quite responsive, and this crop experienced something of a technological revolution beginning in the late 1970s. There was some expansion in area over this period, which accounts for the smaller yield contribution in the 1980s as compared with the previous decade (Table 7.2). Rising demand from the commercial livestock industry also induced greater output. Production over the 1980–92 period increased sharply, marginally outpacing the growth of rice. Yields also began to rise appreciably from the late 1970s, and for the 1969–91 period they actually increased some 10 per cent faster than those of rice.

However, the record of the other crops has been much more mixed. Production of peanuts and soybean has risen quickly from a very small base. The latter's increase has been particularly spectacular—some 500 per cent from 1969 to 1992—but at the cost of prohibitively high protection. Since the mid-1980s, only one producer of soybean meal has been permitted, a firm by the name of Sarpindo, and it benefits from 5 per cent tariff protection together with a 35 per cent surcharge (Tomich, 1992). Its meal is marketed to feedmills through *Bulog* at a price approximately 50 per cent above world prices. Cassava and sweet potatoes have continued to languish: both are regarded as inferior goods, the area planted has shrunk, and yield improvements have been erratic. Moreover, commercialization of the industry has proceeded slowly, and export opportunities have been missed. A notable example of the latter has been that Indonesia was unable to enter the profitable cassava pellet export trade in the manner in which Thailand did.

CASH CROPS

The record in cash crops has been much less impressive than that of rice.[18] As with *palawija* crops in the 1970s, but for different reasons, much of the cash crop sector has an indifferent performance record. Except for the much publicized success of palm oil, and a few minor crops such as cocoa, output growth has often been slow and erratic (Figures 7.7a and 7.7b). Rubber production is a case in point: from the late 1960s until the early 1990s, production on estates rose only 50 per cent, barely keeping pace with population growth and displaying no clear upward trend since the mid-1980s. The record among smallholders has been only marginally better. Production actually stagnated until the early 1980s, but thereafter has displayed greater dynamism. Coffee and tea have expanded quite quickly at certain periods, mainly in response to high international prices. Smallholder coffee output has proven to be quite dynamic, with output more than doubling since the late 1960s. However, estate output has not increased since the early 1980s. Smallholder tea production has grown slowly since the 1980s, while the estate sector has expanded more rapidly.

By far the most dynamic crop has been palm oil. From its revival on a commercial scale, in the 1960s, output rose more than 11-fold from 1968 to 1992. Indonesia is the world's second largest producer of palm oil, accounting for about 23 per cent of total production. It is still well below the premier producer, Malaysia, with 55 per cent of the total, but easily surpasses the number three producer, Nigeria (with 5 per cent). According to some forecasts Indonesia may produce as much as 12 million tons by the year 2010. By this time, with its wage and land cost advantage over Malaysia, it is likely to be the world's largest producer. Palm oil has been free of the supply and demand-side constraints which have bedevilled other cash crops, such as international production quotas (as in the case of coffee), and a heavy-handed and cumbersome state enterprise presence (such as in rubber). Foreign firms have played a more significant role in this industry than in any other major cash crop. Some enterprises have relocated from Malaysia, and in the process introduced that country's more advanced technological capacity into Indonesia.

The yield data underline the patchy performance of the cash crop sector (Figures 7.8a and 7.8b). In the case of the technologically more advanced estates, in no case has there been a doubling of yields as has occurred in rice and maize. In the first decade of the New Order, rehabilitation programs and favourable prices produced a modest rise in yields, but since the late 1970s there has been no clear trend. A similar conclusion applies to tea, while in sugar the picture is confused by the incorporation of smallholder output in the estates sector. In palm oil, the rapid

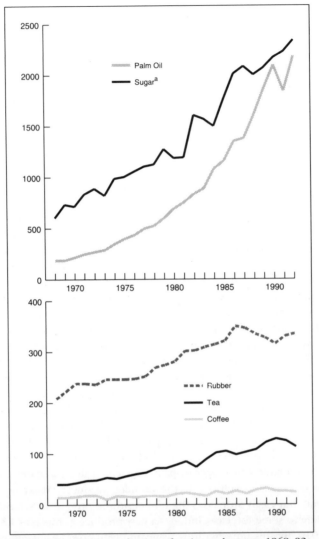

Figure 7.7a Estate production of major cash crops, 1968–92

expansion of new plantings has meant that average yields in the early 1990s are comparable with those of the mid-1970s. However, at the margin, among established, technologically progressive plantations, yields have reportedly risen quickly. In the case of smallholders, remarkably, there has been no appreciable yield increase in any of the major crops, a stark illustration of the failure of agricultural development policy in this arena. Coffee and clove yields appear to be lower now than they were in the late 1960s. These judgements need to be qualified again by the very poor data base, especially concerning the area estimates for smallholders. There is interplanting of crops, new plantings are not always recorded accurately, and during periods of low prices crops may not be harvested. But, notwithstanding these caveats, there can be no doubt that the major conclusion, of a bypassed, technologically stagnant sector, still applies.

Unlike food crops, much of the increased cash crop production has come from an

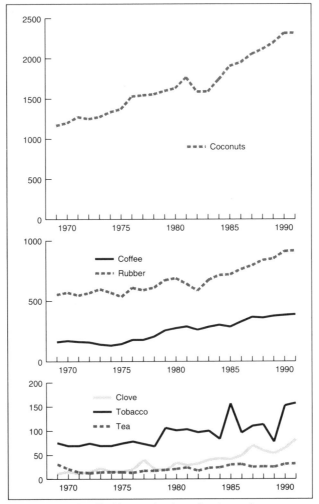

Figure 7.7b   Smallholder production of major cash crops,
1969–91

expansion in area, especially during the 1980s in the case of estates and throughout the period among smallholders (Table 7.2). This applies particularly to the two major crops, rubber and coconuts (when data are available). Among the estates, average yields actually declined in the 1980s owing to rapid area expansion in some instances. In general, the contribution of yield growth was greater in the 1970s as compared with the following decade, owing in part to more favourable international prices—and hence more intensive cultivation—and with the rehabilitation of agricultural holdings and rural infrastructure. The considerable fluctuation in the numbers is, as noted, at least partly the result of the poor quality of the land area data.

There is substantial specialization within the estate and smallholder components (Table 7.3). Only in the case of palm oil and tea are estates the major producers, accounting for more than three-quarters of production in recent years. A sizeable estate sector exists in the case of rubber and cocoa, while for all other crops the producers are overwhelmingly smallholders. As noted above, these shares are

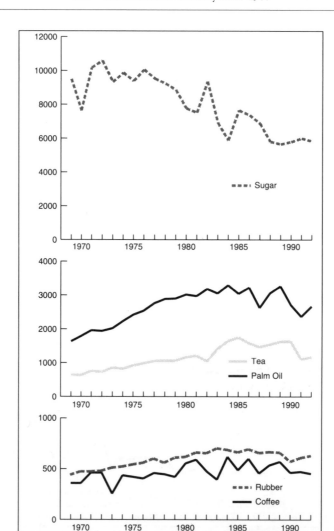

Figure 7.8a Estate yields of major cash crops, 1969–92

somewhat misleading because of the presence of 'large smallholders' (or conversely 'small estates'), and because there are various commercial relationships between larger and smaller units, particularly at the processing stages. Some of these linkages have been promoted by the government, especially in the case of state enterprises, which are expected to assist smallholders in their proximity. Physical yields on estates are often significantly higher, especially in the cases of rubber, palm oil and tea. The quality of the estates' output is frequently higher, and so too are their prices, thereby resulting in still higher gross return per hectare. However, smallholder operating costs are generally much lower, enabling them to be competitive. The estates, particularly those which are state-owned, have also received a range of government subsidies. For these reasons it would be inaccurate to infer from the data in Table 7.3 that social rates of return are higher in the case of the estates.

In a number of respects, the history of the cash crop sector appears to be one of lost opportunities, ostensibly consistent with several gloomy accounts of its development over the twentieth century (see, for example, Stoler, 1985). Prior to 1965, the sector

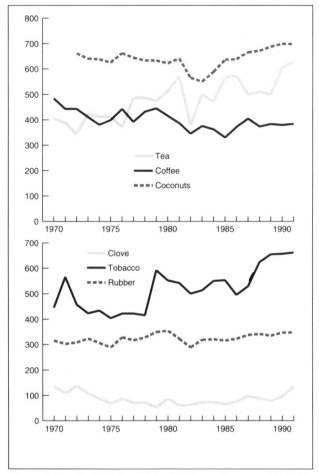

Figure 7.8b Smallholder yields of major cash crops, 1970–91

was impeded by unrealistic foreign exchange pricing (notwithstanding widespread smuggling), by the loss of Dutch technical expertise after 1957–58 (see Mackie, 1961/62), and by the general political uncertainty which discouraged substantial investment in crops not offering immediate yields. Smallholders achieving low yields and producing on an irregular basis consequently provided what little dynamism there was. After 1966 the sector might have been expected to grow more quickly, as a unified foreign exchange rate was adopted, big investments in infrastructure got underway, and the political situation became more secure. International prices in the 1970s were also generally favourable, rubber in particular benefiting from the higher cost of synthetic rubber during the oil boom period.

There were some improvements: in palm oil, as noted; increased yields for most crops produced by the plantations; and smallholder area expansion. But inefficient management of and costly subsidies for the state-owned plantations, insecure land access for some private estates, and ineffective promotional programs for smallholders have all retarded growth. The oil boom also hindered international competitiveness through the squeeze on non-oil tradeable activities. In the 1980s, falling oil prices produced the opposite outcome, via real effective depreciations of the rupiah.

Table 7.3 **Estates and Smallholders—Comparative Data, 1990[a]**

	% Estates		Yields (kg/ha)	
	Production	Area	Estates	Smallholders
Rubber	27	17	631	342
Palm oil	77	64	2,780	1,426
Coffee	7	5	503	382
Cocoa	35	32	356	304
Tea	81	60	1,455	538

[a] For the following crops, smallholders produce at least 95% of output: coconuts, cloves, tobacco, cotton, cashew nuts, various spices. Data refer to the three-year averages, 1989–91.

Source: BPS, *Statistik Indonesia*, various issues.

However, this competitive advantage was nullified somewhat by generally low international prices.

Indonesia's lost opportunities are nowhere better illustrated than in the case of natural rubber. Three countries, Indonesia, Malaysia and Thailand, dominate the industry, producing 75 to 80 per cent of world output in recent decades (and a higher share still, in earlier years). Malaysia has traditionally been the dominant producer, accounting for about 40 per cent of the total until about 1980. Malaysian output began to contract slowly during the 1980s, at which point Indonesia, long the second major producer, might have been expected to become the dominant supplier. However, Thailand's rubber output has grown at an extraordinarily rapid pace, especially in the 1980s (Table 7.4). In the 1960s and 1970s it grew at about twice the Indonesian rate, while in the 1980s it was some seven times faster. Producing about one-sixth of Indonesia's total in 1950 and one-third in 1970, by 1990 it had caught up. In 1992 it was officially declared to be the world's largest producer.

The problems bedevilling Indonesia's smallholder rubber producers have been extensively analysed by Colin Barlow and colleagues.[19] In the early 1970s Collier and Werdaja (1972) pointed to high transport costs, poor port facilities, low quality (at both tapping and processing stages), long marketing chains, and the imposition of export taxes and other levies. Farmers consequently received only a small fraction of the world price, often less than one-half of the percentage accruing to Malaysian producers. A decade later, Barlow and Muharminto (1982) emphasized the biases in government policy, with the estates receiving the major proportion of government loans and extension efforts. Smallholders, they observed, rarely received assistance through extension services. The Nucleus Estates Scheme (NES), launched in the mid-1970s to encourage smallholder production, entailed the use of excessively capital-intensive inputs, which inevitably limited the participation of most small farmers. Despite efforts to integrate estates and smallholders, the yield gaps have widened and spin-offs from the former remain limited. There now appears to be a change in official thinking away from the 'focused' strategy, which has proved too capital and management-intensive, towards a 'dispersal' strategy, akin to the successful Thai

Table 7.4   **Southeast Asian and World Rubber Production, 1950–90**

Year	Malaysia	Indonesia	Thailand	World
Production ('000 ton)				
1950	761	707	114	1,890
1960	764	620	171	2,040
1970	1,269	815	287	3,140
1980	1,530	1,020	501	3,850
1990	1,292	1,175	1,222	5,065
Annual average growth				
1950-60	n	-1.3	4.2	0.8
1960-70	5.2	2.8	5.3	4.4
1970-80	1.9	2.3	5.7	2.1
1980-90	-1.7	1.4	9.3	2.8

Note: Data refer only to natural rubber; n = negligible.
Source: Data kindly supplied by Dr Colin Barlow. (See Barlow, Jayasuriya and Tan, 1994.)

policies which have tailored extension services more carefully to the smallholders' requirements (see, in particular, Barlow and Tomich, 1991).

There is no consistent pattern among the other cash crops. Palm oil, as noted, has displayed the greatest dynamism, boosted in the 1970s by domestic protection and in the 1980s by the entry of several large conglomerates. Sugar, an important export crop during the colonial era, has expanded under the impetus of very high protection. Domestic prices are four to six times those on international markets and, according to Nelson and Panggabean (1991), in 1986/87 the social costs of protection amounted to Rp 465 billion, equivalent then to about 1 per cent of total agricultural value added. The government introduced measures in 1975 to increase smallholder (and *pribumi*) participation, despite concerns about the management and marketing capacities of diffused production units (Mubyarto, 1977). This process was largely completed by the early 1980s (Brown, 1982). But the production and processing stages of the industry remain technologically stagnant and heavily regulated, and interests associated with them constitute a powerful obstacle to reform (Tomich, 1992). There is little economic rationale for the industry to occupy about 300,000 ha of productive *sawah* on Java. The government has been attempting, with mixed success, to shift the industry to the Outer Islands (Brown, 1989).

Indonesia is now the third largest coffee producer in the world, although a good deal smaller than the major Latin American producers, Brazil and Colombia. The industry, found throughout the country but with the largest concentration in southern Sumatra, has grown quite rapidly since the 1960s. For much of the 1980s international prices were favourable, owing mainly to droughts in Brazil, and annual exports averaged some $500 million, or 5 to 12 per cent of non-oil exports. Quotas imposed by the International Coffee Organisation have constrained growth for much of this period, but since 1989 they have been ineffective. The relaxation of quotas might provide an opportunity to expand international market share. However, estate and smallholder yields have fallen and estate yields have shown little increase since 1970 (Figures 7.8a and 7.8b), and remain low by international standards. Moreover,

Indonesia has a reputation as a low quality coffee producer (Bennett and Godoy, 1992; McStocker, 1987).

Clove production has been growing rapidly in response to the booming *kretek* cigarette industry, and Indonesia is the world's largest producer and consumer of this crop. It is almost totally under smallholder cultivation, and is grown principally in Maluku and Sulawesi for sale to Java's *kretek* factories. Marketing chains and price signals appear to have operated quite effectively in the past, but the industry has always been subject to intense regulation (Godoy and Bennett, 1990). Initially this took the form of control over the profitable import trade. But with expanding local supplies the focus has shifted to domestic marketing regulations, including the establishment in 1990 of a controversial procurement arrangement supervised by a company owned by one of the President's sons.

NATURAL RESOURCE MANAGEMENT

Indonesia possesses a vast land and sea area, and a rich ecological diversity. Occupying just 1.3 per cent of the earth's area, it contains about 10 per cent of the world's flowering plant species, 12 per cent of mammal species, 17 per cent of bird species, 25 per cent of fish species, and 10 per cent of remaining tropical rainforest area, the latter second only to Brazil (World Bank, 1994). Yet the issue of natural resource management received very little scholarly or policy attention until the last decade or so. In the first 20 years of Independence, there was no attempt to curb population growth, and indeed former President Sukarno boasted that the country could easily support a population of 250 million or more—a forecast destined to be fulfilled, of course, albeit in vastly different circumstances. Even though the New Order regime has implemented family planning programs vigorously (Hull, 1994), there has been a widespread belief that most of the regions off-Java were 'empty' and could carry much larger populations. More fundamentally, environmental issues have been considered of secondary importance in the face of the daunting economic challenges confronting the New Order. As the West has become more conscious of these issues, many pollution-intensive industries have migrated across international boundaries in search of less restrictive policy regimes. The relocation of certain petrochemical industries from the more advanced Northeast Asian economies to countries such as Indonesia and China is a case in point.

For the first 20 years of the New Order, agricultural development strategies paid little attention to environmental management. In forestry the primary objective was export growth (not to mention the distribution of rents to the favoured few). In rice it was self-sufficiency, with little assessment of the damage caused by indiscriminate fertilizer usage. Upland cultivation of vegetables expanded rapidly, notwithstanding the cost in terms of soil deterioration and even landslides. Even where environmental regulations were introduced, they were rarely enforced with any vigour or consistency. Many of the regulations were complex, and staff were ill-equipped to carry out their mandated functions.[20]

The policy climate began to change during the 1980s. Environmental issues became ever more prominent internationally, and the debate was transmitted to Indonesia through a number of channels. At an intellectual level, the NGO movement became more active, and a number of specialist environmental groups emerged. International bodies such as the World Bank began to pay much more attention to the issue, initiating research on the topic and incorporating an ecological focus in project planning and appraisal. Global issues emerged, such as atmospheric warming and depletion of ozone levels, and with it an international appreciation of the importance of tropical rain forests in countries such as Indonesia and Brazil. A particularly able and respected Minister, Professor Emil Salim, championed the cause, albeit with very limited government resources. An official environmental agency, Bapedal, was established, with offices throughout the country.[21] There was a recognition that in a number of instances environmental and economic objectives converged, and could be pursued simultaneously.

Among the major non-oil natural resource sectors, forestry has expanded the most unevenly and been the source of greatest controversy.[22] Output and exports, mainly from Kalimantan, grew rapidly in the late 1960s in response to high world prices; Indonesia's forests had hitherto remained largely unexploited owing to poor infrastructure and cheaper supplies elsewhere. By 1970 the value of timber exports exceeded that of all the cash crops except rubber (Manning, 1971). Most studies of the industry since 1970 report that forest management and conservation practices have been poor. There have also been frequent allegations of corruption in the awarding of forest concessions, and criticisms of the industry's suboptimal fiscal practices. An important study by Ruzicka (1979), for example, concluded that public forestry revenues were between one-quarter and one-half of what could reasonably be expected from an efficient fiscal regime.[23]

In response to these criticisms, the government in 1980 foreshadowed the phased introduction of a log export ban, accompanied by a range of reafforestation measures. The package was designed to meet conservation objectives, and to achieve increased domestic economic benefits through greater local processing. Forestry output in consequence fell during the first half of the 1980s and by 1985 was a little over one-half of that of the late 1970s. This was accompanied by a boom in plywood exports, which through to 1986 generated about one-half of the country's total manufactured exports (Table 8.3, p. 163). Figure 7.9 charts these developments clearly. With the introduction of the ban, and increased restrictions accompanying the granting of forest concessions, log output declined in the early 1980s. It surpassed 1980 levels only in 1987, but in 1990 was still at only about the 1973 rate of exploitation. Meanwhile, the output of processed timber, principally in the form of plywood and sawn timber, rose sharply, by 800 per cent and 500 per cent respectively over the 1980–91 period.

Thus the export prohibition was clearly successful in its objective of increasing the level of processing in the industry. But the economic benefits of the strategy have been negligible, and forest management is unquestionably one of the weakest areas of the New Order's development record. Rents have been dissipated in the construction of inefficient plywood factories, a condition imposed on award of a concession.[24] Very high timber wastage rates have occurred. Forest management standards have been very poor. Annual deforestation rates in the 1980s have averaged some 850,000 hectares, the result of shifting cultivation, conversion of land to other agricultural activities, and logging and normal fire loss (World Bank, 1988).[25] Regeneration and replanting activities have been limited, the result both of limited lease periods (20 years, as opposed to the customary regeneration cycle of 35 years), and weak and corrupt supervisory capacity by the relevant government agencies. An

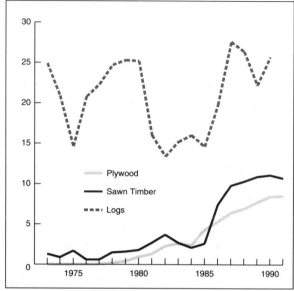

Figure 7.9   Production of forest products, 1973–91

efficient fiscal regime would have almost certainly produced a superior outcome from the viewpoint of both public revenue and environmental concerns.[26] However, powerful vested interests in the timber industry and the Ministry of Forestry have ensured that no such reforms are introduced.[27]

In mid-1992 the ban was finally revoked, partly in response to these criticisms, but mainly because it was inconsistent with GATT rules and it was feared that export restraints such as this might provoke retaliatory action from trading partners. Nevertheless, prohibitive export taxes were introduced in place of the ban, resulting in very little liberalization of substance. In 1988 a similar ban was placed on rattan exports, which was actually more onerous in that there was an additional stipulation that processing was to be in one of the three designated centres, Jakarta, Surabaya, and Medan, all far from the major producing regions. This export ban has not been rescinded, presumably in the expectation that the much smaller volume of rattan exports will not attract international attention.

Research on the uplands of Java points to a similar convergence of environmental and economic concerns.[28] Java's fragile upland ecology is under severe pressure as a result of inappropriate agricultural practices. These include, in particular, the production of temperate vegetables on steep volcanic slopes, a practice which is privately profitable, but socially costly owing to serious erosion problems. Estimates of the costs of erosion are approximate at best. But according to one set of estimates, in the mid-1980s it may have been equivalent to about 4 per cent of the annual value of dryland farm output on Java. Alternatively, the capitalized losses in future productivity are estimated to be equivalent to some 40 per cent of the annual value of upland farm production (Repetto et al., 1989, pp. 48–52). In some instances, high protection (notably for sugar and some vegetables) has encouraged these agricultural activities. The absence of clear land titles—and hence land security for the tillers—acts as a disincentive to careful agricultural management. The commercialization of these activities, and the rise of absentee land owners, appears to be accelerating this lack of interest in land conservation, especially where tenancy arrangements are insecure. The government's extension services are also focused more on lowlands cropping, and thus are not well adapted to the unique upland challenges.

Both fisheries and livestock output have expanded at approximately the same rate as food crops, the real value of production increasing by more than 250 per cent over the 1966-92 period. In the case of fisheries,[29] marine activities dominate, generating about three-quarters of output, although the more labour-intensive inland fishing (such as *tambak*, fresh water breeding) generates more employment. Shrimps, prawns, and fresh and frozen tuna are the major export items. Prawn exports in particular have been rising rapidly, their value doubling in real terms over the 1986-91 period to become Indonesia's second largest agricultural export after rubber, excluding forest products. As with forestry, environmental concerns have become more important, especially the fear of overfishing. Thus trawling was prohibited in western Indonesian waters in 1980, and the ban extended to most other regions in 1983. However, it is estimated that output could be increased three-fold if efficient and environmentally sound management practices were introduced. Occasionally Indonesia's seafood exports have experienced difficulty meeting international health and quality standards.

In the livestock industry, also, there is considerable scope for expansion. The traditional components of the industry are almost exclusively smallholder and have yet to introduce modern veterinary technology and feed practices. Shipping from the major herd concentrations in Sulawesi and Nusa Tenggara to the principal market of Java results in considerable animal weight loss (Kristanto, 1982; Leake, 1980). A commercially oriented poultry industry emerged around major Indonesian cities, particularly on Java, in the 1980s. One obstacle it faces is high feedstuff prices, in no small measure the result of protection for soybean, as noted above.

THE FUTURE AGENDA

What of the future for Indonesian agriculture? Two of the factors which propelled agriculture and especially food crops in the 1970s—technological advance and subsidies from the oil boom—are unlikely to be important in the 1990s and beyond. Expert opinion (see, for example, Ruttan, 1990) holds that dramatic food crop yield increases are not in prospect. Rather, incremental gains will be achieved by mixing inputs, adapting to climatic variations, and obtaining higher yields in upland areas. Java's rice yields are already very high by international standards and a repetition of the doubling which occurred over the past quarter-century seems out of the question. The large subsidies since 1970, in pesticide, fertilizer, irrigation, credit, and research and extension services, are also being reduced. In addition, fiscal austerity since the mid-1980s and a reluctance to consider partial or complete divestment have starved many state-owned agricultural enterprises of much needed capital injections.

Moreover, rapid economic growth and industrialization may be causing fundamental shifts in the comparative advantage of Java–Bali away from food crop production. Higher value added activities, such as manufacturing, poultry, tourism and recreational services, not to mention the inexorable urban sprawl, are placing increasing pressure on agricultural land. These activities are also drawing labour out of agriculture, although there is no evidence yet of sustained increases in real agricultural wages (see Chapter 10). Most of the increased food crop production will therefore have to be generated off Java–Bali. However, yields in these regions are much lower. They average about 70 per cent of the Java–Bali figure, while at the margin some Department of Agriculture estimates assume 3.5 ha of land is required to replace the loss of 1 ha of prime *sawah* on Java. Until recently, yields in the Outer Islands were increasing more slowly than on Java–Bali, reflecting less intensive promotional efforts, inadequate adaptation of research and extension to the different agronomic conditions, and the increased cultivation of marginal rice lands.

There is, however, some room for optimism in assessing Indonesia's likely food equations. In the case of food crops, domestic demand can be expected to grow more slowly as both population growth and demand elasticities continue to decline.[30] (The exception is the demand for animal feedstuffs, a product of the increased commercialization of the livestock industry.) In addition, the removal of some input and credit subsidies in the late 1980s has not had the adverse effect on output that many had expected. Continued reductions in the fertilizer subsidy are also unlikely to have a noticeable effect on rice yields.

In the case of cash crops, and livestock and fisheries, there is considerable scope for expansion also. These are activities in which Indonesia might be expected to retain a comparative advantage for decades to come. The challenge for the 1990s will be to achieve the same successes registered in other non-oil exports, notably manufactures and tourism. It seems likely that the low commodity prices of the 1980s will continue, as many developing countries, driven by the imperative of debt service, attempt to expand exports. The gradual reform of international trading arrangements following the successful outcome of the Uruguay Round in late 1993 may ease Indonesia's international market access problems in some cases. But apart from a few instances such as edible oils, Indonesia has not been greatly harmed by the distortions in world agricultural trade. Indeed it has supported international trade liberalization primarily with a view to enhanced market access for its manufactured exports. Its support of agricultural trade liberalization initiatives such as the Cairns Group has been motivated essentially out of a desire to support its ASEAN neighbour, Thailand (Mangkusuwondo, et al., 1988).

Continuing effective exchange rate management—the reverse "Dutch Disease" effects—will provide a competitive spur to cash crop exports. There is great scope also for increased efficiency: by improving smallholder yields in processing quality, by lowering marketing margins through improved physical infrastructure and better information flows, and by reform of the large but generally inefficient state agricultural enterprises. Indonesia appears to be one of the world's most efficient producers of tropical cash crops. However, it is not uncommon for its smallholder cash crop yields to be less than one-half of those of internationally efficient producers, indicating the magnitude of the potential gains if measures to enhance supply-side efficiency are introduced.

For these gains to be realised, the agricultural sector needs less regulation and more promotion. The sweeping trade and industry reforms of the 1980s hardly affected agriculture. It needs to be emphasized that Indonesia has not embarked on the costly Northeast Asian road of high agricultural protectionism, except for a few relatively unimportant crops such as sugar and soybean (cf. Anderson, Hayami, and Associates [1986]). Anderson (1992, Table 8.3), citing data from Webb et al. (eds, 1990), reports

Indonesia's agricultural producer subsidy equivalent over the 1979–87 period to be 11 per cent. This was higher than a number of developing countries (the figure for Thailand was −4 per cent), but well below that of Korea (61 per cent), the US (30 per cent), and all other OECD countries except Australia. The same source (Anderson, 1992, Table 8.4), cites estimates prepared by Barker, Herdt and Rose (1985) showing Indonesia's 'producer-to-border' price of rice to be very close to unity (0.98) over the 1976–80 period, close to the median figure for Asian rice producers. Timmer (1993) reports a broadly similar set of numbers in his East Asian comparisons.

As noted, domestic prices have never diverged really significantly from international levels, except during the 1972–73 rice crisis. During the 1970s, domestic prices were generally below border prices, whereas in the 1980s the reverse came to apply more frequently. Effective protection for rice producers was almost certainly higher, notwithstanding extensive protection for manufactures, owing to credit and input subsidies. There may indeed have been some justification for modest protection, as a means of overcoming information bottlenecks and quickly inducing farmers to adopt HYVs (Timmer, 1989), and also as a crude but immediate means of recycling oil revenue into rural areas. Yet the arguments for protection for the food crop sector are now much less persuasive. The HYVs have been disseminated effectively, and the exactions imposed on the food crops sector by an appreciating currency and manufacturing protection are either inoperative or much diminished. For political reasons, there may be a case for modest buffer stocks and *Bulog* type open-market operations. But for Indonesia, as for all countries, the most effective means of achieving food security are rapid income and export growth.[31] Such a theme appeared to emerge during a vigorous public debate in early 1992, coinciding with the 25th anniversary of the establishment of *Bulog*. Several participants in the debate, including the respected former Coordinating Economics Minister Professor Widjojo, endorsed the importance of the agency for social reasons while firmly emphasizing the need to avoid Northeast Asian style agricultural protectionism.

The most effective strategy for agricultural development would therefore seem to be a combination of promotional measures—increased agricultural extension and research and large investments in rural infrastructure—and an extension of the deregulatory program. Especially since the mid-1980s austerity, research and extension efforts for the cash crop sector have been starved of resources. Agencies have been forced to commercialize their research work. This trend is not inherently undesirable, but it appears to have reinforced the powerful 'pro-estates' feature of their work, to the neglect of smallholders.[32] Moreover, as several observers have noted, the fertilizer subsidy has dwarfed research and extension efforts, while a greater emphasis on user-pays principles in the case of irrigation would release more funds for continued capital works extension and rehabilitation. According to World Bank (1992, pp. 63–5) estimates, the government's agricultural extension expenditures per employee approximately halved in real terms over the 1985–90 period. Over the same period, the cost of the fertilizer subsidy was on average about 10 times that of development expenditures on research. Related to this issue is the importance of rural infrastructure development to ensure that agricultural markets can function more effectively. The link between rural infrastructure and the efficient development of small-scale agriculture in Indonesia is argued persuasively by Hayami and Kawagoe (1993) in their study of agricultural marketing in a three-village case study of West Java and Lampung.

On the second major policy issue, that of deregulation, notions of self-sufficiency and marketing controls remain deeply rooted in official thinking (especially in the Departments of Agriculture and Industry, although less so now in the latter case). They have resulted in extraordinarily high sugar prices. On occasions they have actually increased domestic rice price volatility, as in the drought year of 1987/88 when the rigid 'no rice imports' policy accentuated price instability. The regulatory regime has also provided the superficial justification for all manner of interventions—cloves is only the most recent glaring example—which rarely assist the notional beneficiaries. There is therefore a strong case for significant agricultural liberalization. The first item is obviously a reduction in agricultural protection, especially in sugar, dairy and meat products, and soybean. A second element would be the abolition of marketing programs which entail compulsory procurements. A third is the phasing out of compulsory cropping requirements for products such as sugar and tobacco. Fourthly, there is a strong case for replacing cumbersome export bans or prohibitive export taxes, as in timber and rattan, with more effective means of rent appropriation. Fifthly, the functions and operations of *Bulog*, which have never been subject to rigorous public scrutiny, need to be evaluated in a transparent manner. Finally, the state agricultural enterprise sector requires a major overhaul to improve standards of efficiency. These reform and promotional measures would, in all likelihood, have little impact on the overall size of the agricultural sector. The food crop sector might contract, but cash crops would become relatively large. Increased food imports would be financed by rising cash crop and manufacturing exports. By the end of the century Indonesia will most likely be a net food importer, but a net agricultural exporter, even if the current regime of agricultural *dirigisme* is not phased out.

CHAPTER 8

The Industrial Transformation

Perhaps more than any other sector of the economy, manufacturing industry has reflected the fortunes and the policy currents of post-1966 Indonesia. Structural and technological change have been extremely rapid. There was a period of inefficient, state-led industrialization during the oil boom decade, but from the mid-1980s export-oriented manufacturing became one of the primary engines of growth. This sector has also been the arena for some of the New Order's major philosophical debates concerning economic strategy. All parties in that debate agree on the importance of rapid industrial growth, but there have been sharp disagreements over the means of achieving this objective. In the 1970s the debate was over the merits of import substitution versus export-oriented industrialization. By the late 1980s the latter school of thought prevailed decisively, and the focus had shifted to whether Indonesia should follow a popular interpretation of the Korean and Japanese approach, entailing "guided industrial policy" and selective state support of heavy, high-tech industry.

Since 1970, it has been common for Indonesia to be grouped with Asia's dragon economies and to be regarded as one of the next Asian NIEs. By the late 1980s such a characterization was appropriate, but for much of the period it was rather misleading. Indonesia shared geographic proximity and high growth with its dynamic neighbours, but little else. These differences were no more sharply evident than in manufacturing. Unlike the nearby export-led economies, Indonesia's manufactured exports were minuscule until the early 1980s. Rather, a highly interventionist regime presided over increasing protection and an expanding state enterprise sector. In many respects over this period, Indonesia had more in common with Brazil and Mexico, albeit at a more infant stage of development, than with Thailand and Malaysia. The story of how Indonesia engineered a decisive shift to the "East Asian model" in the mid-1980s is an important one, and goes to the heart of understanding the bases of the New Order's economic success.

This chapter focuses mainly on the manufacturing sector, its development and the policy environment. There is also a brief discussion of the other major component of industry, mining. The other subsectors, utilities and construction, are alluded to elsewhere in the book. Utilities and construction feature in the next chapter, on services, while oil and gas are of particular relevance to the chapters on fiscal policy and trade (Chapters 4 and 5).

MANUFACTURING INDUSTRY

AN OVERVIEW

In the mid-1960s, much of Indonesia's manufacturing sector had come to a standstill.[1] The country was perhaps the least industrialized of the world's large developing nations. The manufacturing output of much smaller states, such as the Philippines and even Hong Kong, exceeded that of Indonesia. The factory sector was starved of inputs, especially from overseas. Ingrid Palmer (1972), for example, in the most detailed study of Indonesian industry over this period, documented how closely the fortunes of the weaving industry depended on supplies of imported yarn. When supplies were exhausted, many firms, mechanized and handloom alike, simply closed down. This study also drew attention to two other features of industry over this period: the extremely antiquated technology still in use, much of it a relic from Indonesia's early spurt of industrial growth in the 1930s, and pervasive government regulations, which especially governed access to scarce foreign exchange. Power and infrastructure services were deficient, and in many cases almost totally absent. Ironically, however, the regime was not always able to offer much in the way of import protection, as smuggling of certain goods was widespread.

Much of the commanding heights of industry, such as they were, were in the hands of the government, following the wave of nationalizations from 1957 to 1964.[2] There was, not surprisingly, virtually no private investment. Nor was there any foreign equity capital to speak of. The major international connection in the early 1960s was with the Eastern bloc, which supplied technology, equipment and finance in the form of joint ventures and profit-sharing agreements (Gibson, 1966). The post-1966 regime regarded many of these projects as politically inspired, and closed or rationalized a number of them (Sadli, 1972). Others were rehabilitated, most notably in the case of the Krakatau Steel Project, which employed the current Minister of Industry as a senior engineer in the mid-1960s (Arndt, 1975).

The 1964 Industrial Census, which actually refers to 1963, also provided a snapshot of the structure of manufacturing over this period. Conducted in a period of political turbulence and economic disarray, its results should be treated with great caution. But there is little reason to doubt its principal findings, that manufacturing consisted almost wholly of simple resource-based processing and basic consumer goods for the home market. For example light industry constituted 85 per cent and 87 per cent, respectively, of value added and employment. The share of food, beverages and tobacco alone was 53 per cent of output and 44 per cent of employment. Reflecting its extremely labour-intensive nature, textiles generated some 29 per cent of total employment. These data refer only to firms with at least five employees (10 employees in the case of firms without power) and there is no information on the size distribution of industry over this period. But it is reasonable to assume that small and medium firms dominated. Large firms, apart from the state enterprise sector, were actively discriminated against, and except for a few notable instances, entrepreneurs did not contemplate long-term industrial investments when there were always profitable opportunities for speculative forays elsewhere.

With the shift to economic orthodoxy in the late 1960s, manufacturing activity recovered remarkably quickly. Over the 1966–92 period, production rose by an annual average rate of some 12 per cent (Figure 8.1 and Table 8.1). Few countries

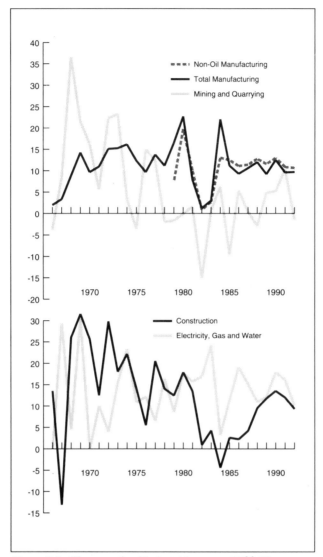

Figure 8.1 The growth of industrial output, 1966–92

have matched such a record outside the dynamic East Asian group. The rate implies a doubling of real output about every six years, approximately equivalent to a ten-fold increase after 1966. From 1969 to 1992 real manufacturing output expanded by at least 9 per cent in all but three years, these occurring consecutively during the slump of 1981–83. Since 1978 a separate non-oil manufacturing output series has been published. This distinguishes between oil and gas processing, in some years accounting for as much as 30 per cent of manufacturing value added, and the rest of manufacturing. During the 1980s, and especially after 1984, it has been this non-oil manufacturing sector which has provided the real industrial dynamism. In every year since 1984 non-oil manufacturing growth has exceeded 10 per cent and, apart from the special case of 1984, it has grown faster than total manufacturing output. Rapid

Table 8.1 **Output of Selected Industrial Products, 1969–91**[a]

Product	Unit	Annual growth (%)					
		1969	*1979*	*1984*	*1991*	*1979–91*	*1969–91*
Consumer goods							
Cooking oil	'000 ton	263	452	267	540	1.5	3.3
Margarine	'000 ton	7.5	18.5	34.1	50.3	8.7	9.0
Kretek cigarettes	bil. sticks	19.0	41.5	79.7	125	9.6	8.9
White cigarettes	bil. sticks	11	28.6	26.9	52.8	5.2	7.3
Yarn	'000 bales	182	998	1,782	4,140	12.6	15.3
Textiles	mil. metres	450	1,910	2,402	5,342	8.9	11.9
Garments	mil. dozen	n.a.	n.a.	26	66.0	n.a.	n.a.
Intermediate goods							
Plywood	'000 sub. metres	n.a.	n.a.	4,249	8,500	n.a.	n.a.
Paper	'000 ton	17	214	543	1,644	18.5	23.1
Fertilizer (all types)	'000 ton	85	2,089	4,427	6,568	10.0	21.8
Soap	'000 ton	133	203	160	232	1.1	2.6
Auto tyres	'000	366	2,898	3,944	8,209	9.1	15.2
Cement	'000 ton	542	4,705	8,854	16,153	10.8	16.7
Glass sheets	'000 ton	n.a.	67.3	152.1	398	16.0	n.a.
Steel ingots	'000 ton	n.a.	122	901	2,091	26.7	n.a.
Aluminium sheets	'000 ton	n.a.	9.5	24.5	41	14.2	n.a.
Engineering goods							
Dry batteries	mil	54.0	462	772	1,224	8.5	15.2
Motor vehicles	'000	5.0	103	154	261	8.1	19.7
Motor cycles	'000	21.4	222	272	436	5.8	14.7
TV sets	'000	4.5	660	773	1,581	7.6	30.5

[a] Data refer to fiscal years; that is, 1969 to 1969/70, etc.
n.a. = not available.

Sources: Nota Keuangan, and *Lampiran Pidato Kenegaraan*, various years.

increases have been recorded in all major industry groups, and for consumer, intermediate and engineering goods industries alike.

There have been at least four subphases within this era of high growth and rapid structural transformation, each one corresponding to different policy emphases and shaped in part by international economic developments. The phases largely mirror those identified earlier in Chapter 2. The initial period of very rapid growth from 1967 to 1973 was driven mainly by liberalization and the return to normal economic conditions. Inflation fell sharply, domestic and international market channels were reopened, there was a large backlog in consumer demand, and consumer spending began to rise quickly under the impetus of high economic growth. There was undoubtedly a shake-out of some traditional labour-intensive and cottage industry, but the broad-based expansion more than compensated for their demise. After the stagnation of 1966–7, real manufacturing output expanded by almost 9 per cent in 1968, while it exceeded 14 per cent in 1969, the initial year of the First Five Year Plan.

The oil boom led to a fundamental reappraisal of industrial policy objectives. It ushered in a second phase, of state-directed industrialization characterized by high but inefficient growth. The boom might have been expected to shift resources out of tradeable goods industries such as manufacturing, through the familiar "Dutch disease" effects discussed in Chapter 5. However, it did not do so for at least two reasons. First, the government began to depart from its liberal trade policies introduced in the late 1960s. More tariffs were introduced, and there was a steady proliferation of non-tariff barriers (NTBs). The second reason was the government began to recycle some of the oil revenue into the state enterprise sector. As noted in Chapter 6, discussion of privatization and divestment disappeared and state commercial investments proliferated, with a lag. These two factors ensured that much of the large increase in domestic incomes over this period fed directly into demand for domestic manufactures.

The decline in oil prices after 1981 triggered a third phase, of policy reappraisal. From 1982 to 1985, before the very sharp fall in oil prices, the response was limited to prudent macroeconomic management and a large devaluation in 1983. Indeed some of the policy initiatives of the previous period remained in place. Huge state investments in oil and gas, planned in an era of abundance, were brought on stream. This explains the extremely large increase of 22 per cent in manufacturing output in 1984, when much of the economy was in recession. The Fourth Five Year Plan, released in April 1984, foreshadowed a major thrust into heavy industry, substantially state-financed, through equity investments and state bank loans. The government also resorted to increased use of non-tariff barriers over this period, many of which were quite blatantly political in their dispensation.

However, after 1985 there was an unambiguous change of direction, leading to the fourth phase of industrial policy and development. For the first time in the history of the New Order, exports and the private sector became the primary engines of industrial growth. A range of bold deregulation packages, described in Chapter 6, combined with continuing firm macroeconomic management, unleashed a surprisingly swift supply response. Non-oil manufacturing output grew on average by more than 11 per cent per annum over the 1985–92 period. Increasingly, Indonesia began to resemble its East Asian neighbours, both in its economic performance and in the causes of that fast economic growth.

That the oil boom decade interrupted Indonesia's adoption of a labour-intensive, export-oriented path is illustrated later in this chapter. It is also evident in the production data of Table 8.1. The output of labour-intensive industries such as textiles grew quickly enough in the 1970s as there was a catchup phase in overcoming the backlog in consumer goods. But these growth rates were maintained, and in some cases (notably garments) increased, during the export phase of the 1980s. At the same time, output of the engineering goods industries slowed appreciably during the 1980s, as the easy phase of import substitution came to an end, and in some cases protection was lowered.

Developments in the manufacturing sector and industrial policy since 1966 are of particular interest because industry has been the focus of so much policy discussion during the New Order. With the possible exception of poverty and equity, no other issue or sector has attracted such continuous and, on occasions, divided debate. The contrast with agriculture and, in particular, the food crops sector, where there has been a broad community consensus on policy directions, is particularly stark. In the 1970s much of the debate focused on the merits of protection. As a tradeable goods sector, manufacturing was one of the first to feel the effects of the liberalization after 1967. But even during this period of comparatively liberal policies, key industrial sectors such as the automotive industry and textiles received significant protection.

By the late 1970s there was a much more pronounced emphasis on a guided industrial policy, featuring extensive industrial intervention.

As oil prices declined in the first half of the 1980s, the assault on this strategy gathered force. A vocal public debate on the origins and effects of the so-called "high-cost" economy emerged. Economists, especially those based at the University of Indonesia, began to publicize the costs of protection, of blunt and pervasive regulatory requirements, and of inefficient state enterprises. They were aided discreetly in their argument by detailed analytical work conducted by consultants to the World Bank and other international agencies. Much of this research never saw the light of day, such was the opposition to it by some senior officials in the Indonesian government. But by laying the intellectual foundations for the public debate, the analysis contributed to the painful process of halting and then decisively reversing the earlier trend towards protectionism.

Just as the debate over the merits of a liberal industrial policy had seemingly been won, however, new and powerful critics of such a strategy emerged. The most important of these has been the Minister for Research and Technology, Professor B.J. Habibie, who since the early 1980s has built up an immensely important bureaucratic and commercial industrial power base, and who for much of this period has been seen as a de facto Minister of Industry. Invited personally by President Soeharto to return to Indonesia, from Germany, where he was a senior executive in that country's aviation industry, he was placed in charge of an expanding empire which included the government's major research initiatives and also a number of high-tech projects. It is the latter which have attracted tremendous debate and, from economists, much criticism. Under the aegis of the Strategic Industries Board (BPIS), Professor Habibie now controls a large number of state enterprises, including aircraft, steel, shipbuilding, ammunitions, and electronics. Very little is known about the commercial performance of these enterprises. They do not publish complete financial statements, nor are their operations subject to the oversight and monitoring of the Department of Finance. Even the official estimates of profitability (which are very low, in the range of 1 to 3 per cent return on capital) give a highly distorted picture of performance, since they do not include a plethora of implicit and explicit subsidies. For example, in the case of the Bandung-based aircraft factory IPTN, the land has been provided at no cost to the firm, and much of its output is sold to other state entities such as one of the nation's domestic carriers, Merpati, or to the Pertamina airline, Pelita Air. Increasingly, also, IPTN has a say in the acquisitions of the national airline Garuda, particularly through offset arrangements.[3]

The rise of Minister Habibie has therefore transformed Indonesia's industrial policy debate. From one focused on the merits of import substitution versus export promotion, the debate has shifted to the far more complex issue of an "orthodox", export-oriented strategy, based heavily on comparative advantage in labour-intensive and resource-based industries, to one which combines elements of this approach with a concerted, state-directed and funded technological leap. By early 1993 it seemed clear that the "Habibie camp" was becoming increasingly powerful. The Minister himself had made a number of strongly critical statements of the technocrats' "gradualist" approach and their emphasis on macroeconomic management. Moreover, the power of the technocrats themselves seemed to be waning, while many key Habibie supporters were either in the new Cabinet or in very senior bureaucratic positions.

So much for this overview of industrial policy and performance. What have been some of the principal features of Indonesia's industrialization over the past two decades? We focus here on structural change, the export boom, ownership issues, size distribution and employment, and spatial dimensions.

RAPID STRUCTURAL AND TECHNOLOGICAL CHANGE

Chapter 2 highlighted the rapid structural change since 1966, and in particular the shift of resources from agriculture to manufacturing. Within manufacturing the process of structural change has been equally rapid. The contribution of light industry to non-oil manufacturing fell sharply from 85 per cent of the total in 1963 to 72 per cent in 1974–75 and 62 per cent in 1985.[4] The decline in the share of the once dominant food, beverage, tobacco, and rubber processing industries has been particularly sharp, their output shares approximately halving over each intercensal period, from 70 per cent to 37 per cent and to just 18 per cent. In addition to this swift structural change, there has been a dramatic increase in the quality and range of products planned. Some of the 1960s manufactures were of such indifferent quality that they could almost be regarded as "non-tradeables". Very few capital and intermediate goods were produced in the mid-1960s.[5]

Table 8.2 provides a more detailed picture of structural change within manufacturing over the 1975–90 period. The year 1975 is chosen as the benchmark since, following the census of the previous year, a consistent size definition of large and medium firms was adopted (firms with a workforce of at least 20 employees), and by this year data quality had improved. The data have been grouped into four major ISIC-based categories, together with oil and gas processing, data for which are published separately in the national accounts.[6]

Focusing first of all on the non-oil segment, the government's push into heavy industry in the 1970s is reflected clearly in the sharply rising shares of the metals goods and heavy processing industries between 1975 and 1980. This was the period when major projects were initiated, such as the Asahan Aluminium smelter in North Sumatra, and the Krakatau Steel project at Cilegon, west of Jakarta, was resurrected. The automotive and electronics industries grew rapidly under the impetus of strong domestic demand growth and rising protection. Light processing industries, mainly wood-based, also grew rapidly. By contrast, the share of traditional industries such as food processing and textiles contracted, although most continued to expand quickly in absolute terms. These changes are observable both in the case of output (value added) and employment.

The period from 1980 to 1985 was one of transition, as noted above. Some heavy industries were still growing quite quickly as large state investments were brought on stream, and the plywood industry became a rapidly expanding source of employment. But by the mid-1980s domestic demand was growing much more slowly, and exports were not yet at the stage of providing a major stimulus to demand. Thus the trends identified in the previous five-year period continued, albeit at a slower pace, and with the notable exception of employment in the timber industry.

In the most recent period, however, there has been a pronounced turnaround. The output shares of the heavy industry and metal goods groups have either levelled off or declined. As the export boom took hold,[7] the share of the footloose labour-intensive group, dominated by textiles, garments and footwear, rose appreciably. The wood

Table 8.2 **Indonesia's Changing Industrial Structure, 1975–91**
(% of total)

Year	Food processing	Footloose labour-intensive	Wood and paper products	Heavy processing	Metal goods	Oil and gas processing
	(31)	(32 + 39)	(33 + 34)	(35 + 36)	(37 + 38)	(353)
I. Output (excl. oil and gas)						
1975	41.2	18.2	7.4	20.3	12.8	
1980	31.7	14.1	10.2	24.1	20.0	
1985	26.0	13.3	12.8	26.3	21.6	
1991	25.2	15.5	17.7	20.9	20.7	
II. Output (incl. oil and gas)						
1975	36.6	16.2	6.6	29.2	11.4	11.2
1980	25.3	11.2	8.1	39.5	15.9	20.3
1985	18.8	9.6	9.2	46.7	15.6	27.7
1991	20.8	12.8	14.6	34.7	17.1	17.5
III. Employment						
1975	37.5	32.8	8.5	12.7	8.5	
1980	33.2	27.3	10.0	16.1	13.4	
1985	30.9	23.4	14.2	20.0	11.6	
1991	21.5	31.8	18.3	17.0	11.4	

Notes: The numbers in parentheses in the column headings are ISIC industry codes. The data in panels I and III refer to large and medium firms (with at least 20 employees). In panel II, the shares from panel I have been combined with the national accounts data. Since the latter refer to all firm sizes, the shares relate to all firms. (This procedure is necessitated by the fact that, especially in earlier years, the non-oil manufacturing value added total was considerably less than the SI figure.) Note that the 1975 oil and gas processing share refers to 1978, the first year such a separate series was released.
Sources: Data are from BPS, *Statistik Industri* (SI), and the national accounts, various issues.

and paper products group also expanded, especially as the furniture and paper and pulp industries have become increasingly prominent. The output share of food industries remained unchanged. Much of the apparent decline in labour intensity (the employment share of these industries contracted noticeably) is due to the growing mechanization of the huge *kretek* cigarette industry.

It is clear therefore that in important respects Indonesia's period of labour-intensive industrialization really got underway only in the mid-1980s, some 20 years after the advent of the New Order regime. In this respect it shares some similarity with China and, to a lesser extent, India, both of which promoted heavy industry early—and for much longer—before emphasizing a labour-intensive growth path. The industrial experience of Asia's three giants differs from the smaller East Asian economies, none of which attempted to promote heavy industry so early in the course of industrialization. The fact that all three countries attempted to travel down this path, for different reasons and at different time periods, underlines one important advantage of smallness, namely that the temptation to embark on costly import substitution is more easily avoided.

The inclusion of oil and gas processing in the statistics accentuates these trends. The magnitude of Indonesia's premature push into heavy industry in the 1970s and early 1980s is revealed by the fact that the share of output of oil, other heavy processing and the metals goods industries rose from 41 per cent in 1975 to 55 per cent in 1980 and 62 per cent in 1985, before declining considerably as labour-intensive and resource-based industries expanded in the late 1980s.

Accompanying and shaping this rapid structural change has been a virtual technological revolution in many industries. As argued in Chapter 2 there has been a flood of new technologies from abroad since 1965, many concentrated in manufacturing. For two decades prior to the New Order (approximately 1940 to 1950 and 1956 to 1966) there was virtually no new manufacturing investment, and during the first half of the 1960s Indonesia increasingly cut itself off from international commerce, technology, and investment. Consequently, the country had an extremely antiquated industrial stock by the late 1960s. Much of the technology was hand-powered, while a good deal of the mechanized equipment had been installed by Dutch interests in the 1930s. These labour-intensive technologies began to disappear quickly, a trend which was exacerbated in some instances by policy measures such as negative real interest rates and other capital-cheapening biases. Rapid technological modernization became a key objective of Minister Habibie and his grandiose plans of the 1980s. But the fundamental driving force of this technological upgrading since 1966 was that the equipment in use before then was so antiquated, and the return to normal economic conditions induced a boom in industrial sector investment.

As documented in Table 2.3, p. 26, manufacturing has become steadily more capital-intensive as compared with the rest of the economy. Value added per worker in 1971 was just 17 per cent higher than the economy-wide average, but it was 41 per cent and 83 per cent higher in 1980 and 1990 respectively. Over the 1971–80 period, real labour productivity grew at an annual average rate of 10 per cent, easily the fastest of the major sectors, and more than treble the rate of the total non-mining economy. At the same time, and further indicative of the shedding of labour-intensive technologies, some two-thirds of the expansion of output was due to rising labour productivity and only one-third to increased labour inputs. Again this was significantly higher than that of the economy as a whole, although not of agriculture. In the 1980s, a different trend emerged. Much of the shedding of labour-intensive technologies had occurred, while the new export-oriented manufacturing industries were almost entirely labour-intensive. Consequently, labour productivity grew more slowly from 1980 to 1990, but still quite quickly, at an annual rate of 5.7 per cent. The increases in labour productivity and in the labour force made almost equal contributions to output expansion over this period.

Rising real labour productivity is evident in all major manufacturing branches (Figure 8.2). Over the 1975–91 period and for firms with at least 20 employees, it rose by approximately 250 per cent for non-oil manufacturing industries. For all two-digit ISIC groups there was at least a doubling, but in a number of instances the increase was very sharp. This was particularly so in the case of basic metals. The rise, almost fifty-fold, reflected the fact that the industry was transformed beyond recognition following major investments in alumina and steel facilities. Other industries where rapid transformations occurred included textiles, clothing and footwear, wood products, paper products, and the miscellaneous group. The textiles case has already been discussed. Although it retains its status as a labour-intensive industry (labour productivity is 80–85 per cent of the non-oil average), labour productivity rose rapidly as the large handloom sector disappeared, and as new more capital-intensive segments such as yarn and artificial fibres emerged. The increases in the cases of wood and paper products also reflect major transformations, most notably the emergence of the plywood and pulp industries, both more capital-intensive than the activities that formerly dominated these sectors.

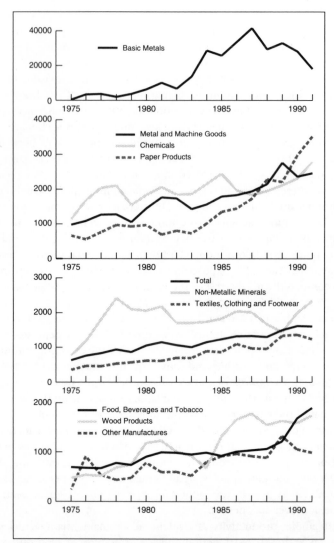

Figure 8.2 Labour productivity in manufacturing, 1975–91

By contrast, the changes have been less pronounced in the other sectors. Labour productivity in chemicals and non-metallic minerals rose quite sharply in the second half of the 1970s, much of it due to sizeable investments in state-owned fertilizer and cement plants. But thereafter there has been no pronounced trend, for a number of reasons. Technological advance in these industries is closely linked to investment which, in a number of sectors, dried up in the 1980s. Moreover, the less technologically innovative state firms are dominant in some of the major activities within these groups. The food, beverages, and tobacco industry, and metal and machine goods, both rose at approximately the same rate as the non-oil total.[8]

It needs to be emphasized that great care should be taken in any international comparisons of these labour productivity trends and levels. Careful analysis by Szirmai

(1994), using a framework known as international comparisons of output and productivity (ICOP), developed by a Dutch-based international research group, underlines such a point. For example, the conversion factor in 1987 derived from this study for the purposes of international comparisons of labour productivity was some 72 per cent of the official exchange rate at that time. Correspondingly, the gap between labour productivity in Indonesia and the US was somewhat smaller according to the ICOP approach, although the Indonesian figure was still very low, just 10 per cent of that in the US. Estimates of real labour productivity growth are also sensitive to this alternative, more accurate approach. Consistent with the argument advanced above concerning the 1980s labour-intensive industrial growth phase, Szirmai found that over the 1980–90 period, Indonesian labour productivity did not increase relative to that in the US.

THE EXPORT BOOM, 1980 TO THE PRESENT

Until the late 1970s, Indonesia's manufacturing firms sold virtually all their output on the domestic market. During the 1970s, manufactures never exceeded 3 per cent of total merchandise exports, and in most years the percentage was a good deal less than even this. There was, moreover, no expectation that a manufacturing export boom was around the corner. Instead the prevailing philosophy was one of export pessimism, that Indonesia would never be able to compete with its neighbouring NIEs. The intersectoral effects of the oil boom, Indonesia's industrial and commercial infancy, and the costly and cumbersome regulatory framework all contributed to this pessimism. Finally, the domestic market was growing rapidly, and protection was on the increase. As long as high oil prices propelled the economy, there was little incentive for firms to break out of this cosy arrangement and begin to look outward.

The initial attempt at export promotion seemed to confirm these pessimistic prognostications. Following the November 1978 devaluation, there was a short-lived increase in manufactured exports, but it was soon swamped by the effects of the second round of oil price increases. It was not until the early 1980s that there was a renewed effort to promote manufactured exports, as outlined in Chapter 5. The results were quite spectacular: manufactures (narrowly defined, see next paragraph) rose from 2.3 per cent of merchandise exports in 1980 to 47.5 per cent in 1992. In value terms, the increase over this period was from $501 million to $16.1 billion. Particularly important in the export drive were the two devaluations, in 1983 and in 1986, and the drawback scheme introduced in May 1986.[9] Other initiatives, such as the customs reform, the liberalized foreign investment code, and the banking reform of November 1988, also played a key role.

From 1980 to 1992, manufactured exports grew at an annual average rate of 20 to 30 per cent in real terms (Figure 8.3). The precise rate of growth depends on how "manufactures" are defined, whether using the conventional narrow definition (of items SITC 6–8 less SITC 68), or a broader concept which more closely corresponds to the national accounts definition, ISIC 3. As Figure 8.3 demonstrates, the two series have diverged considerably in some years, with the narrow series, which is dominated in recent years by the high growth, footloose items, displaying faster increases in

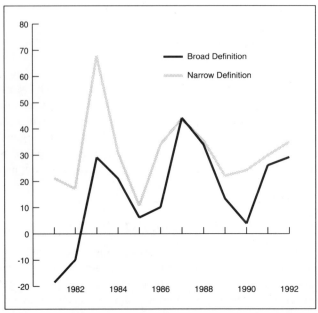

Figure 8.3   The growth of manufactured exports, 1981–92

most years. But whatever series is used, the increase has been remarkable. Nor have the high growth rates been the result of the small initial base year figures. For both series, the increases in 1991 and 1992 were among the highest of any year.

Until the late 1980s, some doubted the significance of these impressive figures. Initially, there were reasonable grounds for some scepticism concerning the durability of the export boom, for at least two reasons. The first was that one item, plywood, dominated the picture, so much so that it accounted for almost 50 per cent of the total in the mid-1980s (Table 8.3).[10] This was of course a special export item, a case of enforced export substitution following the log export ban introduced progressively from the early 1980s. Forest concessionaires were forced to export the timber in processed form, which they were able to do by virtue of Indonesia's market power as a supplier of tropical hardwood and because of the very low rent appropriation in the industry. The second ground for scepticism was that the next two major export items, garments and textiles, were quota-governed, under the MFA (Multifibre Arrangement). Until the late 1980s, Indonesia had unfilled export quotas for these products. Providing exporters could meet minimum quality, price and delivery standards, these firms were virtually guaranteed a market, especially as the more advanced NIEs faced binding and restrictive quotas.

By the late 1980s, however, it was apparent that Indonesia's export success was not a transitory phenomenon. Plywood exports were growing quite slowly, in response to demand and supply-side constraints, and its share of manufactured exports had fallen to just 22 per cent in 1992 (Table 8.3). A proliferating array of labour-intensive manufactures rapidly became very important, with this group's share of the total rising from 38 per cent in 1988 to 62 per cent in 1992. Garments and textiles continued to dominate, but several other items quickly became significant: footwear, exports rising from $1 million in 1980 to $1.3 billion in 1992; electronics,

Table 8.3   **Major Manufactured Exports, 1980–92**
($ million or %)

	1980	1982	1984	1986	1988	1990	1992
Labour-intensive							
Total	287	323	826	1,054	2,061	4,634	9,963
Percentage of all manufactures	57	40	45	40	38	51	62
Major items							
Clothing (84)	98	116	296	522	797	1,646	3,164
Woven fabrics (652-9)	43	43	183	287	571	1,132	2,494
Footwear (85)	1	3	5	8	82	570	1,324
Electronics (76-77)	94	117	214	29	41	204	935
Furniture (82)	3	2	5	9	70	286	491
Yarn (651)	3	1	17	20	109	109	344
Toys and sporting goods (894)	n	n	n	n	n	57	218
Glass and glassware (664-5)	3	3	10	13	75	80	101
Resource-intensive							
Total	119	354	832	1,209	2,575	3,324	4,131
Percentage of all manufactures	24	44	45	46	47	37	26
Major items							
Plywood (634)	68	316	791	1,127	2,368	2,791	3,501
Cement (661)	26	8	13	41	80	100	114
Leather (611)	6	7	7	15	68	64	61
Capital-intensive							
Total	97	131	181	377	839	1,083	2,023
Percentage of all manufactures	19	16	10	14	15	12	13
Major items							
Paper products (64)	5	2	20	33	128	154	341
Steel products (672-9)	8	8	7	58	269	188	230
Fertilizer (562)	35	10	37	127	134	193	184
Rubber tyres (625)	n	n	2	11	45	66	96
Total, all manufactures	501	809	1,839	2,639	5,476	9,041	16,061
Three largest as % of total	52	68	71	73	68	61	57
Manufactures as % of total exports	2	4	8	18	28	35	48

Notes: 1. The following definitions are used:
  Resource-intensive–SITC items 61, 63, 66 (excluding 664-6), 671.
  Labour-intensive–SITC items 54, 55, 65, 664-6, 695-7, 749, 76-7, 793, 81-5, 89.
  Capital-intensive–SITC items 5 (excluding 54 and 55), 62, 64, 67 (excluding 671), 69 (excluding 695-7), 7 (excluding 76-8), 86-8. This classification was developed by Krause (1982), and subsequently modified by Ariff and Hill (1985) for ASEAN, and by the author for Indonesia.
  2. SITC codes for the major exports are in parentheses.
  3. 'n' indicates less than $1 million. Numbers do not always add, owing to rounding.
Sources: BPS, *Ekspor*, Jakarta, various issues.

after subsiding in the mid-1980s; toys and sporting goods, exports of which were negligible until 1989; and several other items.

By the late 1980s the export boom appeared set to last also because garment and textile exports continued to grow quickly even after Indonesia had hit quota limits under the MFA. In such circumstances, supply-side efficiency became the crucial arbiter of commercial success. Apart from generally modest quota increases, most of the growth now had to come from expanding non-MFA markets, outside the governance of quotas, and through improved quality and a shift to higher value items, since the quotas are based on physical quantities and not values. The fact that Indonesia's exports of these items continued to grow quickly in the early 1990s was powerful testimony to its suppliers' growing international competitiveness. It was only when the prolonged OECD recession began to have an impact on export demand that the pace slackened off, in 1993. This period also coincided with a slowing in the reform momentum, and a rising incidence in domestic regulatory impediments.

In evaluating the manufacturing export record, it is important, finally, to emphasize the comparative advantage and international dimensions. By the early 1990s, it was clear that Indonesia was following the East Asian route with its emphasis on labour-intensive manufactures. As noted, these items constituted over 60 per cent of the total by 1992 (Table 8.3), and they are likely to increase their share over the 1990s. By contrast, capital-intensive manufactures are now relatively unimportant, at about 10 to 13 per cent of the total, and much of this figure contains a significant natural resource component. Indonesia's natural resource endowments will ensure that its export composition differs somewhat from that of its resource-poor East Asian neighbours. But, over time, the differences will become somewhat smaller. It is important also to emphasize that Indonesia still belongs to the "late-comer" group of East Asian exporters. Its total manufactured exports are still just a fraction of those of China and the NIEs, with the exception of Singapore. The differences are manifest also in Indonesia's concentration in labour-intensive items and, within these, in low value added products. For example, within the important textiles and garments group, Indonesia's unit values for finely specified products are consistently among the lowest in East Asia. In addition, reflecting its more recent export orientation, less intensive foreign investment penetration, and comparative industrial infancy, Indonesia's intra-industry trade indices are also generally low by regional standards.[11]

OWNERSHIP AND CONCENTRATION

As noted in Chapter 6, ownership has always been a sensitive issue in Indonesia. There is a large state-owned sector, the foreign investment policy environment has swung from liberalism to quite intense regulation and back again, and there has always been a mistrust of "bigness" and concentration, albeit less so when these features are part of the government apparatus.

Within these parameters, manufacturing ownership patterns reflect the interplay of "policy" and "industrial economics" factors. As demonstrated in Table 8.4, foreign investors are prominent in industries where, if entry is permitted, they are able to exploit their advantages in technology (petro-chemicals, synthetic fibres, motorcycles, sheet glass, electronics), brand names (white cigarettes, pharmaceuticals, breweries), and knowledge of international markets (footwear). In this sense, the Indonesian record conforms quite closely to the predictions of the standard industrial organization theory of foreign investment, which invokes firm or industry-specific attributes to explain interindustry variations in foreign ownership.[12]

There was a sudden rush of foreign investors into Indonesian manufacturing after 1967, and again after 1987, but in aggregate foreign ownership remains quite modest. Indeed, as illustrated in Table 8.4, there is no instance where foreign-owned firms are the dominant group, at least as far as equity shares are concerned. In the first decade or more of the New Order, foreign investors were in a strong position *vis-à-vis* domestic firms. The latter, still recovering from the ravages of the Sukarno era, lacked international commercial experience, together with modern managerial and technological competence. By the late 1980s, the situation was altogether different. Domestic investors took advantage of the policy liberalizations even more than foreign

Table 8.4   **Ownership Shares in Indonesian Manufacturing, 1988**
(% of each industry's value added)

	Industry	Private	Government	Foreign
311	Food products	53.9	36.7	9.4
312	Food products	53.8	18.6	27.6
313	Beverages	39.2	34.2	26.6
314	Tobacco	95.9	0.8	3.3
321	Textiles	68.1	7.1	24.8
322	Garments	98.0	0.2	1.8
323	Leather products	99.1	0.9	0
324	Footwear	86.9	0.2	12.9
331	Wood products	83.3	3.7	13.0
332	Furniture	91.8	1.8	6.4
341	Paper products	50.2	10.1	39.7
342	Printing and publishing	64.4	24.3	11.3
351	Basic chemicals	14.6	72.6	12.8
352	Other chemicals	54.6	7.8	38.6
353/4	Oil and gas processing	0	100.0	0
355	Rubber products	47.5	34.9	17.6
356	Plastics	91.2	0.3	8.5
361	Pottery and china	76.3	0.5	23.2
362	Glass products	88.5	3.6	7.9
363	Cement	24.8	61.5	13.7
364	Structural clay products, Other non-metal	91.4	1.5	7.1
369	Manufacturing	95.9	4.1	0
370	Basic metals	6.0	89.1	4.9
381	Metal products	50.8	22.4	26.8
382	Non-electrical machinery	31.9	31.0	37.1
383	Electrical equipment	59.9	13.8	26.3
384	Transport equipment	59.0	13.8	27.2
385	Professional equipment	77.0	0	23.0
390	Miscellaneous	88.3	0.2	11.5
Total				
	Excl. oil and gas	59.1	24.2	16.7
	Incl. oil and gas	43.8	43.8	12.4

Source: Unpublished data from BPS.

firms, as evidenced by the surge in domestic investment approvals over this period (Figure 5.3, p. 76). In the financial sector the domestic firms' response to the 1988 liberalization was stronger still (Figure 9.4, p. 189). By international comparisons, also, Indonesia has never been a particularly large recipient of foreign investment.[13]

The ownership data reported in Table 8.4 of course greatly understate the extent of foreign involvement in Indonesian manufacturing for a number of reasons. Most firms in the manufacturing sector have some kind of commercial involvement with foreign parties. Some of these arrangements are particularly intense, especially in the automotive industry in which foreign ownership is precluded in a number of sectors. These are instances of "control without ownership"; local firms produce foreign brand models to tightly specified requirements of the local partner. In other cases the foreign connection is a good deal weaker, being confined essentially to marketing arrangements. In the recent garment export boom, for example, foreign investment shares have been very low (less than 5 per cent of total investment), but foreign partners have played a crucial role in connecting Indonesian garment firms to world markets.

As noted in Chapter 5, history and strategic development priorities have shaped the development of the large state enterprise sector in manufacturing. History has been important in that many enterprises were formerly Dutch-owned. They were nationalized in 1957–58 and, while a few were returned to their original owners in the late 1960s, most have remained in government hands since then. During the oil boom decade there was a deliberate strategy to expand the state enterprise sector, by using oil revenue to develop a range of heavy industries. Thee and Yoshihara (1987, p. 343) aptly characterize the government's industrial objectives up to the mid-1980s as "upstream socialism, downstream capitalism". In the mid-1980s the push for heavy industry waned but, as noted, several high-tech projects under Professor Habibie's umbrella of companies continued to prosper. These two factors explain state invest-ments in industries as diverse as oil refining, LNG, sugar refining, cement, fertilizer, aircraft, spinning and weaving, and machine goods.

Domestic private firms, the third ownership group, are generally smaller, less capital-intensive and found more commonly in labour-intensive, consumer goods industries than the state or foreign groups. The differences are, however, narrowing over time, especially with the advent of large and diverse domestic conglomerates. Technology-intensive industries are no longer the preserve of foreign firms, since these indigenous operations now have the capacity and know-how to acquire modern technology from abroad. Nevertheless, the sizeable medium- and small-scale sector will always remain in domestic private hands, thus pulling down the average size and capital intensity of these firms.

A final feature of ownership patterns is high levels of concentration in many industries (Table 8.5). Figures calculated from the 1985 Industrial Census indicate that 19 per cent of industries exhibited very high levels of concentration, where the four largest firms produced 70 per cent or more of industry output. These industries accounted for 28 per cent and 54 per cent of non-oil and total manufacturing output respectively in that year. Taking the 40 per cent threshold of seller concentration (that is, the output share of the four largest firms), the share of manufacturing produced in such highly concentrated industries is higher still. These figures, it should be emphasized, understate the true dimensions of concentration. They are plant-level estimates, with the result that multi-plant operations under one umbrella are enumerated separately. And they ignore the fact that many of Indonesia's large conglomerates have vast holdings across many industries, so that nominally distinct firms may in fact be owned by the same group.

High concentration in small economies still in their industrial infancy—a broadly accurate description of Indonesia until about a decade ago—is not all that surprising, nor even necessarily of great concern. However, in Indonesia, especially through to the late 1980s, the issue was important because this concentration was combined with very high levels of protection in many instances. It was thus the absence of competitive pressures either domestically or from abroad which concerned economists. Since then, the issue of concentration has become less serious for at least two reasons. First, the trade reforms have exposed most industries to at least some international competition, in the process hastening restructuring and increasing efficiency. Secondly, the major industrial growth has occurred in labour-intensive, export-oriented industries which, in almost all cases, are characterized by low levels

Table 8.5   **Seller Concentration, 1985**[a]

Concentration ratio (Share of four largest plants, %)	Excl. oil & gas					Incl. oil & gas	
	Industries			Value added		% of value added	Cml. %
	No.	% of total	Cml. %	% of total	Cml. %		
90–100	12	10.1	10.1	17.7	17.7	46.7	46.7
80–89	4	3.4	13.5	6.0	23.7	3.9	50.6
70–79	7	5.9	19.4	4.5	28.2	2.9	53.5
60–69	15	12.6	32.0	11.8	40.0	7.6	61.1
50–59	15	12.6	44.6	7.4	47.4	4.8	65.9
40–49	13	10.9	55.5	6.8	54.2	4.4	70.3
30–39	19	16.0	71.5	17.4	71.6	11.3	81.6
20–29	16	13.4	84.9	14.1	85.7	9.1	90.7
10–19	9	7.6	92.5	10.7	96.4	6.9	97.6
0–9	9	7.6	100.0	3.7	100.0	2.4	100.0
Total	119	100		100		100	

[a] Data refer to shares of the four largest plants in each industry, for all firms with a workforce of at least five.

Cml. = Cumulative shares.

Source: Hill (1990a, p. 97)

of concentration, and for which in any case notions of seller concentration are irrelevant. Where the issue continues to be of public policy importance is in instances of politically sanctioned monopolies insulated from international competition through protection, and from domestic competition through regulatory entry barriers.

SIZE DISTRIBUTION AND EMPLOYMENT GROWTH

There has been a clear trend towards industrial agglomeration in Indonesian manufacturing. The average size of large and medium firms (defined as at least 20 employees) rose from 92 to 161 persons from 1974 to 1990. The increase since the mid-1960s would have been much greater still, but over the longer period there are no reliable data available which employ consistent definitions. Notwithstanding this trend, a continuing feature of Indonesian industry from the colonial era (1930s) to the chaos of the early 1960s and to the rapid growth since the late 1980s has been the extraordinary diversity of Indonesian manufacturing. Enterprises range from multi-million dollar industrial plants employing best-practice technology, often enclave in nature, with large foreign inputs and integrated within the international economy, to small, seasonal household units rarely employing wage labour and selling only within the immediate neighbourhood. Both are engaged in manufacturing, but they are as different as multinational banks and occasional rural moneylenders in the finance industry. Although it is clearly inaccurate to label this diversity as ''dualism''—the phenomenon is best seen as a continuum from large to small—sharp differences will persist for many decades until labour markets begin to tighten and low-wage cottage enterprises are driven out of business.

Related to this issue are two hotly debated features of Indonesia's industrialization: trends in small-scale industry (SSI) and in employment. Critics of the New Order's

Table 8.6   **Estimates of Manufacturing Employment by Size Group, 1975 and 1986**

Size group (Persons employed)	1975		1986		Annual growth (%)
	('000)	(% of total)	('000)	(% of total)	
> 20	1,025.7	(30.4)	1,869.0	(30.6)	5.6
5–19	442.8	(13.1)	840.5	(13.8)	6.0
<5	1,904.4	(56.6)	3,400.8	(55.7)	5.4
Total	3,372.9	(100)	6,110.3	(100)	5.6

Source: These data are from Hill, 1992a, p. 246. See this source for an explanation of estimation procedures on which the data are based.

record contend that manufacturing growth has generated too few jobs and that it has led to the demise of small and cottage industry. It is true that, as noted above, the much-delayed introduction of new technologies from the late 1960s resulted in the disappearance of many traditional technologies, and that capital-cheapening fiscal incentives may have hastened this process. But there is no empirical evidence which supports either of the above allegations. On the contrary, small firms appear to have grown quite quickly, at least from the mid-1970s to the mid-1980s, and employment growth has been rapid.

In the case of SSI, the only reasonably complete secondary data on trends come from the 1974/75 and 1986 Industrial Censuses. The data suggest that there was very little change in the size distribution of manufacturing, at least as far as employment patterns are concerned (Table 8.6). The employment share of large- and medium-sized firms remained unchanged, that of small firms rose marginally, while the cottage sector declined very slightly. Cottage industry employment still accounts for over one-half of total employment. However, these figures need to be treated with great caution, as the cottage industry data base is extremely weak. The data in Table 8.6 for these firms are calculated as a residual from labour force surveys, after subtracting the more reliable estimates of factory sector employment. The picture is a good deal clearer for firms with a workforce of at least five employees. The evidence suggests clearly that firms with a workforce of five to 19 employees grew nearly as quickly in terms of both output and employment as those with 20 or more employees. Approximate estimates for the 1985–90 period suggest a continuation of these trends during the manufacturing export boom (Hill, 1992c, Table 9).

It also appears that small firms have been participating in this export boom. The database here also is rather weak, but estimates prepared by the Department of Industry suggest small industry exports rose from $137 million to $2.1 billion over the 1983–92 period (Table 8.7). According to these figures, small firms have kept pace with larger units in their export growth, and the share of the former has actually risen for the period as a whole. As with larger firms, textiles, clothing and footwear have been extremely important, and by 1992 constituted almost 60 per cent of the SSI total. Plywood, by contrast, has been unimportant, since most of the forest concessionaires have established plants which are larger than the official definition

Table 8.7   **Small Industry Exports, 1983–92**
($ million or %)

	1983	1985	1987	1989	1992[a]
Total	137	248	673	1,020	2,124
Percentage of all manufactures	10.0	12.1	17.3	14.5	13.2
Composition (% of total)					
Textiles, clothing, footwear, leather	40.6	63.2	28.7	37.8	57.3
Food	8.5	3.7	10.4	11.6	8.2
Chemicals and building materials	20.8	15.2	9.0	5.6	16.9
Other[b]	30.1	17.9	51.9	45.1	21.2

[a] Preliminary data.
[b] Including handicrafts.

Source: Lampiran Pidato Kenegaraan, various issues.

of small industry. Very little is known about small enterprise export activity. The strong export performance does *a priori* question the conventional wisdom that pecuniary economies of scale are important in international markets.[14] It is likely though that a good deal of the garment exports are undertaken through international and domestic subcontracting networks involving larger firms.

These trends, based admittedly on rather weak data, are contrary to popular perceptions. There is a widespread sentiment that, during both the import substitution and export-oriented phase of industrialization, small firms have been pushed aside by larger units. Such a trend is generally observed during the course of early-stage industrialization, and so it would not be so surprising if it were occurring in Indonesia. That smaller units have not apparently experienced a sharp decline in relative importance may be attributed to their capacity to find niches in specialized manufacturing activity. Smaller firms are particularly important in labour-intensive industries, where scale economies are less important, or where they are better able to serve local market segments.[15] It is therefore likely that the emphasis on export orientation will ensure that these firms continue to play an important role in the next few decades.

The policy debate over SSI has frequently lacked coherence. The fundamentally important observation of Little (1988) that the dynamic East Asian economies which have generally eschewed special SSI programs have a good record of employment creation, while in South Asia the reverse has applied—in terms of both policy and outcomes—seems to have been missed in much of the debate. There have been frequent calls for special assistance programs for SSI in Indonesia, especially after most of the (generally unsuccessful) subsidized credit programs were abolished. The government has maintained a wide range of programs, including enforced sub-contracting (the so-called *bapak angkat*—literally "foster parent"—scheme), mandatory deletion requirements in the automotive industry, and additional obligations imposed on state enterprises. Although the subsidized credit programs have been abolished, 25 per cent of banks' outstanding loans must be allocated to small and medium enterprise. Other programs of assistance are run by various government agencies.[16]

This is not the place to assess these policies. But it is doubtful whether they have had any marked impact. Moreover, these initiatives have frequently failed to address some of the more fundamental impediments to the development of an efficient SSI sector. Training programs have not been well targeted or developed in most instances. Small firms have often not been able to avail themselves of government facilities and programs because of complicated bureaucratic procedures. There has also been a tendency to approach small industry as an issue of social welfare, rather than one of economic efficiency and firm dynamics. The decision in the March 1993 Cabinet to include small enterprise with cooperatives in the administrative structure of government exemplifies such an approach.

Another contentious issue in Indonesian industrialization, where much of the criticism has been misguided, concerns employment trends. Manufacturing employment growth has been quite rapid over the New Order period. From 1961 (a reasonable proxy for the mid-1960s) to 1990, the share of manufacturing in total employment approximately doubled, for both the country as a whole and on Java (Table 2.2, p. 22). During the 1980s, manufacturing provided one-quarter of the new jobs in Java, just surpassing the contribution of trade, and much larger than any other sector. Factory sector employment grew even more rapidly, at an annual rate of 9.1 per cent from 1974 to 1990, resulting in a quadrupling in absolute numbers employed (0.66 million to 2.66 million) over this period. As noted above, there are no reliable data on small industry employment after 1986, but at least over the 1975–86 period, employment growth among these firms was quite rapid. It is true that much of this manufacturing employment growth is not really occurring in the modern factory sector (see Table 8.6), which still provides jobs for no more than 4 per cent of the total workforce. Also, the employment record could have been better in the oil boom decade if there had not been a bias against labour intensity. But some of the more dismal prognostications of the past concerning employment generation in manufacturing have not been realised.[17]

SPATIAL DIMENSIONS

Regional patterns of economic activity are examined in more detail in Chapter 11. But it is worth emphasizing here two major features of Indonesia's spatial dimensions as they pertain to industry. First, Java's share of factory-sector (non-oil) manufacturing output and employment appears to have been declining steadily since the 1960s. In 1963 the island generated some 83 per cent of factory sector output, but by 1985 this figure had declined to 74 per cent. Including oil and gas processing in the latter year, Java's share falls sharply, to just 52 per cent of the total. Java's population share, around 60 per cent, lies between these two estimates. There is of course nothing inherently desirable in the island's population and industry shares being similar, and much of the Outer Island industry is enclave and highly localized in nature. But these figures do at least dispel simple notions of "overconcentration" of manufacturing activity on Java.

The second important spatial dimension concerns regional patterns of industrialization and specialization. The provinces of Java are in general more industrialized than most other regions of the country. The share of manufacturing in regional output is higher, the share of employment in the agricultural sector is lower, and they have a more diversified industrial base. These propositions are illustrated in

Table 11.2, (p. 220) columns 11 to 14. Particularly instructive are the data on manufacturing output per square kilometre, where the Java figure exceeds that of other regions by a large margin. In some Outer Island provinces manufacturing is a large share of output, exceeding the 17 per cent figure of less industrialized Central Java in three of the four provinces of Kalimantan, for example. But these figures are deceptive, for in a number of the latter instances the industrial base is rather "thin", in both a spatial and an industrial composition sense. Wood products, essentially plywood, account for over one-half of manufacturing output in some provinces.

This latter feature draws attention to a related, very important, spatial dimension, namely the evolution of regional comparative advantage. It is no exaggeration to state that Java and a few scattered pockets elsewhere have specialized in footloose, labour-intensive manufactures, whereas almost all industry off-Java has a much stronger natural resource component. During the import substitution era of the 1970s, it made sense for footloose industries to locate on Java to be close to markets, the bureaucracy (as the dispenser of licences and privilege), and the better commercial–industrial infrastructure. In the 1980s, labour-intensive exporters located there for similar reasons. Proximity to government offices has been just as important in the booming garment industry for firms requiring export quotas. Java's ports and harbours are generally superior, and its international communications and access to foreign buyers are also better. Moreover, its unskilled wages are usually no higher than elsewhere. Consequently, Indonesia's major labour-intensive industries—garments, textiles, footwear, electronics—are located overwhelmingly in Java.

Equally, the Outer Islands' specialization in resource-based industries is clearly evident (Table 11.2, column 13). Plywood is dominant in several provinces, rubber processing activities are important, huge energy-intensive installations such as fertilizer plants are found in a number of instances, while processed agricultural produce is important in those provinces with a strong cash crop sector.

Two additional features of these regional patterns need to be emphasized. The first is that there are three significant cases of footloose industry off-Java. In Bali, akin to Java in its factor endowments, garments and handicrafts, both heavily tourism-related, are important. Batam, administratively in the province of Riau, is attracting much industry from Singapore as part of that region's "growth triangle" (see Pangestu, 1992). Finally, in North Sumatra, the largest regional economy outside Java, the local market is sufficiently large to support a variety of consumer goods industries. In time also, there may be a migration of labour-intensive industries from nearby Penang, especially if the proposed triangle involving Northwest Malaysia, Sumatra, and Southern Thailand develops. Conversely, resource-based industries have not disappeared entirely from Java. Sugar processing is still significant in East and Central Java. *Kretek* cigarettes and steel—both marginal candidates for inclusion in the resource-based category—are very important components of industry in East and West Java respectively. The government's ban on unprocessed rattan exports, and accompanying restrictions of processing sites mainly to Java, has pushed this industry and associated downstream activities such as furniture away from the Outer Islands.

The second feature is that there are pronounced intra-regional industrialization patterns, which are not readily discernible from the provincial data. On Java, for example, manufacturing is almost entirely a northern and north-central phenomenon, principally around the island's two major industrialization poles, greater Jakarta and greater Surabaya, together with smaller centres around Bandung and Semarang.

Outside Java, as noted, much of the manufacturing activity is enclave in nature, with one locality or even a small number of industrial plants accounting for the bulk of manufacturing output.[18]

THE MINING INDUSTRY

The value of mining output has fluctuated sharply since the mid 1960s, especially so during periods of price turbulence (Figure 8.1, p. 153): witness the large increases in 1972-73 and again in 1991, and the contraction in 1982 and again in 1985. Within the mining industry, oil and gas dominate output, in recent years accounting for approximately 80 per cent of value added. This figure is declining steadily, however. In the late 1970s, for example, oil and gas contributed about 97 per cent of the industry's value added. During the 1980s, several non-oil mining industries grew very rapidly.

Summary output trends of the major minerals are presented in Figure 8.4. There has been surprisingly little variation in the physical volume of oil output since the early 1970s.[19] Oil output rose rapidly in the late 1960s as the commercial environment improved and in response to increasing prices. Thereafter, there has been no significant trend; in fact the peak output years of 1977-78 have not been surpassed. The lack of growth reflects fundamentally supply-side constraints, though on occasion adherence to OPEC quotas has also constrained production growth. Some time in the next two decades or so, and in the absence of major new discoveries, Indonesia will cease to be a net oil exporter. Since the mid-1980s, low international oil prices have meant that it is not economic to explore less accessible fields. During the oil boom decade, Pertamina implemented a reasonably effective system of oil taxation through a system known as "production sharing", which ensured that most of the windfall gains from higher prices accrued to Indonesia (though not to the government in the mid-1970s, owing to the misappropriation of funds within Pertamina). The oil companies were given exploration rights in exchange for a contract in which revenues were divided on a predetermined basis, for much of the period 85 per cent: 15 per cent shares to Pertamina and the companies respectively. On a number of occasions these fiscal negotiations became quite acrimonious and resulted in a decline in exploration activity and output.

By contrast, natural gas output continues to rise rapidly. Commercial production from the two major sites, Aceh and East Kalimantan, commenced in 1974, as a by-product of oil production. After increasing by more than 300 per cent in the second half of the 1970s, output levelled off in the early 1980s, before rising sharply again as additional gas "trains" were brought into production. In the late 1970s LNG exports were overshadowed by oil, being only about 10 per cent of the latter's value. By 1991, however, the value of net LNG exports exceeded that of oil for the first time. Unlike oil, gas reserves are projected to last for many decades. Increasingly gas is being substituted for oil as a source of domestic energy, through the expanding gas grid on Java, and with the construction of several huge fertilizer plants around the gas fields. Nevertheless, Indonesia is likely to continue exporting gas well into the twenty-first century, long after it has ceased to be an oil exporter. Most of the LNG

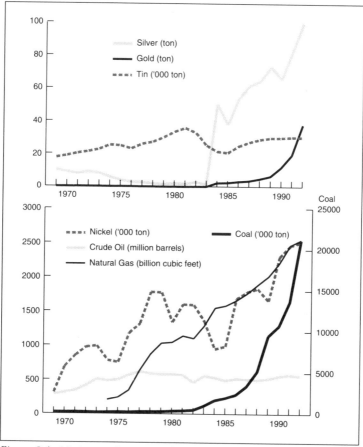

Figure 8.4   Mining production, 1969–92

is exported to the resource-poor Northeast Asian countries in the form of long-term supply contracts.

The performance of the non-oil mining industries has varied considerably. Two of them, coal and gold, have experienced boom conditions since the mid-1980s, for broadly similar reasons. State enterprises dominated some of these industries in the past, notably in the case of tin and coal, but recently there has been a retreat from state involvement. In two industries, copper and nickel, huge foreign-owned projects in inaccessible regions of eastern Indonesia were the major growth stimuli. The fortunes of these industries have also been shaped by fluctuations in international prices and by international cartels, the latter too in retreat since the mid-1980s.

Coal production has grown at a spectacular rate since the early 1980s, from a little under one million tons in 1983 to an estimated 21.1 million in 1992. Indonesia is thought to have vast coal resources, of as much as 30 billion tons, located primarily in southern Sumatra and East and South Kalimantan. Much of the country has not been adequately explored. Commercial coal mining commenced in the 1840s, and at the outbreak of the Pacific War Indonesia was a significant producer. Thereafter the

Table 8.8   **Energy Consumption by Source, 1968–92**
(% of total)

	1968	1973	1978	1983	1988	1992
Oil	84.9	87.4	82.5	74.7	64.3	64.8
Gas	11.6	7.5	14.6	19.4	21.1	20.3
Coal	1.8	0.9	0.5	0.5	7.0	8.0
Hydro	1.7	4.3	2.5	5.2	6.9	6.4
Geothermal	0	0	0	0.2	0.7	0.5
Total	100	100	100	100	100	100
	(41)	(77)	(154)	(224)	(293)	(406)

Note: The figures in parentheses refer to total energy consumption, in millions of oil barrel equivalents.
Source: Lampiran, various issues.

industry languished, owing to the inhospitable exploration and production environment, the exclusion of foreign investment, and the absence of infrastructure investment. It was not until 1986 that the pre-war production peak of 2 million tons was overtaken.[20]

Ironically, the industry has really only begun to flourish again in an era of low energy prices. Three interrelated factors explain the extremely rapid growth in production and exports from the mid-1980s. First, the industry was opened up to foreign involvement, in the form of both equity investment and technological ties. Many of the very large projects were initiated under such auspices, including the largest single investment, the Australian-British Kaltim Prima mine. Secondly, liberalized entry facilitated the huge infrastructure investments necessary, particularly in East Kalimantan where the development of ports and bulk-loading operations have been important. Thirdly, although international prices have been low, resulting fundamentally from conditions in the international oil market, there are no institutional demand-side constraints such as cartels and quotas. Indonesia has been able to compete on the basis of its competitive exchange rate and its accessible, high-quality reserves. It has an additional competitive advantage deriving from the fact that its Kalimantan coal has a low sulphur content. As with LNG, its major customers are the resource-poor countries of Northeast Asia, with whom it has signed a number of long-term contracts.

The development of the coal industry is also having an impact on Indonesia's energy supply equations. From 1968 to 1992 Indonesia's energy consumption rose 10-fold (Table 8.8). Given the more than four-fold increase in economic activity (real GDP) over this period, this implies a doubling of the ratio of energy consumption to GDP, hardly surprising given the extremely low level prevailing during the 1960s. In the late 1960s oil and gas, principally the former, supplied almost 97 per cent of the country's commercial energy, but by 1992 their share had fallen somewhat, to 85 per cent; the share of oil fell significantly, being partially compensated by the switch from oil to gas. Indeed, over the entire period, the largest incremental growth came from LNG, as major commercial exploitation was directed to industrial and commercial use. The share of coal also rose significantly from the mid-1980s, reflecting both the rapid increase in output and a conscious strategy to substitute coal for oil in energy-intensive projects such as cement plants. Hydro-electric power, too, has become more important, mainly owing to the large but troubled Asahan Project in North Sumatra.

The other element in the future energy equations is of course the controversial possibility of nuclear power. As the government presses forward with a program of diversification from oil and gas, the nuclear option is under active consideration. The government has announced its decision, in principle, to construct a $2 billion, 600 megawatt plant at Muria, northern Central Java. One of the leading proponents of the initiative is Professor Habibie, who has in the past advocated that Indonesia should build up to 12 such plants. It is not clear at this stage whether the Muria plant will go ahead. It is encountering stiff opposition from increasingly active environmental groups, which maintain that the region is geologically unstable. Economists oppose it also, because they fear that the project will not be subject to rigorous economic analysis (not to mention the scope such "megaprojects" afford for corruption), because nuclear energy appears to be on the wane worldwide, and because Indonesia possesses ample alternative energy sources.

The tin industry, by contrast, has been plagued by difficulty, mostly self-inflicted. Tin production is still below the 1940 level of 40,000 tons, and during the 1980s was largely stagnant apart from a modest recovery in the middle of the decade (Figure 8.4). Indonesia is one of the world's four major producers, accounting for some 15 per cent of global output. The industry is dominated by the state tin company, PT Tambang Timah, and for many years output was constrained by Indonesia's membership of the international tin cartel. Following the latter's collapse, and facing an era of state enterprise fiscal austerity, the company underwent drastic surgery. Almost 50 per cent of its workforce is to be retired and per unit production costs are scheduled to fall by about one-third, achievements which are indicative of the extent of overstaffing and inefficiency in much of the state enterprise sector. Even in an era of prolonged low prices, Indonesia is likely to be a competitive tin exporter following these reforms.

Production of gold and silver has risen sharply since the mid-1980s. An unknown proportion of the production comes from small-scale illegal mining activities, which were not reported at all until about 1984; data weaknesses still render the figures extremely approximate. Unlike coal, international price movements in gold over some of this period have been favourable. But like coal, a more liberal investment and exploration code has stimulated production. Relatively few work contracts were issued in the 1970s and early 1980s, but in 1986 and 1987 alone some 94 contracts were issued, mostly to small- and medium-scale Australian miners. In the case of nickel, the industry's fortunes have been tied to the huge Canadian Inco mine at Soroako, South Sulawesi. Commencing in 1973, the mine has had a chequered history, profitability reportedly squeezed by low international prices and, until the mid-1970s, high (unexpectedly so at the time of project planning) energy prices. The mine became profitable only in 1987 at which time industry output, after stagnating from 1979 to 1987, began to rise appreciably. Under current expansion plans, the mine is likely to become one of the largest in the world.

Output of the other major mineral, copper, comes mainly from the huge Freeport mine in Irian Jaya, the development of which is graphically described in Wilson (1981; see also Manning and Rumbiak (1989) for a discussion of the mine in the broader regional setting). The Freeport mine assumes particular significance in Indonesian economic policy history since it was the first major foreign investment project agreed upon following the introduction of the government's 1967 DFI regulations. Thus, even though manufacturing was quick to dominate non-oil DFI inflows, Freeport was seen as a test case of the new regime's commitment to a liberal investment code. The regime was keen, in the words of its principal negotiator of the time, Professor Moh. Sadli, to "bag its first contract" (see the quote on p. 99).

The Services Revolution

AN OVERVIEW

The services sector has played a crucial role in underpinning the growth of tradeable goods activities in agriculture and industry, in generating employment opportunities and foreign exchange earnings (notably in the case of tourism), and in providing an increasingly wide array of personal and community services as incomes rise. It has consistently produced 35 to 40 per cent of GDP, and in most years over 45 per cent of non-oil GDP, up from 35 per cent in the mid-1960s. Over the 1967–92 period services output has grown rapidly, in all years in excess of 4 per cent and for half the period at more than double this rate (Figure 2.1, p. 12). Its expansion has been more "even" than that of agriculture and industry, where international prices, climatic factors and changes in policy regimes have resulted in a more erratic growth path. Throughout the entire New Order period, and in each of the four principal economic phases identified in Chapter 2, it has always generated at least 40 per cent of the incremental expansion in GDP (Table 2.1, p. 21). Also, value added in services has always exceeded the combined total of value added in the more publicized food crop and manufacturing sectors by a significant margin, even in the early 1990s after the latter sector had grown strongly for 25 years. Accompanying this growth has been rapid structural transformation within many service industries, a transformation resulting in the fact that many of the service activities of the early 1990s bear little relation to those of the mid-1960s.

Services have also been a major source of employment growth. Consistent with the theory of economic development, the share of services in total employment has risen in each intercensal period since 1961, from 19 per cent to 33 per cent in 1990 (Table 2.2, p. 22). Of the three major sectors, it has always absorbed by far the largest increments to the workforce, for the periods 1961 to 1971 and from 1971 to 1980 in excess of 50 per cent of the total. Both these shares and increments have been larger still for Java, reflecting the island's key role as a service provider to the nation. During the 1970s labour productivity in services rose more slowly than that of most other sectors, even agriculture, but in the following decade the pace of change picked up considerably, and was close to that of non-mining GDP as a whole (Table 2.4, p. 27).

Several features of the services sector in Indonesia, and in neighbouring high-growth economies, deserve emphasis.[1] First, reflecting advances in transport and communications, and a more liberal international environment, many services are traded increasingly across international boundaries. Some examples of these traded services are given below. They are everywhere evident among the highly skilled members of the labour force in Indonesia's major cities, where Sri Lankan accountants, Taiwanese technicians, Philippine's musicians, and Australian athletic coaches provide services not readily available domestically. Reverse flows are also expanding, in the form of unskilled workers from Indonesia seeking employment abroad, principally in the neighbouring high-wage economies of Malaysia and Singapore, but also in more distant regions such as the Middle East. These examples point to a second important feature of services, especially as it relates to their international trade: namely, being personnel-intensive, proximity exerts a more powerful influence on regional composition than is the case with merchandise trade. Accurate data on services trade by country are not available, but it is almost certainly the case that the Western Pacific, from Japan through to Australia, occupies a more prominent position in Indonesia's services trade as compared with its merchandise trade. This phenomenon leads directly to a third feature, namely the special role of Singapore as, in effect, the services "capital" of Southeast Asia, through its efficient provision of an increasingly diverse array of high value services to the rest of the region. Although poorly documented,[2] Singapore plays this role in transport, health, telecommunications, information technology, and many business services.

Fourthly, and related to the first point, the framework for the analysis of the spectacular growth of Indonesia's non-oil merchandise exports is in important respects applicable to the growth of newly emerging service exports. A good example is the growth of the tourist industry. A combination of competitiveness, delivered through real effective depreciations in the 1980s, and a series of deregulation measures, which eased entry and lowered business costs in the industry, spurred much of the growth. Financial services are another instance where deregulation produced dramatic, albeit somewhat unpredictable, results.

Finally, the public sector plays a particularly important role in services. It is the sole or significant provider of many of them—defence, justice, health, statistics, and physical infrastructure. Government ownership is sizeable in several cases, such as banking and civil aviation. Moreover, the government is a major employer of skilled labour, particularly in countries at early stages of development, such as Indonesia.[3] Thus public sector wage and hiring policies have a substantial impact on the highly skilled component of the labour market, in addition to the general impacts of the labour market regulatory programs.

Yet, for all its importance, there have been few detailed studies of Indonesia's service industries, investigating industry structure, competition and regulation, and performance. This reflects in part statistical deficiencies. Output and efficiency are often very difficult to measure, most obviously in the case of rent and accommodation, and public administration and defence, but also in retail and wholesale trade and even financial services. This sector is also extremely diverse: for example, "trade" extends from the modern new shopping complexes of Jakarta to itinerant traders in remote areas outside Java, while "finance" embraces both multinational banks and also occasional small-scale rural moneylenders. Data on international services trade, to be examined shortly, are even more inadequate.

But, to some extent, this lack of attention is also indicative of a widespread tendency to regard services as ancillary to, and dependent for its growth on, tradeable goods activities. The literature on services draws attention to this tendency, as articles examining services often employ subtitles such as "the neglected sector" or the "forgotten sector". The lesson from Indonesia, as elsewhere, is quite the reverse: a more efficient and diverse services sector has made an effective contribution to rising efficiency in the goods sectors, to enhanced consumer welfare, to rapid employment growth, and more recently to increased exports.

Within services, trade (including also hotels and restaurants) has always been a dominant subsector, producing on average about 40 per cent of sectoral value added. The government sector, essentially measured by public service salaries, is the next largest with 15 to 20 per cent of the total. By the late 1980s transport and communication (13 to 14 per cent of the total) and financial services (10 to 11 per cent) had become sizeable, followed by the miscellaneous group other services (8 to 9 per cent) and accommodation (6 to 7 per cent). Growth among these subsectors has fluctuated considerably since the late 1960s (Figure 9.1). The key and direct role of the government is highlighted in these figures. Very high growth rates were recorded, with a lag, following the oil price increases of the 1970s. Particularly notable were transport and communications, banking, and public administration, sectors which were major recipients of government's efforts to recycle oil revenue. Conversely, the slowdown in the mid-1980s reflects, in part, the impact of fiscal austerity in the public sector.

The transport and communications industry grew at a spectacular rate over the 1971–83 period as first aid and then oil revenue was poured into long neglected physical infrastructure. The revolution in light commercial road transport further hastened this growth. The public administration subsector also expanded quickly over this period, as civil service numbers and especially remuneration rose significantly.[4] The accommodation subsector likewise grew rapidly. The control of inflation induced a renewed confidence in the banking sector, which was ravaged by the events of the early and mid-1960s. Monetization increased quickly, and much of the government's oil revenue was channelled through state banks during the 1970s. Another episode of high growth in financial services commenced in 1989, in the wake of the banking deregulation of late 1988, and double-digit growth was recorded in each year from 1989 to 1992. Somewhat surprisingly, the other services group expanded slowly, at around 5 per cent. Trade grew steadily in line with the expansion of commercial activity. The absence of peaks and troughs which are characteristic of some other subsectors is at least partly due to the fact that the policy regime has been more stable. A major transformation got under way in the 1980s with the proliferation of large shopping complexes in prosperous urban areas, extending also to the establishment of market complexes in smaller towns and rural areas.[5]

As noted above, statistics on international trade in services suffer from both conceptual and empirical shortcomings. They suggest that Indonesia is a large net importer of services. During the 1980s exports grew more rapidly than imports, but in recent years the latter were still almost three times the former (Table 9.1). The major problem with these balance of payments data is that "invisibles" include both non-factor services (such as tourism) and factor services (such as investment income), and the total cannot be equated with services trade. Invisibles also include some official aid transfers, which ought properly to be included as capital movements (for an exposition of these issues, see Arndt, 1989). For these reasons, little significance can be attached to the aggregate figures in Table 9.1. An additional problem is that some of the factor services data also embody traded non-factor services. Examples include royalty payments and financial services.

However, while many of the major items of services trade are not separately

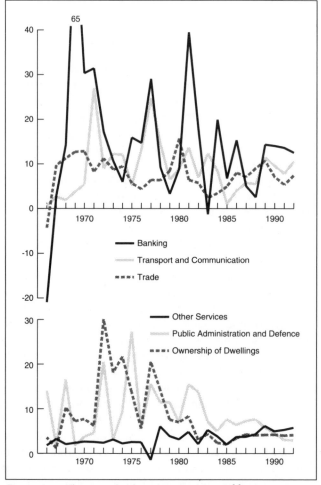

Figure 9.1 The growth of services output, 1966–92

enumerated, the balance of payments data do shed light on some of Indonesia's trade in non-factor services, and these items are listed separately in the table. For example, not surprisingly, Indonesia is a large net importer of "shipment" services, primarily freight and insurance on freight. In fact no exports are recorded under this item, although in practice a small amount of the country's trade is carried by Indonesian-registered liners. Similarly, Indonesia records a large deficit in "other transport", mainly port fees and passenger services. By contrast, exports of travel services, principally tourism, have been growing rapidly. These exports were negligible until the mid-1970s, but then began to grow very rapidly, overtaking imports (that is, Indonesians travelling abroad) in 1986, and by 1989 being some 125 per cent larger than the latter. As will be discussed shortly, expenditure-switching measures (successive devaluations, and from late 1982 a hefty departure tax) and several promotional measures explain this rapid transformation. From 1981 to 1988 travel imports actually declined in nominal terms, while exports rose by almost 500 per cent.

In the following sections I examine developments in selected service sector activities in more detail, choosing in turn physical infrastructure and transport,

Table 9.1 **Estimates of Services Trade, 1966–92**
($ million)

	Total		Shipment	Other Transport		Travel	
	Export	*Import*	*Import*	*Export*	*Import*	*Export*	*Import*
1992	3,044	7,040	2,900	87	797	2,729	1,166
1991	2,852	6,494	2,699	81	671	2,515	949
1990	2,488	6,056	2,343	70	686	2,153	836
1989	1,875	5,439	1,772	54	486	1,628	722
1988	1,369	4,606	1,502	44	314	1,283	592
1987	1,065	4,440	1,354	41	256	924	511
1986	844	4,256	1,290	39	280	647	570
1985	844	5,135	1,392	42	324	548	591
1984	570	4,239	1,648	49	362	460	514
1983	546	4,311	2,046	50	284	396	522
1982	504	4,867	2,052	69	324	280	562
1981	499	4,998	1,910	68	291	229	603
1980	327	3,477	1,479	60	236	173	400
1979	315	2,889	1,099	41	178	209	366
1978	234	2,349	1,003	30	165	149	274
1977	114	1,840	984	28	133	40	131
1976	111	1,668	902	26	117	41	137
1975	93	1,306	725	21	85	34	90
1974	71	952	597	12	60	28	87
1973	52	544	303	7	36	21	57
1972	45	430	167	4	22	18	43
1971	28	355	149	7	28	10	36
1970	16	316	142		5	5	19
1969	11	287	127		3	3	13
1968	9	223	93		3	2	16
1967	2	186	86	1	10		4
1966	27	221	75	1	8		18

Note: Blanks indicate no data reported, or zero.
Sources: IMF, *Balance of Payments Statistics Yearbook*, various issues, and *International Financial Statistics*, various issues.

tourism, and financial services. Despite data limitations and the sparse scholarly literature, the key themes of rapid structural transformation, a large public sector impact, and deregulation in the 1980s are clearly evident.

PHYSICAL INFRASTRUCTURE AND TRANSPORT

The expansion of services is nowhere better illustrated than in the case of physical infrastructure, transport and communication. Following the defeat of regional insurrections in the late 1950s the Jakarta government had achieved unchallenged political control over the nation. But Indonesia hardly functioned as a national economic entity, owing to the steadily deteriorating transport and communication network. The quality of inter-island transport services, excluding air, had declined. There were few significant investments in land transport in the increasingly populous regions off Java. Java's once excellent rail network was in a ramshackle state.[6] The fleet of commercial transport vehicles was ageing and inadequate, while power generation supplies were insufficient for household requirements, let alone industrial demands.

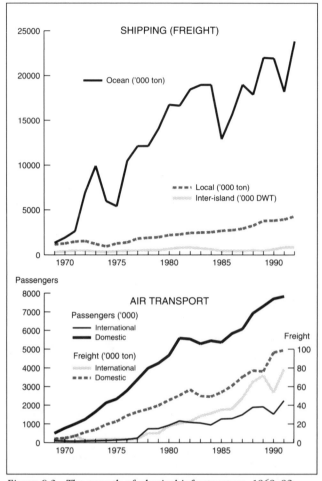

Figure 9.2 The growth of physical infrastructure, 1969–92

The expansion in physical infrastructure since the late 1960s has been extremely rapid in most cases (Table 9.2 and Figure 9.2). Many of the increases from the late 1960s to the early 1990s have been exceptional: 2,600 per cent in the number of buses, and a similar magnitude in domestic air freight, 1,300 per cent in the case of power generation (over a 20-year period) and almost 1,900 per cent in the number of motorcycles, and a still larger increase in the volume of international telephone calls. Some of these increases reflect the low initial base figures, that is, the abysmal state of infrastructure in the 1960s.[7] However, it is important to note that there are a few instances—bus numbers, electricity production—where the pace of expansion actually accelerated in the 1980s. In other cases, notably telecommunications, the increases reflect technological breakthroughs and are part of a rapid global expansion, which to some extent would have occurred even in the absence of large infrastructure investments.

There have been a few instances where expansion has been slow, such as in rail and local sea-transport. But on the whole the trend has been one of high growth, continuing from the catch-up phase of the late 1960s and 1970s right through to the 1990s. Moreover, these aggregate figures do not provide a

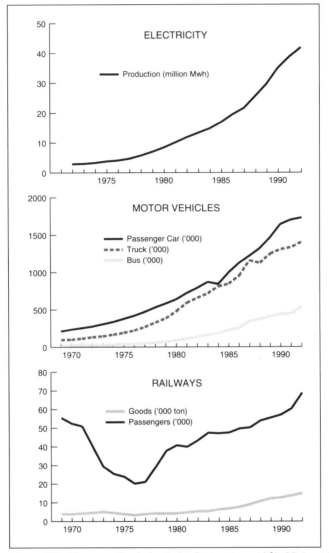

Figure 9.2   The growth of physical infrastructure, 1969–92 (cont.)

comprehensive picture of the improvement in the range and quality of transport and communication services. For example, quality, comfort, and safety have improved considerably in the case of air and sea transport. International and interregional telecommunication connections are immeasurably better, aided by the country's Palapa satellite system.

Within the rapidly expanding transport sector, performance has been somewhat mixed.[8] Road transport has expanded the most rapidly, owing to the vast improvement in road conditions, especially off-Java, the introduction of relatively inexpensive light commercial vehicles (known universally as "colts"), and the growth of other 4- and 2-wheeled transport. The industry is responsive to consumer needs, providing services ranging from modern and well-equipped long distance buses to colts servicing urban and short-distance intercity networks. The "transport

Table 9.2   **Indicators of Physical Infrastructure, 1969, 1980, 1992**

Indicator	Unit	1969	1980	1992[b]	Annual growth (%)		
					1969–80	1980–92	1969–92
Road transport							
Buses	'000	20	86	542	14.2	16.6	15.4
Trucks	'000	96	478	1,405	15.7	9.4	12.4
Passenger cars	'000	212	639	1,729	10.6	8.6	9.6
Motorcycles	'000	328	3,881	6,414	25.2	4.7	14.5
Railways							
Passengers	'000	55.4	40.7	68.7	−2.8	4.5	0.9
Goods	'000 ton	4.0	4.3	14.9	0.7	10.9	5.9
Sea freight							
Ocean	'000 ton	1,343	16,752	23,831	25.8	3.0	13.3
Local	'000 ton	1,162	2,200	4,282	6.0	5.7	5.8
Capacity (inter-island)	'000 DWT	318	668	844	7.0	2.1	4.5
Air transport							
International							
Passengers	'000	99	923	2,238	22.5	8.4	15.2
Goods	'000 ton	3.3	17.8	78.7	16.6	14.5	15.5
Domestic							
Passengers	'000	499	4,664	7,831	22.5	4.8	13.3
Goods	'000 ton	4.1	45.3	98.9	24.4	7.4	15.6
Electricity production	mil. mWh	2.9[a]	8.4	41.9	14.2	14.3	14.3
International phone calls	mil. mins.	0.3	8.9	134.1	37.0	35.2	36.2

[a] Data refer to 1972.   DWT = dead-weight ton
[b] In some cases data refer to 1991.   mWh = megawatt hours.

Source: BPS, *Statistik Indonesia*, various issues.

revolution" is manifested in the fact that it is now possible to travel from the northern tip of Aceh to Sumbawa (east of Lombok) by road and vehicular ferry. Cities as far apart as Medan-Surabaya are now served by frequent bus connections.

Another manifestation of the revolution, disturbing to some, is the demise of *becak* (rickshaw) transport, and even bicycles. *Becak* have now become little more than providers of residual urban and fringe-urban transport, a trend hastened by urban authorities who frequently regard them as incompatible with a modern transport system and as embarrassing reminders of Indonesia's "backwardness".[9] The number of cyclists in major urban centres has declined rapidly owing to a combination of factors: the danger posed by a congested road system and sometimes fast-moving motorized transport, a public transport network which is cheaper and more accessible and, with rising incomes, a shift to motorized transport especially motor cycles.

Despite these major improvements, some notable deficiencies remain in the transport networks. The underinvestment in public transport on major urban arterial routes, the result in part of fare and zoning restrictions, is everywhere evident. Governments have been slow to address the long-term implications of the emergence of megacities in Java, and their need for efficient urban rail networks. Major intercity highways carry extremely high transport volumes. Automobiles are expensive, probably a desirable outcome given the negative externalities associated with their growth. Yet these high prices are not the result primarily of deliberate fiscal measures designed to tax the large negative externalities associated with automobile use in congested urban environments, but rather of inefficiencies resulting from extremely high protection for the industry.

In sectors dominated by state enterprises—notably rail and to a much lesser extent shipping—transport has expanded more slowly. The stagnation in the rail sector for much of the New Order period is clearly evident from the statistics above. Rail transport is hampered by underinvestment in stock and tracks, and less flexible management and service delivery, than private sector competitors in road transport. The rail system is still managed partly as a welfare agency in which the managing authority is unable to recoup its operating and capital costs. Overstaffing remains rife. The record in rail is particularly puzzling since Java, where most of the network is located, is well suited to such transport given its long-established rail infrastructure and dense commuting populations. Inter-island shipping was retarded in the 1960s and 1970s by the government's desire to protect its inefficient corporation *Pelni*, by barriers to entry, and by limited port infrastructure (Dick, 1987). However, regulatory reforms of 1985 and 1988 have increased competitive pressures and, combined with rising public and private sector fleet investments, greatly improved services.

Physical infrastructure bottlenecks eased from the late 1970s as the first round of large investment projects from the oil and aid inflows came on stream. Slackening economic growth in the mid-1980s further reduced demand pressures. However, the government was unprepared for the sudden and strong growth which emerged in the late 1980s, in response to the liberalizing reforms. In the latter period, the situation became just as critical as in the early 1970s and, as in neighbouring Thailand, it threatened to choke off economic growth. Unlike the 1970s, moreover, the government's fiscal options were quite restricted. Its external debt obligations were "squeezing" the revenue side of the government's budget, and constraining its capacity to borrow on international capital markets.

From about 1989, the government had no choice but to turn to the private sector, in power, telecommunications, roads, and ports.[10] The results so far have been mixed. There has been some expansion of capacity, almost certainly at a pace quicker than the state authorities acting alone would have achieved. But there have also been problems. The state infrastructure agencies have retained control of all projects, reserving the right to vet projects and set operating rates. Often the rates have been set so low and approval procedures so cumbersome that private sector investment has been discouraged.[11] A second problem has been a lack of transparency in awarding private sector contracts. Several major toll-road and power projects have been secured by such politically powerful figures as the President's children and the country's leading conglomerate, the Liem (Salim) group. It is of course quite possible that these investors are best placed to run the projects efficiently. But not surprisingly the absence of open tendering procedures has led to public suspicion of nepotism.

TOURISM

Tourism has witnessed spectacular growth since the mid-1980s (Figure 9.3). While Indonesia has always been famous for the fabled tourist island of Bali and many other scenic and cultural attractions, tourism languished in the 1970s for much the same reasons as other non-oil exports. The oil boom, operating through the exchange rate, made Indonesia a comparatively expensive country to visit, especially given the range of amenities on offer. There was no urgency to develop the industry, the government's lack of interest being reflected in tight regulations pertaining to visas, aircraft landing rights, and investments in tourism facilities. Such planning as existed, especially for Bali, attempted to target high-income tourism, neglecting the most important and rapidly growing tourist class segment. As a result, international tourism expanded quite slowly, the numbers barely doubling between 1974 and 1983. Little consideration was given to the potential for domestic tourism growth.

Declining oil prices and the evident success of tourism elsewhere prompted a major policy rethink in the early 1980s. As a result, tourism began to grow rapidly (Figure 9.3), and for the decade as a whole Indonesia recorded the highest rate of growth in inbound tourism of any ASEAN country.[12] Tourism emerged as a major source of export growth alongside that of manufactures, and for similar reasons.[13] Real effective devaluations conferred a competitive edge. Visa-free entry for nationals of many countries was introduced, and points of entry for international airlines extended. An important example of the latter was that flights from the east (notably Australia) were now permitted to terminate in Bali. A proliferation of training programs and institutes augmented the skills of the industry's workforce. A package of measures introduced in December 1987 simplified the previously complex procedures for investing in the industry. The arrivals data in Figure 9.3 do overstate the growth of the industry somewhat. As Batam has been opened up and the "growth triangle" concept promoted, visitors to that island, mostly from Singapore, have grown rapidly: from 84,500 (11 per cent of total inflows) in 1986 to 655,600 (26.4 per cent) in 1992. The average length of stay of most of these visitors is much less than those from more distant sources; many are day-trippers. Nevertheless, even allowing for this factor, the growth of the industry has been impressive. Reflecting the importance of proximity in internationally traded services, Western Pacific countries have been the major source of tourists. In recent years, the most important have been Singapore, Japan, and Australia, with shares averaging 21 per cent, 12 per cent, and 11 per cent of the total respectively; ASEAN in total now provides over 40 per cent of the tourists. The Singapore, Australian, and ASEAN figures are much higher—approximately double—than their merchandise trade shares with Indonesia.

Domestic tourism was also stimulated by a range of factors. One was the general development of the industry and its amenities, including a range of accommodation facilities and prices. Domestic airline services have expanded very rapidly, as noted. New services and competitors have been introduced. Finally, the costs of outward tourism have risen sharply. The real effective devaluations have pushed up costs of overseas travel. And since December 1982 an exit tax (*fiskal*) has been imposed on Indonesian citizens, set initially at Rp150,000 and increased progressively.[14] As Table 9.1 shows, the combined effect of these measures was to restrain outbound tourism while strongly promoting inward flows.

A number of major challenges remain if the growth of tourism is to be sustained.[15] There is still an excessive concentration on Bali, although diversification is occurring steadily. The environmental (and cultural) sustainability of the industry continues to be a topic of debate, especially in the increasingly crowded resorts on Bali. Shortages in trained personnel and in some amenities remain. Domestic and international transport networks are not well integrated in some instances. In the case of high-class tourist facilities, there are frequent allegations that the local community derives little of the economic benefits. But there seems little doubt that tourism is likely to be a major source of export and employment growth for many years, rivalling that of labour-intensive manufacturing industries such as textiles and garments.

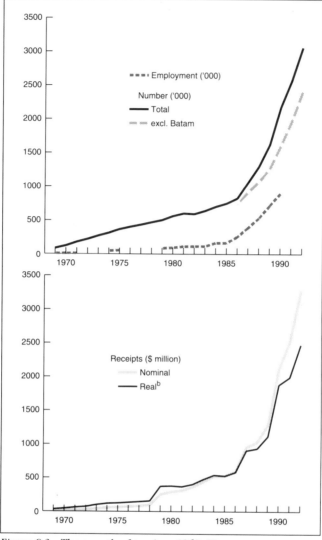

Figure 9.3   The growth of tourism, 1969–92

FINANCIAL SERVICES

Developments in the financial services industries also reflect a mix of rapid growth and regulatory reform. As noted in Chapter 3, government regulations were particularly important in shaping the industry's development through until the late 1980s. The control of inflation in the late 1960s led to increased holdings of liquid assets and renewed faith in the banking industry. But the government kept a firm hand on all banks, paradoxically despite the introduction of a very open international capital market. State banks were little more than agencies for the central bank until 1983, with little incentive to compete and innovate. The entry of private banks, both foreign and domestic, was virtually prohibited from the early 1970s. Similarly, the growth of the insurance industry and a properly functioning stock market was stifled until the late 1980s.

Although the banking industry grew rapidly from the early 1970s, its structure was to change little for the next 15 years (Table 9.3 and Figure 9.4). For example, from 1969 to 1988 the number of state banks remained the same, while their branches increased by 38 per cent—an amazingly low figure considering that the economy expanded by over 300 per cent during the same period. While the number of domestic private bank branches more than doubled, the number of these banks actually declined in the 1970s, as the government imposed prudential regulations in an attempt to improve credit-worthiness. An inheritance of the 1960s was that many of the smaller private banks were little more than extensions of trading firms; some were owned by political parties or cooperatives (Grenville, 1981). A similar rationalization occurred in the case of savings banks and people's credit banks. No new foreign bank licences were issued, while their branch network was also very limited and heavily restricted. Likewise, development banks expanded quite slowly. These trends are reflected in the deposit shares of the three major ownership groups in the formal banking sector (Figure 9.4).[16] During the 1970s there was very little change in ownership structure, the principal trend being minor expansion of the two domestic groups at the expense of foreign banks. In the 1980s, the private bank share began to increase still further, attracting custom mainly from the state banks. The minor banking reforms of 1983, the reduction in the volume of subsidized credit being channelled through the state banks, and general fiscal austerity in the state enterprise sector all contributed to this trend.

However, the major watershed was the banking reforms of 1988, which for the first time enabled the private banks to offer genuine competition. The private banking sector responded vigorously to the new opportunities, expanding at a frenetic pace. In little more than four years, from March 1989 to June 1993, the number of their branches almost doubled, compared with the leisurely 24 per cent increase in state bank branches. These changes translated into a rapidly increasing share of deposits, which in 1993 overtook the state bank figure (the latter excluding the development banks). The state bank share is now little more than half the figure of the early 1970s, and its continuing decline signals a further retreat in the state's direct influence in the economy. This is a remarkable transformation when it is recalled that the state bank share was almost 10 times that of domestic private banks just two decades earlier. Foreign banks also expanded after the 1988 reforms, but only at a pace sufficient to ensure that they retained market share. Small rural banks continued to expand quickly, but data on their aggregate significance in the financial sector are not readily available. Although small in total, they have injected much-needed flexibility into rural credit markets.

The story of the insurance industry mirrors that of the banking sector in important respects. It too was heavily regulated until 1988. No new licences for foreign non-life insurers were issued after 1975, the number of domestic non-life insurers was frozen from 1974 to 1982, while only three companies (two government owned) were permitted to offer reinsurance services (Nehen, 1989). The reforms of October 1988 quickly changed the structure of the industry, as new domestic private entrants especially began to out-compete the hitherto protected state firms. The industry remains in its infancy, and is very small compared with that of industrialized economies.[17] However, it is likely to grow rapidly in line with rising incomes, a better developed legal–commercial environment, and a large pool of qualified professionals.

Table 9.3   **Number of Banks and Branches, 1969–93[a]**

		1969/70	1978/79	1988/89	1993/94
General banks					
State	banks	7	7	7	7
	branches	625	707	860	1,069
Domestic private	banks	138	83	94	152
	branches	295	279	1,536	2,923
Foreign	banks	11	11	11	39
	branches	15	20	21	75
Regional development banks					
Banks		25	26	27	27
Branches		61	144	326	431
Savings banks					
Banks		12	5	3	3[b]
Branches		18	12	82	127
People's credit banks		8,408	5,718	7,501	7,632

[a] Data refer to the end of each financial year (31 March 1970, etc., except for 1993/94 which is 30 June of that year).
[b] 1992/93

Source: Nota Keuangan, various issues.

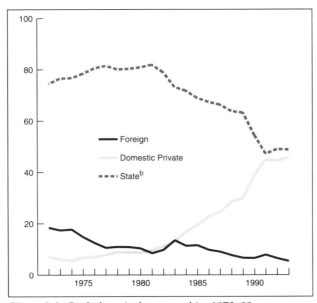

Figure 9.4   Bank deposits by ownership, 1972–93

Another aspect of growing financial sophistication has been the development of the stock market. Jakarta's stock market remains small by regional standards,[18] its market capitalization as a percentage of GDP being less than 10 per cent of that of either Singapore or Kuala Lumpur (Table 3.1, p. 40). But it has developed rapidly in the last few years. Re-established in the late 1970s, its activities were heavily restricted initially, and one state-owned entity dominated trading. Here also the major stimulus

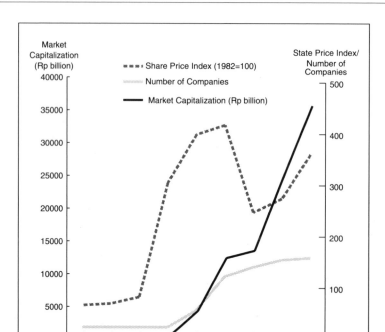

Figure 9.5   The Jakarta stock exchange, 1985-93

occurred in late 1988, when entry was eased, and taxation reforms encouraged investment on the stock market. The market sprang to life following the reforms, and in just two years (1988-90) the number of listed companies rose by 400 per cent and market capitalization by 2,500 per cent (Figure 9.5).

For a period the Jakarta exchange was hailed internationally as one of the most promising of the newly emerging stock markets. Foreign portfolio investment flowed in, attracted by Indonesia's boom conditions of the late 1980s, while Indonesian business increasingly began to see equity capital as a means of raising finance more cheaply than loan capital, especially as monetary policy resulted in very high interest rates over this period. As an added attraction of this form of capitalization to firms, most offerings ensured that major corporate owners of publicly floated projects still retained effective control. In the early 1990s, however, the stock market's fortunes fluctuated sharply. Share prices crashed in 1991, recording the steepest decline in the composite price index of any significant market in the world. The decline occurred partly as a correction to the euphoria generated in the previous two years. But lack of prudential supervision was a more important factor. Insider-trading and other market manipulations were revealed to be rife. Frequently, financial documentation of public companies was poorly prepared, inadequately audited and quite misleading. Chastened by these developments, and aided by improved—though still deficient— monitoring, the market recovered in 1993 and became somewhat less "casino-like" in its operation.

Poverty, Inequality and Social Progress

The previous chapters have assessed the New Order's record according to essentially economic criteria. It is important also to examine levels of and trends in a range of social indicators—poverty incidence, inequality, nutritional standards, wage levels, and standards of education and health. These are the focus of the four sections in this chapter. Social developments are important for at least three reasons. First, and obviously, they are the most tangible yardstick of the fruits of economic development. Improvements in economic indicators convey little meaning in the absence of these indicators. Improvements in economic measures, also, are pointless unless they are accompanied by commensurate improvements in the social field. Secondly, there is a clear and powerful nexus between the two series. Higher incomes provide the capacity for better nutrition and education, for example. Conversely, better standards of health, education, and nutrition are likely to result in higher productivity and efficiency. Thirdly, social advances contribute to community cohesion and harmony. Economic development is an inherently uneven and disruptive process. Traditional social organizations are uprooted and obligations weakened. Personal mobility and choices expand rapidly. In the process, some individuals (not to mention regions and ethnic groups) advance more quickly than others, while traditional supports—especially for the poor—may cease to be effective. Broad-based development is therefore essential if the process of national economic development is to proceed without interruption over a period of decades for a poor country such as Indonesia to ensure that all its people enjoy a decent standard of living.

There is a perception in some quarters that social development in Indonesia has lagged far behind economic development. While there are important instances where social progress has been rather slow, the major conclusion of this chapter is that, by and large, social indicators have kept pace with those in the economic realm. In this respect, Indonesia's record is consistent with that of East Asia, as the only region in the developing world to score well according to both criteria over a period of several decades (World Bank, 1993).

POVERTY AND INEQUALITY

Equality (*pemerataan*), and social justice more generally, has been one of the central objectives of the New Order regime, as enunciated for example in the *Trilogi Pembangunan*.[1] After the initial stabilization phase, this objective has been emphasized strongly, in each *Repelita* and in numerous presidential and other official statements. But in part because it has become almost a political slogan, "equality" has rarely been given a great deal of empirical content. For different groups and over different periods of time, the concept—not to mention the measures—has varied. For academics, the statisticians at BPS, and increasingly the government, "poverty" has been defined and analyzed as persons below variously defined poverty lines, while "distribution" has come to be measured by assorted indices of inequality. In the first decade of the regime, before the green revolution and the spending effects of the oil boom had a major impact, much of the discussion and analysis focused on rural areas, especially Java, where several detailed case studies pointed to a seemingly hopeless situation (see Chapter 7). Moreover, a recurrent distributional theme has been the regional dimension, as discussed in the next chapter: a few resource-rich provinces earning the lion's share of national exports and government revenues, especially during the oil boom. More recently that concern has focused on the underdeveloped and distant eastern provinces being bypassed by the rapidly growing western economy centred around Java and Sumatra. A final component has been the ethnic dimension, a recurring theme in modern Indonesian history. Anti-Chinese sentiment has simmered beneath the surface (see Chapter 6), often manifesting itself in boom periods such as the mid-1970s and early 1990s when Chinese corporate wealth became a topic of much public discussion.

Trends in poverty and equality are also of great analytical interest. Indonesia's record of poverty alleviation is regarded as an international success story. The country's progress has been praised by the World Bank,[2] apparently confirming its status as an aspiring member of the unique East Asian club. How has a regime, heavily managed politically, been able to deliver such an outcome? The good record is especially commendable, and puzzling, in view of the exogenous shocks experienced by the economy since the 1970s. The oil (and aid) booms of the 1970s placed enormous resources at the disposal of powerful individuals in a centralized and authoritarian political system, in which the poor rural constituency hardly appeared to have a voice. Conversely, the large and abrupt cutbacks in government expenditure during the mid-1980s might have been expected to bear more heavily on the poor.

Tables 10.1 to 10.3 provide a summary picture of trends in poverty and equality. The longer series on equality shows no significant change for the whole country over the 28-year period to 1993 (Table 10.1).[3] It is the relative constancy of this ratio which underpins the New Order's good equity record. The data suggest that there has been no fundamental change in the distribution of household expenditures. Expenditure shares since 1969 confirm this picture (Table 10.3). The share of the poorest group, by quintile or decile, has changed very little, apparently falling slightly in the late 1970s, but rising through the 1980s to a figure slightly higher than that of 1969/70. At the other end of the spectrum, there has been almost no change in the share of the high expenditure groups. Thus, if the data are correct, all groups have benefited in approximately equal measure, and rapid economic growth is the essential determinant of sharply falling poverty incidence.

There was an increase in the Gini ratio (Table 10.1)—hardly significant—in 1978, at the height of the oil boom, followed by a steady decline and levelling off through the 1980s. For all but the first two years inequality is lower in rural areas, a common pattern owing to the concentration of high income earners and spenders in cities. The urban ratio shows very little change over the whole period, peaking in 1978 at the height of the oil boom. In rural areas the ratio displays a continuous decline after 1978, more or less coinciding with the acceleration of rice production. By 1993 it

Table 10.1   **Trends in the Gini Ratio, 1964–65 to 1993[a]**

	Urban	*Rural*	*Total*
1964–65	0.34	0.35	0.35
1969–70	0.33	0.34	0.34
1976	0.35	0.31	0.34
1978	0.38	0.34	0.38
1980	0.36	0.31	0.34
1981	0.33	0.29	0.33
1984	0.32	0.28	0.33
1987	0.32	0.26	0.32
1990	0.34	0.25	0.32
1993	0.33	0.26	0.34

[a] Based on household expenditure data.

Sources: Unpublished BPS data for 1978–93, and Booth (1992, p. 335) for 1964–65 to 1976, based on *Susenas* data. I am most grateful to Dr Abuzar Asra for assistance in the preparation of this and following tables.

was very low. As a corollary, the incidence of poverty has fallen sharply: the *percentage* of the population in poverty in both rural and urban areas in 1993 was about one-third of that in 1976. The *numbers* in poverty approximately halved over this period, falling at a slower rate owing to population increase. In particular, rapid urbanization explains why the absolute numbers of urban poor were more or less equally numerous over this period, in spite of the sharp decline in percentage terms. Combining these figures with earlier poverty estimates (for example, as reported in Booth, 1992a, p. 343), Indonesia's record on poverty alleviation has been a resounding success.

The real success story appears to begin in the late 1970s. Critics of the regime's first decade conceded that there were significant output gains, but argued that distribution had deteriorated and poverty hardly abated. In the first decade of the New Order, the government's attention was focused heavily on economic stabilization and recovery, and the rehabilitation of physical infrastructure. This was also the period when the pace of technological change was particularly rapid, as traditional technologies began to disappear in the newly liberal economic environment (Chapter 2). One careful analysis of the expenditure data up to 1976 concluded that the picture was "a blurred and confused one", although "[t]he fruits of the rapid economic growth that has taken place in urban Indonesia ... have been unequally distributed among the urban population" (Booth and Sundrum, 1981, p. 214, 202). Other writers (for example, Dapice, 1980) argued that cautious conclusions of this genre were probably too optimistic and that some people were becoming worse off.[4] In addition, he emphasized a concern to which we return shortly, namely the increasing disparity between per capita expenditure as recorded by *Susenas*, and personal consumption expenditure as estimated in the national accounts; he also argued that the problem of understatement in the former series was becoming more serious. The despair of the 1960s, as reported for example by Penny and Singarimbun (1973), and the notion of a looming Malthusian catastrophe, were still fresh in observers' minds. Analysis of macro-level food supply and nutritional data, to be assessed in the next section, added to the pessimism.[5] Economists and anthropologists

Table 10.2   Trends in Poverty Incidence, 1976–93

Year	Numbers in poverty (millions)			% of Population		
	Urban	Rural	Total	Urban	Rural	Total
1976	10.0	44.2	54.2	38.8	40.4	40.1
1978	8.3	38.9	47.2	30.8	33.4	33.3
1980	9.5	32.8	42.3	29.0	28.4	28.6
1981	9.3	31.3	40.6	28.1	26.5	26.9
1984	9.3	25.7	35.0	23.1	21.2	21.6
1987	9.7	20.3	30.0	20.1	16.4	17.4
1990	9.4	17.8	27.2	16.8	14.3	15.1
1993	9.1	16.4	25.5	14.2	13.1	13.5

Source: BPS (1991), and as for Table 10.1.

Table 10.3   Expenditure Shares, 1969–93
(% of total)

	1969/70	1976	1978	1980	1981	1984	1987	1990	1993
Quintile									
1	7.5	8.0	7.3	7.7	8.3	8.0	9.2	8.9	8.9
2	11.5	11.5	10.8	11.8	12.2	12.8	11.7	12.4	11.5
3	15.9	16.0	14.8	16.0	15.6	15.3	15.6	16.2	15.5
4	22.5	22.0	36.5	22.2	21.8	22.0	21.8	20.6	21.4
5	42.6	42.5	45.3	42.3	42.1	42.0	41.7	42.0	42.8
Decile									
1	3.0	3.5	2.8	3.3	3.5	3.4	3.7	4.0	3.7
10	27.3	27.3	30.5	27.8	27.6	27.1	27.0	26.8	28.1

Note: Rankings are from the lowest (1) to highest (5 or 10) expenditure groups. The numbers refer to shares of each group in total expenditure.
Source: BPS, Statistik Indonesia, various issues, based on Susenas data.

over this period were also pointing to the labour-displacing effects of major changes in rice harvesting and processing technology, to institutional changes which were, purportedly, weakening traditional rural "safety nets" for the poor, and to the widespread incidence of *ijon* (indebted) labour. We also return to this issue shortly.

But the mood changed in the 1980s. Some of the pessimists of the 1970s now began to observe tightening rural labour markets and even rising real wages (see, for example, Collier et al., 1982), a trend unimaginable a decade earlier. The rice economy began to expand dramatically. Each new round of household expenditure survey data (the *Susenas*) reported significant declines in poverty incidence, even during the recession of the mid-1980s, and the figures were quickly and prominently reported in the press. Moreover, the conclusions appeared to be robust, as more sophisticated quantitative analyses all pointed in the same direction. For example, one detailed study concluded that:

> No matter where one draws the poverty line, or what poverty measures one uses (within a broad class), aggregate poverty (measured in terms of income) unambiguously fell between 1984 and 1987. (Ravallion and Huppi, 1991, p. 68)[6]

Table 10.4   **Estimates of Private Consumption, 1969–93**
(Rp billion)

	Susenas	National accounts	$\frac{(1)}{(2)} \times 100$
	(1)	*(2)*	*(3)*
1969/70	1,949	2,428	80.3
1976	7,223	10,500	68.8
1978	9,488	15,126	62.7
1980	14,814	25,595	58.6
1984	30,674	54,066	56.7
1987	44,617	71,988	62.0
1990	64,721	106,312	60.9
1993	98,015	175,078	56.0

Notes: Care should be taken in making the comparison. The *Susenas* have been undertaken at
   different periods of the year. For the first comparison, *Susenas* refers to the financial year
   1969/70, whereas the national accounts data refer to the calendar year. 1993 data are
   preliminary.
Source: BPS, *National Accounts; Pengeluaran Untuk Konsumsi Penduduk Indonesia;* and
   Statistik Indonesia, various years.

How robust are these data, and the conclusions that inequality has not worsened
and poverty incidence has fallen rapidly? They conflict with much popular sentiment,
and with some scientific assessment. At least five qualifications are variously attached
to these favourable conclusions. These caveats may dilute some of the strongest
assertions concerning poverty decline, but they do not invalidate the fundamental
proposition that the New Order's equity record is a comparatively good one.

First, the results depend crucially on a single data set, and one which is
increasingly politicized.[7] There is no independent verification of the data, nor are
there any databases of comparable complexity and sophistication against which the
results may be monitored. There is obvious under-reporting in the expenditure data
owing to the fluctuating but sizeable discrepancy between average expenditure from
the *Susenas* and per capita personal consumption expenditure from the national
accounts. As Table 10.4 shows, the apparent undercoverage of *Susenas* worsened
during the 1970s, before stabilizing in the 56 to 62 per cent range during the 1980s
and early 1990s. It is impossible to determine the impact of these errors and
omissions on the aggregate picture of inequality and poverty. No doubt there is
under-reporting at the top end, but such a phenomenon may also be under-reporting
across-the-board. It is important to emphasize also that BPS is a highly professional
statistical organization, and there has never been any allegation of systematic bias in
its distribution data. It is also accessible to serious researchers, even to the point of
making available lightly edited data tapes. Moreover, undercoverage is a general
phenomenon in these surveys, by no means confined to Indonesia. Nevertheless, the
data do underline the importance of interpreting the poverty and inequality series
cautiously.

Secondly, some rural researchers, mainly anthropologists, continue to report case
studies of immiserization. Indeed, one of the puzzles of the record since 1970 is that
the results of the macro (*Susenas*) data depict a positive picture of improvement,
while some of the micro studies continue to portray a much more gloomy story.[8]

According to these analyses, which focus almost entirely on rural Java, there has been increasing landlessness, a growing trend towards "exclusionary" labour contracts, the adoption of labour-saving technologies, the demise of traditional rural institutions which provided some protection for the very poor, and, for small farmers, unequal access to new technologies, credit, and government services. The results of these developments are seen as rising inequality, rural polarization, and possibly even increases in absolute poverty.

While the possibility of increasing rural poverty cannot be dismissed, especially in poorly endowed, bypassed regions, not all the rural research points in this direction. Much, though not all, of this research was conducted in the 1970s, before the strong growth in rice production and the vast improvements in rural infrastructure had an impact, and certainly well before the phase of labour-intensive industrialization. Some of the studies essentially provided snapshot pictures of rural poverty, although a number were based on intensive study over a period of time. By the late 1980s, a new series of intensive rural studies was emerging which challenged many of the findings of the pessimistic school. Several studies were particularly valuable in that they consisted of resurveys of villages first examined more than a decade ago, and in some instances more than two decades earlier. It is useful to briefly summarize some of the results.[9]

The principal studies are Edmundson (1994), Hardjono (1993), and Singarimbun (1990, 1993). Their research sites cover a wide geographic area—East and West Java and Yogyakarta respectively—and offer generally similar assessments. All conclude that there has been a general improvement in living standards, and few if any instances of rising impoverishment. They do, however, suggest that incomes have risen more slowly than those in urban areas, and that inequality may have risen. Singarimbun (1990, 1993) provides a very rich source of information in that he was able to resurvey the original village in Yogyakarta used in the Penny-Singarimbun research. He found that, over the 1972–89 period, average family income (in rice equivalent terms) had risen by about 37 per cent, and the percentage of the population who were "very poor" had declined from 44.3 per cent to 28.3 per cent. Hardjono's findings relate to a somewhat different time period (1982–93), and to a more industrialized village, south of the West Java capital, Bandung. But her conclusions are broadly consistent. Surveying earnings in agricultural activities and weaving, she found that "rice wages" (that is, earnings deflated by rice prices) rose in all cases, by about 50 per cent for unskilled factory workers and for hoeing, and about one-half of this rate for weeding.[10] Edmundson (1994) also provides a very detailed case study from a village in East Java surveyed on a number of occasions between 1971 and 1991. Although the sample size was necessarily small (46 individuals), the findings are similar to the first two studies. He too found a trend towards reduced inequality, with both rich and poor enjoying rising prosperity in most instances, but with the poor on average experiencing a more rapid rate of improvement.

As with the secondary data, the results of these micro studies have to be interpreted cautiously. The number of respondents is generally small, and specific local factors are present in all three field locations. But they are consistent both with the macro-level poverty data, with other social indicators to be surveyed shortly, and with the government's "pro-active" rural development strategies, including the rice success story from the late 1970s (Chapter 7). All three studies offer a sober assessment, of still very low incomes and widespread poverty, and of rates of improvement which are lagging behind the more dynamic urban areas. It is not surprising that living standards are rising more slowly in these villages, since the process of economic development entails the transfer of resources into higher productivity activities, many of which are urban-based. But viewed from the vantage point of the early 1990s, the gloomy prognostications of the 1970s literature do not appear to have eventuated.

The third point which needs to be stressed in evaluating the macro-level poverty and inequality data is that the latter refer only to household expenditure and, in some years, incomes. Other components of distribution are not considered. For example, there are no reliable estimates of the distribution of wealth in Indonesia. Agricultural wealth distribution is relatively even, with no clear trend towards rising inequality in land ownership or tenancy patterns, at least in the period between the agricultural censuses of 1973 and 1983 (Booth, 1988, pp. 52–60; Manning, 1988).[11] In non-agricultural sectors, wealth would almost certainly be more unequally distributed, especially with the rise of the commercial-industrial conglomerates in the 1980s.

A fourth qualification is that the incidence of poverty is obviously sensitive to the measure used. There is no consensus over the appropriate definition in Indonesia and elsewhere—on absolute or relative definitions, on rice-based or monetary measures, on ''objective'' or ''subjective'' concepts.[12] The most commonly used poverty lines in Indonesia are lower than many other countries, and alternative definitions have generated a considerable range of estimates.[13] Also, the figures above do not measure the intensity of poverty, merely assigning the population to groups of ''poor'' and ''non-poor''. The World Bank (1990) report on poverty addressed this issue, illustrating the sensitivity of the estimates to the threshold chosen. Many of the ''non-poor'' are, in reality, in the precarious ''near-poor'' position. Raising the poverty line by just 10 per cent, for example, increases the numbers in poverty by a similar percentage. Finally, there is debate over the desirability of region-specific poverty lines, disaggregated further into rural and urban areas (Bidani and Ravallion, 1993).[14] Nevertheless, as the quote from Ravallion and Huppi (1991) shows, and other writers have demonstrated, debate over poverty lines does not invalidate the fundamental conclusion of a significant decline, whatever index is used.

A fifth point to emphasize, especially important in the political context, is that perceptions often matter more than scientifically informed poverty measures. When President Soeharto invited 30 of Indonesia's most prominent businessmen—almost exclusively ethnic Chinese—to his Tapos ranch in March 1990, he was responding to a widespread public perception that non-*pribumi* business groups were benefiting disproportionately from the commercial boom which commenced in 1988 (on this point see Tjondronegoro, Soejono, and Hardjono, 1992). In fact, they may have been—although workers in manufacturing and banks and *pribumi* partners and senior managers have also benefited considerably. But the politics of envy often overrides careful economic analysis.

What factors explain Indonesia's comparatively good record on distribution and poverty alleviation since 1966? While it is not possible to offer precise empirical quantification, at least three appear to have been critically important. The first, the legacy of history, is that initial conditions were favourable. In the mid-1960s, there were no major concentrations of private wealth, either in agriculture or in the commercial-industrial sectors. The colonial era and the first 20 years of Independence did not witness the accumulation of vast, land-based rural agglomerations. Moreover, what there were—mainly foreign-owned estates—were run down and later nationalized over the 1958–65 period. Thus the commanding heights of the economy in 1965, such as they were, were almost entirely in the hands of the state. In this respect, Indonesia was quite unlike the Latin American countries or, closer to home, the Philippines and Malaysia, with their large concentrations of private agricultural wealth. It has much more in common with Taiwan and Korea, both noted for their even income distribution. Indonesia's experience therefore appears to provide empirical confirmation for the proposition that initial conditions play a key role in determining subsequent distributional outcomes, and that it is much more difficult to redistribute once the process of rapid economic growth has commenced.[15]

A second factor is that Indonesia's growth trajectory has been conducive to equitable outcomes, in at least two important respects. The strong performance of the rice sector has been the first of these. The food crop sector tends to be associated inherently with more even distributions of wealth and income, owing to the technologies employed, to cultivation practices, and to the predominance of smallholders. The contrast with cash crops, particularly the plantation sector, is clearly evident. And, as we have seen, there is no evidence that the green revolution has exacerbated rural inequalities, so that a buoyant rice sector has directly injected purchasing power into rural households, rich and poor alike.[16]

The other feature of Indonesia's post-1965 development with important employment and equity implications has been the growth of export-oriented, labour-intensive manufactures since the mid-1980s. Although criticized by some as a form of exploitation and "sweated labour", this growth path has been critical to the success of the Asian NIEs in achieving equitable growth (World Bank, 1993). For the poor, who by definition lack any form of capital, the surest means of raising their living standards is through enhancing their earning capacity. This entails, on the supply side, improving education and health standards, and on the demand side expanding employment opportunities. The most effective means of hastening the approach of the "turning point" in the labour market, when conditions of labour surplus begin to disappear, is such a labour-intensive strategy.[17] Here also, therefore, Indonesia shares common features with Japan, Taiwan and Thailand, all states with comparatively good equity records.

A third important factor has been public policy. The New Order regime has been criticized for paying insufficient attention to poverty and inequality. These criticisms are justified in a number of areas. There has never been a serious attempt to introduce a progressive structure of taxation. The politically powerful receive all manner of special privileges and perquisites, some quite blatant in nature. The poor, lacking any political power, have sometimes been treated shamelessly, such as in the relocation of urban squatters, or the eviction of tenant farmers from their land.

Conversely, some government policies have been pro-poor. The rice success story is an obvious example, as was more generally the government's capacity to channel a significant proportion of the windfall oil revenues into rural areas, including local development projects and employment-generation programs. The major emphasis on education, and greatly improved standards of basic literacy, is another important example. Large investments in infrastructure have assisted poor farmers, by reducing marketing margins and thereby achieving higher returns. Such a point is emphasized in the three-village study of Hayami and Kawagoe (1993). These investments have also facilitated personal mobility, enabling the poor to migrate more easily in search of better employment opportunities. Another factor, frequently overlooked, is that firm macroeconomic management has indirectly assisted the poor, since it is generally this group which is least able to protect itself from the ravages of high inflation. In addition, the government made a concerted effort to insulate poorer households during the difficult period of fiscal stabilization of the mid-1980s. In sum, therefore, while the record could have been much better, public policies have played a not insignificant role in poverty alleviation since the mid-1960s.

NUTRITIONAL STANDARDS

The above analysis has focused primarily on monetary measures of poverty and inequality. Trends in nutritional standards and food consumption patterns provide additional evidence on the record of social progress. There can be little doubt that nutritional standards among the poor were grossly inadequate in the mid-1960s, and that hunger was endemic and widespread. The following quote from a knowledgeable researcher at this time illustrates the gravity of the situation:

> *The greater parts of Java and Nusa Tenggara, accounting between them for 70 per cent of Indonesia's total population, must be regarded as malnutrition areas. The regions whose condition is fairly satisfactory are the minority, only 30 per cent. (Napitupulu, 1968, p. 69)*

Since then the situation has improved markedly, owing to rapidly rising incomes and the strong food crop performance. Nutritional intake has risen significantly, and changes in food consumption patterns bear all the hallmarks of increased incomes and a nascent middle class. The clearest indicator of these changes is rising food supplies. From the early 1960s to the late 1980s Indonesia's average per capita calorie and protein supplies have risen dramatically, by about 45 per cent and 50 per cent respectively (Table 10.5). In the early 1960s Indonesia's food supplies per capita were desperately low, the *national average* being actually lower than the minimum levels required for subsistence (see Note 5). Protein supplies were similarly low. Indonesia was also well below the developing country averages in most respects. By 1969–71 Indonesia was still below these averages in all cases. But there were evident improvements, especially in calorie supplies which had risen by over 11 per cent during this period. Presumably most of these increases were concentrated in the late 1960s, since rice production had fallen in some years earlier in the decade. The big improvements occurred mainly in the 1970s, coinciding with the expansion of the rice sector. Over this decade, calorie supplies rose by about 22 per cent, and Indonesia overtook the averages of both developing Asia and all developing countries. Average protein supplies also rose appreciably, although they were still behind the other two groups. These improvements continued through the 1980s, albeit at a slower pace.

Trends in the patterns of household expenditure and food consumption confirm this picture of improved nutrition (Tables 10.6 and 10.7). The proportion of household expenditure on food has fallen steadily since 1969–70, with most of the decline accounted for by the cereals and tubers group (Table 10.6). Correspondingly, the share of non-food items has risen, the sharpest increase being for housing and utilities. Within the food group, a number of important trends are discernible, again consistent with significant improvements in living standards (Table 10.7). Consumption of the preferred staples has risen appreciably. The increases were concentrated in the 1970s to some extent, especially for rice and wheat. This trend,

Table 10.5   **Trends in Food Supplies**

	1961–63	1969–71	1979–81	1988–90
Daily calories per capita				
Indonesia	1816	2019	2462	2605
Developing Asia	1825	2029	2245	2442
All developing countries	1940	2117	2324	2473
Daily protein per capita				
Indonesia	37.1	41.3	51.0	56.3
Developing Asia	46.1	49.1	53.3	59.2
All developing countries	49.7	52.4	56.3	60.6

Source: FAO, *1992 Production Yearbook*, 1993.

of a decelerating rate of increase observed in the 1980s, is likely to continue in the 1990s, to a point where income elasticities of demand approach zero, and may even become negative, for all but the poorest groups of society.[18] Such a trend is clearly evident in the case of the inferior staples, cassava and sweet potatoes. Per capita consumption of both of these items has declined steadily since the late 1960s. The largest increases are likely to occur in meat and dairy products, and to a lesser extent fruit, vegetables and fish, consumption of which has risen throughout the New Order period. Meat in particular is the converse of the rice story: apparent consumption barely rose in the 1970s, but it increased strongly in the 1980s as the size of the middle class expanded rapidly.

Thus the nutritional and food consumption data provide considerable empirical support for several of the propositions advanced in this book. They constitute an important and most tangible indicator of social progress over the course of the New Order. They are consistent with the favourable poverty and equity picture depicted in this chapter. This is because food consumption patterns are inherently more evenly distributed than those of both income and expenditure, especially so in the case of staples. The data are also consistent with the strong growth in incomes, manifested in declining consumption of inferior staples, and growth in the consumption of preferred staples and meat and fish. Of course, many challenges remain in this area. The incidence of malnutrition, both mild and severe, is still widespread, especially in poor rural communities and in some regions off-Java. There have been great improvements in calorie intake, but Indonesia's protein intake remains modest even by developing country standards. It is also possible that the food supply data in Table 10.5 overstate the increase since the 1960s.[19] Yet in spite of these caveats, the record remains a most impressive one.

TRENDS IN WAGES

Trends in wages are another indicator of economic welfare under the New Order, albeit one of limited import. About 40 per cent of the workforce are in regular wage employment, and so wage data do not necessarily tell us very much about earnings and welfare in the informal sector, in many agricultural and service activities, and in cottage industry. It is also very difficult to obtain reliable long-term wage data

Table 10.6   Household Expenditure Patterns, 1969–93
(% of total)

	1969/70	1976	1978	1980	1981	1984	1987	1990	1993
Food	77.2	73.8	68.1	69.3	61.5	63.2	61.3	60.4	56.9
Cereals and tubers	33.9	32.1	26.5	25.6	21.9	20.6	18.7	19.0	14.7
Prepared food	3.9	4.0	4.6	4.6	3.4	6.2	6.5	5.1	7.7
Non-food	22.8	26.2	32.0	30.7	38.5	36.8	38.7	39.6	43.1
Housing and utilities	8.2	10.1	13.6	12.2	14.4	17.4	17.1	16.2	18.0

Source: BPS, *Statistik Indonesia*, various issues, based on *Susenas* data.

Table 10.7   Trends in Food Consumption[a]
(kg/year)

	Rice	Maize	Wheat	Cassava	Sweet potatoes	Soy-beans	Pea-nuts	Sugar	Fruit	Vege-tables	Fish	Meat
1968–70	99.7	20.0	3.4	70.1	18.4	3.3	2.1	6.9	26.2	16.7	10.0	3.4
1978–80	122.4	23.4	6.5	63.3	13.6	4.8	2.9	10.6	27.1	15.6	11.3	3.5
1986–88	141.7	29.8	9.8	54.3	11.3	7.4	3.0	13.6	34.1	21.4	14.1	5.8

[a] Refers to annual human consumption.

Source: World Bank (1992, p. 15), based on FAO data.

which purport to measure the wage rates of the unskilled. Observed trends in real wages reflect not only the returns to unskilled labour but also occupational shifts, capital accumulation, changing skill composition, and the intensity (hours worked) and tenure of employment. Moreover, in labour surplus conditions, certainly an accurate characterization of Indonesia, one would not expect real wages for the unskilled to rise. There can be little doubt that Indonesia is still at least a decade or two away from the Lewis "turning point" when labour markets begin to tighten and broad-based real wage increases are experienced. Much of the emotive criticism of the New Order and the alleged "exploitation" of labour is based on a misunderstanding of the fundamental supply and demand determinants of wage trends.

Nevertheless, used carefully, wage data are at least a partial indicator of economic welfare. Wage series which focus on unskilled occupations and adjust for hours and conditions of work are a reasonably good indicator of the living conditions of poorer groups in the community. Moreover, annual series provide a more detailed and timely picture than the periodic *Susenas* surveys. The latter are conducted at intervals of two to three years, and some of the findings have been the subject of serious criticism, especially in the 1960s and 1970s. There may also be less under-reporting in the wage data. Therefore, notwithstanding the limitations alluded to above, they are worthy of examination as an additional dimension of the welfare picture. They also provide a vivid contrast with the situation before 1966. In comparing the periods before and after 1966, Papanek (1980b) points to the irony that the earlier regime espoused workers' rights and generally fostered trade union development, but almost certainly presided over a period of declining real wages. By contrast, the regime since 1966 has kept workers' associations closely in check, but workers' conditions have generally improved.

The following analysis focuses mainly on wage trends in the lower segment of the labour market. To the author's knowledge there are no detailed series on professional and managerial wages, which in any case are of little relevance to the issue of poverty. It is likely that wage inequality rose in the early years of the New Order, and again in the late 1980s, both periods in which skills were at a premium and attracted high scarcity rents. But with the partial exception of some intensive field research on intra-industry wage differentials (most notably by Manning, 1979), some surveys of elite managerial incomes (as for example reported in Chapter 6, Note 33), and some estimates of earnings by education (see Table 10.11), the database is too weak to support any detailed analysis of this phenomenon.

The first issue to address in the analysis of wage trends is the selection of wage series. A number of informative short-run series exist, but they provide at best a "snap-shot" picture of trends during the past quarter century. To obtain a longer run picture, therefore, it is necessary to examine those series which extend over at least 10 years, even if they do not always achieve high standards of consistency. Most of these series commence in the early 1970s. The database of the late 1960s is a good deal weaker, and in the high inflation period preceding it, monetary aggregates were extremely suspect.[20] For the purposes of analysis, six wage series are selected, two each from agriculture and industry, one from services (construction), and a low echelon civil service series (Figure 10.1). Within manufacturing, "textiles" (which includes textiles, garments, footwear and leather products) is selected as the major unskilled labour intensive industry. The civil service series—and to a lesser extent that of estates—is of course institutionally determined to a considerable degree. But it reflects government thinking on wage policy, and there are some spillover effects to the private sector. The rice and construction series are probably the best barometer of labour market conditions, in rural and urban areas respectively. The findings of the major recent studies of wage trends are used to supplement these data.[21]

Allowing for institutional factors, the series display a reasonably consistent and coherent picture. There is some growth of real wages during the 1970s, especially for civil servants, whose wages were still catching up from the steep declines experienced in the 1960s, and who were the direct beneficiaries of government's vastly enlarged fiscal coffers. But until the late 1970s the increases in other sectors were modest, particularly allowing for the fact that the biggest jump in manufacturing wages, in 1974, is probably the result of the change in coverage of firms. During the late 1970s and early 1980s, all series suggest an upward movement. From 1978 to 1983, for example, the respective increases for textiles, all-manufacturing, construction and estates workers were 37 per cent, 47 per cent, 39 per cent and 39 per cent. The increase for civil servants was less, in part because of the earlier significant increases and in part because of the government's more cautious fiscal approach during the second oil boom period. Rice wages rose more slowly although, unlike most of the other series, they continued to rise through to the mid-1980s; the increase from 1980 to 1986 (27 per cent) was not too far short of that of the other five.

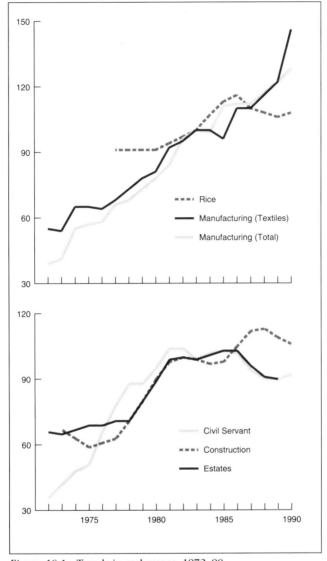

Figure 10.1   Trends in real wages, 1972–90

During the 1980s, also, the picture is one of broad consistency. Civil servants' wages dropped to levels of the late 1970s in response to fiscal austerity, including a freeze on wages in a number of budgets. Estates wages followed a broadly similar trend. Construction and textile wages also declined, marginally, in the mid-1980s. The former was most likely the direct consequence of the government's freeze on capital works projects, while in the latter case the industry was affected by the slowdown in domestic demand. For rice wages the decline occurred a little later, while for all-manufacturing there was virtually no decline, presumably because of compositional shifts in industrial structure. Then, towards the end of the decade, most series show a fairly flat trend, or at best a modest increase. The conclusion of Jones and Manning (1992, p. 379) therefore sums up the situation aptly:

> *Unskilled wage rates, particularly in rice and construction, stagnated for much of the 1970s but began to rise—quite sharply in some sectors such as manufacturing and estate agriculture—towards the end of the decade and in the early 1980s. They appear to have levelled off again, and in some cases declined from around the mid-1980s.*

All series show an increase over the longer period. All-manufacturing, textiles and the civil service were at the high end (with annual growth rates of 6.8 per cent, 5.6 per cent and 5.3 per cent, respectively), while rice, estates, and construction (1.3 per cent, 1.8 per cent and 2.7 per cent respectively) were a good deal lower. These conclusions are therefore broadly consistent with the positive picture of poverty alleviation and comparatively modest inequality depicted above. The workforce has undoubtedly benefited from the New Order's economic growth. Real wages may not have grown as fast as GDP, although in manufacturing and the civil service the overall rates of increase have been broadly comparable. There is no evidence of immiserization in agriculture or in the informal construction sector. Moreover, the improvement in welfare has been greater than that suggested in Figure 10.1 for at least two reasons: there have been structural shifts in employment, from insecure, casual employment to more permanent wage-labour in the formal sector; and the amount of available work has almost certainly risen, with the result that total earnings have increased faster than wage rates.[22]

A complete explanation of these trends is beyond the scope of this chapter. However, notwithstanding the data limitations, the trends do correspond to a *priori* expectations to a striking degree, and are consistent with the interplay between institutional and market factors in determining wage outcomes. Wages have expanded the most in the late 1960s, late 1970s/early 1980s, and again (at a more subdued rate) from the late 1980s. During periods of low growth, such as the mid-1980s, or periods of capital-intensive growth, such as the mid-1970s, the growth appears to have been much slower. Thus the "labour intensity of growth", to use Papanek's (1993) phrase, appears to have been crucial in poverty alleviation and wage growth. It seems clear that the strong growth in the rice sector—the largest source of employment for most of the New Order—had an immediate and direct bearing on the labour market, since with a minor lag the increase in rice wages coincided with the jump in production. The construction boom of the 1970s and late 1980s also appears to have had a direct impact on wages in that sector. In both these sectors, also, government public works programs may have had an additional impact on wages. In the case of public sector wages, there is a clear correlation between wage growth and the government's fiscal position. Trends in the manufacturing sector are somewhat more difficult to explain, but the stagnation in the mid-1980s is clearly associated with the recession over that period, and the limits to import substitution.

Several additional points need to be emphasized in this discussion of the wage data. First, the wage series demonstrate the importance of supply-side factors in hastening the process of structural adjustment in the economy. The shift from agriculture to the industrial and service sectors is commonly regarded as being mainly the result of demand-side factors (but see Martin and Warr, 1993). However, the much slower growth of agricultural wages has clearly been an additional, important factor in facilitating the intersectoral transfer of labour. Secondly, in addition to the caveats mentioned above, it needs to be stressed that the results are sensitive to the selection of wage deflators, particularly for the slow growth agricultural wage series. This comment applies especially to the 1980s, when rice prices increased more slowly than either the 1970s or the general cost of living indices. It may be appropriate to weight rice more heavily in the regimen of the rural poor, but the point remains that for these series it would be possible to generate a very flat series—and possibly even a decline—depending on the selection of deflator.[23]

Thirdly, it needs to be emphasized that the growing internationalization of the Indonesian economy will have important effects on the labour market. These effects, also, are too complex to discuss in this section in any detail. Export orientation will stimulate the demand for labour and hasten the approach of labour scarcity. But it will also place greater competitive pressures on the labour market, as Indonesian firms compete with those from China, Vietnam, and other low-wage countries. The net effects will undoubtedly be beneficial so long as the growth momentum is maintained, but they will pose considerable challenges in the area of labour relations. The situation in the 1990s and 1970s differs markedly in this respect. In the earlier period firms sold almost entirely in the highly protected and concentrated domestic market. They could thus afford to adopt a benign—indeed generous—approach to wage settlements, base rates of which were still low as a result of the decline in the 1950s and 1960s. In the 1990s, the discipline of export orientation is imposing a powerful constraint on such a cosy "compact", and it has been an important factor in the upsurge in industrial unrest (see Manning, 1993a).

An additional factor in this internationalization process is that Indonesian workers are seeking employment abroad on an unprecedented scale, with estimates that there may be up to one million currently overseas, principally in Malaysia. This process will also begin to have an effect on labour markets, both in increasing labour demand and in enhancing the acquisition of skills. Remittances are likely to become an increasingly significant factor in the Indonesian economy, as they have been since at least the 1970s in South Asia and the Philippines (Athukorala, 1993).

Finally, there is the issue of labour market regulation and policy. An important characteristic of Indonesian labour markets is that they appear to operate efficiently. Spatial barriers to mobility are increasingly unimportant, as information flows and the state of physical infrastructure continue to improve. Trade unions are politically weak and poorly organized, notwithstanding the recent upsurge in activity. Until recently also, government labour market regulations have not been onerous and enforcement is generally sporadic. Social barriers to employment are minimal.[24] Consequently, variations in wage levels between and within industries probably reflect differences in skill composition and capital intensity more than any other factors.[25]

The principal form of regulation has been through the direct mechanism of setting public sector salaries. As noted in Figure 10.1, these salaries rose rapidly in the 1970s but, except for the most recent budget, they have since stagnated, and the pace of manufacturing wage increases had caught up by the early 1990s. However, during 1993-94 the government appeared to signal a significant shift in labour policy, including a much more interventionist minimum wage strategy. At the end of 1993, the government announced that minimum wages in the Jabotabek area (Jakarta and surrounding districts) were to rise by over 40 per cent, with smaller increases elsewhere; enforcement was also to be more vigorous. The government took this decision in response to pressure both from at home and abroad: domestically, to deflect criticism that the primary beneficiaries of the post-1986 liberalization have been non-*pribumi* business conglomerates, and internationally in response to US criticism over labour rights and conditions, including the link to market access. There is an understandable desire to push up wages, for both social and political reasons, especially as Indonesian wages are a good deal lower than those elsewhere in ASEAN.[26] At low levels, also, there may be productivity-enhancing effects, particularly if some of the increase can be directed towards improved amenities such as medical, educational, or nutritional facilities. However, during the phase of labour surplus, what matters for the Indonesian workforce is a rise in the wages bill rather than in wage rates. There is a very real danger that a premature increase in wages will have adverse employment effects, both in deterring new investments and in encouraging existing firms to adopt more capital-intensive technologies.

EDUCATION AND HEALTH

The final set of social indicators are education and health achievements. These too are very important, both as a tangible manifestation of improved living standards, and owing to their ''interactive'' nature: better education standards are likely to contribute to improved health and nutrition, and so on. Levels of education and health generally improve over the course of economic development, but there is a special role for government here, on both equity and efficiency grounds. Especially for basic education and health programs, there are likely to be high social returns to investments, the impact of which will invariably be pro-poor. Governments also have a role in setting standards and otherwise regulating these industries. This section examines, in turn, the record on education and health, focusing on both achievements to date and major policy issues. These two sectors present contrasting case studies in the New Order's social achievements. The record in education is well documented, it is clearly a positive one, and public policy has generally been well directed. None of these propositions applies to the same extent to health, although there has been some progress in this area.

Tables 10.8 and 10.9 and Figure 10.2 provide an overview of educational achievement during the New Order period.[27] Enrolment ratios have risen considerably for all age groups since 1971 (Figure 10.2). The greatest increases have been concentrated in the youngest and oldest age groups, where in some cases there has been a doubling of ratios. Among the age groups broadly corresponding to senior primary school and junior secondary, the increases have been less. But they are still commonly of the order of 30 per cent or more. Reflecting the government's priorities, the sharpest increases in primary-age enrolments occurred in the 1971–80 period, and by 1990 near-universal enrolment had been achieved for the age groups eight to 11 years. In the 1980s, the emphasis shifted to secondary education, and the proportionate increases for teenagers in this decade were greater than that at the primary age-level.

Table 10.8 extends this analysis back to 1961 (probably a more accurate picture of the situation in 1965–66) and assesses also the gender gap in educational achievement. The percentage of the population in 1990 with no schooling was much smaller—a little over one-quarter of that in 1961. Correspondingly, the percentage with

Table 10.8   **Educational Attainment by Gender, 1961–90**

	Year	No schooling	Incomplete primary	Primary	Secondary	Tertiary
		Percentage of population with:				
Male	1961	55.7	22.6	16.7	4.8	0.2
	1971	32.4	29.4	27.1	10.4	0.7
	1980	21.8	35.9	25.5	15.9	0.9
	1990	12.2	24.3	32.2	29.2	2.1
Female	1961	79.6	11.2	7.3	1.9	n
	1971	57.0	21.2	16.5	5.1	0.2
	1980	41.4	30.4	18.8	9.1	0.3
	1990	25.4	24.9	28.1	20.6	1.0
Total	1961	68.1	16.7	11.8	3.3	0.1
	1971	45.2	25.1	21.6	7.7	0.4
	1980	31.9	33.1	22.1	12.4	0.6
	1990	18.9	24.6	30.1	24.8	1.6

n = negligible.

Notes: Primary, secondary and tertiary data refer to completed education at that level. Secondary includes both upper and lower levels. Tertiary includes both universities and academy. Data refer to the population aged 15 years and above.
Source: The original source is BPS, *Sensus Penduduk*, 1961, 1971, 1980 and 1990. The data for 1961, 1971, and 1980 are reported in Hugo et al., 1987, p. 282. I am indebted to Gavin Jones and Pat Quiggan for providing the 1990 data.

completed primary and secondary schooling has risen sharply, by 150 per cent and 650 per cent respectively. The tertiary educated population has risen faster still, from the minuscule proportions of the 1960s. Male education achievement is higher than that of females. But the gender gap is comparatively modest by the standards of developing countries, and it appears to be narrowing. The proportion of primary educated males was 2.3 times that of females in 1961, but by 1990 it was just 15 per cent higher. Similarly, the secondary educated male advantage has fallen from 150 per cent to 40 per cent over the same period. The gap does widen at higher levels of education, but here also appears to be narrowing over time. Only for the "no schooling" category are females recorded as being seriously disadvantaged, much of it a reflection of past educational shortcomings.[28] These educational advances are reflected in steadily rising literacy rates (Table 10.9). The marked differences by age group are yet another indication of educational progress. Literacy rates fell sharply by age group in 1971, and even in 1980, so that in both years the rates for the 15 to 24 age group were more than double those of their parents' generation. By 1990 the educational progress under the New Order was beginning to have an impact on all groups. There was near-universal literacy for the youngest age group, and the figure was above 70 per cent for all but the oldest group.

How does Indonesia's record of education and science compare internationally? In its literacy rate and educational enrolment ratios it is broadly comparable with neighbouring countries, after adjusting for per capita incomes and "educational history" (Table 10.10). Its illiteracy rate in 1990 was actually lower than that of Malaysia, but much higher than Korea, the Philippines or Thailand. Its primary enrolment ratios were higher, a reflection of its catch-up phase and of over-age

Table 10.9 **Literacy Rates by Age Group, 1971–90**
(% of each age group)

Age	1971	1980	1990
15–24	80.1	85.4	94.7
25–34	61.9	77.7	89.0
35–44	47.8	62.0	70.9
45+	31.1	39.7	58.0

Source: The original source is BPS, *Sensus Penduduk*, 1971, 1980, 1990. I am indebted to Gavin Jones and Pat Quiggan for providing these data.

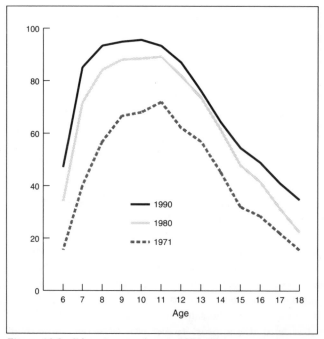

Figure 10.2 Education enrolment, 1971–90

children attending these schools. However, its secondary rates were still substantially lower than the others, with the surprising exception of Thailand, and its tertiary rates were almost the lowest. Indonesia appears to spend a good deal less on education than the other countries. As a percentage of GNP, public expenditure in 1990 was by far the lowest—less than one-third of the figure for the next lowest country, the Philippines, and just one-sixth of that of Malaysia. In its budgetary allocation, also, Indonesia is by far the lowest in the group. Moreover, education in Indonesia appears to have received a lower priority around 1990 as compared with 1975. In all the other countries, by contrast, the educational expenditure percentages either rose or were largely stationary over this period. It is possible that these figures understate Indonesia's educational effort.[29] But it is still striking that, when the country aspires to "near-NIE" status, education expenditure as a share of total government outlays appears to be just one-quarter and one-fifth of that of Malaysia and Korea, respectively.

According to indicators of advanced education and R&D, also, Indonesia is generally behind the other countries in the comparison. Its tertiary education resources appear to be devoted disproportionately to the humanities, with one-half of the students taking courses in this area, as compared with a more common figure of one-third (except for Malaysia, the figures for which do not include the very large numbers of students abroad). Enrolments in the sciences and commerce are, correspondingly, a good deal lower. The Indonesian figures are now rather dated, but it is unlikely that the percentages have changed markedly since 1984. In the case of R&D, and notwithstanding the much publicized efforts of Minister Habibie, in the late 1980s Indonesia's expenditures were not notably superior to those of its ASEAN neighbours, although there may have been a somewhat greater concentration of resources than in the Philippines and Thailand. Here also the comparison with Korea, commonly regarded as a model for Indonesia's industry and technology policy, is salutary.

There can be little doubt that the private returns to schooling are significant. Average monthly earnings of the educated, especially the highly educated, are very high compared with those with little or no education (Table 10.11). These earnings rise monotonically with educational attainment in all four years for which data are available. The biggest incremental increase, not surprisingly, occurs between those with no schooling and primary education, and between the secondary and tertiary educated. It is clear, however, that the general rise in educational standards is compressing these differentials. In the mid-1970s the premium attached to tertiary education was very large indeed, with the tertiary educated earning more than nine times that of the no-schooling group and more than four times that of the primary educated. Both supply and demand-side factors contributed to this outcome. This was the peak of the oil boom period, when the demand for skilled labour was acute. However, reflecting underinvestment from previous generations, the supply of highly skilled labour was very limited, in addition to which employment of expatriates was severely restricted. Moreover, wages in the public sector, which as we saw in Chapter 6 is a major employer of skilled labour, were rising rapidly and probably reached their peak in terms of public-private wage relativities over this period. For all these reasons, this group was able to command scarcity rents on a scale unlike that of any generation of tertiary educated Indonesians before (and most probably after) them. The value of these rents declined steadily during the 1980s, and by 1990 the differentials were less than one-half of those of 1977. The differential for high school graduates was always much lower, and it too fell throughout the period.

These figures are suggestive, albeit very crudely, of the high returns to education in Indonesia since the 1960s. The data are too aggregated to provide a detailed picture. For one thing, it would be necessary to break down the tertiary group by discipline and educational institution. The returns for the graduates of marketable disciplines such as commerce and engineering, and of the elite universities, would be very much higher. Indeed, contrary to the picture presented in Table 10.11, the differential for this group may have actually widened in the early 1990s, when the financial boom in the private sector led to an acute skills shortage in certain areas, and to salaries which are high even by Southeast Asian standards.

For another thing, the returns to education need to standardize for several additional variables which affect income. A number of studies have estimated returns to education in Indonesia employing a Mincer-type earnings function which attributes earnings to education, along with other variables such as experience and gender.[30]

Table 10.10 **Comparative Education and Scientific Indicators**

	Indonesia	Malaysia	Philippines	Thailand	Korea
Illiterate, %, 1990[a]	18.4	21.6	6.4	7.0	3.7
Enrolment, %, 1991[b]					
Primary	116	93	110	113	107
Secondary	45	58	74	33	88
Tertiary	10	7	28	16	40
Public education expenditure[c]					
as % of GNP					
1975	2.7	6.0	1.9	3.5	2.2
1990	0.9[d]	5.5	2.9	3.8	3.6
as % of budget					
1975	13.1	19.3	11.4	21.0	13.9
1990	4.3[d]	18.3	10.1	20.0	22.4
Tertiary students by field of study (%)					
Humanities[e]	49.7	41.7	27.9	29.1	32.1
Sciences	18.2	28.1	21.3	18.3	35.2
Commerce	13.9	21.5	21.6	29.9	16.0
(year)	(1984)	(1990)	(1991)	(1989)	(1990)
R&D personnel per					
million population[f]	181	327	90	104	1,343
(year)	(1988)	(1988)	(1984)	(1987)	(1988)
R&D expenditure, % of GNP	0.2	0.1	0.1	0.2	1.9
(year)	(1988)	(1989)	(1984)	(1987)	(1988)

[a] % of population aged 15 years and above.
[b] Enrolments as a percentage of the relevant age group.
[c] Indonesian data for 1990 refer to 1988.
[d] In this year, data refer only to expenditure by the Department of Education and Culture.
[e] Includes teacher training and social–political science.
[f] Refers to scientists and engineers engaged in R&D, per one million population.

Source: United Nations Educational, Scientific and Cultural Organization (UNESCO), *Statistical Yearbook 1993*, and earlier editions. Enrolment data are from World Bank, *World Development Report 1994.*

These studies generally find high rates of return, much higher than the typical benchmark figure used for project evaluation. Figures in the 15 to 25 per cent range are not uncommon, and reflecting past underinvestments, the rates for Indonesia are often higher than the typical developing country figures. In most cases the returns are highest at lower levels of education, after which they fall steadily. Social returns are usually lower, since the private returns include educational subsidies. However, the social returns may be higher than those calculated to the extent that the studies do not capture the externalities resulting from a better educated community. Conversely, some of the earlier very high figures have been questioned by Behrman and Deolalikar (1993), whose analysis it should be noted is based on data from the recession year of 1986. They argued that these figures were inflated by a failure to control for "unobserved" household and community variables, such as schooling quality, ability, and motivation. According to their estimates, private and social rates of return on education are still acceptably high, but lower than most of the earlier figures.

Indonesia's education policy-makers face many challenges in the 1990s and beyond. Near-universal primary school education enrolments have been achieved. The next

Table 10.11   **Average Monthly Earnings by Education, 1977–90**
(Index: no schooling = 100)

	1977	*1982*	*1986*	*1990*
Primary	225	190	174	151
Junior High	333	285	259	236
Senior High	341	349	338	281
Junior Diploma		n.a.	342	304
Senior Diploma	} 963	491	455	456
University		578	580	501

n.a. not available.

Notes: Categories refer to completed schooling levels. The Junior and Senior High School data refer to the General streams.
Sources: Data are from BPS, *Sakernas* 1977, 1986 and 1990; and *Susenas* 1982. I am indebted to Chris Manning and Abrar Yusuf for supplying these data.

step in the government's quantitative agenda, that of universal junior secondary school attendance by the end of the *Repelita* VI (1999) appears to be well on schedule. By the end of the decade, with population growth slowing and basic educational objectives fulfilled, at least quantitatively, the major emphasis will be on quality, together with issues of public sector funding, and of targeted and effective intervention. The issue of aggregate public sector funding is in one sense relatively straightforward. Even allowing for possible understatement in the comparative data, and for a more sober assessment of the returns to educational investment, Indonesia's public expenditure figures appear very low. Labour market bottlenecks have become serious since the late 1980s, contributing to slower growth, and requiring firms to recruit on the expensive international labour market for skilled labour. Middle-level technical labour, a key ingredient in rapid industrialization, has also been in short supply. Therefore, through whatever means possible, the case for raising public sector educational expenditure is a strong one.

In addition, however, the reform agenda is a very large one. One issue concerns targeting particular areas of disadvantage, both in terms of funding and tailoring specific programs. The government has been quite successful in this respect in the past, particularly through its emphasis on primary education (van de Walle, 1992). However, there remain particular pockets of disadvantage, notably in gender achievement (despite the improvements to date), and in more remote rural areas. Owing to the distances involved, these problems are more serious in regions off-Java, including Kalimantan and much of Eastern Indonesia. Some of the latter provinces historically enjoyed quite high standards of education, partly owing to the role of mission education (Jones, 1976), but they have fallen behind with the general growth of the education system since 1970, and now no longer possess any advantage. Dropout rates are also higher among poorer socioeconomic groups, owing to the relatively higher costs of foregone earnings in remaining in school.

It is generally recognized that school resources, curricula, and educational instruction methods are also in need of reform. Most surveys of educational resources point to excessively high pupil-teacher ratios, especially for public schools in more remote regions. They also find that supplementary resources are very limited, including libraries, computer equipment, and science laboratories. Moreover, teaching methods emphasize rote learning, at the expense of individual inquiry and initiative; "curiosity-led" educational techniques are rarely employed. Teachers' salaries are so low that moonlighting is essential, and there is little opportunity for upgrading and refresher programs. Considerable research has been undertaken into the system of higher education,[31] where many of these problems are evident. Academic salaries are very low. There is inadequate recognition of research achievements. Most of the interface with students, in teaching and assessment, is undertaken by inexperienced junior staff. Promotion is based mainly on seniority, and there is little mobility between institutions. Except at the most prestigious institutions, the educational background of teaching staff is rather weak, with as little as 5 per cent of those in public universities possessing a PhD (known in Indonesia as an S3) degree or its equivalent. As noted above (see also World Bank, 1991), vocational and technical areas of education have received little priority, with the result that employers usually discount scientific qualifications from Indonesian universities.

With the government unable to keep pace with the demand for education, the private sector has been the major source of growth. There are, for example, approximately 1,000 private institutions of higher education, in number and in enrolments now exceeding those in the government system. In many instances, private institutions have proved to be much more adept at responding to the demand, especially in the provision of sought-after and marketable qualifications.[32] The government has, however, displayed a certain ambivalence towards this sector, on the one hand recognizing its inevitability, but on the other failing to provide any clear guidance, much less assistance. In some cases there is suspicion that the private sector represents bastions of Christian, non-*pribumi* privilege, or oppositional Islamic politics. Whatever the motive, the government has been slow to provide accreditation to these institutions, it has hindered their capacity to recruit badly needed teaching staff from abroad, and it has failed to reform cumbersome procedures for assessment. Ironically, these problems have arisen even when the private institutions are demonstrably superior to most government universities, and often when the major teaching services are provided by government university lecturers.

The record on health reveals much slower progress. It also appears that public expenditure has been less effectively focused and less pro-poor and pro-rural than that of education.[33] Health indicators have improved considerably, but no faster than would be expected on the basis of rising incomes, greatly improved nutrition, and the wider availability of medicines. Indeed, according to one very widely used indicator, the infant mortality rate (IMR), the progress since the 1960s has been rather slow and, especially in the 1980s, a matter of some controversy. IMRs were estimated to be about 130 per 1,000 live births in the late 1960s (Table 10.12). According to these estimates, they fell gradually through to the late 1970s, followed by a sharp decline over the next five years, to be around 70 in 1982-83. In fact it is almost certain that the decline in the latter period was overstated, and the figure reported in the late 1980s, also around 70, is a more accurate estimate. The figure for rural areas has been consistently higher than urban areas, by some 30 to 40 per cent, but it has declined at about the same rate. The recorded decrease represents a considerable decline, but no faster than that of other countries (Table 1.3, p. 6). Indeed, infant mortality is one of the few areas where Indonesia's comparative record is not particularly impressive, both in its current level and its rate of decline over the

Table 10.12   **Estimates of Infant Mortality Rates**[a]

Source	Reference period	Total	Urban	Rural
1971 Census	late 1960s	132	104	137
1976 Survey	early 1970s	110	95	113
1980 Census	late 1970s	112	88	112
1985 Survey	early 1980s	71	57	74
1990 Census	late 1980s	69	52	77

[a] Data refer to deaths of infants up to age 12 months per 1,000 live births.

Sources: Hull (1994, Table 3.5) for late 1980s; World Bank (1990, p. 87) for remaining estimates.

past quarter-century. There are moreover serious regional imbalances, with some of the poorer provinces, notably West Nusa Tenggara, recording levels up to twice the national average (see Chapter 11).

These problems have been compounded by three additional factors. First, there was a decline in public health expenditures during the 1980s. Corner and Rahardjo (1993, pp. 5–6), citing World Bank research, show that government spending on health in the late 1980s was very low, both as a percentage of the budget and of GDP. As with education also, these percentages declined through the decade. The utilization of health services was also low by international standards: Indonesia has only 0.6 hospital beds per 1,000 population, which is low by any international standard, and about one-quarter of the ASEAN ratio. Secondly, the government has been rather late in adopting preventative health measures. In 1987, for example, some 47 per cent of the population had never been immunized. There were in addition clear socioeconomic correlates in this case, since 58 per cent of the rural poor had never been immunized, as compared with 26 per cent of the urban non-poor (World Bank, 1990, p. 90). Finally, and contrary to the case of education, public funds are not well targeted. Public funding of hospitals absorbs a large proportion of the health budget, much larger for example than rural health centres and services. Yet hospital services are used overwhelmingly by the better off. Hospital admission rates for the urban non-poor are some five times those of the rural poor, although the same disparity is not so evident in the case of outpatient services.

The policy agenda for health, as with education, is therefore a large one. More public funds are required. More emphasis needs to be placed on preventative medicine, especially in rural areas. The problem of high infant mortality needs to be tackled more vigorously, combining elements of an improved public health system with better sanitation and water quality, and possibly also more attention to parental education. There is also much scope for more effective targeting of public funds, including especially a needs-based system of charging for public hospitals.

The Regional Dimension: Patterns and Issues

THE IMPORTANCE OF THE REGION IN INDONESIA

In most country studies, the regional dimensions of economic development would hardly deserve serious attention. Most of East Asia's success stories have been small, compact nation states, indeed city-states in two cases. In large high-income countries such as the US and Australia, regional differences are evident. Nevertheless, internal economic integration is generally highly developed owing to efficient infrastructure services, and regional income differentials are ameliorated by long-established fiscal equalization mechanisms.

In Indonesia, however, as in other giants of the Third World, such as Brazil, China, and India, the *daerah* (region) has always been a major preoccupation. No country arguably is as diverse as Indonesia in its ecology, demography, economy and culture. Certainly no other country resembles Indonesia in its unique geography as the world's largest archipelagic state. The nation's motto, *Bhinneka Tunggal Ika*, freely translated as "Unity in Diversity", symbolizes the importance attached to the achievement of national unity, while recognizing regional diversity. National unity was a central component of the Independence struggle, and it has been accorded the highest priority by all regimes since 1945.

The colonial administration exacerbated regional differentials through the promotion of a highly uneven development strategy focusing on intensive agricultural development of Java and the development of extractive enclaves, centred mainly on plantations and petroleum, off-Java. Post-independence governments have been grappling with the daunting challenges of establishing central authority throughout the archipelago and of ensuring reasonably uniform development patterns for cosmopolitan urban dwellers and traditional, isolated shifting cultivators alike. The national integrity of the country was challenged in the regional revolts of 1957–78, when disaffection with rule from Jakarta, and more generally Java, manifested itself in open revolt in parts of Sumatra, Kalimantan, and Sulawesi. Although these revolts were put down relatively quickly, and political control from the centre was firmly established in most regions by 1960 (Mackie, 1980), regional economic integration during the first quarter-century of Independence was quite limited. It is perhaps no exaggeration to state that Indonesia has only become a national *economic* entity since 1970. Smuggling and the evasion of Jakarta's controls were rampant in the 1950s and early 1960s. Indeed, some regions, notably the east coast of Sumatra, were more strongly integrated with the economies of Malaysia and Singapore.[1] Regional price variations were large, even for basic goods such as rice. Labour mobility was constrained by the poor state of physical infrastructure. The financially crippled central government lacked the capacity to undertake the task of nation-building. Information flows were weak.[2]

By contrast, regional development has, by and large, been one of the success stories of the New Order regime. Aided by the oil bonanza and by large inflows of aid, there have been vast investments in transport facilities, communications, and other physical infrastructure. Many of the barriers to regional commerce have been largely overcome. People and goods move around the archipelago as never before. It is possible, for example, to travel by bus from the northern tip of Sumatra to Java, Bali, Lombok, and beyond with the aid of vehicular ferry. All the provincial capitals and most other significant urban centres can be reached by air in one day from Jakarta. Such achievements would have seemed incomprehensible in the mid-1960s. The major barriers to integration are now primarily intra- rather than interregional in nature, especially in the hinterlands of Kalimantan, Sulawesi and Irian Jaya.

Notwithstanding these achievements, the topic of regional development is important principally because of the persistence of extraordinary diversity. In 1990 the per capita regional product of the richest province (East Kalimantan) was some 16 times that of the poorest (East Nusa Tenggara). Even removing the oil and gas sector, the differentials are very considerable. The population density of the province (or, more formally, the Special Region) of Yogyakarta was over 900 persons per square kilometre in 1990, and in some densely populated rural areas of Java the figure exceeds 1,000 persons. In remote Irian Jaya, by contrast, the corresponding figure is four, while in two of the provinces of Kalimantan it is nine. During the peak of the oil boom, to give another illustration of the uneven distribution of factor endowments, two of the nation's 27 provinces generated over 60 per cent of merchandise exports. According to social indicators, also, the differences persist. The infant mortality rate in the province of West Nusa Tenggara is some four times that of Jakarta. Per capita tertiary enrolments in the major educational centres of Jakarta and Yogyakarta are about eight times those of a number of provinces off-Java.

The regional issue is important for a number of other reasons. One is political. Along with ethnicity, no issue is politically more sensitive in Indonesia than the inviolability of the nation state. Although rarely discussed in such terms, Indonesia faces major challenges in an era when nation states are crumbling and regional sentiment is becoming ever more assertive.[3] Some of the problems arise from the highly uneven distribution of natural resources and of the requirement that revenue from these natural resources accrues almost entirely to the nation as a whole rather than to subnational units. Thus there is, not surprisingly, dissatisfaction in the mineral-rich provinces of Irian Jaya, Aceh, East Kalimantan, and Riau: natural resource rents accrue to foreign or state-owned companies, inexperienced domestic businesses are often pushed aside by national companies in bidding for large development projects, and despite the apparent affluence, as measured by average per capita incomes, social indicators are often quite poor. Another layer of discontent arises primarily from historical factors. Two provinces, Irian Jaya and East Timor, were incorporated after Independence, in controversial circumstances never fully accepted by important sections of the local community. Another, Aceh, has a long history of resistance to any form of external authority. Most of the centres of disaffection are distant from, and feel neglected by, Jakarta. The issue is further complicated by the fact that in at least two of them, Aceh and Irian Jaya, both sources of disaffection—the historical legacy and the presence of enclave mining activities—have been at work.

The third reason the region is particularly important in contemporary Indonesia has to do with spatial dynamics. For much of Indonesia's history, the regional problem has been seen primarily as one of the extreme imbalance between Java, with about 60 per cent of the nation's population crowded onto a little over 6 per cent of its land area, and the rest of the country. As noted earlier, there was a sense of Malthusian despair which permeated much of the literature on the island's socioeconomic conditions and prospects. Especially in the densely populated central districts, none of the usual palliatives—off-farm employment, agricultural intensification, reduced fertility and out-migration—were seen then to be sufficient to overcome the gloomy "economic arithmetic" advanced by Penny and Singarimbun (1973) and others. By contrast, the prospects of the so-called Outer Islands were viewed much more favourably, if only because of their superior land/labour ratios. Social indicators may not have been much better and there was little industrialization. But extensive agricultural growth remained an option because in many areas the land frontier had not been reached.

By the 1990s the regional problem manifested itself in quite different forms. As we shall see shortly, the economy of Java–Bali performed creditably during much of the New Order, and such growth was accompanied by a dramatic improvement in social indicators. Propelled by the new export-oriented growth industries, labour-intensive manufactures and tourism, the future of this regional economy now seems much rosier than that of the poorer provinces in Eastern Indonesia. The latter, traditionally poor, distant and neglected, have been growing more slowly than the richer provinces to the west. Consequently, as emphasized in the President's 1990 budget speech, the major regional challenge facing the nation is now the gap between east and west.

More generally, an understanding of the dynamics of the regional component enriches our understanding of the development process in Indonesia. Indonesia is the sum of its 27 provinces for the purposes of statistical compilation. But it is much more than this. The major parameters at the national level—exchange rate policy, macroeconomic management, social and physical infrastructure development—determine the overall course of development. Yet their impact at the local level varies. Even in such a centralized system of government, there is a capacity for autonomous growth, building on local comparative advantage, a propensity to extract concessions from the centre, the quality of local government, and perhaps a measure of good luck. These local factors will inevitably become more significant as the fiscal and administrative power of the central government recedes.

Related to these regional dynamics is a fourth factor which underlines the importance of the issue. Namely, how should regional relations be managed? How much decentralization should there be, consistent with the overriding objective of preserving national unity and integrity? According to one persuasive school of thought, there is the argument that "[a]rchipelagic in geography, eclectic in civilization, and heterogeneous in culture, [Indonesia] flourishes when it accepts and capitalizes on its diversity and disintegrates when it denies and suppresses it" (Geertz, 1971, p. 19). Yet Indonesia has a strongly centralized system of government. There are deep-seated and widely held fears that in such a diverse country still only 50 years old, decentralization could lead to unacceptable regional inequalities, a splintering of the national socioeconomic fabric, and possibly even the break-up of the modern Indonesian nation state.

There was, moreover, a case for the adoption of a highly centralized mode of governance in the late 1960s. There was such a backlog in the development of physical infrastructure that national coordination and supervision was required. Regional administrative and absorptive capacities were very weak, especially off-Java. Indonesia quickly had to develop structures to utilize very large amounts of foreign aid, within a nationally coherent framework. The country was buffeted by powerful centrifugal forces, such as the oil boom and the development of other resource-based enclaves off-Java. By the late 1980s, however, a new set of regional policy issues had emerged. In an era of low oil prices, the central government did not have the capacity to fund regional development on the extravagant scale of the oil boom decade. Local, region-specific factors became much more important determinants of provincial performance. At the same time, another of the key rationales for highly centralized development policy, namely weak administrative capacity in the regions, was now much less important. Provincial and even subprovincial government agencies are now relatively well-staffed, partly owing to a conscious effort to upgrade the local planning agencies (the *Bappeda*). It is a measure of the complexity of the issue, both in its political and technical dimensions, that initiatives to promote the devolution of economic and administrative authority have been so long under discussion but so slow to be implemented. A major regional policy package has been under consideration since at least 1987 but, by late 1993, very little of substance had been announced. We return to this issue later in the chapter.

Two additional points need to be stressed at the outset of this chapter. First, the regional database, which barely existed up to 1970, is much improved and is now quite sophisticated. Comprehensive regional accounts are prepared, in addition to a wide range of financial, production and demographic data. Indonesia now has one of the best sets of regional socioeconomic statistics of any developing country. This makes the task of analyzing regional development issues and canvassing alternative policy approaches much easier.

Secondly, however, although these data are generally compiled on a provincial basis, "region" and province are not necessarily synonymous. For some issues several provinces may be grouped together. If the focus is high population density, for example, the appropriate unit of analysis is Java–Bali. Aceh, Riau and East Kalimantan all face common problems associated with the presence of rich mining enclaves. For Maluku and East Nusa Tenggara it is distance from Jakarta and major centres of commerce, while for Central Kalimantan and Central Sulawesi it is physical infrastructure and access to major markets. In other cases, regional issues manifest themselves at the subprovincial level. In West Java there are sharp differences between the rapidly industrializing north, more an extension of the Jakarta economy, and the lagging south. The economy of the island of Batam is becoming ever more closely enmeshed with that of Singapore, and its major development challenges are quite unlike those of the rest of the province of Riau on the main island of Sumatra. In North Sumatra there is a marked cleavage between Medan, Asahan and the plantation economy, and much of the rest of the province. The data do not always correspond to these and many other regional, subprovincial divides, but it is important to be sensitive to them.

Table 11.1   Indicators of Regional Development: Economic

	GRP 1990 Rp billion	GRP per capita, 1990 RP '000	GRP per capita, real growth 1973-90 (%)	Net exports as % of GRP,[a] 1989	% of Exports[b] 1976	% of Exports[b] 1991	% of Foreign Investment,[c] 1967-92	% of Domestic investment, 1968-92[x]	Relative prices 1991,[d] (average = 100)	Bank deposits as % of GRP, 1990[e2]
	(1)	(2)	(3)	(4)	(5)	(6)	(7)	(8)	(9)	(10)
Sumatra										
Aceh	8,290	2,448	12.5	66.8	0.2	10.7	1.9	1.6	87	4
excl. oil	2,897	737	6.4							13
North Sumatra	10,833	1,063	5.3	10.3	7.1	6.1	7.4	3.1	95	24
West Sumatra	3,297	829	7.1	19.9	0.7	0.7	0.1	0.8	79	16
Riau	13,231	4,493	-3.2	48.8	43.2	17.3	5.0	7.1	123	5
excl. oil	2,672	907	3.4							22
Jambi	1,414	709	3.3	20.0	0.8	0.9	—	1.5	79	17
South Sumatra	8,268	1,304	3.4	9.5	4.4	2.4	2.2	2.6	97	18
Bengkulu	795	684	7.2	-13.8	—	—	0.1	0.3	92	12
Lampung	3,217	540	2.5	19.8	1.5	1.2	1.1	1.6	94	15
Java-Bali										
Jakarta	22,855	2,481	5.9	71.2	11.2	26.1	28.5	8.9	99	245
West Java	31,358	917	5.5	18.8	1.8	0.9	30.3	35.8	87	19
Central Java	21,689	673	6.0	9.6	0.7	2.5	4.2	7.7	93	14
Yogyakarta	1,901	654	4.2	-28.1	—	—	0.1	0.6	83	33
East Java	29,161	769	5.8	2.7	1.6	7.9	6.0	9.2	73	21
Bali	3,018	1,090	8.0	-1.1	0.1	0.6	4.0	2.6	101	33

Table 11.1 Continued

	GRP, 1990 Rp billion	GRP per capita, 1990 RP '000	GRP per capita, real growth 1973–90 (%)	Net exports as % of GRP,[a] 1989	% of Exports[b] 1976	% of Exports[b] 1991	% of Foreign Investment;[c] 1967–92	% of Domestic investment, 1968–92[x]	Relative prices 1991,[d] (average = 100)	Bank deposits as % of GRP, 1990[x2]
	(1)	(2)	(3)	(4)	(5)	(6)	(7)	(8)	(9)	(10)
Kalimantan										
West Kalimantan	2,743	860	6.0	−5.6	1.2	1.9	0.2	3.1	110	16
Central Kalimantan	1,376	998	5.8	−8.0	1.0	0.4	0.5	0.4	109	11
South Kalimantan	2,326	887	4.5	32.0	1.1	2.1	1.0	1.3	96	15
East Kalimantan	10,770	5,821	4.8	55.4	17.6	12.5	3.1	4.6	139	3
excl. oil	4,410	2,383	4.7							19
Sulawesi										
North Sulawesi	1,507	593	4.8	−6.6	0.2	0.2	0.6	0.9	83	22
Central Sulawesi	982	581	4.7	9.2	0.2	0.1	0.1	0.6	90	14
South Sulawesi	4,241	610	5.2	3.9	0.3	1.6	2.3	0.9	99	21
Southeast Sulawesi	821	616	5.0	4.7	0.4	0.2	0.1	0.5	89	10
Eastern Indonesia										
West Nusa Tenggara	1,290	383	4.6	−5.8	—	—	0.1	0.6	82	13
East Nusa Tenggara	737	361	4.7	−16.5	0.1	—	0.1	0.3	108	15
East Timor	269	364	4.7[q]	−14.4	—	—	0	—	133	22
Maluku	1,463	809	5.1	33.3	0.6	1.3	0.1	1.1	121	17
Irian Jaya	2,047	1,247	0.7	52.5	4.0	2.5	0.8	2.4	136	13
excl. mining	1,217	742	6.3							19
Indonesia	196,919	1,098	3.6		100	100	100	100	100	44
excl. mining	171,471	956	5.0							52

Table 11.2   Indicators of Regional Development: Sectoral-Infrastructure

	Manufacturing as % of GRP, 1990[f]	MVA, Rp mil. per km², 1990[g]	Major manufacturing industry, 1985[h] (and % of total)	Agriculture as % of employment, 1990	Decline in agricultural employment share, 1971–90 (%)	Rice yields, 1991[i] ('000 kg/ha)	Cash crops as % of agriculture, 1990[j]	Buses per 1,000 persons,[k] 1990	Motor cycles per 1,000 persons, 1990	Asphalt roads, 1990 (km/kb²)
	(11)	(12)	(13)	(14)	(15)	(16)	(17)	(18)	(19)	(20)
Sumatra										
Aceh	11.1	39.9	basic chemicals (46)	66	16.5	39.9	14.2	0.6	36	64
excl. oil		5.8								
North Sumatra	17.7	27.8	food products (32)	61	19.9	38.3	39.6	3.5	49	157
West Sumatra	12.1	8.0	cement (38)	60	16.2	45.6	10.8	2.9	25	119
Riau		8.7	metal products (28)	58	16.4	29.5	26.8	1.3	39	25
excl. oil	7.7	2.2								
Jambi	17.0	5.4	wood products (61)	70	11.4	29.6	27.6	2.2	32	50
South Sumatra	20.3	18.5	basic chemicals (46)	65	12.4	31.9	37.3	3.4	42	51
Bengkulu	3.0	1.1	rubber products (78)	71	18.9	31.9	23.2	1.6	23	108
Lampung	11.1	10.8	food products (49)	70	14.7	37.5	31.5	0.7	16	112
Java-Bali										
Jakarta	26.4	140.0[r]	transport equipment (17)	1	72.2	n.a.	n.a.	20.5	97	n.a.
West Java	23.2	158.1	basic metals (21)	37	39.8	49.8	12.0	1.4	14	276
Central Java	16.7	61.9	textiles (32)	48	24.8	51.3	8.8	0.6	32	420
Yogyakarta	10.3		food products (24)	46	19.8	46.5	6.9	0.8	65	676
East Java	21.0	127.6	tobacco products (37)	50	27.0	52.4	18.1	3.1	40	330
Bali	5.3	28.8	food products (28)	44	36.3	51.9	6.4	0.9	84	679

Table 11.2 Continued

	Manufacturing as % of GRP, 1990[f]	MVA, Rp mil. per km², 1990[g]	Major manufacturing industry, 1985[h] (and % of total)	Agriculture as % of employment, 1990	Decline in agricultural employment share, 1971–90 (%)	Rice yields, 1991[i] ('000 kg/ha)	Cash crops as % of agriculture, 1990[j]	Buses per 1,000 persons,[k] 1990	Motor cycles per 1,000 persons, 1990	Asphalt roads, 1990 (km/kb²)
	(11)	(12)	(13)	(14)	(15)	(16)	(17)	(18)	(19)	(20)
Kalimantan										
West Kalimantan	18.7	3.5	wood products (71)	73	17.9	22.9	21.7	0.7	30	16
Central Kalimantan	10.2	0.9	wood products (93)	62	25.4	20.8	16.7	0.1	20	7
South Kalimantan	17.2	10.6	wood products (52)	54	24.2	28.3	10.1	0.4	45	62
East Kalimantan		16.5		43	34.3	22.2	3.2	3.4	52	7
excl. oil	20.2	5.6	basic chemicals (49)							
Sulawesi										
North Sulawesi	5.7	4.5	transport equipment (76)	56	18.3	39.6	32.9	3.5	17	173
Central Sulawesi	5.8	0.8	wood products (93)	68	14.5	31.2	29.5	1.0	25	28
South Sulawesi	6.9	4.0	food products (46)	58	16.3	43.1	11.8	1.4	33	92
Southeast Sulawesi	2.3	0.7	food products (55)	68	20.2	30.5	22.5	0.5	15	74
Eastern Indonesia										
West Nusa Tenggara	2.9	1.9	food products (45)	54	21.4	43.5	7.2	0.4	17	123
East Nusa Tenggara	2.3	0.4	wood products (33)	75	11.7	25.9	9.0	1.1	10	60
East Timor	1.7	0.3	other chemicals (100)	74	14.4	26.2	35.7	1.6	25	26
Maluku	14.0	2.7	wood products (94)	62	22.3	22.8	18.9	0.6	9	32
Irian Jaya	4.3	0.1		72	n.a.	26.0	5.4	2.5	18	4
excl. mining			wood products (97)							
Indonesia		20.3								
excl. mining	18.4	13.0	tobacco products (17)	50	24.7	43.5	15.8	2.6	34	61

Table 11.3 **Indicators of Regional Development: Social-Demographic**

	Population		Density, 1990 (persons per km²)	Education enrolments per 1,000 persons, 1990		Infant mortality rate, late 1980s[l]	% of Population in poverty, 1990[m]	Minimum wage, 1992 (daily, Rp)	Monthly expenditure > Rp 60,000, 1990 (% of pop.)[s]
	Total, 1990 ('000)	Annual growth, 1971–90 (%)		Primary	Tertiary				
	(21)	(22)	(23)	(24)	(25)	(26)	(27)	(28)	(29)
Sumatra									
Aceh	3,416	2.83	62	157	9.9	57	11.5	2,133	3.0
excl. oil									
North Sumatra	10,256	2.33	145	182	10.8	59	12.1	2,550	4.3
West Sumatra	3,999	1.91	80	174	12.3	71	13.4	1,750	6.4
Riau	3,306	3.75	35	161	4.1	65	13.1	2,700	9.6
excl. oil								(5,550)[s]	
Jambi	2,016	3.73	45	172	3.7	71	11.2	2,100	5.8
South Sumatra	6,377	3.30	61	170	4.6	70	14.6	1,600	6.1
Bengkulu	1,179	4.41	56	208	6.0	68	24.6	1,300	5.2
Lampung	6,006	4.14	181	194	4.4	69	28.2	1,750	3.1
Java-Bali									
Jakarta	8,254	3.15	13,945	127	33.9	38	1.3	2,500	41.2
West Java	35,381	2.62	764	136	4.8	89	17.6	2,100	8.2
Central Java	28,522	1.41	834	143	4.4	63	24.7	1,600	3.3
Yogtakarta	2,913	0.83	919	137	35.4	41	17.2	1,250	8.3
East Java	32,504	1.28	678	120	7.8	62	21.8	2,250	4.6
Bali	2,778	1.43	500	137	12.9	49	12.2	2,000	8.9

Table 11.3 Continued

	Population			Education enrolments per 1,000 persons, 1990		Infant mortality rate, late 1980s[l]	% of Population in poverty, 1990[m]	Minimum wage, 1992 (daily, Rp)	Monthly expenditure > Rp 60,000, 1990 (% of pop.)
	Total, 1990 ('000)	Annual growth, 1971–90 (%)	Density, 1990 (persons per km²)	Primary	Tertiary				
	(21)	(22)	(23)	(24)	(25)	(26)	(27)	(28)	(29)
Kalimantan									
West Kalimantan	3,239	2.52	22	171	4.5	80	33.8	1,800	6.2
Central Kalimantan	1,396	3.70	9	199	3.9	56	18.7	1,600	5.3
South Kalimantan	2,598	2.26	69	141	6.3	91	8.7	2,275	5.8
East Kalimantan excl. oil	1,877	5.07	9	179	6.6	56	14.0	1,600	16.3
Sulawesi									
North Sulawesi	2,479	1.95	130	154	11.9	63	18.8	2,000	6.1
Central Sulawesi	1,711	3.36	25	180	5.7	89	24.9	1,100	3.1
South Sulawesi	6,982	1.57	90	163	12.9	69	23.1	1,750	4.4
Southeast Sulawesi	1,350	3.41	49	181	5.6	76	28.8	1,599	3.7
Eastern Indonesia									
West Nusa Tenggara	3,370	2.26	167	153	6.3	145	27.6	1,257	3.1
East Nusa Tenggara	3,269	1.88	68	179	4.2	74	45.6	1,800	1.8
East Timor	748	2.98[t]	50	134	1.1	82	n.a.	2,000	5.1
Maluku	1,856	2.85	25	182	5.9	75	29.0	1,800	4.6
Irian Jaya excl. mining	1,641	3.07	4	155	5.3	79	12.6	2,400	7.2
Indonesia excl. mining	179,322	2.17	93	148	8.3	69	19.6		7.1

Table 11.4 Indicators of Regional Development: Government

	Govt. as % of GRP,[a] 1989	Local revenue as % of GRP,[c] 1989–90	Per capita development grants 1991/2[b] (Rp '000)	Public servants per 1,000 persons, 1990	Local revenue as % of total revenue	
					Province, 1990	Kabupaten, Kotamadya 1989
	(30)	(31)	(32)	(33)	(34)	(35)
Sumatra						
Aceh	5.0	0.72	6.0	25.2	11.8	6.2
excl. oil						
North Sumatra	8.2	0.99	2.0	21.2	20.3	16.5
West Sumatra	10.5	0.98	5.0	28.5	29.5	10.8
Riau	1.9	0.88	6.8	21.7	13.4	7.2
excl. oil						
Jambi	9.8	0.94	10.1	25.2	15.5	5.3
South Sumatra	8.0	0.58	3.9	19.0	24.2	6.6
Bengkulu	20.7	1.06	15.5	30.1	11.9	8.5
Lampung	15.9	0.94	4.8	15.1	13.0	15.2
Java–Bali						
Jakarta	6.6	2.29	2.3	43.3	62.7	n.a.
West Java	9.7	0.86	0.6	14.9	22.0	27.7
Central Java	12.9	0.99	0.7	18.1	16.3	26.3
Yogyakarta	18.1	1.35	6.2	34.9	17.1	23.1
East Java	10.2	0.89	0.6	16.4	24.7	23.9
Bali	12.1	1.80	6.5	28.2	31.3	29.0
Kalimantan						
West Kalimantan	9.9	0.73	7.9	20.3	10.1	13.7
Central Kalimantan	9.9	0.38	18.3	32.5	33.1	5.3
South Kalimantan	9.0	0.83	7.5	27.9	10.8	13.6
East Kalimantan	2.9	0.76	15.2	27.2	20.8	12.3
excl. oil						
Sulawesi						
North Sulawesi	18.2	1.56	7.7	34.4	11.4	19.2
Central Sulawesi	14.1	0.89	12.4	28.1	6.2	10.1
South Sulawesi	13.9	1.20	3.0	26.1	26.8	9.6
Southeast Sulawesi	20.5	0.66	14.4	31.9	8.5	4.2

Table 11.4 Continued

	Govt. as % of GRP[a] 1989	Local revenue as % of GRP[o] 1989–90	Per capita development grants 1991/2[p] (Rp '000)	Public servants per 1,000 persons, 1990	Local revenue as % of total revenue Province, 1990	Local revenue as % of total revenue Kabupaten, Kotamadya 1989
	(30)	(31)	(32)	(33)	(34)	(35)
Eastern Indonesia						
West Nusa Tenggara	15.3	1.10	5.6	18.7	16.0	7.6
East Nusa Tenggara	18.9	1.53	6.2	23.0	16.3	7.2
East Timor	23.9	0.94	24.4	30.3	4.6	2.9
Maluku	11.4	0.85	12.0	29.5	9.3	5.8
Irian Jaya	7.0	0.55	24.3	36.7	4.9	3.2
excl. mining						
Indonesia		1.11		21.0	26.4	15.9
excl. mining						

Notes and Sources:

a Net exports of goods and services as a percentage of GRP.

b Percentage of merchandise exports.

c Approved investment, excluding oil and financial services.

d Indices of relative prices with the national average equal to 100. The data are derived from estimates of a bundle of goods and services regarded as meeting minimum physical needs (KFM, *Kebutuhan Fisik Minimum*), as reported in *Business News*, 6 September 1991.

e Deposits in the formal banking sector, excluding rural credit banks.

f Non-oil manufacturing as a percentage of non-oil GRP.

g Manufacturing value added (Rp million) per km[2].

h The largest non-oil manufacturing industry in the province at the three-digit ISIC classification, and its share of provincial manufacturing value added.

i Includes both wet- and dry-land rice (*padi sawah* and *padi ladang*).

j Value added of cash crops, both estates and smallholders, as a percentage of provincial agricultural value added.

k Includes minibuses (colts).

l Deaths before age 1 year per 1,000 live births, as reported in Hull (1994, Table 3.5).

m Refers to the 'adjusted headcount indices' as calculated by Bidani and Ravallion (1993) from *Susenas* (National Socio-Economic Survey) data.

n Government current expenditure as a percentage of GRP.

o Revenues raised by provincial and second-tier (*kabupaten*, municipalities) governments as a percentage of non-oil GRP.

p Development grants (*bantuan pembangunan*) from the central government to provincial governments.

q 1983–90 only.

r The ratio for Jakarta is Rp 10,214 million/km[2].

s The figure in parentheses refers to Batam Island.

t 1980–90 only.

n–Negligible (less than 1 per cent).

Additional Sources: BPS, *Pendapatan Regional Propinsi-Propinsi di Indonesia*, various issues; BPS, *Statistik Indonesia*, various issues; BPS, *Buletin Ringkas*, various issues; and other unpublished BPS statistics; Republic of Indonesia, *Nota Keuangan*, various issues; and Bank Indonesia, *Statistik Ekonomi-Keuangan Indonesia*, various issues.

PATTERNS OF REGIONAL DEVELOPMENT

This section illustrates Indonesia's regional diversity, in its economic, structural, social and demographic dimensions, with the aid of the data assembled in Tables 11.1 to 11.4, and drawing on the material in Hill (ed., 1989).

AN OVERVIEW OF THE REGIONAL ECONOMIES

As has always been the case, Java dominates Indonesia's economy. In 1990 it contributed 62 per cent of the country's non-oil GDP (Table 11.1, column 1), very close to its population share. Its share of total GDP was somewhat lower—54 per cent—but the latter figure is misleading since much of the oil revenue from the Outer Islands flows to and through Jakarta. By contrast, the economies of Eastern Indonesia are very small indeed. With the exception of South Sulawesi, in some respects the administrative and commercial capital of the region, no provincial economy east of Bali and Kalimantan constitutes more than 1 per cent of national non-oil GDP. Also with the exception of South Sulawesi, none of the eastern provinces has a GRP larger than the small Java province of Yogyakarta.

Within Java, Jakarta and West Java stand out. Jakarta's GRP is actually the third largest in the nation (excluding oil), and exceeds that of Central Java even though the latter's population is 3.5 times larger. Jakarta is similar in magnitude to the combined total of all the eastern provinces and Kalimantan (again excluding oil). Jakarta and West Java together constitute the greatest economic concentration, with almost one-third of the nation's non-oil GDP and over one-half of that of Java; much of West Java is an extension of the Jakarta economy. Within other regions, also, several provinces stand out. North and South Sumatra are easily the largest non-oil economies on that island, generating some 37 per cent of its total. South Sulawesi is some 56 per cent of the four provinces on that island. East Kalimantan produces 63 per cent or 26 per cent of Kalimantan's GRP, depending on whether oil is included.

These regional disparities reflect both population concentration and disparities in regional incomes. On the face of it, the latter are very sizeable (Table 11.1, column 2). The richest province, East Kalimantan, has a per capita GRP some 16 times the poorest, East Nusa Tenggara. Here also, oil makes a big difference, and for the four mineral-rich provinces in particular the total GRP per capita series is a quite misleading indicator of provincial economic welfare. Excluding oil and abstracting from interregional price variations, the differences narrow considerably. Three of the four mining provinces fall below the national average. Only two provinces, Jakarta and East Kalimantan, have a per capita GRP more than double the national average. The per capita GRP of the richest province, Jakarta, is still almost seven times that of the poorest, however. Three other provinces are in a band 10 to 35 per cent above the national (non-oil) average: the tourist island of Bali, once considered a poor province, and the major cash crop economies of North and South Sumatra. At the other extreme, most of the poor provinces are concentrated in the east. None of the Sulawesi provinces has a per capita GRP as much as two-thirds the national (non-oil) average. By contrast, only one province in all of Sumatra, Java, and Kalimantan—the special and serious case of Lampung—does not exceed the latter threshold. The three Nusa Tenggara provinces, the poorest in the nation, are further behind. All have a limited natural resource base, all are distant from major commercial centres, and none has a per capita GRP more than 40 per cent of the national (non-oil) average.

Have these regional disparities been widening or narrowing? We address this complex and unresolved issue below. But on the surface, at least, patterns of economic growth have been reasonably even. The data in Table 11.1, column 3 suggest no clear correlation between per capita GRP and economic growth. Over the 1973–90 period, most provinces grew within a band of one percentage point either side of the national non-oil average. This applies to all of Java (with all but Yogyakarta being above the average), Kalimantan, Sulawesi, Nusa Tenggara, and Maluku. Among the above average exceptions, Bali was the star performer with the fastest growth rate. The high figures for Aceh and Irian Jaya presumably reflect the spillover from the mining boom, in such activities as construction. The Irian Jaya data need to be interpreted cautiously since much of that economy is still subsistence in nature. Surprisingly, the poorest performers are concentrated among the provinces of central and southern Sumatra, with Lampung performing worst of all. The high rate for Bengkulu should be discounted somewhat in view of its low starting point.

Export patterns reflect a combination of local resource endowments and the availability of physical infrastructure. They also give a first approximation of the mineral rich economies' "export surplus" and their contribution to the country's balance of trade. In all four (that is, Aceh, Riau, East Kalimantan, and Irian Jaya), exports are almost 50 per cent or more of GRP (Table 11.1, column 4). Only Jakarta matches this figure, which in the latter case arises because of its superior port facilities, through which much of the exports from neighbouring West Java and southern Sumatra flow (Azis, 1989). Several poor provinces, notably the Nusa Tenggara, record a negative figure, equally indicative of their subsidization by the richer provinces. These provinces are in effect running a current account deficit, both internationally and with the rest of the country.

There have been major changes in regional export composition since the mid-1970s, the peak of the oil boom period (although before Aceh's gas exports had come on stream). In 1976 Riau provided 43 per cent of merchandise exports; combined with East Kalimantan the total was over 60 per cent, about four times the Java share. By 1991, however, with manufactures dominating and oil receding in importance, Java's share of exports had risen sharply and was approaching 40 per cent (Table 11.1, columns 5 and 6). Jakarta was easily the most important export province. Exports from Eastern Indonesia have been very small throughout the period, with minerals from Irian Jaya the principal exception.

Jakarta and West Java have attracted much of the private investment, both foreign and domestic, since 1967 (Table 11.1, columns 7 and 8).[4] Excluding oil and finance, Jakarta and West Java have attracted almost 60 per cent of approved foreign investment over this period. Most of the West Java investment has been adjacent to Jakarta, extending out to the major centres of Cilegon and Bandung. By comparison, foreign investment in Java's other major growth area, East Java, has been surprisingly small, merely 10 per cent of the Jakarta-West Java total. Central Java has attracted even smaller amounts, comparable in value to that of Bali, with less than one-tenth of its population. Only North Sumatra and Riau, the latter mainly Batam, have attracted significant volumes off-Java. In the case of domestic investment, West Java emerges as even more important, with more than one-third of the national total, and about four times the next two recipient provinces, Jakarta and East Java. Perhaps reflecting their local knowledge, domestic investors have been somewhat less Java-centric than foreigners, since 65 per cent of the former's investment has been concentrated there, as compared with the foreign share of 73 per cent. In both cases, Eastern Indonesia has attracted very little investment.

Two other features of the regional economies deserve comment. First, internal economic integration, as measured by declining regional price disparities, is now much stronger than it was 20 years or more ago.[5] These disparities are still evident (Table 11.1, column 9), being concentrated in more distant provinces such as Maluku, and the mining economies. The latter typically display higher prices, often because the spillover effects of the mining enclaves, which push up the general supply price of labour. East Timor is a special case incorporating both the effects of distance (not relieved by its proximity to the high-cost economy of Northwest Australia) and a heavy presence of government employees who receive compensating local allowances. In Riau, also, there is the effect of both the mining sector and, in the case of Batam, proximity to high-wage Singapore. Inter-regional price disparities are much greater still for the hinterland districts of sparsely-populated provinces.

The second feature concerns the relative size of the formal commercial banking sector, proxied by bank deposits as a percentage of GRP (Table 11.1, column 10). Here Jakarta's role as the nation's financial centre is illustrated starkly. Its figure is fully seven times that of the next two provinces, Bali and Yogyakarta, both coincidentally major tourist centres. The high figure for Jakarta reflects not only its financial sophistication, but also the fact that government accounts and company headquarters are maintained there. Apart from the capital's dominance, no clear regional patterns are detectable. Surprisingly, there does not appear to be a strong correlation between this variable and per capita GRP, or the share of non-agricultural sectors in GRP.

REGIONAL ECONOMIC STRUCTURE

These regional differences are reflected in quite distinct economic structures and specialization. In manufacturing, discussed in Chapter 8, these differences are particularly evident. Jakarta, West Java and East Java are the nation's most industrialized provinces, as measured by the share of manufacturing in (non-oil) GRP (Table 11.2, column 11). Only Central Java and North Sumatra are of any significance, apart from these three, in possessing a reasonably large and diversified industrial base. Quite high figures are recorded in a number of provinces off-Java, in South Sumatra, parts of Kalimantan, and even Maluku. But these are rather misleading, since they reflect the impact of a small number of very large industrial plants (typically a fertilizer factory) or one resource-based activity (usually plywood). Manufacturing plays a very minor role in Eastern Indonesia, and is less than 7 per cent of GRP in all cases. It is also small in the service economies of Bali and Yogyakarta. As already discussed in Chapter 8, there is a clear pattern of manufacturing specialization, with the provinces of Java concentrating on footloose industries, and most of the Outer Islands possessing resource-based activities (Table 11.2, column 13). These differences are illustrated further by patterns of manufacturing intensity (Table 11.2, column 12). The ratios of manufacturing activity to land area for the three big provinces of Java are typically at least 10 times that of the off-Java provinces, and more than 50 times that of the majority of Eastern Indonesian provinces.

The differences are similarly evident in agricultural patterns. With the obvious exception of Jakarta, only in West Java did agriculture employ less than 40 per cent of the workforce in 1990 (Table 11.2, column 14). Reflecting the strength of industry and services, the agricultural share is below the national average in all of Java–Bali, as it is in the special case of East Kalimantan, owing to timber processing and to mining-related services. In most of the other provinces, agricultural employment shares are well above the national average, especially in some of the agrarian eastern provinces where it still absorbs more than 70 per cent of the workforce. The shift out of agricultural employment is also more rapid in the higher growth, industrializing economies, and much slower in the east (Table 11.2, column 15).

Agricultural structure also varies considerably across provinces (Table 11.2, columns 16 and 17). Reflecting ecology, local dietary preferences and the impact of government programs, rice yields vary considerably. These figures of course understate the differences greatly since they refer to province-wide averages. The figures in the highest-yield province, East Java, are more than double those of several provinces in Kalimantan and Eastern Indonesia. Equally the yield data illustrate the considerable diversity outside Java and Bali. In several of the traditional rice growing areas, yields are not so far below those of West Java and Yogyakarta. Examples include the important rice-surplus economies of West Sumatra and South Sulawesi, and West Nusa Tenggara, half of which is more akin to Java–Bali in its ecology (the island of Lombok), while the other island (Sumbawa) has a dry climate and arid soils more akin to neighbouring East Nusa Tenggara.

On the other hand, Sumatra has long displayed a much stronger cash crop specialization (Table 11.2, column 17). In all but Aceh and West Sumatra, these crops constitute a significantly larger share of agricultural output than is the case nationally. They have a particularly large and diversified presence in North and South Sumatra, the latter almost entirely as smallholders, the former with a mix of both plantations and smallholders. These crops are also significant in most of Sulawesi (coconuts, cocoa, cloves), West Kalimantan (rubber), and East Timor (coffee). On Java, cash crops have historically been most important in East Java, but they are likely to decline in importance in the near future as rapid industrialization alters that province's local comparative advantage.

Infrastructure supplies also reflect, and have shaped, patterns of economic activity. In the case of transport vehicles (Table 11.2, columns 18 and 19), Java is well ahead of the rest of the nation, if account is taken of the fact that much of the island's bus fleet is registered in Jakarta. Motorcycle ownership appears to be correlated quite closely to per capita incomes, in addition to tourism (Bali and Yogyakarta) and concentrations of student populations (Yogyakarta). Java's road networks are much more highly developed, along with those of most of Sumatra, and pockets elsewhere, such as North Sulawesi (Table 11.2, column 20). The very low levels in Irian Jaya and much of Kalimantan underline the poor internal economic integration of these regions.

SOCIAL AND DEMOGRAPHIC PATTERNS

Table 11.3, columns 21–23 emphasize Indonesia's uneven demography. In particular, 61.5 per cent of the population reside on Java–Bali, with only 7 per cent of the land area. The population density of the least densely settled Java province, West Java, is still more than four times that of the highest figure off Java–Bali, Lampung. The latter has long been the focus of transmigration, and spontaneous settlement, until in the mid-1980s it was declared a "closed" province, at least for the official program, in recognition of its serious ecological and economic problems. A small percentage of Java's population increment may have been transferred to this province, but in the process its socioeconomic indicators have deteriorated to a point where they are generally poorer than those on Java.

Population growth has been high in Jakarta and West Java, the former primarily owing to in-migration, the latter reflecting traditionally high fertility levels. But otherwise population growth on Java–Bali has been below the national average, as socioeconomic changes and effective family planning initiatives have brought fertility down sharply (Hull, 1994). Outside Java, population growth rates have been noticeably below the national average only in a few instances—North and South Sulawesi, East Nusa Tenggara, and West Sumatra—the result either of out-migration or falling fertility. Very high rates have been recorded in major regions of in-migration such as Lampung, and East and Central Kalimantan. High population growth has been a feature of much of Sumatra, with five of the eight provinces recording growth rates of over 3 per cent from 1971 to 1990. In demographic perspectives, Sumatra has always been overshadowed by Java. Yet in 1990 its population totalled 36.6 million persons, about double that of Malaysia. If it were an independent entity it would rank among the 20 most populous developing countries in the world. It is heading inexorably towards a population of 55 to 60 million in the next quarter-century.

Social indicators reveal a mixed picture. Primary education has spread rapidly and evenly throughout the nation since 1970. At least in quantity terms, though much less so in quality, no region is clearly lagging behind (Table 11.3, column 24). Indeed, in several Outer Island provinces enrolments per capita are actually higher than on Java, the result of both more youthful populations and a catch-up from earlier neglect. As would be expected, the pattern is much more varied at the tertiary level (Table 11.3, column 25). Jakarta and Yogyakarta emerge clearly as the major centres, at least on a per capita basis. Higher figures in some Outer Islands provinces also reflect their role as major regional centres of higher education, such as in the cases of North Sumatra and South Sulawesi. In other cases, notably West Sumatra and North Sulawesi, the higher figures reflect a history of stronger educational achievement. According to this indicator, the east is not so disadvantaged. Indeed, in a number of instances education systems based around mission schools were quite well developed historically (Jones, 1976), although by 1990 this advantage had probably been overtaken by the large state expansion. The most disadvantaged province according to this indicator was East Timor, where a state university has only recently been established.

In health achievement, the record is rather mixed (Table 11.3, column 27). Infant mortality rates are generally below the national average on Java–Bali. The achievement of Yogyakarta is particularly notable: in spite of being one of the poorest provinces in the country in economic terms, its infant mortality rate is lower than all provinces except Jakarta. Conversely, the rate of the strongly industrializing province of West Java is the second highest in the nation and more than double the Yogyakarta figure. Intra-provincial divides (in West Java) and access to good public health facilities (in compact Yogyakarta) explain much of the difference, and they illustrate that social indicators are not necessarily correlated with economic indicators, both within and between countries. All of Eastern Indonesia records an above average infant mortality rate, again with the conspicuous exception of North Sulawesi. Most serious of all is the rate in West Nusa Tenggara, which is more than double the national average, and some 60 per cent higher than that of the second highest province in Eastern Indonesia.

There are also no consistent correlates of interregional variations in poverty incidence, and regionally the picture is very mixed. All of Sumatra is well below the national average, except for the two southern provinces of Bengkulu and Lampung. The latter's very poor socioeconomic status has already been remarked upon. Most of Kalimantan is also below average, except for the poorest province, West Kalimantan. It is noticeable, however, that in spite of East Kalimantan's very high per capita GRP, its poverty record is not markedly superior to the rest of the island, providing *a priori* support for the view that high-income enclaves in the province have resulted in substantial intra-regional inequality. Apart from Jakarta, where absolute (but certainly not relative) poverty has almost disappeared, all of Java is closely bunched around the national average, East and Central Java just above it, West Java and Yogyakarta a little below. Although Java has more people in poverty than any other region in the country, its ranking is no worse collectively than the Outer Islands. In neighbouring high-growth Bali, poverty incidence is one of the lowest in the country. That poverty is particularly serious in Eastern Indonesia is illustrated by the fact that only two provinces there do not rank above the national average—North Sulawesi is marginally below it, while Irian Jaya is much lower. Poverty and per capita incomes are highly correlated for the province of East Nusa Tenggara, in that it ranks highest on the former and lowest on the latter.

These poverty data need to be treated as approximate estimates at best. The samples from the *Susenas* data are rather small for the less populous provinces, with the result that the figures fluctuate considerably between enumerations. In some years, for example, Irian Jaya has recorded among the highest poverty incidence, yet according to the 1990 round it was ranked very low. In some official publications, several smaller provinces have been grouped together in poverty estimates. Moreover, the figures do not indicate the intensity of poverty. They estimate what percentage of the population is below a specified poverty threshold, but they do not measure how far those in poverty fall below that line.[6] There is known to be considerable variation in intra-regional inequality,[7] although there is no clear evidence that such inequality is correlated systematically with per capita income. One might surmise that inequality is greater in the high income provinces, and some support for this proposition is given in Table 11.3, column 29. Putting aside regional price differentials, by far the largest concentration of high spenders is located in Jakarta: the percentage of the population spending more than Rp60,000 per month in 1990 was almost six times the national average. East Kalimantan is clearly in second position, followed by a cluster of two of the other mining provinces and Bali. The low figures for most of Eastern Indonesia are presumptive evidence of lower inequality in these provinces, together with their much higher poverty incidence.

To return to the question posed at the beginning of this section, have there been any significant trends in regional inequality over the course of the New Order? The evidence in Table 11.1 (columns 2 and 3) suggests a reasonably even pattern. Some of the high-income provinces have grown slowly, while in other cases there has been a catch-up as a number of poor provinces have grown quite quickly. There is no case of a high-income province growing much faster than the national average, or conversely of a poor province falling sharply behind.

This pattern of reasonably even regional development is corroborated by several studies which have calculated "Williamson" indices of regional inequality. As noted earlier, initial estimates of regional accounts were rudimentary in nature (Arndt, 1973; Kerr, 1973). Esmara (1975) was the first researcher to analyse the data systematically. He estimated the index (which generally falls within the 0–1 range, although it is not constrained to unity) for Indonesia in 1972 to be very high, at about 0.95. However, if the oil and gas sectors were excluded it fell to about 0.52, while the exclusion of three high income provinces (East and Central Kalimantan and Riau) resulted in a halving, to 0.26. According to Esmara, this placed Indonesia among the "low regional inequality" countries for which data were available from the 1950s and 1960s.

As the regional database improved, empirical research during the 1980s extended in three directions. First, calculating trends in regional inequality, especially during and after the oil boom; secondly, examining the social dimensions of regional inequality, and comparing social and economic performance across provinces; and finally, probing the sectoral dimensions of regional inequality.

Most studies agree that there was no significant increase in inequality during the decade from the mid-1970s.[8] Much depends on the treatment of the rich oil provinces here: including them, the income- (production) based index of inequality may be as high as 0.9. However, estimates which exclude mining altogether (and even a smaller number of exceptional provinces), or are based on personal expenditure data, are much lower, in the range 0.18–0.25. The latter figures are much more plausible since they exclude high-income enclaves, revenues from which accrue mainly to the central government, to the state oil company Pertamina, or to foreign investors. A further modification, introduced by Akita and Lukman (1994), combined the provinces of Jakarta and West Java (as much a single economic entity as, for example, Surabaya and the rest of East Java); this also had the effect of lowering the index of inequality. It is therefore accurate to portray Indonesia through this period as a "moderately low" regional inequality case. For all the criticisms of Indonesia's regional development structures, and a substantial unfinished policy agenda to be discussed shortly, this is a remarkable achievement. There have always been powerful centrifugal forces at work in a country of Indonesia's vast diversity. The oil boom, several smaller commodity booms (for example, timber), the recent rapid growth of manufactured exports, and large inflows of foreign aid, to name just a few, have all had uneven spatial impacts.

Two qualifications should be attached to this positive assessment. First, the most serious regional development challenge now lies in Eastern Indonesia, and secondly the government's capacity to sustain generous funding for these provinces after the collapse of oil prices is under great strain. As government revenue fell after the mid-1980s, so too have its regional expenditures. Correspondingly, as the centrally imposed financial straitjacket has weakened, local factors have become more important determinants of regional economic growth. As noted, this has been particularly important in Java, with its services and footloose manufactured exports, in Bali's tourist industry, and in other provinces in Western Indonesia with a strong resource base.

What of the post oil boom period? Regional inequality might have been expected to increase given the central government's fiscal austerity (and, therefore, its diminished capacity to promote fiscal equalization), together with increased regional economic autonomy, especially on Java. In fact, however, according to the estimates of Akita and Lukman (1994), there was virtually no change in the aggregate indices

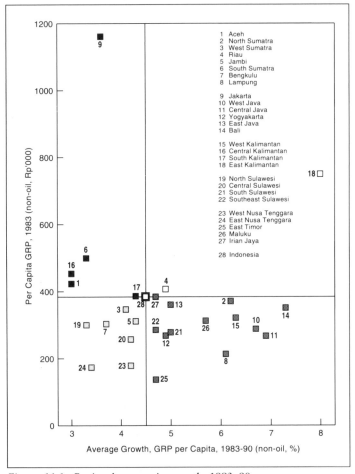

Figure 11.1   Regional economic growth, 1983–90

over the period from 1983 to 1990. The index for all sectors declined somewhat, from about unity to 0.82 in 1990, while the index for non-mining sectors was broadly constant, in the 0.54–0.56 range. Figure 11.1 further examines the picture in the post-oil boom phase by correlating provincial per capita (non-oil) GRP in 1983 with economic growth over this period. The trend of reasonably even regional development is corroborated according to these figures. Indeed 17 of Indonesia's 27 provinces fell into the top left quadrant (above average income, below average growth) or bottom right quadrant, indicating a continuation of these equalizing tendencies for the majority of cases. Just two were in the top right quadrant (high growth, high income), one of these, Riau, marginally so in both counts. Another, Irian Jaya, was very close to both national averages.

The really serious cases, below average in both respects and therefore falling further behind the rest of the nation, include seven provinces: West Sumatra, Jambi, Bengkulu, North Sulawesi, Central Sulawesi, and West and East Nusa Tenggara. Two more, East Timor and Lampung, might be added to this list in view of their very low incomes and special circumstances. This is especially so for East Timor, since its economic growth was only marginally above the average, and its per capita GRP in 1983 was the nation's lowest. It is clear that these provinces must be the subject of special government assistance if the objective of national unity is to be maintained. Four of these provinces are actually in Sumatra, which underlines the point that poverty and sluggish economic growth are not entirely an Eastern Indonesia phenomenon. But socioeconomic conditions are generally much weaker in the east, as indicated by lower per capita GRP and inadequate social indicators. All nine eastern provinces were below the national per capita (non-oil) GRP in 1983, and of the five which recorded above average growth rates, only one, Maluku, grew appreciably faster. The three Nusa Tenggara provinces score particularly poorly. Not only were their per capita GRPs far below average, but they also grew slowly. Eastern Indonesia poses a special development challenge, these three provinces the most serious of all.

The record of social progress across regions, the second research theme, is generally impressive (Hill, 1992b). Here also, the precise results depend on the methodology. There have been attempts to develop a composite social development index. But these involve arbitrary weighting and calibration exercises and also obscure important variations among social indicators for certain provinces. Inequalities in education and health indicators are in most cases remarkably and consistently low, as noted above. These outcomes reflect the impact of concerted government attention to these areas, particularly at the level of primary education, and historical strengths in some poor regions. The inequality of poverty incidence, being less amenable to direct policy intervention, remains a good deal higher than education and health indicators. As noted, the poverty estimates are less reliable in the smaller provinces.

The association between economic and social performance across provinces and over time is surprisingly weak, and should constitute a major item on Indonesia's regional research agenda. There are cases where economic and social indicators are both good (Jakarta being the prime example) or both poor (Lampung, the Nusa Tenggara provinces). However, there are many instances where the correlation is not strong. There are cases of good social indicators and lagging economies, such as, North Sulawesi and West Sumatra. Conversely there are relatively high income economies which display indifferent social indicators. Surprisingly, West Java is perhaps the most notable of such cases. Islam and Khan (1986) pointed to another dimension of this pattern, as noted above, by correlating poverty incidence and inequality (within each province) on the basis of 1976 data. They found that there was generally a linear correspondence between the two measures, with all but four provinces being in the low (poverty)–low (inequality), medium–medium or high–high categories.

What explains Indonesia's comparatively good record on regional development? Part of the answer is in the third strand of empirical regional research, in which the inequality indices have been calculated at a sectoral level. Booth (1986) undertook such an exercise, finding as would be expected a much lower index for agriculture. Thus the strong performance of agriculture—in particular food crops—has contributed indirectly to the good regional outcomes.[9] More generally, for all its faults, the rigid, highly centralized system of government administration has, in a suboptimal fashion, ensured reasonable uniformity in delivering government services. Programs in education, health and physical infrastructure on a national scale have been implemented. The government's fiscal equalization measures, and its recycling of the windfall revenues from a few mining enclaves through routine and development budget expenditures, have ensured that all provinces have shared in the oil (and foreign aid) bonanzas to some extent. It is to this issue, meeting the challenge of regional development goals in a rapidly changing environment, that the final section of this chapter is devoted.

The Regional Policy Agenda

Under its constitution, Indonesia has a unitary system of government in which subnational tiers of governance have little administrative or financial authority. The course of history since Independence has further centralized power in the hands of the Jakarta government. The latter's authority, and it suspicion of local autonomy, was heightened at the time of the unsuccessful regional separatist attempts in 1957–58. During the New Order period, large inflows of aid and oil revenue have strengthened Jakarta's financial clout immeasurably. The key role of the armed forces, which also have a highly centralized command structure, has placed still more power at the centre.[10] Yet, at the same time, the regional policy agenda has altered significantly, beginning in the 1980s. In the early years of the New Order, provincial administrative capacity was in many cases so weak and the bottlenecks to regional economic integration so large that a strong centralized system was inevitable, and probably necessary. Moreover the oil boom occurred just six years after the Soeharto government had assumed office, before there had been any opportunity to create new regional structures. By the late 1980s, none of these arguments constituted a powerful case for retaining the current centralized system: Indonesia is a national economic entity as never before, regional administrative capacity is now much stronger, and the government's fiscal position is tight.

It is testimony to the complexity of regional issues—political, economic, administrative, social—that the government has been so slow to move on reform. Since at least the mid-1980s, various policy packages have been under active consideration. Increasingly the government has begun to focus on the second tier of regional administration, the *kabupaten* and municipalities (*kotamadya*). In the process this has undoubtedly delayed announcement of the reform measures, as there has been a major effort to build up bureaucratic capacity at this level. Nevertheless, in spite of high-level awareness of the urgency of change, virtually no new initiatives have surfaced over this period. Rather, there has been tinkering at the margin: minor alterations in the regional grants formulae, incremental changes in the regions' fiscal autonomy, and small steps towards greater civil service mobility among the provincial governments.

One of the most pressing policy issues is regional finance. Under the current system, the central government is the primary revenue collecting agency. It then disburses funds to lower level governments, termed in Indonesia Dati (*daerah tingkat*) I (provinces) and II (municipalities and *kabupaten*). The current system still remains fiscally quite generous to the regions. But there has never been a clearly stated rationale for allocations across provinces. For example, in one of the major allocations, to be referred to shortly, Azis (1992a, pp. 396, 404) concludes that "[n]o explicit mention of regional capacity or needs is made in the criteria . . . [and] a systematic rationale is lacking in the planning of Inpres Dati I allocations". Moreover, subnational governments are placed in a straitjacket, having no authority to alter their fiscal mix, and no incentive to enhance efficiency of tax collections.[11]

Central government disbursements to the regions occur primarily through two mechanisms, the *Inpres* (*Instruksi Presiden*, Presidential Instruction) allocations and the DIP (*daftar isian proyek*, list of project proposals). As noted in Chapter 4, *Inpres* grants to the provinces were introduced in 1973 to compensate for the abolition of the *Alokasi Devisa Otomatis*, under which grants were tied in part to foreign exchange earnings. During the oil boom period, they quickly came to be regarded by the government as a convenient means of rapidly disbursing funds to the regions. As a result, total allocations rose sharply and the number of such schemes proliferated (see Tables 4.3 to 4.6 pp. 56–60).[12] These programs were cut back during the austerity of the mid-1980s, but as an indication of the importance the government attaches to the *daerah*, allocations began to rise quickly again from the late 1980s as fiscal circumstances improved.

The absence of a coherent allocation formula is illustrated by the fact that the annual grants have changed frequently. As Azis (1992a, p. 396) notes, beginning in fiscal year 1981–82, the "5 plus 22" criterion was introduced, whereby 22 provinces received the same amount (then Rp 9 billion), while another five received a slightly larger amount (Rp 11 billion). In 1988–89, the formula was changed again, to one in which all provinces received the same amount. Owing in part to the fixed administrative costs inherent in a cumbersome centralized system of management, small provinces have generally benefited more from the system than larger ones. As an incidental by-product, these arrangements have avoided a pro-Java bias which, given modern Indonesia's political economy, might otherwise have emerged. The result has been that the three large Java provinces receive less funding than smaller provinces off-Java (and incidentally Yogyakarta). Since several of the smaller provinces are also among the poorest group, there has also been some pro-equity bias, albeit rather weak, in the allocations. At the same time, larger, economically more powerful provinces have been able to develop their own funding resources to a greater extent, in part because, as noted above, the commercial activities on which subnational taxes may be levied are found disproportionately in these regions.

Some of these propositions are illustrated in Table 11.4, columns 30–35. First of all, the government presence, as measured by public sector expenditure, is larger in small provinces (column 30). Ironically, apart from the special case of the four mineral economies, this ratio is lowest of all in the seat of national government, Jakarta, where the private sector is the main engine of growth, often of course with public sector patronage. In large, dynamic economies, such as East and West Java and North and South Sumatra, the government share is also modest, at 10 per cent or less of GRP. By contrast the share is more than double the Jakarta figure in East Timor (the highest share of all, reflecting its special circumstances, including a large military presence), all of Sulawesi, both Nusa Tenggara provinces, Bengkulu, Lampung, and Yogyakarta. Civil service numbers follow this trend in most cases, owing to the fact that the government has established an administrative structure which in some respects is invariant to the size of the province (column 33). Thus, for example, in the smaller provinces listed above, civil servants are relatively twice as numerous as is the case in the nation's most populous province, West Java. In Jakarta and East Timor, again for obvious reasons, the ratios are the highest.

Yet another indicator of the bias towards small provinces in these regional flows is per capita development grants (column 32). Since many of these grants are paid in the form of a lump sum, regardless of provincial population or per capita income, the small provinces receive much larger amounts on a per capita basis. Thus, Yogyakarta received Rp 6,200 per capita in 1991–92, while neighbouring Central Java, with generally inferior social indicators, received Rp700 per capita. The booming economy of Bali received more than either East or West Nusa Tenggara.

As argued above, the bias towards small provinces has had the incidental effect of avoiding a pro-Java bias and, to the extent that most (but not all) of the small provinces are also among the poorest, of being moderately progressive in effect. The equity implications of these grants have been addressed rigorously by Azis (1990) and Ravallion (1988). The latter study, for example, found only a weak negative correlation between per capita *Inpres* grants and per capita personal consumption for 1985, concluding that the revealed allocation pattern could be characterized as exhibiting a "mild absolute-inequality aversion". Azis (1990) undertook a broader study of these expenditures and arrived at a similar conclusion.

The revenue patterns of both tiers of local government also reflect this combination of size, per capita incomes, and economic structure. On the face of it, the correlates between local revenue as a percentage of GRP are not altogether obvious (column 31). It would be expected that small and poor provinces would not have the capacity to raise significant local revenues. While this is true in some instances, there are several exceptions. For example, East Nusa Tenggara had one of the highest ratios in the nation, and both North and South Sulawesi are above the national average. Yet the sizeable figures for some of the small and poor provinces in turn reflect the large role of the government in these economies. A clearer perspective on the financial autonomy and capacity of these provinces is illustrated in columns 34 and 35, which record local revenue as a percentage of total expenditure. Here their reliance on the *pusat* is obvious. Among the nine provinces of Eastern Indonesia, the share of local revenue averaged 11.5 per cent and 7.8 per cent of total revenue for the first and second tier of governments respectively. These figures were both less than one-half of the national average. If the strongest eastern economy, South Sulawesi, were removed, the east-west disparity would be greater still.

These numbers highlight one of the fundamental dilemmas of Indonesian regional policy since the mid-1980s. The government is a major force for economic development in these poorer provinces, and yet Jakarta has faced severe fiscal constraints since the collapse of oil prices. The data also indicate the lack of coherence in regional strategies, since there is a large government presence in, and higher per capita grants to, relatively prosperous provinces, such as Bali and Yogyakarta, in which economic and/or social indicators are above the national average.

The government's challenge in the arena of regional finance is to walk a tightrope between the contending claims of national unity and regional autonomy. A return to some form of the old ADO (*Alokasi Devisa Otomatis*) system, which linked central government grants to export earnings, would have serious interregional equity implications, and exacerbate the inequalities between east and west (or, more particularly, between the mineral regions, together with North and South Sumatra, Jakarta–West Java, and possibly East Java–Bali, versus the rest of the nation). The solution will presumably lie in a package of measures comprising some revenue-sharing, a limited devolution of revenue and expenditure responsibilities, and a stronger link between tax effort and revenue. At the same time, even though the central government will continue to face severe fiscal constraints during the 1990s, owing to its debt-service obligations, more decentralized regional finance arrangements would also need to be accompanied by the introduction of some minimum, nationally devised social, economic and infrastructure targets, below which no province will be permitted to fall.

The regional development policy agenda is, of course, not just about fiscal relations. There is also a strong case for greater emphasis on regional comparative advantage. The notion of self-sufficiency, especially in agriculture, is deeply entrenched in Indonesia, and it embraces not only national thinking but also aspirations at the *daerah*. Many provinces have developed a mentality in which there is emphasis on local supply and demand equations, whether it be food, tertiary graduates, or a range of manufactures. Related to this is a Jakarta-based emphasis on nationally implemented programs which does not always incorporate sufficient recognition of regional variations in ecology, agronomic conditions and institutions. The regional surveys in Hill (ed., 1989) provide numerous illustrations of the failure to exploit regional comparative advantage, and of the tendency to transplant Java-oriented programs to other parts of the archipelago.[13]

A final and related aspect of the reform process concerns the trade and regulatory regimes. Although they generally do not incorporate explicit regional goals, there are often unintended side-effects. High protection of footloose consumer goods industries entails a tax transfer from the Outer Islands to Java, to the extent that most of these industries are located around Java's major industrial complexes. Intricate licensing procedures constitute a sometimes powerful centralizing bias towards Jakarta, the seat of political and bureaucratic power. Export procedures and investments in port infrastructure contain a similar bias, although the reforms introduced in the second half of the 1980s did remove some of the constraints. Some regulations are blatantly discriminatory, such as the requirement that rattan must be processed in certain designated centres, mainly on Java; another example is the notorious clove marketing monopoly. Rigid pricing structures, notably for power, also disadvantage some energy-rich provinces, mainly outside Java.

In sum, the record of regional economic development since 1965 is generally a creditable one. Despite continuing tension in distant provinces (most notably Aceh, Irian Jaya and East Timor), the government has delivered a measure of economic and social progress across all provinces. The challenge for the 1990s and beyond will be to build on these achievements by fashioning a strategy emphasizing a measure of regional devolution and greater sensitivity to conditions in the *daerah*. It is likely that Eastern Indonesia in particular will be a major challenge for decades to come, and that a fundamental requirement of maintaining national integrity will be special programs of assistance targeted to these poor provinces.

Conclusion:
Looking to the Future

A BRIEF LOOK BACKWARDS

Indonesia was characterized as the "chronic dropout" in the early 1960s. Before that it was the home of dualism and backward-sloping supply curves. In the 1970s, with the spectacular exception of oil, notions of export pessimism were pervasive. Yet over the past quarter-century Indonesia has unquestionably been one of the better performers in the Third World. Since 1966 it has experienced the first sustained period of economic development in its modern history. In one of the most decisive breaks with the past anywhere, the economic stagnation, accelerating inflation, and declining living standards of the 1960–66 period have given way to rapid growth, macroeconomic stability, and rising prosperity. Real GDP has risen almost five-fold over this period, resulting in an increase of more than 300 per cent in per capita GDP. There have been commensurate improvements in a range of socioeconomic indicators, including rising educational levels, and declining infant mortality and poverty incidence.

Structural change has been rapid, with the share of manufacturing in GDP rising almost three-fold over this period. Indeed, in the long sweep of economic development, Indonesia passed three milestones in the early 1990s: in 1991 manufacturing output exceeded that of agriculture for the first time, and notwithstanding the latter's impressive growth; by 1990 the share of the labour force in agriculture fell to 50 per cent; while manufactured exports have now overtaken those of both oil and minerals and agriculture and, depending on definitions, total more than 50 per cent by value. Moreover, within these three broad sectors, structural and technological changes have been very rapid.

By international standards, also, Indonesia's record looks good. Its growth rate may not have been up to those of the Highly Performing Asian Economies (HPAEs, an acronym recently introduced by the World Bank, 1993). But it has not been too far behind. And it compares very favourably with any other region or country outside East Asia. The detailed comparative work cited in Chapter 1 underlines this point. In particular, in the comparison with countries possessing similar natural resource endowments—the OPEC group—its experience is impressive. In its social achievements, too, Indonesia's comparative record is good, if not outstanding. Its daily calorie supplies have risen faster than any other country in the sample referred to above. Health and education improvements have at least kept pace with these countries, although the increases are not markedly superior.

Two additional, interrelated aspects of Indonesia's record since 1966 deserve comment. First, Indonesia has developed a capacity to confound its critics, even the best-informed ones. And secondly, the New Order regime has displayed a tremendous resilience, and an ability to respond deftly and effectively to looming economic crises. So far, these crises have surfaced in the middle of each decade. Very few observers and practitioners, both inside and outside the country, expected the economy to respond so strongly to the dose of economic and political orthodoxy in 1966–67. Viewed from a 1965 perspective, who would have dared to predict that real GDP growth would actually exceed the rate of inflation early in the following decade! In the mid-1970s, the state oil company Pertamina had accumulated debts at one stage of some $10 billion, equivalent then to about one-third of GDP. Yet here too a swift and effective rescue operation was mounted. Then in the mid-1980s crisis, the only one of the three precipitated by external events, falling oil prices shaved some 15 per cent off GDP. Once again the government acted decisively, averting a looming debt scenario by introducing far-reaching reforms which by the end of the decade had pushed growth back up to 7 per cent, for the first time spurred on by manufactured exports.

As noted above, Indonesia seems to have attracted an unusually large band of pessimistic observers. The government brought down inflation much faster than expected. Rice self-sufficiency was achieved in the mid-1980s, whereas such an achievement seemed impossibly optimistic a decade earlier. In the 1980s, the liberalizing reforms—which in many cases pushed aside powerful vested interests— set Indonesia at last on the road to high-growth, East Asian style export-oriented industrialization, again contrary to the expectations of most informed opinion at that time. The 1980s also began to reveal clearly the longer-term trends in equity and social indicators of the New Order. Once more, careful analysis on the whole debunked popular notions that the benefits of growth had been highly skewed.[1]

LOOKING FORWARD[2]

So much for the past. What of future prospects? Can Indonesia's development momentum be sustained, not just for a few more years but for decades, to ensure all Indonesians have a decent standard of living? In this concluding section, I will not engage in an exercise of "crystal-ball gazing". I will not try to predict actual outcomes, such as growth forecasts and so on, for the 1990s and beyond. Even the most skilled econometric modellers do not have an especially good track record here for Indonesia. Rather, I will attempt to answer this question by identifying the major parameters, or "conditioning factors", which are likely to have an important bearing on outcomes over the next decade and more. I focus mainly on economic issues, but also attempt wherever possible to inject a political economy flavour. The analysis rests on the assumption that the international economy will continue to be supportive, that is, that Indonesia will continue to have access to international markets for goods, capital and technology. Finally, I am also assuming that the government will continue to be an effective macroeconomic manager, as it has been since the late 1960s.

At the outset, it needs to be emphasized that, for all its success, Indonesia is still a very poor country. It is in the World Bank's "low-income" group of countries, with a per capita income of just over $600 in 1991. In some of its structural characteristics,

Table 12.1   **Indonesia in East Asian Perspective**

	Korea	Malaysia	Thailand
(a) When were other countries at Indonesia's 1991 level of development?			
Per capita GNP			
'actual' (= $610)	1957	1956	1970
'PPP-adjusted' (= $1,998)	1972	1963	1978
Manufacturing output first exceeding agricultural output (Indonesia in 1991)	1973	1984	1981
50% of labour force in agriculture (Indonesia in 1990)	1970	1973	n.a.
(b) When will Indonesia catch up to others' 1991 per capita GNP?			
(1991 per capita GNP)	(6,330)	(2,520)	(1,570)
Assuming Indonesia's growth in GNP per capita to be:			
High (5.5%)	2035	2017	2009
Medium (4.0%)	2051	2027	2015
Low (2.5%)	2088	2046	2029

Memo item: comparative growth rates (GNP per capita)

	Indonesia	Korea	Malaysia	Thailand
1965–91	4.5	7.0	4.1	4.5
1980–91	3.9	8.7	2.9	5.9

n.a.–not available.

Notes: 'PPP' refers to 'purchasing power parity'. Indonesia's 1991 PPP figure is in 1985 prices, extrapolated forward from the latest estimate, for 1988.
Sources: Output and employment shares are from a variety of country sources. GNP data are from World Bank, *World Development Report*, various issues. The PPP series are from the PENN World Tables, originating from the United Nations International Comparisons Program.

the Indonesian economy in the early 1990s resembles that of (South) Korea in the early 1970s. This is so in respect of per capita GDP (in Purchasing Power Parity terms[3]), and the shares of agriculture and manufacturing in GDP and employment (Table 12.1). The comparisons with periods of recent Thai and Malaysian economic history are not so clearcut, other than generally—though not always—reflecting their latecomer status. Thus Indonesia appears to be at least two decades behind Korea, and somewhat less in the case of its two lower-income neighbours.

Taking the "medium-growth" scenario (very close to the actual record for 1980 to 1991), for example, the simple growth extrapolations reported in Table 12.1 suggest Indonesia would not catch up to Thailand's current level until the year 2015, while the Malaysian and Korean levels would be a further 12 and 36 years away respectively. As the top two lines of the table illustrate, however, the catch-up period is a good deal less—perhaps as little as half—than that suggested by a simple extrapolation of GNP per capita measured at official exchange rates, owing to the relative price effects discussed in Note 3. Nevertheless, Indonesia's growth rates in the 1980s were well below the Korean rate since 1965. They are closer to the Thai and Malaysian rates over the longer period, although they have been at least two percentage points lower since the post-1988 boom in Southeast Asia. Calculations of this sort are very much back-of-the-envelope exercises, but they do underline the magnitude of Indonesia's development challenge. It will take decades of growth to put Indonesia well into the middle-income league of countries. Moreover, these figures are based on scenarios of sustained growth, without a serious or prolonged faltering of the growth momentum.

They abstract from all manner of possible obstacles: a deep and widespread global economic depression; a major environmental catastrophe; a period of political instability, the latter a not unlikely prospect given that economic growth is an inherently disruptive process, and especially as the end to President Soeharto's long rule is now in sight.

The following factors seem to be particularly pertinent in discussing future prospects. If serious problems arise in one or more of these areas, the growth momentum and the process of rising living standards could be retarded significantly.

MAINTAINING THE REFORM MOMENTUM

The old adage, in Jakarta and many other parts of the world, that "bad times make good policies and good times frequently the reverse", appears relevant to the Indonesia of the early 1990s. The bold and decisive pace of reform of the second half of the 1980s appears to have slowed noticeably in very recent years. There are a number of quite plausible explanations for this. Rising inflation preoccupied and distracted the government in 1990–91, as officials imposed tight monetary policies to cool an overheated economy. The politically "easy" reforms were, understandably, enacted first, and we are left now with the most intractable areas, where the political opposition to reform is much more fierce. There is (probably) not the same presidential backing for further reforms now, as the economic recovery from the precarious period of the mid-1980s is clearly well established. There is usually a slowdown in Indonesia's decision-making processes before and immediately after parliamentary and presidential elections, including a reluctance on the part of some senior officials to push hard for politically unpopular reform and a delay as the new Cabinet begins to function effectively. The 1991–93 period was such a period (although the more desperate years from 1986 to 1968 were not, by and large), when very little in the way of significant reform was introduced. Heavily managed though its political system is, even in Indonesia "electoral cycles" do have a bearing on the dynamics of reform.

Yet, although the immediate economic challenges are not as great now as they were from 1985 to 1987, the case for continuing the reform momentum in the 1990s is just as pressing as it was then. This is so primarily because Indonesia needs to reform quickly just to keep pace with the international commercial environment, and because there remains a sizeable agenda of unfinished policy reforms.

(i) OTHER COUNTRIES ARE REFORMING QUICKLY: Indonesia has to push ahead with reforms just to stand still, comparatively speaking. More than any other post-war period, the international marketplace is replete with countries, large and small, engaged in the export of labour-intensive manufactures. In the 1960s and 1970s the Asian NIEs, and a few others in Latin America and southern Europe, had this market largely to themselves. In the current environment, Indonesia has to compete with the two Asian giants. One, China, is growing at a phenomenal speed of around 12 per cent per annum in recent years and its major export-oriented zones in the south reportedly growing at a fantastic 20 per cent per annum. The other, India, is much more hesitant in its reform thrust, but at least it has taken a huge step in its reform endeavours by making the rupee virtually fully convertible. The Philippines, too, took this long-overdue step in September 1992. Also in the immediate region, Vietnam has began to liberalize more quickly and effectively than many had expected. Now that its relations with the US are normalized, foreign capital and technology will pour in, giving it a decisive lift. Elsewhere, Latin America is beginning to move ahead, notably in Chile and Mexico, and these countries have the added advantage—it remains to be seen whether it is psychological or real—of preferential access to the North American market.

These changes in the international environment mean that many countries are trying to do the same thing as Indonesia. There will be price-depressive effects in the areas of major competition, in much the same way that commodity prices were low during the 1980s in part because many Third World countries attempted to service their debts by exporting more of a narrow range of mineral and other commodities. The reforms elsewhere mean that Indonesia will have to maintain an attractive and uncomplicated business environment if it wants to attract investment—not just for foreign firms, but to keep its own firms at home rather than going abroad, as many have begun to do over recent years.

Of all the challenges from the new exporters, that from China will undoubtedly be the greatest. First, China's very size means that it has a major impact. It has very quickly reached the NIEs in the volume of its exports. It has the commercial-diplomatic power to ensure international market access, whatever its human rights record at home. Perhaps even more important, China's economic success in the south and its unambiguous adoption of a market-based capitalist economy is having profound ripples through Southeast Asia, and especially in Indonesia and Malaysia. In these countries, the ethnic Chinese business community commands a commercial influence out of all proportion to its size, yet of course it has long been something of a pariah class, lacking in political influence.

For some of the disaffected in this group, the option in the past was to migrate, to Singapore or beyond the region entirely. For the first time since 1949, however, they are welcome back to a China which is commercially at least as hospitable as their current location, and probably more so, and where they do not have to suffer the stigma of being a politically vulnerable "alien class". A newly assertive Chinese business class is likely to emerge in Indonesia and its neighbours, a process dubbed by some as the "resinification of Southeast Asia". Chinese business interests are likely increasingly to demand an end to the overt discrimination in business and social life from which they currently suffer. If these demands are not met, the possibility of the movement of capital and a highly skilled business class back to China, with potentially devastating commercial implications for Indonesia, cannot be discounted.[4,5]

(ii)   A SIZEABLE UNFINISHED AGENDA: Significant though the reforms to date have been, the process is far from complete. Consider, for example, the following issues:

Tackling the state enterprise sector: The bold and far-reaching economic reforms of the late 1980s largely bypassed the state enterprise (SE) sector. In December 1986 the President instructed the then Coordinating Economics Minister, Professor Ali Wardhana, to report on financial conditions in SEs. For the next few months these enterprises were in the headlines, as those with a vested interest in the outcome of any reforms adopted a high public profile. The orthodox economics view, espoused by staff from the technocratic departments and some academic economists, was that reforms were overdue and a major overhaul was necessary. International organizations such as the World Bank also argued the case for reform. Staff in the line departments frequently took a contrary view, as did most—but not all—senior officials in the SEs.

In the event, very little came out of this debate. The SE sector began to shrink in relative terms because, owing to the government's fiscal austerity over this period, there was very little new investment in these firms, while the private sector was growing strongly. However, there was not one significant case of disposal or privatization among the 200 or so SEs. In this respect, Indonesia has been a striking exception to the winds of privatization that have swept through the world economy since the mid-1980s. To be fair, the government has attempted to reform these firms by insisting on improved financial reporting, and by pushing ahead with a program of "corporatization", which attempts to place state firms on the same footing as their private counterparts in financial and organizational management. There have been a few instances where the firms were in such an acute financial position that major surgery was essential. The state tin corporation is one such example, an instance where feather-bedding could not be sustained following the collapse of world tin prices and with it the international cartel. The reforms introduced in 1991–92 appear to have worked well, generating a marked increase in labour productivity and efficiency.

But such instances of major reforms are all too rare, and following the collapse of Bank Summa in late 1992 the pressure for reform of SEs may have abated. Defenders of the status quo point to this event as evidence that there is nothing inherently desirable about private, over state, ownership. In principle they have a point. An additional complicating factor in the reform process in Indonesia is of course the delicate ethnic equation. The fear that the most likely buyers of any SE put up for divestment would be either the country's major Chinese business conglomerates or the newly created empires of the President's children and others close to the "inner circle" has swayed much community opinion against reform. Opposition to reforms in the senior echelons in the bureaucracy is not infrequently motivated by financial considerations, as these officials hold lucrative directorships in SEs, and often retire to take up a senior management position. The collapse of the stock market in 1991, thereby rendering the option of disposal through public floats much less attractive, further stalled the process.

The history of state enterprise performance in Indonesia, as in so many other countries, is not a particularly encouraging one. These firms have invariably performed poorly by whatever yardstick is chosen—strictly financial criteria, or broader "development" objectives which many of their defenders see as the key reason for their existence. The problem, seemingly universal, is that governments are reluctant to allow these firms to compete in an unfettered manner, without subsidy and without restriction. Despite some recent reforms, most Indonesian SEs still have very little operational autonomy. They receive considerable subsidies, but they also have a plethora of restrictions imposed upon them which stifles commercial incentives and initiative. The government therefore faces a major dilemma here: it can ill-afford to leave such a large sector of the economy, accounting for as much as 35 per cent of non-agricultural GDP, untouched by the reform process. Yet its reform options are politically constrained. The best that may be hoped for, given these constraints, is a combination of continued liberal reform, more direct links between SE performance and staff incentive systems, and a transparent and accountable system of subsidies where they are granted.

Promoting a predictable and transparent policy regime: Another area largely unaffected by the 1980s reforms is the regulatory regime, and the operation of the bureaucracy in general. There have been some notable achievements over the course of the New Order, including the institution of an open capital account, a very clean and efficient drawback scheme for exporters from 1986, the customs breakthrough of April 1985, and conversion of NTBs to tariffs after 1985. There have also been some attempts to improve the efficiency of government departments and to recognize that, especially at senior levels, government salaries are often far below the levels prevailing in the private sector. But in the day-to-day operations of most government departments, little appears to have changed. A study commissioned by the World Bank in 1981, but never officially released, laid out the problems in great detail: the lack of precise objectives, and those that were enunciated were frequently in conflict with one another; the complexity of seemingly simple procedures; the costs such a complex and unpredictable regime imposed on business; and the general lack of trust between business and government.

For all the regulations which exist on the statute books, however, Indonesia is a rather "lawless" society. There is no firmly established history of press, legal and judicial independence. The press plays a major role as a guardian of civil liberties in some cases, but its ability to publish frankly on certain subjects is curtailed. Courts provide little protection for individuals or companies in the face of high-level intervention from the country's political or military wings. A new legal code to replace the antiquated system currently in use, and inherited from the Dutch colonial era, has been in preparation for many years. While this may go some way to overcoming the present deficiencies, the changes need to extend into the political–military–judicial nexus to be really effective. Investors need to be assured that they have an equal opportunity of success in tendering for a government project. If banks wish to resume the assets offered as collateral by a defaulting debtor, they need to be confident that they can do so quickly and cleanly. Those buying shares on the stock market need to be confident that certified financial data are reasonably accurate. A firm wishing to secure title to a proposed industrial site needs to be able to do so quickly. Partly for these reasons, Indonesia is still regarded as a "high-cost economy", especially by foreign investors who are unfamiliar with it. To remain attractive to international business, Indonesia needs to aim for nothing less than "Singapore-style" bureaucratic efficiency. Moreover, while deregulation, in the sense adumbrated above, remains a key issue, *more* regulation is required in certain areas, such as the prudential supervision of banks and the management of the stock market, to provide the business community with a predictable and stable business environment.

Cronyism—or where business and government get too close: There is nothing wrong with close business–government relations. Indeed, this has been a feature of many of the East Asian economic success stories. In Indonesia's case, too, the notion of such a "partnership" is popular, to redress the perceived ethnic imbalance in business circles, and owing to the battered state of domestic business in the wake of the Sukarno regime. Moreover, in the 1960s and 1970s there may have been a case for a significant government business role to quickly recycle the windfall oil revenue gains and to demonstrate to hesitant investors, foreign and domestic alike, that the country was a secure place in which to invest. The other side of the coin, of course, is that such a relationship can manifest itself in nepotism, cronyism and straight-out corruption. Where political and military power is heavy centralized—in fact personalized—where civil service salaries are low, and where the press is unable to report freely on certain topics, as in Indonesia, these problems are likely to surface.

There have been many notable achievements during the tenure of the New Order in combating corruption, as noted above. But the battle is never won. Corruption, both petty and large-scale, is a common occurrence in Indonesia. It emerged in virulent form in the late 1980s as the business interests of the children of the politically powerful began to grow dramatically, spurred on by all manner of government-sanctioned licences, monopolies, and other privileges. Some of these business empires—Bimantara, Humpus, to name only the two most prominent—are barely a decade old, but already they rank among the largest corporations in Southeast Asia. In some cases they have gained public notoriety, as in the clove monopoly, introduced ostensibly to assist small clove growers, and under which a central bank-financed board has been given the national monopoly for trade in this commodity. The "mega projects" issue, discussed below, raises similar concerns. Rent-seeking in forestry and in land acquisition and zoning is the rule rather than the exception. There are countless other examples of this sort, which appear to have flourished during the country's "good times", mainly the oil boom decade from 1973 and the strong industrial export growth period, from 1987 to the present.

It is important to keep these developments in perspective. Indonesia's macroeconomic management remains reasonably tight. Its response in "near-crisis" situations has been exemplary. Public comment, press exposure, and even to some extent parliamentary scrutiny of corruption is increasingly direct and sophisticated.[6] And its strongly growing exports of labour-intensive manufactures have been basically insulated from this crony politics. It would be tragic indeed, however, if in the 1990s the major achievements of the past 27 years were to be undone by the blatant greed of a few.

(iii) WILL LIBERALISM ALWAYS BE A DIRTY WORD? As argued above, it was the adoption of liberal, market-oriented reforms in the 1980s which enabled the Indonesian economy to recover from the hyperinflation and economic decline of the mid-1960s, and the adverse exogenous shock of the mid-1980s. Yet the country faces a fundamental dilemma in adhering to the principles of a liberal economy because notions of "liberalism" and "capitalism" are still very unpopular with a significant section of the population. One of the central philosophical problems of the New Order has been to define its economic ideology and to forge a community consensus around this philosophy. Of course, putting aside the official rhetoric concerning *Panca Sila* (the nation's five guiding philosophical principles), in practice the government has been first and foremost a pragmatic regime, responding to economic challenges in a largely orthodox manner. But Indonesia is the home of the "Middle Way", as former Vice President Hatta put it in the 1950s (Higgins, 1958), wishing to eschew both capitalism and communism. The notion of a cooperative-based economy and society still has tremendous appeal, a sentiment adroitly exploited by the President in his "Tapos meeting" of March 1990, when he instructed the heads of the country's 30 leading business conglomerates, almost all ethnic Chinese, to divest a portion of their equity to cooperatives. In the event, and underlining the national ambivalence on this subject, very little of substance resulted from the meeting. In a similar vein, debate over the interpretation of Article 33 of the Constitution still continues: was it intended that the government should control the economy in the sense of regulating it, or should it actually own the commanding heights?

Like many other newly independent states emerging from a turbulent colonial history, anti-capitalist sentiment was very powerful in the first two decades or so after Independence. But what has ensured that such feelings remain so popular today, almost 50 years on, is the delicate ethnic divide between the non-*pribumi* (mainly ethnic Chinese) groups, numbering no more than 4 per cent of the population but dominating much of the corporate sector of the economy, and the rest of the community. Although the evidence overwhelmingly suggests that all groups have prospered since the mid-1960s in roughly equal proportions, the Chinese business success has been spectacularly obvious in the emergence during the 1980s of big business conglomerates, and as Indonesia has become more obviously "capitalist".

Owing to religion, Indonesia does not have the "Thai option", whereby there will be a gradual assimilation of the Chinese community through intermarriage. It has avoided, probably wisely, the Malaysian route under its New Economic Policy, from 1970 to 1990, of instituting rigid ethnic targets for shares in ownership, employment, and much else. But the continuing ethnic schism will put great pressure on the political structure and it will inevitably result in the adoption of second-best policies in a number of areas. Inefficient state enterprises may not be reformed as quickly as they could be. Cooperatives will continue to be promoted officially, even though there is little evidence to suggest that they are commercially viable. The business manipulations of the politically powerful will tend to be overlooked by some because "at least they are *pribumi*". The strategy obviously has to be raise the living standards of the entire community, so that such divides no longer matter. But that is a long-term process which will take generations to achieve.

INDUSTRY POLICY AND "HIGH TECH": THE HABIBIE FACTOR

A major policy and analytical issue is to what extent East Asia's industrial success is the result of "industry policy". According to one popular interpretation of Northeast Asian development, particularly that of Japan and Korea, a key factor has been far-sighted activist regimes, in which governments have anticipated dynamic comparative advantage, allocated and directed resources accordingly, and "picked winners".[7] Such views receive much support in Indonesia, obviously because of Northeast Asia's undeniable success, but also because it reinforces widespread community and official distrust of markets and liberalism. But as argued in several chapters of this book (especially Chapters 6 and 8), the notion that selective industrial promotion policies explain Indonesia's industrial success receives very little empirical support. Protection has subsidized inefficient industries, and well beyond the stage of infancy. It has also taxed some of the most successful exporters in the past, notably the garment industry. State enterprises have not played a major developmental role. Subsidized credit has helped many firms, but the schemes have been plagued by corruption and it is not obvious that they have been a decisive factor in industrial growth.

The challenge of industrial policy is nowhere better illustrated than in the case of Professor B.J. Habibie, Minister of State for Research and Technology, Head of the Strategic Industries Board (BPIS), and now the Cabinet's longest-serving member after the President himself. He has a bold vision of Indonesia taking a quantum leap in technology into the twenty-first century, in contrast to the more cautious, evolutionary approach of the technocrats. As the de facto Minister for Industry he is likely to have a major bearing on industrial policy and performance in the 1990s.

Habibie's role raises a complex set of political and economic factors. There is little doubt that Indonesia needs to develop its technological capacities, especially in the area of education and firm-level skills. But at what cost? The Habibie "vision", while forward-looking in many respects, is an unknown and uncosted one. His theme that Indonesia cannot just rely for its success on the gradualist approach of the technocrats evokes widespread public support. In important respects his views, personal ties to the President, and his "think big" approach resemble those of the former President Director of Pertamina, Dr Ibnu Sutowo. Habibie's strategic industries already account for a significant percentage of Indonesia's state enterprise sector outside the finance and energy sectors. No public information is available on their economic performance. The "profit" figures reported are virtually meaningless, since they make no allowance for capital costs or for the large explicit and implicit subsidies conferred upon them. The very limited independent work on this subject, constrained by inadequate access to key financial data, suggests that financial performance has been poor and that there have been major managerial and absorptive problems.[8]

It is the absence of any public accountability, and the Minister's extraordinarily close access to President Soeharto, which in the long run are the sources of major concern for those wishing to curb his burgeoning empire. The Minister's power now extends well beyond his own portfolio. He was not elevated to the status of "Coordinating Minister" in the new Cabinet of March 1993, as was widely expected. But several of his supporters were awarded key portfolios, and others moved out of his Agency into senior positions in other departments.[9] These changes, coupled with the appointment for the first time of a non-economist to head the planning agency (Bappenas), the creation of a new "MITI" to coordinate trade and industry policy, and the departure of some of the key technocrats from the last Cabinet, have alarmed many. These concerns were not allayed, further, by Habibie's strong attack on the technocrats in January 1993, when he stated that Indonesia now had to emphasize technology policy over its macroeconomic preoccupation of the past 25 years. Such strong statements by a Cabinet Minister in Indonesia are unusual, and it was interpreted by many commentators as an attempt to change significantly the direction of economic policy.

EXTERNAL DEBT

As noted above, Indonesia avoided a debt crisis in the mid-1980s by taking swift and effective action to curb uneconomic public borrowings and to restore international competitiveness. The lesson of the 1980s debt crisis, more generally, is that countries encounter difficulty in servicing international borrowings only if they adopt inappropriate economic policies. As the East Asian NIEs demonstrated in the 1970s, it is possible for countries to continue to grow strongly, and to borrow abroad, even in adverse international circumstances such as a sharp decline in the terms of trade. What matters essentially is that when countries borrow abroad, the funds are invested in projects where the rates of return exceed the borrowing rate.

Indonesia accumulated debt rapidly in the 1980s as it adjusted to the declining terms of trade. Its external debt is officially estimated to be about $85 billion and its debt-service ratio about 35 per cent. The size of this debt and, in particular, the size of the current account deficit since 1990, have been a major topic of public debate and a preoccupation of economic policy-makers. These figures are extremely approximate, however, and are a probable underestimate. The true figure for the external debt is thought to be in excess of $100 billion, making Indonesia the Third World's largest debtor after Brazil. Much of the uncertainty concerning the size of the debt is a result of the fact that, with an open international account, accurate figures on private external debt are not available.

The issue of external debt has two main components. The first is the importance of an efficient export sector, including essentially a competitive exchange rate, which ensures that Indonesia has the foreign exchange earning capacity to service the debt. In this respect, Indonesia's record is a good one. There were sharp real depreciations of the exchange rate in the 1980s, and the maintenance of a competitive rate since then. The second, more complex, component concerns the use to which the borrowed funds are put. It is here that there is some cause for concern. In both the public and private sector there are investments for which rates of return may be below lending rates. In the public sector, much of the concern focuses on the state enterprise sector and its many loss-making operations. Included here are the borrowings of the state banks, and the huge heavy industry projects, mainly under the umbrella of Professor Habibie. In physical and social infrastructure projects, there may also be some grounds for concern, although these sectors typically display high social rates of return, and so if problems emerge they are more likely to be related to administrative and implementation shortcomings.

Finally, there are private borrowings abroad. In a competitive and undistorted environment, the external borrowings of private firms should, in principle, be no cause for alarm.[10] The particular problem in Indonesia in recent years has been that many of the proposed "private sector" projects have a strong government connection. Most have, or would have, borrowed from the state banks, while in many cases those with powerful political connections have been the major backers. Most of the so-called "megaprojects" which surfaced in the period from 1990 to 1992 were in these categories. Some may indeed have been viable investments. But there was a widespread suspicion that they would have required public subsidy, and that the manner by which this subsidy was to be procured would not be transparent or open to public scrutiny. None of the projects released an independently commissioned feasibility study. Most were thought likely to secure preferential financial access, either through subsidized loans from the state banks or through international borrowings and aid funds with a government guarantee. And although there was no official pronouncement on the subject, it was thought likely that all projects would obtain special trade privileges, in the form of tailor-made import duty exemptions and tariff protection.

In these circumstances, and given the nature of the business interests involved, the technocrats were forced to depart from one of the fundamental tenets of New Order economic policy in September 1991. This entailed the establishment of the committee to vet international borrowings by all state entities, including the state banks.[11] There is a very real danger that, the longer the committee continues, this clumsy, sub-optimal strategy is resulting in a permanent departure from the doctrine of an open international capital account. The technocrats will, no doubt, face a continuing struggle in the 1990s to stave off other attempts by politically powerful interests who wish to "privatize profits but socialize losses".

HOLDING THE COUNTRY TOGETHER

Besides ethnic cleavages, discussed above, the other significant divide in Indonesia is the spatial dimension. Indonesia's diversity, combined with a history of disaffection in certain regions of the country, poses particular challenges for the central government. There are divides between "inner" and "outer" Indonesia, between East and West, and between the four major mineral exporting provinces (Aceh, East Kalimantan, Riau, and Irian Jaya) and the rest of the country. In addition, in three provinces (Aceh, East Timor and Irian Jaya) there are unique historical factors which form the bases of disaffection.

In view of this potentially explosive cocktail, it might be considered an achievement that the country has actually held together since Independence. As noted in Chapter 11, the regime has embarked on a very deliberate program of regional development which, although centralized and heavy-handed in its implementation, has ensured that all regions have benefited from rapid national development, at least in some measure. Yet the regional factor continues to be a potent one. During the 1990s it will pose a different kind of challenge to that which surfaced a decade or two ago.

First, international events have changed the intellectual environment. With the break-up of the former USSR and Yugoslavia, the notion of the nation state is no longer sacrosanct. For Indonesia, merely 50 years old as a nation, after a bitterly contested struggle for Independence, the proposition that it could splinter is of course a shocking one. But for the disaffected in the *daerah* (region), still few in number, examples abroad could provide a spur to their own campaigns. A second challenge arises from the fact that the central government does not have the financial resources on the scale it possessed in the 1970s oil boom. Therefore, its capacity to "buy" its way out of regional protests through financial largesse is a good deal more limited now.

Thirdly, the nature of Indonesia's export-oriented development has significant implications for the country's spatial patterns of development. The Javanese economy, which has performed consistently well through the New Order, has been stimulated further by the manufactured export boom. With the exception of plywood and fertilizer, and the Batam industrial complex, virtually all the new industrial exports are produced in Java-Bali. This has not been the result of any conscious government directive (apart from a few minor instances such as rattan processing), but rather because Java's subnational comparative advantage lies in this area—it has the unskilled and skilled labour, the physical infrastructure, and the entrepreneurs.

In consequence, Indonesia's major regional challenge is no longer rural poverty in Java, as it was portrayed in the 1960s, but the increasingly by-passed areas of Eastern Indonesia. It is unlikely that these provinces will attract much industry in the next decade or two, apart from a limited amount of simple resource-based processing, based on timber, fisheries and some food and cash crops. These regions do not have a significant wage-cost advantage over Java, they are distant from major national and international centres of commerce, and their physical infrastructure is poor. Just as many poor and isolated nation states are dependent on aid and remittances, so too are the poorer provinces of Indonesia's East going to have to be supported financially by the richer western provinces, and the international community, for the foreseeable future. There is much in addition that can be done through the provision of public amenities (roads, ports, schools, health services, etc.), and through the introduction of programs which build on local resources and initiative. But it is important not to lose sight of the fact that, whereas Java and much of the West will be able to, in effect, fund itself through the export-oriented industrialization phase, if Indonesia is to hold together the East will continue to require special support.

CONTINUING TO ENHANCE SUPPLY-SIDE CAPACITIES

Indonesia is likely to remain a low-wage country for decades to come. One of the lessons of the East Asian success stories is that wages will rise in a sustained, broad-based fashion only after the labour market begins to tighten and the "labour surplus" begins to disappear, in the manner envisaged in the classic Lewis model. Policies which seek to interrupt this process, by pushing up wages prematurely, are likely to retard the pace of labour absorption.

However, there is much that the government can do, through education, training, and technological development, to enhance labour productivity, thereby both raising living standards and facilitating international competitiveness. This issue is particularly pertinent since a tier of new exporters is emerging with wages which may be even lower than those in Indonesia. Indonesia can hardly compete with these countries on the basis of low wages. Moreover, as the country begins to diversify its industrial base and its range of manufactured exports, a broader range of industrial and commercial skills will be required. Serious supply-side constraints have emerged during all boom periods since 1966. It needs to be remembered, moreover, that during the post-1988 East Asian economic boom, Indonesia recorded the slowest growth among the HPAEs. It is reasonable to conjecture that this slower growth was, to a significant degree, the result of the country's serious supply-side bottlenecks.

This process of industrial upgrading can be achieved partly by a liberal commercial regime which permits the uninterrupted flow of goods, technologies and people, and which provides incentives for longer-term investments and innovation. In this respect, Indonesia scores reasonably well. But in addition the government will have to do more than it has in the past to develop supply-side capacities. Even in well-functioning markets, private agents are likely to underinvest in education, not to mention R&D, principally because they are often unable to appropriate all the benefits from such investments. In countries such as Indonesia, where investors' time horizons are very short, the problem could be more serious. The social and private returns from investment in education, in Indonesia and elsewhere, have been estimated to be very high. This alone would justify more resources to this sector, at all levels, than the current somewhat meagre amounts. There is also a sound case for developing a more effective industrial extension service, akin to that employed in agriculture, to ensure the widespread adoption of new and more efficient technologies. Finally, it is crucially important that all forms of infrastructure—roads, power, telecommunications, ports, urban services—be available in sufficient quantities and at comparable prices and quality to international best-practice. The issues of what agencies provide these services, and whether they be publicly or privately owned, are not of great importance, although given the record of government agencies as cumbersome, inefficient, and slow to respond to demand, there is a strong case for greater private sector involvement here.[12]

AN INDONESIA WITHOUT OIL?

Some time in the next two decades or so, barring unforeseen developments, Indonesia will no longer be a net exporter of oil and gas. The timing of this switch from net exporter to net importer is difficult to predict as much depends on Indonesia's rate of economic growth (and therefore its energy consumption), its domestic pricing and conservation policies, and world energy prices. The date of the crossover will continue to recede, because the closer the country gets to this point, the greater will be the pressures for conservation.[13] Indonesia will continue to be a natural gas exporter in this period, but will begin to import oil in at least equivalent quantities. The country will also continue as a resource-based exporter, selling coal, copper, tin, nickel and other metals abroad.

There are at least two reasons for believing that the exhaustion of oil exports will not interrupt the pace of economic development in Indonesia. First, the country has already adjusted to a decline in the importance of oil of a roughly similar magnitude. In 1981, at the peak of the oil boom, oil and gas constituted over three-quarters and two-thirds of the country's exports and government revenue, respectively. Following the oil price decline and the successful structural adjustment period, a decade later these shares had fallen by approximately one-half, while respectable growth rates have been maintained. If Indonesia can maintain the pace of adjustment, at this rate a diminished oil surplus some time early in the next century should pose little difficulty. The second reason is, obviously, that East Asia is full of resource-poor development success stories. These successful economies managed to grow quickly even when, as in the 1970s, they experienced adverse terms of trade movements. Rapid export growth resulted in rising income terms of trade (that is, the quantity increase exceeded the price decrease) even as their price terms of trade declined. The lesson from this and other episodes of economic development is that natural resources are not a key factor in explaining intercountry variations in economic performance.

THE MANAGEMENT OF NATURAL RESOURCES

The management of Indonesia's natural resources raises complex issues of fiscal appropriation, administrative capacity, and trade-offs between material living standards and environmental amenities. The following paragraphs identify some, but by no means all, of these issues.

There is little doubt that Indonesia's record of forest management is a poor one; in fact, it is perhaps the most significant item on the negative side of the regime's ledger of development performance. As noted in Chapter 7, the fiscal regime has resulted in a major undercollection of forest rents. Corruption has been blatant and widespread. The management of the forests, and replanting programs, have been weak. On both economic and environmental grounds there is a strong case for reform of the fiscal regime, to increase government revenue and to provide a better incentive for forest management. Given the nature of vested interests in the industry, however, it is most unlikely that reform is possible within existing institutional structures. As with the 1985 customs revolution, there would have to be a complete overhaul, and a new administrative agency. Similar comments apply to the management of public lands, the sale and lease of which are consistently underpriced (World Bank, 1994).

Another complex case of environmental management concerns Java's uplands. Owing also to lax supervision, and inappropriate agricultural activities such as the production of temperate vegetables, the loss of forest cover and erosion are serious problems. Their consequences are becoming increasingly evident, in widespread flooding, loss of top-soil and leaching. Here also, weak supervisory capacity is a major cause of these problems. Moreover, the complex pattern of land titles provides very little security for agricultural tenants, who therefore have no incentive to adopt better conservation practices. An additional challenge in Java's ecology has been coping with the unintended consequences of the fertilizer and pesticide subsidies, the latter now abolished. Excessive fertilizer use has generated significant negative externalities, including the pollution of waterways previously used for fishing, and in some instances soil degradation. Uncontrolled industrial pollution of the air and waterways also generates other significant negative externalities, notably in its impact on public health.

The government has begun, in a limited fashion, to enforce regulations concerning industrial and commercial emissions. There is an obvious case for such an approach on the grounds that such negative externalities should be taxed at their source, wherever possible. This could include, for example, introducing effluent charges, full-cost water charging, and urban congestion provisions in major cities (Ahmed, 1991; World Bank, 1994). Moreover, the costs of imposing better environmental standards are quite low in many instances, and so there is scope for the government to enforce standards at modest social and private cost. The real issue here is how far the government ought to proceed in this direction. What environmental standards should be set? High quality environmental amenities are, inevitably, something of a luxury good. Indonesia could aspire to the very highest of OECD standards, for example, but the cost would be high.[14] Somehow, the community has to decide on a trade-off between costs and quality of life. The example of the now rich Northeast Asian countries—and indeed of all the OECD bloc—is something akin to "growth first, environmental clean-up later". The choices do not have to be so stark, of course. As noted, the costs of improved environmental quality may be quite modest. In some industries, such as tourism, there is a compelling commercial incentive to maintain and improve standards. And obviously, severe cases of degradation have to be tackled. But it would be foolish to pretend that trade-offs do not exist. Equally, the administrative implications of environmental regulation need to be addressed. The costs of supervision will be significant, especially among small firms. And as in so many other cases of regulation, a poorly paid and ill-equipped staff may simply impose an additional layer of exactions on firms, without achieving environmental goals.

ENSURING INTERNATIONAL MARKET ACCESS

It hardly needs to be stated that the maintenance of Indonesia's export-oriented strategy requires an accommodating international environment—one in which world demand for the products Indonesia wishes to export is expanding, and in which the country faces no major institutional constraints. Indonesia has done well out of the international economy since 1965, as a commodity exporter, aid and capital recipient, and most recently as an industrial exporter. There have been periodic recessions, but for most of the period the international economy has grown, albeit at a slower pace than the first quarter-century after World War II. Indonesia's terms of trade have fluctuated considerably, putting pressure on macroeconomic management to cope with exogenous shocks. There have also been a few irritants in its international commercial relations, such as trading partners' tariffs for certain commodity exports which escalate according to the degree of processing, and the soon to be phased-out Multi Fibre Arrangement which initially assisted but more recently restrained the growth of textile and garment exports. But by and large the international environment has been a benign and supportive one, a fact which does not sit easily alongside the considerable reservation—indeed hostility—towards the notion of closer international engagement in some Indonesian quarters.

Barring a major and prolonged slowdown in, or fragmentation of, the international economy, external conditions are unlikely to be a serious constraint on Indonesia's future growth. The strong export growth from 1989 to 1992 during a period of international recession illustrated that efficient exporters can survive in such circumstances. Although export markets will become increasingly competitive, the resolution of the Uruguay Round of international trade negotiations in late 1993 offers emerging international exporters such as Indonesia the reasonably strong and durable prospect of a transparent and accessible global market environment. Further supporting this picture of qualified optimism is Indonesia's location in the high-growth East Asian region, and its strengthening ties to these economies through institutional mechanisms which emphasize open regionalism. But to take advantage of these opportunities, Indonesian firms and bureaucrats will have to be nimble and clever, in negotiating international arrangements and in assisting nascent exporters to identify new commercial opportunities.

A frequently overlooked factor is that the need to ensure international market access should have a beneficial effect on the pace of domestic reform. Now more than ever before Indonesia's trade and regulatory interventions are under scrutiny, especially by the US, but more generally within the GATT/WTO framework. Indonesia cannot complain about, or bargain over, export constraints abroad so long as it maintains such barriers at home. This is a comparatively new element in the country's trade policy formulation process. The export industries are now very significant in Indonesia's political economy equations, and if these exporters complain that their operations in certain markets abroad are being hindered by other restrictions at home they are likely to be listened to. It seems clear that this consideration has been a factor in the country's recent trade liberalizations and that it will become more important in the future. Nationalists may not like this new form of international engagement, but there is little they can do about it if the export sector is to continue as a major engine of growth.

A SUMMING UP

It would be inappropriate to finish a book about a successful economy with a checklist of problems. It needs to be emphasized again that the record since 1966 is much better than the great majority of developing countries, and than Indonesia's record at any time in its history up to 1966. The improvement in economic and social indicators over this period far exceeds the expectations of even the most optimistic observers at the beginning of the regime. And as emphasized throughout this book, the capacity of the regime to weather, and respond decisively to, adverse economic circumstances is unparalleled. Barring any catastrophe, political, economic or ecological, it is not unreasonable to project a continuation of Indonesia's development momentum. The real issue is whether the country proceeds at the high speed East Asian pace, resulting in a dramatic improvement in living standards, or is closer to the Third World norm of slower economic progress. That is, whether the economy grows at 7 to 8 per cent per annum, which implies a quadrupling in real per capita GDP every 25 years or so, or around 4 to 5 per cent, in which case the increase takes closer to 50 years. The issues identified in this concluding chapter are likely to be central to determining which path Indonesia takes. If they are not resolved, there will still be economic progress. But Indonesia's ascent to the status of a significant middle-income economy will be delayed, and community living standards will grow more slowly.

CHRONOLOGY OF MAJOR ECONOMIC EVENTS, 1965 TO 1993

1965

December   'New' rupiah introduced, equivalent to 1,000 'old' rupiah; petroleum prices increased 250-fold; Indonesia ceased to meet foreign exchange commitments

1966

March   Soeharto assumes formal executive authority

April   Indonesia applies for readmission to United Nations; Deputy Premier Sultan Hamengkubuwono delivers a frank assessment of economic conditions

June   Arrival of IMF mission

September   First major meeting with non-communist creditors, in Tokyo

October   Major stabilization and rehabilitation program announced; import licensing system partially dismantled; 'export bonus' scheme liberalized

December   Further meeting with creditors, in Paris

1967

January   New foreign investment law announced

February   First official meeting of IGGI, in The Hague

July   Major foreign exchange liberalization

August   Banking crisis

September   Widespread rice shortages reported

November   New mining law enacted

December   Major reorganization of state enterprises; new banking law introduced

1968

April   Large increases in prices of petroleum products and utilities

May   Major overhaul of 'export bonus' scheme

September   Positive rates on bank deposits instituted

November   Domestic investment law introduced

December   Eight commercial banks established

1969

April   *Repelita* I commences; start of financial year shifted from 1 January to 1 April

May   Further reorganization of state enterprises

September   *Ekonomi dan Keuangan Indonesia* resumes publication

December	Inflation effectively brought under control (17 per cent for the year)

1970
April	Major trade policy package—devaluation, elimination of most multiple exchange rates, simplification of export and import procedures; elimination of international capital controls; some import bans introduced in the automotive industry
May	*Bimas Gotong Royong* discontinued, replaced with *Bimas Nasional* and *Inmas*
December	Final and complete unification of the exchange rate

1971
April	Import ban on CBU automobiles imposed for Java and Sumatra
August	10 per cent devaluation of rupiah, now pegged to US$
September	Import duties on 459 items reduced

1972
December	Serious rice shortage evident—rice prices doubled August–December

1973
June	The Investment Coordinating Board (BKPM) established
August	International petroleum prices begin to rise steeply, quadrupling in next six months
November	Preferential treatment by state banks for small *pribumi* borrowers announced

1974
January	Malari protests occur; import ban extended to all CBU vehicles; state bank medium-term credits henceforth available only to firms with significant *pribumi* participation; non-oil foreign investment regime tightened
March	Regional development strategy announced, including establishment of Bappedas; state enterprises transferred from the Department of Finance to 'technical' departments
April	*Repelita* II commences; anti-inflation package announced, including increased interest rates and ceilings on (state) commercial bank credit

1975
February	Pertamina unable to repay or refinance its short-term debt
April	Major shift in sugar strategy announced, encouraging small-holder production
May	Bank Indonesia ceases publication of its weekly and monthly bulletin (resumed September 1976)
July	Soeharto and the Japanese Prime Minister sign the Asahan agreement

October	Imports of 23 varieties of textiles banned

1976

February	First ASEAN Summit held, in Bali
March	President Director of Pertamina, Ibnu Sutowo, 'dismissed with honour'
April	Export promotion package introduced, most export taxes reduced to 5 per cent
August	Regulations relating to 'Third Generation' mining contracts announced

1977

February	Investment licensing regime becomes more transparent; petroleum investment incentive packages become more attractive
June	Government announces intensified anti-corruption campaign
August	Jakarta Stock Exchange reopened; first major LNG shipment, from Bontang (East Kalimantan) to Japan

1978

January	Deposit rates reduced, and banks' reserve requirements cut from 30 per cent to 15 per cent
June	Smallholder development program introduced, including Nucleus Estates Scheme and several crop-specific initiatives
November	50 per cent devaluation of the rupiah; extensive price controls introduced

1979

January	Export Certificate (*Sertifikat Ekspor*) scheme introduced
April	New tax package introduced, affecting company, sales and excise taxes, and tariffs; *Repelita* III commences
September	Second round of large increases in international petroleum prices commences
October	Stage I of PT Krakatau Steel starts production

1980

January	Presidential Decree 14A favours *pribumi* in government procurements
May	Ban on log exports announced, to be introduced in several phases; 50 per cent increase in domestic petroleum prices
July	Indonesia's first textile trade dispute occurs, with the United Kingdom

1981

November	Automotive industry plan envisages full local content by 1985

1982

January   Domestic petroleum prices increased by 60 per cent; new trade promotion package announced, including counterpurchase and export credits

March   Emergency OPEC meeting agrees to production cutbacks

November   Import licensing in the form of approved importer system (*Tata Niaga Impor*) commences; sharp increase in departure tax, from Rp 25,000 to Rp 150,000

1983

January   70 per cent increase in domestic petroleum prices

March   Rupiah devalued by 28 per cent

May   Deferral of major public sector projects, valued at $5 billion

June   Major banking reform—controls over state bank deposit rates removed, some credit ceilings abolished, liquidity credit scheme scaled down

July   Huge Asahan Project officially opened

September   First domestically produced aircraft (CN-235) displayed

December   Wide-ranging quantitative import restrictions introduced

1984

January   50 per cent increase in prices of domestic petroleum products

February   *Kupedes* (Village Credit Scheme) launched by Bank Indonesia; Bank Indonesia introduces discount facilities to encourage open market operations

March   Foundation stone of controversial Cold Rolling Steel Mill at Cilegon laid

April   *Repelita* IV commences; major tax reform package introduced, including simplification of direct tax rates and abolition of most investment incentives, and announcement that value added and land and building taxes to be phased in

June   Large investments in petroleum refining come on stream, doubling capacity

September   Capital flight precipitates money market crisis, overnight interbank rate exceeds 80 per cent

November   Further restrictions on public sector procurements (*Keppres* 29, 30) announced

1985

February   New short-term debt obligation (promissory note) facility introduced

March   Reform of the tariff schedule, including introduction of 60 per cent ceiling on tariffs

April   Wide-ranging public debate on the 'high-cost economy' commences; value added tax takes effect; *Inpres* 4 announced: customs responsibilities substantially handed over to Swiss Surveyor SGS, and partial deregulation of domestic and international shipping

June	Further import restrictions announced; government acquires 30 per cent shareholding in the financially troubled PT Indocement
November	Soeharto announces Indonesia has achieved rice self-sufficiency

1986

January	International petroleum prices plunge to below $20/barrel; government announces austerity budget; new land and building tax takes effect
May	Spot and contract prices for Minas crude fall to below $11/barrel; *Sertifikat Ekspor* scheme replaced with duty free and drawback facilities for exporters
September	45 per cent devaluation of the rupiah
October	Major import liberalization package, comprising shift of some 321 items from NTB to tariff protection
November	Presidential Decree on rice ecology bans the use of 57 varieties of pesticides and announces Integrated Pest Management program
December	Soeharto instructs Coordinating Economics Minister to undertake thorough review of the state enterprise sector

1987

January	Further import liberalizations announced, affecting textiles and iron and steel
February	New rice intensification scheme (*Supra-Insus*) launched
June	Capital flight precipitates monetary crisis, and first *Gebrakan Sumarlin* results in interbank rates of up to 45 per cent; foreign investment regulations liberalized; the textile export quota system is liberalized
August	Strategic Industry Board (BPIS) established, affecting 10 key industries and headed by Minister Habibie
December	Major liberalization package effecting imports (further shift from NTBs), foreign investment, the stock market, and tourism

1988

July	Ban on the export of unprocessed and semi-processed rattan
October	Major financial sector reforms enacted—entry provisions liberalized, reserve requirements reduced, and a withholding tax on bank deposits imposed
November	Deregulation of foreign investment, shipping and imports (plastics and steel) extended
December	Further liberalization of the financial sector

1989

January	Civil service salaries frozen for third successive year
April	*Repelita* V commences
June	Measures to increase state enterprise efficiency introduced

August	Stock market reforms enable foreign companies to acquire up to 49 per cent of listed companies' shares

1990

January	Further banking reforms, including removal or phasing-out of most refinance subsidies
March	Soeharto calls a meeting with the owners of 31 major business groups and requests that they divest up to 25 per cent of their equity to cooperatives
May	A further trade reform package
August	Beginnings of short-lived increase in international oil prices
September	Bank Duta, one of the largest private banks, announces foreign exchange losses of $420 million

1991

January	Politically powerful private group given the monopoly to purchase and distribute cloves
February	Second *Gebrakan Sumarlin* removes Rp 10 trillion of liquidity from the system; new banking regulations introduced, entailing greater prudential supervision
June	Additional trade reforms introduced
September	Coordinating committee established to vet overseas borrowings of state entities

1992

March	Indonesia terminates all official Dutch aid; a new donor consortium, the Consultative Group on Indonesia, is established
April	100 per cent foreign ownership of firms permitted in certain circumstances; controversial Chandra Asri petrochemical plant receives approval
May	The prohibition on log exports is removed and replaced by very high export taxes
December	Bank Summa, a large private bank, is liquidated; in consequence, the Soeryadjaya family loses control of the Astra group

1993

January	Significant increase in, and some restructuring of, public service salaries
March	New Cabinet installed, with apparent decline in the power of the technocrats
June	Minor trade reform package introduced, mainly directed at the automotive industry
October	Further minor simplification of the foreign investment regime
December	Large increases in minimum wage announced, over 40 per cent in the case of the Botabek (fringe Jakarta) and Bandung regions

NOTES

CHAPTER 1

[1] The term employed was *Manipol Usdek*, *manipol* being an abbreviation of *Manifesto Politik*, and *USDEK* an acronym of the five guiding principles listed above.

[2] The popular slogan in this case was *Berdikari, berdiri diatas kaki sendiri*, or literally standing on one's own feet.

[3] The standard references on the economy before 1966 include Higgins (1957), Mackie (1971), and Paauw (1963). Glassburner (ed., 1971) and Tan (ed., 1967) contain valuable collections of essays. The best collection of statistics over the 1960–65 period is contained in *Report of Bank Indonesia for the Financial Years 1960-1965*, released in 1967. As explained in the Report's introduction, no annual reports were issued over this period " . . . because of the decision of the Minister of Finance . . . of 6 January 1961 which prohibited the Bank Indonesia from publishing any monetary/banking statistics or annual reports". Most of the data in this paragraph are taken from this Report.

[4] That this achievement was recognized internationally was illustrated by the fact that when Colombia discovered oil, the country's senior economic policy-makers examined the Indonesian record closely, to the point of conducting a high-level international conference on the lessons from Indonesian development at Bogota in March 1994.

[5] These were Algeria, Ecuador, Nigeria, Trinidad and Tobago, and Venezuela; surprisingly Mexico was not included in the study. The Indonesia chapter in this volume was written by Bruce Glassburner.

[6] For a recent and comprehensive survey and assessment of Indonesian politics since 1966, including an extensive bibliography, see Mackie and MacIntyre (1994).

CHAPTER 2

[1] A note on Indonesian national accounts statistics is appropriate here. Although their quality has improved enormously since the mid-1960s, one continuing limitation is that the Central Bureau of Statistics (Biro Pusat Statistik, BPS) has never published a consistent, long-term (20 years or more) series. The published constant price series employ several base years. This is to be expected, but there has never been a long-term series published for *any* set of constant prices. Revisions to the current price series are also frequent. The data employed in this section are based on spliced series, calculated backwards from the last estimates. It needs to be emphasized, therefore, that while these long-term series use official data, they should be regarded as "author's estimates" since no such spliced series is available. For some additional comments on BPS data, see Footnote 15 below.

[2] Note here that these are constant-price estimates, and so the effects of rising oil prices are not captured directly in mining output.

[3] The "non-oil" series in Figure 2.3 refers to GDP less value added in mining. This is because there are no published estimates of non-oil GDP prior to the mid-1970s, so the first best approximation is non-mining GDP. The non-oil series published since the mid 1970s refers to GDP less value added in oil, gas and their industrial processing. It is the latter series which is unavailable for the earlier period. Both the non-mining and the non-oil series therefore exclude oil and gas mining. The difference is that "non-oil" also excludes oil and gas processing, whereas "non-mining" excludes non-oil mining. For the period when data are available, the two series move closely together. For example, in 1992 non-mining GDP totalled Rp 224.2 trillion, as compared with Rp 223.2 trillion in the non-oil case. It is possible that there was a greater divergence in the late 1960s, when oil refining capacity was small. But on grounds of long-term

consistency, there is no practical alternative to the non-mining series. Note that the latter is used also in Figure 2.6.

[4] The obvious caveats associated with interpreting the data in Figure 2.3 need to be emphasized here. These include, in particular, the fact that service exports are not included, and the ratio compares value added and gross value of output. It is probable that the "domestic value added" component of exports fell during the 1980s, in the switch from resource-based commodity exports to footloose manufactures, and that therefore the reported rise in the non-oil series is exaggerated. On the other hand, the inclusion of services data, if available, would boost the export ratio.

[5] The data in Figure 2.3, incidentally, underline the perils of including Indonesia in comparative cross-country studies which seek to determine a causal relationship between rates of export and economic growth (for example, see Ram, 1985), and illustrate why Indonesia has been an outlier in such studies, at least for the period since 1966 as a whole, though not for the subperiods 1966 to 1980 and post-1985.

[6] Indonesia's true investment ratio is a matter of some controversy. The data in Figure 2.4 include changes in stocks which, as a proportion of GDP, have been as much as 8 percentage points. Their inclusion therefore pushes up the investment ratio considerably, and also the ICORs over this period. Official Indonesian data generally record the investment ratio without stock changes, whereas most World Bank data sources include stocks in the figure.

[7] Anne Booth (pp. 6–10) explores the issue of Indonesia's high ICOR in the August 1989 *BIES* Survey. She cites concern in government circles at the sharp rise in the ICOR in the first half of the 1980s.

[8] Recall that these are current price series, so the effects of the oil price increases translate directly into sectoral shares.

[9] For detailed analyses of employment patterns in Indonesia during the New Order, see Jones (1994) and Jones and Manning (1992), and references cited therein.

[10] The transport sector also grew very rapidly over this period, and for similar reasons, but there was not the same employment growth, presumably again because of the backwash effects, in this case occurring in labour-intensive activities such as *becak* (trishaws), and the *prahu* (sail boats) inter-island shipping network.

[11] Before leaving the topic of structural change, one final issue should be noted, namely its determinants. The broad dimensions of these changes are well known, but their precise determinants much less so. In a recent paper, Martin and Warr (1993) have addressed this issue, constructing a simple model of structural transformation to decompose the determinants of the declining share of agricultural output into relative price effects on the demand side (notably that of Engel's Law), and supply-side factors such as relative factor endowments and differential rates of technological progress. They found that, contrary to the general presumption in the literature, demand-side factors were rather weak, having much less effect than capital accumulation and rapid technological progress in agriculture.

[12] Benjamin Higgins, a long-term knowledgeable observer, characterized the situation thus: " . . . net capital consumption has been going on in Indonesia for at least thirty-five years". (*BIES*, March 1972, p. 23)

[13] The figures in Tables 2.3 and 2.4 are suggestive rather than conclusive. For one thing, total factor productivities would provide a more accurate estimate of technological change. Another reason is that sectoral categories are highly aggregated. A more intensive investigation of the data would, for example, disaggregate manufacturing into large and small subsectors (as done, for example, in Hill, 1990a), agriculture into food crops, cash crops and other activities, and the various service sectors into finer subcategories.

[14] This is so notwithstanding the short-lived divergence in 1990 and 1991, owing to the Middle East dispute at this time.

[15] One additional criticism directed at the growth record is that the quality of Indonesia's

national accounts data is so poor that no strong conclusions can be drawn. Such a criticism is misdirected, both because the BPS is a highly professional and independent body, and because independent verification of important series (such as trade, investment, and tourism) is possible. This is not to deny that particular statistical series have been the subject of debate among economists and statisticians, however. Numerous illustrations could be mentioned in this context. For example, in the late 1980s it was revealed that Indonesia had been undercounting its manufacturing output, since BPS had been unable to keep up with the proliferation of new firms. It is believed that official petroleum output may have understated actual levels in some years as Indonesia sought to evade OPEC quotas on a minor scale. Some of the estimates of services value added are regarded as at best approximate, owing to inherent difficulties of measurement. Trade and accommodation are cases in point. Estimates of forestry output are also regarded as unreliable, owing to widespread corruption and lax supervision in the industry. These and other examples do not invalidate the broad picture, however. Indeed, in some instances (when *under*reporting is known to occur) they reinforce it, especially given BPS's well-deserved reputation for openness, as indicated by its willingness to disseminate the tapes of its various series and to engage in discussion with researchers and other users.

CHAPTER 3

[1] The then Foreign Minister, Dr Subandrio, is reported to have dismissed an economist's concern about macroeconomic management with the remark "[T]he fact that you regard economic problems as important shows how your mind has been corrupted by Western liberalism". The economist was Professor Emil Salim, a distinguished Minister for most of the New Order period. I owe this observation and quote to H.W. Arndt.

[2] The statement was made by Rachmat Saleh, and is quoted in Bolnick (1987, p. 582). The reference is to McKinnon (1973), and is used in this context to denote the public's complete lack of confidence in the currency, rather than simply the existence of disequilibrium interest rates.

[3] In addition to *BIES* Surveys, there are a number of detailed studies of monetary policy and performance over this period. Arndt (1971) studied the banking system during the peak inflation period and immediately thereafter. Grenville (1981) provides a detailed study up to the late 1970s, while Arndt (1979) focuses particularly on monetary policy instruments during the 1970s, and Nasution (1983) examines the development of financial institutions. Woo and Nasution (1989) provide a lengthy study of macroeconomic policy through to the early 1980s, in the context of external debt management, while Woo, Glassburner and Nasution (1994) provide a detailed analysis of the period up to 1990, as part of the World Bank comparative macroeconomic project referred to in Chapter 1. Cole and Slade (1992) trace financial developments over the whole period, and Binhadi and Meek (1992) provide a more technical discussion of monetary policy developments in the 1980s. Pangestu (1991c) assesses the 1980s record in an ASEAN context. Odono et al. (1988) survey financial development through to the mid-1980s, while Boediono and Kaneko (1988) investigate the factors affecting inflation over the same period. McLeod (1992) assesses the recently enacted Banking Law. A major book on the development of Indonesia's financial system is being prepared by Ross McLeod.

[4] An obvious word of caution in interpreting trends in interest rates is that in the 1970s there was a multiplicity of lending rates according to the various priority sectors. There was hardly an "interest rate". The 12-month deposit rate is selected in Figure 3.1 for illustrative purposes only.

[5] Although, of course, the price mechanism intruded. Throughout this period of negative rates it was common knowledge that illegal payments to secure state bank loans were widespread and necessary (McLeod, 1980).

[6] The data are from Bolnick (1987), who provides an overview of the programs. The acronyms refer to *Kredit Investasi Kecil* and *Kredit Modal Kerja Permanen* which refer respectively to credit for fixed and working capital.

[7] As discussed in Chapter 5, there was no balance of payments justification for the devaluation. Rather, the measure was apparently undertaken to promote non-oil tradeable activities, and in

the belief among some officials that the real international oil price would either decline or, at best, not increase in the medium-term future.

[8] These included Central Bank Certificates (SBI, *Sertifikat Bank Indonesia*) introduced in February 1984 and designed to mop up excess liquidity, and a short-term debt facility (SBPU, *Surat Berharga Pasar Uang*) introduced in February 1985 as a means of injecting short-term liquidity when required. H.W. Arndt provided an early assessment of the June reforms in the August 1983 *BIES* Survey.

[9] The intervention was quickly dubbed *Gebrakan Sumarlin* (Sumarlin Shock Therapy), in deference to the Acting Minister's dramatic steps. It was repeated on a larger scale in February 1991 by Dr Sumarlin, at this time the substantive Minister of Finance. The immediate effect in the latter instance was similar, although arguably the setback to the reform process—by then almost eight years in progress—was greater.

[10] For a detailed medium-term review of the impact of the reforms on the financial sector, see the August 1993 *BIES* Survey by Ross McLeod, especially pp. 17-31.

[11] In particular, the operation of the facility over this period had the effect of undermining domestic monetary policy. This occurred because Indonesian firms had a strong incentive to borrow abroad, a result of the fact that domestic lending rates exceeded the sum of the swap rate plus the foreign lending rate, even allowing for the fact that the latter (e.g. the Singapore Sibor) was generally higher for Indonesian borrowers owing to sovereign risk factors.

[12] For a more technical discussion of the many complex issues associated with monetary policy management over this period, see several *BIES* "Surveys", in particular by Ross McLeod (August 1993), John Conroy and Peter Drake (August 1990), Stephen Parker (April 1990), and Anwar Nasution (August 1991). See also Binhadi and Meek (1992).

[13] Andrew MacIntyre and Sjahrir summarize the main features of the Summa debacle and its ramifications in the April 1993 *BIES* Survey (pp. 12-16). They view the case as " . . . probably the biggest crisis in Indonesia's modern banking history". Internal lending, to companies controlled by the bank's owners, was one of the major problems, a practice in direct violation of central bank prudential regulations. Despite mounting evidence that the bank was in trouble, as late as July 1992 Summa was still being permitted to service government-related projects, a task usually restricted to financially sound institutions.

[14] A related issue concerns the balance between monetary and fiscal policy in achieving stabilization objectives. This is a complex question beyond the scope of this book, but an argument can be made for the proposition that Indonesia has relied too heavily on monetary policy. Fiscal policy has rarely been countercyclical, as we shall see in the following chapter. This situation has arisen for a number of reasons. First, there has been the (self-imposed) "balanced budget" constraint, even allowing for the fact that this has not resulted in balanced budgets in the economic sense of the term. Secondly, government expenditure processes are such that it is not easy to quickly "fine-tune" the budget to have the desired macroeconomic impact. Finally, in the absence of fiscal instruments such as government bonds, government deficits have an immediate and direct impact on the money supply.

[15] Arndt (1979) and Grenville (1981) provide the best surveys of monetary policy developments over this period.

[16] There has been considerable debate in the literature concerning the impact of concessional credit, especially for small firms. Undoubtedly, many firms benefited from credit subsidies. But corruption was widespread, and the real issue is whether this form of assistance was critical to business development and whether the funds might not have had greater development impact if channelled into other areas, such as physical infrastructure and education. Bolnick (1982, 1983, 1987) and Bolnick and Nelson (1990) present broadly sympathetic analyses of these schemes, whereas McLeod (1983) offers a more critical assessment. The KIK/KMKP programs were finally abolished in 1990. To ameliorate political opposition to the change, the government introduced a new regulation requiring that 20 per cent of the loan portfolios of all banks be to "small" borrowers. In practice, banks have met this requirement mainly by extending larger volumes of consumer finance.

[17] It needs to be emphasized that the "other transactions" include a significant though unknown volume of credit for state entities, and that therefore the statement concerning the government's fiscal rectitude requires qualification. In order to maintain both its "balanced budget" and support for its state enterprises, the government simply shifted funding for them from the budget to directed loans from the banking system. It is revealing, for example, that the "other" share was very high during the oil price peaks in 1973 to 1976 and 1980-81. We return to this issue in the next chapter.

[18] The following quotation from Professor Sumitro Djojohadikusumo, one of Indonesia's foremost policy-makers and academics, is indicative of official thinking since 1966 (Sumitro, 1986, pp. 38-39):

> In 1954/5, I was a strong protagonist of foreign exchange controls. I felt that we only had the State to fight against the "big five". Then I saw what happened under Ali Sastro and Soekarno. In 1983 there was a movement towards the reimposition of exchange controls. I went to the President and argued strongly against it. I know how easy it is to smuggle goods and I know that those who are close to the sources of power will get their hands on the foreign exchange'.

[19] For example, the MIT's Professor Rudiger Dornbusch, one of the international debt gurus, with extensive experience especially in Latin America, called in 1990 for a partial closure of Indonesia's capital account at a Jakarta seminar. His comments were swiftly rebutted by economists in Indonesia.

CHAPTER 4

[1] The general literature on fiscal policy in Indonesia is now substantial. Developments through to the late 1970s are analyzed in detail by Booth and McCawley (1981) and Glassburner (1979). Asher and Booth (1992) focus primarily on the 1980s, as does Nasution (1989). Boediono (1990) provides a policy-maker's perspective on fiscal policy throughout the New Order period. Asher (1989) provides an overview in an ASEAN context. Informed studies of taxation policy include Gillis (1985, 1989), Kelly (1989, 1993), Lerche (1980), and Uppal (1986). Each April *BIES* Survey contains a detailed analysis of the President's budget speech, which is delivered to Parliament in early January. There is also a substantial regional finance literature, which is referred to in Chapter 11.

[2] Unless otherwise indicated, this section follows Indonesian government convention and data presentation, with all data since 1969 on a fiscal year basis, that is, 1 April to 31 March. In the text and tables, calendar years are used as shorthand for fiscal years. For example, "1975" refers to the period 1 April 1975 to 31 March 1976.

[3] Addressing the 1992 annual conference of the Indonesian Economics Association in Banjarmasin, the Finance Minister Mar'ie Muhammad, speaking then in his capacity as Director-General of Taxation, observed that it would be an "extraordinary achievement" (*prestasi luar biasa*) if NODR as a percentage of non-oil GDP could be raised to 20 per cent by the end of Repelita VI, in 1999. A simple extrapolation of the data in Figure 4.6 suggests this target should be met comfortably if the current vigorous prosecution is maintained.

[4] According to one estimate, in 1990 there were about 40 million households in the country, but less than one million taxpayers (Boediono, 1990).

[5] Development expenditures fell from 54 per cent of the total in 1983 to 35 per cent in 1987, the latter identical to the share in 1969, before rising to over 40 per cent again in the early 1990s (Figure 4.8).

[6] Indeed, as Tabor (1992) points out, the official estimates, as reported in Table 4.2 understate the true value of the economic subsidy. This arises because of input and capital subsidies, the former mainly on gas and electricity, which the fertilizer producers receive.

[7] The comments of Chris Manning in the April 1992 *BIES* Survey (p. 22) on the 1992-93 budget are very pertinent in this respect: " . . . as the domestic tax net broadens and deepens, business groups are being increasingly drawn into the budget process . . . Business and middle class groups in particular have began to take a greater interest in how funds are squeezed from them

and how they are used . . . Increasingly, fiscal self-reliance is likely to be accompanied by more pressure for political participation in the allocation of state funds".

[8] It is also worth observing that the data clearly illustrate the changing form of civil service remuneration. In 1969, salaries and pensions constituted little more than one-half of total personnel expenses, a reflection of the fact that, in the wake of the 1960s inflation, civil servants received a significant proportion of their income in kind, principally in the form of rice. These payments have been all but eliminated over the past two decades. In addition, though, the rising share of salaries and pensions in the total figure also reflects to some extent the ageing of the civil service and the increase in pension payments.

[9] Some of these issues are discussed in more detail in Emmerson (1988). There is reported to be considerable discontent among the armed forces concerning budgetary constraints, especially as they impinge on equipment purchases. A 1991 report in the respected weekly magazine *Tempo* (12 October, p. 97, as cited in "Current Data on the Indonesian Military Elite, 1 July 1989-1 January 1992", *Indonesia*, no. 53, 1992, p. 97) was particularly revealing. The report noted that over 50 per cent of the maintenance allocation from the routine budget was required just for the country's 12 F-16 planes. From 1983 to 1991 the number of generals was cut by over one-half. The air force could muster only three of the eight attack squadrons it believed were necessary for minimal national security. It should be noted that these budgetary pressures are likely to intensify as the Minister for Research and Technology, Professor Habibie, steps up his efforts to compel the armed forces to procure from the ammunition plant (PT Pindad) under his purview.

[10] A fourth innovative series of fiscal estimates is that prepared by Booth and McCawley (1981, pp. 157–8) and Asher and Booth (1992, p. 62), who attempt to calculate the "domestic deficit", that is, the difference between domestic revenues and expenditures. This complicated process involves assigning crude though plausible foreign and domestic shares to all revenue and expenditure components, The series suggest, if anything, a *pro-cyclical* fiscal policy: very large domestic deficits during the oil boom period, some exceeding 10 per cent of GDP, followed by much smaller deficits, and even modest surpluses, in the late 1980s.

[11] Three factors appear to have been behind the decision to create these reserves. First, with inflation rising there was a need to adopt a cautious fiscal stance. Secondly, senior economic officials were becoming alarmed about the prospect of the "megaprojects" getting off the ground, and the fact that they had the potential to destabilize macroeconomic management should the government be required to extend financial support to them. Thirdly, there was a concern that Indonesia might experience difficulty maintaining real levels of international aid. The country was graduating out of concessional World Bank assistance, US aid was falling in real terms, while other donors appeared to be attaching greater conditionality. (It was the latter of course which precipitated the rejection of Dutch aid in March 1992.) There was also growing apprehension at the extremely heavy reliance on Japan as the principal donor.

[12] It should be emphasized that there is nothing inherently undesirable in such a "dependence". If Indonesia can continue to obtain capital and technology at below the international supply price, it clearly makes sense to do so. The more important issue is to begin to prepare for the time—still presumably at least two decades away—when it will graduate into full middle-income status and therefore cease to be a major aid recipient. The argument that it makes economic sense for Indonesia to continue receiving aid of course abstracts from the political issue, namely that a significant chord of nationalist sentiment in Indonesia is opposed to reliance on overseas aid.

[13] The five were equiproportional budget retrenchment, increased government investment and reduced government current expenditures, the converse of the second experiment, accelerated devaluation, and monetary contraction and expansion.

CHAPTER 5

[1] For various estimates of smuggling in the 1960s, see Richter (1970) and Simkin (1970). Pitt (1971) provides a particularly detailed overview of commercial policy issues over this period.

A legacy of the pervasive 1960s smuggling is that Singapore still does not publish its trade with Indonesia.

[2] For an excellent review of changing perceptions of the value of international economic engagement, and debate in Indonesia, see Mangkusuwondo et al. (1988).

[3] For an early, semi-official account of the operation of IGGI see Posthumus (1971). When Indonesia announced the cessation of Dutch aid, this group became the Consultative Group on Indonesia (CGI), the chair shifting to the World Bank and the meeting from The Hague to Paris.

[4] On the sequencing issue, much of it concerned with the Latin American economies, see for example Edwards (1984) and McKinnon (1991).

[5] There is no comprehensive study of Indonesia's trade patterns and policies since the mid-1960s. Rosendale (1981), based on a doctoral dissertation completed in the late 1970s, provides a particularly detailed analysis of the balance of payments in the first decade of the New Order. Warr (1992) focuses on the oil sector and adjustment issues, primarily in the 1980s, while Woo and Nasution (1989) examine debt, trade, and macroeconomic adjustment issues through to the mid-1980s.

[6] However, this comment does not apply to LNG exports, the volume of which has grown steadily, owing to its more recent discovery and exploitation, and to less binding OPEC restrictions.

[7] In the case of natural rubber, prices rose in response to the rising cost of synthetic rubber, while coffee—and consequently tea—prices increased in 1977 owing to world-wide shortages.

[8] There have been important exceptions, such as sharply rising gold prices in the 1985-87 period, which stimulated a spurt in exploration and production, much of it located in Kalimantan.

[9] The data in Figure 4.10 are presented on a calendar-year basis, whereas those in Table 5.1 refer to fiscal years. This explains the minor discrepancies between the two series.

[10] "Net resource flows" refer to capital disbursements (that is, drawings on loan commitments) less principal repayments. These are approximately equivalent to lines 4 + 6 less line 5 in Table 5.1, allowing for some differences in classifications and calendar-fiscal year presentations. "Net transfers" are defined as net resource flows less interest payment (or disbursements less debt service payments). Interest payments are grouped within the somewhat misleading "services trade", line 2 of Table 5.1, an issue to which we return in Chapter 9.

[11] In principle the Bank of International Settlements collects such data, but here also the data on short-term debt are incomplete.

[12] This also is a probable understatement in view of Indonesia's open capital account and unrecorded short-term borrowings abroad by the private sector.

[13] Growth in real GDP per capita over the 1980s was −1.4 per cent in Mexico and −3.8 per cent in Nigeria, compared with 3.2 per cent in Indonesia.

[14] For extended commentaries, see several *BIES* Surveys over this period, in addition to McCawley (1980) and Rosendale (1976, 1981). In fact, of course, as shown in Figure 5.1 there was a substantial real effective appreciation over this period, the result of a constant nominal rate against the dollar in the face of inflation rates appreciably higher than Indonesia's trading partners.

[15] For a good analysis of events immediately following the devaluation see the March 1979 *BIES* Survey by Howard Dick.

[16] For discussion of these issues, see Arndt and Sundrum (1984), and Warr (1984, 1986, 1992).

[17] The qualification to the series is that, as Warr (1992) has pointed out, this index is a rather poor measure of the change in relative prices, since there is no clear delineation between non-tradeables and tradeables. He further demonstrates (p. 153) that, while the two series generally move in the same direction, they do diverge considerably, especially after the 1986 devaluation.

Regrettably, no internationally consistent series of such relative prices are available, so Indonesia's record according to this comparative yardstick cannot be examined.

[18] One other and unrelated qualification to this otherwise successful record of exchange rate management has been a puzzling fixation on the US dollar. This might have been understandable in the 1970s, to avoid any commercial uncertainty and in view of the dollar's then dominance in international transactions. But it is more difficult to understand in the 1980s when Indonesia's economy has become so much more strongly integrated within East Asia. For most of the 1980s, the dollar–rupiah rate has moved in a gradual and predictable fashion, in contrast to the marked fluctuations in, for example, the yen–rupiah rate. Ross McLeod emphasizes this point in the August 1993 *BIES* Survey.

[19] Indonesia's foreign investment statistics are a maze for the unwary. Briefly, two series are published: one by Bank Indonesia which purports to measure all realized flows on a balance of payments basis; and the other by the Investment Coordinating Board (*Badan Koordinasi Penanaman Modal*, BKPM) which refers to approved figures for foreign and domestic firms. The BKPM data do not include investments in oil, gas and financial services, but in all other respects they overstate the total considerably because some approved projects are subsequently cancelled or scaled down, while the "foreign" total also includes domestic borrowings and equity capital. The realized totals are therefore the most accurate measure of actual equity capital inflows, whereas the approvals data are useful as an indicator of investor interest and business confidence. See Hill (1988, Appendix) for details.

[20] The exception was 1992 when tight monetary and credit conditions appeared to discourage domestic investors, while the foreign figure was somewhat misleadingly boosted by two extremely large projects, which are thought in any case to incorporate significant domestic capital participation.

[21] See the Appendix Tables in Hill (1990b) for comparative data through until the late 1980s.

[22] The BE essentially took the form of direct balance of payments support. Donor country currency was provided to Bank Indonesia, which was then sold to Indonesian importers in the free foreign exchange market for imports of goods on a priority list. The rupiah funds thus accruing were used as counterpart funds in the government's development budget.

[23] The only qualification one would attach to this judgement now is Indonesia's decision to suspend all Dutch aid from March 1992. The Netherlands had been an important actor in aid to Indonesia after 1967, both as a donor and as chair of the intergovernmental group, IGGI. However, persistent criticisms of Indonesia's human rights record, particularly from Dutch Development Cooperation Minister Pronk, together with lingering sensitivities from the colonial past, prompted President Soeharto to personally take the decision. Two years after the event there is no evidence that the decision has jeopardized other aid flows.

[24] One feature of the data in Figure 5.5 which deserves to be noted is that the OECD data, used here, and the IMF data used in one of the series in Figure 5.3 differ substantially in their estimates on foreign investment. The OECD provides the most comprehensive foreign aid data. However the IMF foreign investment data are thought to be more accurate.

[25] Of course the contrary view, of such prominent aid critics as Peter Bauer, is that aid postpones difficult decisions, as regimes are, in effect, propped up by aid programs, with the eventual result that the needed adjustments become ever more painful. By and large, the Indonesian experience with foreign aid does not correspond to this caricature, although doubtless it is relevant in some cases.

[26] One careful study by Pack and Pack (1990) demonstrates econometrically that for the 1966–86 period foreign aid did not displace development expenditure, nor did it lead to a reduction in domestic revenue-raising. They also conclude that aid was not fungible, in the sense that it was spent on the designated categories, and was not diverted into other purposes.

[27] Knowledge of markets, international trading channels, and consumer preferences are more important in the case of manufactures than for undifferentiated primary commodities. These factors explain the much higher Singapore percentage in the manufactured export total.

[28] The declining share of plywood in manufactured exports from the late 1980s in turn explains the fall in Japan's share of total manufactures. Indonesia's inability to sell more labour-intensive manufactures to Japan has been a consistent source of friction between the two countries. Japan's formal trade barriers are low, it is a major investor in Indonesian manufacturing, and it is not a signatory to the MFA (on the import side). Although informal trade barriers are probably significant, at least as important has been the failure of Indonesian exporters to come to grips with the peculiar intricacies of the Japanese marketing system and with consumer preferences.

[29] For further analysis of trade flows and trade intensities in the Western Pacific context, see Drysdale (1988).

[30] An obvious limitation of the figures in Table 5.6 is that the cumulative data do not allow for inflation. Consequently, they exaggerate the importance of recent investments, such as those from the NIEs, and understate the significance of earlier investments, especially those from Japan.

[31] The major difference of course was that, reflecting overall policy parameters in Indonesia, Japanese investment in the earlier period was almost entirely import-substituting, in contrast to the stronger outward orientation of the NIEs' projects.

[32] An indication of this understatement is the author's attempt to compute country shares of foreign investment including and excluding the oil sector over the 1967–84 period. For BKPM sectors, the US and Japanese shares were 5 per cent and 68 per cent respectively. However, the inclusion of oil altered these shares dramatically—for all sectors the corresponding figures were 58 per cent and 21 per cent (Hill, 1988, p. 55).

[33] Investment intensity indices (defined analogously as those for trade) for US and Japanese investments in ASEAN and Indonesia, calculated by Pangestu (1987) through to the mid 1980s, portray a similar picture. The index for Japan was as much as four times that for the US.

[34] An elaboration of the country shares of aid in Figure 5.14 is necessary. These data are produced according to the format of the OECD's Development Assistance Committee and attempt to measure the genuinely concessional component of resource flows. This approach therefore increases the relative importance of countries (such as Australia) which give all or most of their aid in grant form. It also results in a much smaller share for international agencies such as the World Bank, where lending programs to Indonesia now contain only a very small concessional component. These data are a much more useful indicator of aid flows than the gross figures often reported at the annual IGGI meetings, and cited widely in the Indonesian press. The latter do not indicate the "effective aid equivalent" totals; moreover, they are pledges, which often differ from gross actual flows.

[35] The relative importance of the US as a donor is of course understated in Figure 5.14 to the extent that it contributes through international institutions, particularly the World Bank. By the same logic the Japanese share would also expand, especially since it is the major funder of the Asian Development Bank, whose activities in Indonesia have been expanding rapidly in recent years.

[36] For a comprehensive analysis of AFTA, see the various contributions in Imada and Naya (eds, 1992).

[37] The nature of the relationship has changed rapidly since the 1960s and 1970s, when Singapore provided basic processing facilities (for example, for oil and rubber) and was a major point of transshipment. As Indonesia developed competence in these fields, the key to Singapore's success has been to maintain its advantage in increasingly advanced manufacturing and service activities.

[38] As noted in Table 5.6, by 1992 Singapore's cumulative investments in BKPM sectors exceeded those of both the US and Germany, although they are the smallest of the four NIEs.

[39] The few scholarly studies include Kuntjoro-Jakti and Tjiptoherijanto (1983), Kuntjoro-Jakti et al. (1983), and Thee (1984).

[40] According to the same source, Indonesia received 12.5 per cent of Japan's aid in 1990, up

from 6.3 per cent in 1985 (before the sharp decline in oil prices), though below the 1980 figure of 17.9 per cent.

[41] As one observer of Japanese aid to Indonesia has put it: "Japanese suggest that an almost Messianic belief in the market is overdone by the US" (Kingston, 1993, p. 47).

CHAPTER 6

[1] A recent attempt to articulate the country's economic ideology is that of the Indonesian Economists' Association, ISEI (1990). This pamphlet, prepared at the request of President Soeharto and released in mid-1990 at the peak of an emotional debate concerning the role of cooperatives, is understandably ambivalent on many key issues. While endorsing an international- and market-oriented strategy, it is also at pains to emphasize the importance of the state enterprise sector and the need to avoid "free fight liberalism". The report also endorses the importance of cooperatives: " . . . in the system of Economic Democracy, [they] are the main vehicle for all economic activity, particularly for small economic concerns". Curiously, it has nothing direct to say on the issue of conglomerates and the role of non-*pribumi* business.

[2] To quote Professor Sadli again: "The policy of industrialization is still improperly integrated with trade policy. That is because the two camps, one favouring high protection and the other favouring more competition, are equally strong" (Sadli, 1988, p. 364).

[3] Writing shortly after the devaluation, in the March 1979 *BIES* Survey, Howard Dick (p. 43) observed, appropriately: "[T]here is a fundamental inconsistency between adopting a market solution to structural disequilibrium and relying upon administrative controls to implement structural change".

[4] In the case of mining, the growth figures are based on constant price series, but falling prices in the 1980s had an impact on production through the lower incentives for exploration and production. In *Repelita* II-IV the fortunes of the transport and communication sector were closely related to the government's budgetary circumstances, and so the much smaller actual figure in *Repelita* IV is explained by fiscal austerity over that period. Conversely, the higher actual figure in *Repelita* V is partly the result of stronger private sector activity in this sector.

[5] Econometric modelling of the Indonesian economy is still at a rather rudimentary stage of development. However, simple and reasonably robust models have been developed at the University of Indonesia (see Azis, 1993) and the Department of Finance/Harvard group (see Devarajan and Lewis, 1991).

[6] The best general studies in this field include Azis (1994), Battacharya and Pangestu (1993), Bresnan (1993), Glassburner (1978), Mackie and MacIntyre (1994), Pangestu (1991a), Sjahrir (1987), and Soesastro (1989). All these contributions benefit from an intimate knowledge of economic policy-making processes, and first-hand acquaintance of the key officials in the bureaucracy. An important set of papers on this subject was presented to the "International Conference on Economic Policy Making Processes in Indonesia", held at Bali in September 1990, especially including the keynote address by former Coordinating Economics and Finance Minister, Professor Ali Wardhana. The volume of papers in the "Harvard" volume (Perkins and Roemer eds, 1991) include several rich studies of Indonesian policy processes. Some of the most detailed work has been undertaken by political scientists, including MacIntyre (1991, 1992), Chalmers (1988) and Wibisono (1989), and there is the beginning of cross-fertilization between economists and political scientists in this field.

[7] Previously there was no publicly available list of the sectors open to investment; potential investors had to enter into protracted negotiations with the Investment Coordinating Board (BKPM, *Badan Koordinasi Penanaman Modal*), in the course of which they discovered whether in principle a proposal might be submitted for consideration.

[8] A curious feature of the March 1992 liberalization was that one of the so-called mega projects, the Chandra Asri petrochemical plant, was resurrected as a fully foreign-owned enterprise, even though its major backers were three prominent Indonesian businessmen. The principal caveat concerning 100 per cent foreign ownership related to minimum size restrictions.

[9] This point should not be overemphasized. Mistrust of foreign ownership is still widespread. The shift from highly protected import substitution to export orientation on the part of foreign firms has also introduced new tensions. One obvious example concerns those, mainly from the Asian NIEs, engaged in the export of labour-intensive manufactures. Intense international competition in these industries imposes a much tighter cost discipline on firms than was present during the era of protection (and high domestic concentration in many industries). The pressure on wages, combined with the introduction of sometimes harsh systems of industrial relations by NIE investors, has resulted in increased industrial unrest and public criticism of these firms (Manning, 1993a).

[10] For good overviews of the state enterprises sector during the New Order, see Habir (1990), Mardjana (1993), and Pangestu and Habir (1989). McCawley (1971) provides a particularly detailed case study of a state enterprise—the state electricity company (PLN)—in the 1960s and cites other studies over this period.

[11] These data of course greatly understate the infusion of resources directed to the state enterprise sector. They do not include, for example, concessional credit through the state banking system, foreign aid, and a plethora of hidden and indirect subsidies.

[12] For comprehensive analyses of the Pertamina episode, see Glassburner (1976), McCawley (1978), and several of the *BIES* Surveys over this period.

[13] Ibnu Sutowo disappeared from the public scene for a period, but his visibility, and that of his family businesses, rose dramatically during the 1980s and early 1990s. That he has continued to be an "insider" in the New Order regime, albeit a flamboyant and somewhat maverick one, was revealed in a survey of the country's leading *pribumi* business people published in the magazine *Info Bisnis* in November 1993. According to the survey, Ibnu Sutowo topped the list in terms of the assets value of his group (Nugra Santana), estimated to be about Rp 500 billion and covering a very wide range of business sectors. If the figures are reasonably accurate— clearly they are subject to a wide margin of error—Ibnu's business empire thus exceeds that of some of the more prominent *pribumi* entrepreneurs, such as the President's children and the Soedarpo and Bakri groups. Alternative estimates of the size of Indonesia's leading business groups, presented in Table 6.7, are not consistent with the *Info Bisnis* ranking, however.

[14] The Minister of Industry over much of this period later recorded his disappointment that a number of ambitious industrial projects his department was proposing were blocked by the technocrats either in Cabinet or through direct representations to the President (Soehoed, 1988, pp. 45-6).

[15] His third comparison, comparing the performance of a state enterprise, PT Perkebunan XIV, under the supervision of different departments, highlighted a feature of state enterprises neglected in much of the analysis. When the company was transferred from the Department of Agriculture to the Department of Finance its performance improved markedly, a finding which underlines the scope for improvement "within the system".

[16] Mardjana (1993, Ch. 4) contains much discussion of these issues. One topic on which there has been comparatively little research concerns the views of senior state enterprise managers themselves. They might be expected to support the status quo. Yet it is clear that at least some of them support reform. Many are reportedly frustrated with the constraints under which they operate, and would be willing to forego the subsidies they currently receive in exchange for greater autonomy (including, perhaps, higher salaries).

[17] This concern was accentuated further by the sale in early 1990 of a tyre company, PT Intirub, to a large conglomerate closely associated with the President's family.

[18] Not that all private firms suffered during this period, as the following quote from one knowledgeable observer in 1965 emphasizes: "The fate of resident private business under 'Guided Economy' has been a paradox. It is true that the ideology of the government has generally been hostile to capitalism in any form . . . Yet the economic role of [private business] groups has diminished little if at all . . . Private business retains a considerable field of operations despite the nationalisation of the bulk of the technically advanced sector" (Castles,

1965, pp. 29–31). The relevant phrase for the current discussion is the last one; most private operations were small-scale in nature.

[19] Major studies of Indonesia's conglomerates include Mackie (1990, 1992), Muhaimin (1991), Robison (1986), Sato (1993), and Yoshihara (1988). Owing to the rapidly changing business scene, academic studies have tended to date quickly, and the press has often provided illuminating and penetrating analyses of business groups. Some of the Indonesian press reports have already been alluded to. Major foreign press coverage includes articles in the *Asian Wall Street Journal* (by Stephen Jones, Richard Borsuk and colleagues, for example, in 24–26 November 1986, one of the first press exposes of its kind, and 12 March and 12 May 1992), and the *Far Eastern Economic Review* (by Adam Schwarz and colleagues, for example in 30 April 1992). This topic is discussed and written about much more openly in the late 1980s and early 1990s, as compared with the mid-1980s and before. It needs to be emphasized that all financial data in Table 6.7 and in these studies are extremely approximate.

[20] As a further indication of the approximate nature of these data, the rankings presented in Table 6.7 differ from those referred to in the source in Note 13 above. The latter are more recent, but this factor alone is unlikely to account for the difference.

[21] There are obvious exceptions to this statement. Two of the top 11 conglomerates are engaged primarily in *kretek* cigarette manufacturing. However, even these operations are becoming more diversified, and they are still consistent with the pattern of initial specialization, followed by diversification.

[22] This paragraph draws on a most informative case study by Sato (1993), the most recent and comprehensive scholarly case study in English of a leading conglomerate. See also *Asian Wall Street Journal*, 25–26 February 1994.

[23] Pitt (1991) provides a detailed account of developments over this period.

[24] The importance of the scheme in these exports is illustrated by the following data on exports under Bapeksta, as a percentage of total exports in each case:

	Food & beverages	Textiles, clothing, footwear	Wood products	Paper products	Chemicals, plastics, etc. products	Basic metals	Machine goods
1987	1	9	15	9	1	1	3
1988	5	28	37	31	5	42	20
1989	6	30	45	43	8	31	36

Source: Bapeksta.

[25] These packages were dubbed *paket* in Indonesia, and each was given an acronym indicating the month of its introduction, for example Pakto (*Paket Oktober*). These acronyms quickly extended the already colourful lexicon of economic jargon, institutions, and major policy decisions in Indonesia.

[26] Soesastro (1989, p. 84) quoting former Coordinating Economics Minister, Professor Ali Wardhana, one of the driving forces behind the reforms.

[27] World Bank, *Indonesia: Selected Issues of Industrial Development and Trade Strategy*, Annex 3, *Industrial Licensing*, Washington, D.C., 1981. Amazingly, more than a decade later the report has not progressed from the Bank's "white cover" (highly restricted) series of publications, owing to Indonesian government objections to this and other sections of the report. Interestingly enough, in spite of the very cordial relations between the government and the Bank, no major Bank report on the country's industrial trade and regulatory regime has been published in the past 15 years, for this reason. This includes the 1981 report, together with one prepared in 1993 and at least two others during the 1980s.

[28] Another important constraint is the acute shortage of legal expertise, both in the judiciary and in private legal practice. In 1992, for example it was estimated that there was one lawyer per 152,300 persons, a ratio far lower than Japan (1 per 9,090) not to mention the US (1 per

320) or Australia (1 per 380) (*Australian Financial Review*, 3 February 1994). It is tempting not to make too much of this point given that Japan has performed remarkably well even with a much higher ratio than the US and Australia. But clearly Indonesia's ratio is indicative of serious shortages.

[29] There is a good deal less concentration now on the issue of *cukong*, of what some saw as an unsavoury business alliance between senior army officials and Chinese business groups. By contrast, the business dealings of politically prominent families, especially the sons and daughters of the President, have received much more attention since the mid-1980s, as noted above.

[30] At the risk of labouring the obvious, some definitional difficulties need to be emphasized. Blatant cases of fraud are straightforward. But what of the sometimes complex means of civil service compensation, discussed below? Is a *pribumi*-first policy in the field of commercial contracts and loans, explicit or implicit, corruption or positive discrimination? Then there is the widespread practice—by no means confined to Indonesia—of senior military officials retiring to lucrative private sector positions, sometimes in a nominal capacity. As an illustration of the latter phenomenon, at least in the early days of the New Order, Weinstein (1976, p. 389) reported the following: "One Indonesian army general involved in numerous joint ventures asserted that his actual 'capital' contribution [to a joint venture with a foreign firm] was his ability to see the President on a day's notice".

[31] Economists and political scientists have often recognized that economic policy and implementation options are bound by administrative capacity, but all too frequently this point is overlooked in the literature, especially by those belonging to the interventionist school. Myrdal (1968) placed considerable emphasis on this point, in his discussion of "hard" and "soft" states. The recent World Bank (1993) analysis of the East Asian "miracles" also dwells on this point, particularly in contrasting Northeast and Southeast Asia.

[32] It is probably the case that real civil service compensation declined during much of the 1980s, owing to the freeze on salaries during the austerity budgets in the middle of the decade and the sharp cuts in development expenditure, the latter often constituting a means of supplementing low base salaries (see Figure 10.1). However, salary structures are so complex that one hesitates to state the above conclusion with conviction, especially as it relates to the most senior personnel.

[33] For example, estimates published in the magazine *Warta Ekonomi*, 29 June 1992, as cited in Habir (1993, pp. 174-81), give some illustration of the differentials. According to this survey, it was not uncommon for such executives to be earning in excess of Rp 200 million ($100,000) per annum, and in a small number of instances the figure exceeded Rp 500 million.

[34] Dr Dorodjatun Kuntjoro-Jakti, Dean of the Faculty of Economics, cited by Habir (1993, p.169).

[35] For discussion of the changes, see the *BIES* Surveys by Ross McLeod, August 1993, and Chris Manning, April 1992.

[36] Some of the contributors to Hill (ed., 1991) emphasize this point. See in particular the chapters by H.W. Arndt, Ruth Daroesman, Mayling Oey-Gardiner, and Thee Kian Wie.

CHAPTER 7

[1] Another controversial topic concerns equity in the agricultural sector, particularly the distribution of landholdings, the growth of employment opportunities, and the alleged decline in custom-based rural distributional institutions. These issues are addressed later in Chapter 10.

[2] These two quotes are taken from Booth (1988a), pp. 4 and 6, respectively.

[3] As an illustration of these fluctuations, Mark Mitchell, formerly an adviser to *Bulog*, has modelled rainfall in October–November and the subsequent wet season *sawah* crop in January–April. He found rainfall to be a very good predictor of the area of *sawah* harvested and of total rice production.

[4] *Bimas* is *Bimbingan Massal*, or Mass Guidance Program.

5 *Bulog* is *Badan Urusan Logistik*, or State Logistics Board.

6 These were the BUUD, *Badan Usaha Unit Desa*, or Village Organizational Unit, and KUD, *Kooperasi Unit Desa*, or Village Cooperative Unit.

7 Important studies of rice over the first decade of the New Order include Afiff et al. (1980), Birowo and Hansen (1981), Fox (1991), Mears and Moeljono (1981), and Timmer (1975). Booth (1988) and Pearson et al. (1991) examine developments over a longer period, while Tabor (1992) focuses primarily on the 1980s.

8 In a similar vein, Timmer (1993, p. 175) records the amazement of delegates to the Food and Agriculture Organization (FAO) at the President's detailed knowledge of technical, agronomic issues on the occasion of the latter's receipt of an international award in recognition of the country's rice production achievements.

9 Woo (1991) is one of the few authors to focus systematically on this issue.

10 During this period, there was much public debate over whether rice production trends signified a decisive break with the past or were primarily the result of these fortuitous factors. Writing in late 1980, Peter Warr (*BIES* Survey, November 1980, p. 10) summarized this discussion and demonstrated that the trend in production " . . . strongly suggests that there has been a shift in the underlying trend".

11 See Timmer (1993, pp. 170-2) for an interesting account of this period. He concludes that "*Bulog* activities were badly disrupted during the episode".

12 For an analysis of the most recent initiative, the *Supra-Insus* scheme, see Sawit and Manwar (1991).

13 It needs to be emphasized that the fertilizer data in Figure 7.5 refer to the entire food crop sector and not just rice. However rice has been by far the largest user, so the trends identified are broadly accurate.

14 To quote the assessment of one careful analyst of fertilizer application rates: "There is serious technical and price inefficiency in the use of fertilizer in Indonesia. Average application rates on rice are excessive in many provinces when judged by nutrient uptake, agronomic recommendations, and economic criteria. The problem is most common on Java . . . " (Roche, 1994, p. 16).

15 The latter figure is from Tabor (1992, pp. 177-83) who also points out that over the years 1985-86 to 1987-88 these subsidies exceeded the value of the agricultural and irrigation development budget. Moreover, the official fertilizer subsidy estimate understates the real economic subsidy owing to the concessional energy prices paid by fertilizer producers.

16 At the risk of stating the obvious, area expansion in Table 7.2 for Java refers to an increase in the cropping intensity ratio, that is, from single and double-cropping per year to higher multiples. The physical area under rice has almost certainly contracted, owing to pressures of urbanization, industrialization and other activities. Accurate cropping data are not available, but it is likely that a good deal of the "area expansion" off-Java does consist of physical area expansion rather than increased cropping intensity.

17 Two comprehensive volumes on *palawija* crops are Falcon et al. (1984) and Timmer (ed., 1989), which examine cassava and maize respectively.

18 A word of caution is necessary in interpreting the words "estates" and "smallholder". The usual definitional cutoff is 25 ha, which implies that the former may range from relatively small family holdings to vast corporate operations. Moreover, smallholders often engage in both tree and annual crop cultivation. I owe this observation to Colin Barlow. In spite of the confusion, the presentation of statistics requires that these somewhat misleading categories are employed here.

19 See for example, Barlow, Jayasuriya and Tan (1994), Barlow (1991), Barlow and Jayasuriya (1984), Barlow and Muharminto (1982), and Barlow and Tomich (1991). See also Collier and Werdaja (1972).

[20] For excellent general surveys of environmental issues see Hardjono (ed., 1991), Hardjono (1994), and World Bank (1994).

[21] *Bapedal* is an acronym for *Badan Pengendalian Dampak Lingkungan*, Environmental Impact Management Agency. McAndrews (1994) provides a comprehensive assessment of the agency's early operation, pointing both to its early achievements and the obstacles which need to be overcome to pursue its mandate effectively. Among the latter, McAndrews identifies the lack of coordination with other arms of government, the difficulty in attracting highly qualified staff, the establishment of regional offices, international and domestic funding sources, and the issue of enforcement, especially in the context of Indonesia's uncertain legal environment.

[22] Important studies of forestry over the course of the New Order include Gillis (1988), Hardjono (1994), Pearce, Barbier and Markandya (1990, Ch. 5), Potter (1991), Repetto et al. (1989, Ch. 11, sec. A), and World Bank (1988).

[23] The situation has apparently improved little since then. Press reports in 1991 of research conducted by Dr Rizal Ramli and colleagues indicated that the returns through the 1980s have been similarly low.

[24] According to one estimate (Gillis, 1988), inefficient processing operations resulted in a loss of rents of about $136 million per annum over the 1979–82 period.

[25] In addition, an extremely serious fire in East Kalimantan and the neighbouring Malaysian state of Sabah destroyed some 3 million ha in 1982–83.

[26] See Lindsay (1989) and references cited therein for a discussion of these issues, together with Ahmed (1991) and World Bank (1994).

[27] Indeed the head of several timber associations, Mohamad (Bob) Hasan, has been labelled— not inaccurately—the de facto Minister of Forests, in view of his close contacts at the highest political levels. Estimates of the size of Mr Hasan's own timber concessions range up to 2 million ha.

[28] See in particular Hardjono (1991), Nibbering (1991), Pearce, Barbier and Markandya (1990, Ch. 4), Repetto et al. (1989, Ch. 11, sec. C), and World Bank (1994), on which this paragraph draws.

[29] Sections of this paragraph draw on Rice (1991) and Tomich (1992).

[30] Informed estimates (for example, Pearson et al., [1991, Ch. 7]) suggest domestic demand for rice will grow by 2 to 2.5 per cent annually through the 1990s.

[31] The one possible qualification to this argument might be if Indonesia's rice imports were again to become so large that it became a price-maker on the thin international market. This does not seem in prospect in the 1990s.

[32] The references in Note 19 above document this issue in considerable detail. A curious additional illustration of misplaced research efforts is given by Tomich, Hastuti, and Bennett (1993), who note that the main government coffee research station is located in East Java, whereas the largest concentration of smallholder coffee producers is in southern Sumatra!

CHAPTER 8

[1] For a picture of Indonesian manufacturing in the mid-1960s, see Soehoed (1967), who was later to become an influential policy-maker and Minister of Industry during the New Order period. McCawley (1981) is the standard reference on industrial development in the 1970s, while Donges, Stecher and Wolter (1974) provide much information and analysis of the New Order's early industrialization record. Poot et al. (1990) quantitatively examine industrialization up to the mid-1980s. Hill (1990a) analyzes the results of the Industrial Censuses, while Hill (1992a) focuses principally on developments from the late 1970s.

[2] For what the figures are worth, the *Sensus Industri 1964* (1964 Industrial Census) reported that, compared with private firms, government-owned industrial enterprises employed nine times more people per firm while their installed power capacity was some 14 times greater.

[3] The rise of Minister Habibie, and his impact on industrial policy-making, is one of the most fascinating but poorly documented features of the New Order policy environment. Schwarz (1994) provides an interesting account of his political career. McKendrick (1989, Chs 2 and 3; 1992) contains the most detailed account of the aircraft company; see also Hill and Pang (1988). The World Bank's 1993 report on the Indonesian economy also contains extensive discussion of the Minister's commercial operations, and of his technology strategy more generally. No accurate financial records of his operations have ever been published. The Minister appears to be able to operate a personal fiefdom, immune to financial constraints and accountable only and directly to the President. There are striking parallels, in the Minister's "think big" approach and Presidential connections, with Pertamina's former President Director Ibnu Sutowo, although there is no evidence so far that the Minister is destined for the same fate, of "dismissal with honour" from the government service.

[4] The three years are chosen since they represent the only industrial censuses conducted in Indonesia after Independence. The decline is faster still if oil and gas processing is included. Data for this industry are not available for 1963 but output would have been small. In 1985 the light industry share with oil and gas included was 46 per cent of output. Data in this paragraph and footnote are from Hill (1990a).

[5] As a partial and understated illustration of this phenomenon, the number of industrial products separately identified in official statistics rose almost three-fold from 1969 to 1989, from 35 to 102.

[6] It is appropriate at this juncture to comment upon the paucity of detailed Indonesian industry case studies. For example, until Hasibuan (1993), there was not a book published on industrial economics for university students during the New Order, nor are there any major, book-length industry case studies. Chapman (1992) on footwear and steel and Hill (1992d) on textiles and garments are among the few published industry studies. Many consultant reports on various industries have, however, been written.

[7] Poot (1991) analyzes the sources of demand growth of the major industry groups through until the mid-1980s. At the time of writing, the most recent input-output table available to him was 1985, which was too early to capture the effects of the export boom.

[8] The data in Figure 8.2 need to be interpreted with care for a number of reasons. First, they exclude small and cottage industries, for which no clear, disaggregated trends are available. Secondly, fluctuations in the series, at least in the short run, may well reflect the state of business conditions as much as trends in labour productivity. Finally, and most importantly, because reliable capital stock estimates are not available, there are no estimates of trends in total factor productivity. It is unlikely that total factor productivity has risen as quickly as labour productivity. During the 1974–84 decade, when there were large investments in inefficient state enterprises, heavily subsidized state bank credit programs, and indiscriminate protection, it is probable that total factor productivity growth was low in some instances. A doctoral dissertation in preparation by H.H. Aswicahyono at the Australian National University will resolve this issue.

[9] This is not the place to investigate in detail the relative importance of these two factors in explaining the export success. It would be difficult in any case to separate out the effects owing to the interactive nature of the measures. It was probably the case that the drawback scheme had a greater impact on import-intensive exports where domestic value added was comparatively small. Notable examples are garments and footwear, where by the late 1980s as much as 30 per cent of exports were channelled through the drawback facility. The latter's impact was even larger than this figure would suggest because exporters used the facility as a bargaining tool in negotiating with domestic suppliers of inputs. By contrast, in resource-based industries such as pulp and cement, where domestic value added constituted a larger share of the export price, the devaluations probably had more impact. But, to repeat, both measures were extremely important in the overall picture of export success.

[10] The share of plywood in manufactured exports peaked at 49 per cent in 1987, a year not recorded in Table 8.3.

[11] For example, in 1990 Indonesia's intra-industry trade index for manufactures (at the 3-digit

SITC level) was 0.19, compared with 0.71 for Singapore, 0.58 for Malaysia, and 0.39 for Thailand (Drysdale and Garnaut, 1993, pp. 208-9).

[12] Aswicahyono and Hill (1993) demonstrate that this body of theory stands up reasonably well to empirical scrutiny in the case of Indonesian manufacturing. The most awkward issue confronted in this sort of exercise—in Indonesia as in many other countries—is how to incorporate the policy factor in quantitative analysis. Government policy shapes ownership patterns in a variety of ways, including direct investment, the regulatory framework, and the trade policy regime. Many such interventions are extremely difficult to incorporate in modelling exercises.

[13] See, for example, the comparative data in the appendix figures of Hill (1990b). In its foreign investment inflows, Indonesia is closer to the experience of South Korea and the Philippines, neither of which has been a major recipient. Of course, as with trade shares, these kinds of intercountry comparisons need to adjust for country size, since international transactions are a smaller fraction of economic activity in large countries than is the case for smaller countries.

[14] Based on a firm-level analysis of the 1986 Industrial Census, however, and lending support to the story in Table 8.7, Hill and Kalirajan (1993) found that export orientation was a significant correlate of firms' technical efficiency. Note in this context that the definitions of "small industry" employed by the Central Bureau of Statistics and the Department of Industry do differ.

[15] According to the 1986 Industrial Census, the share of firms with a workforce of 5-49 employees contributed some 15 per cent of non-oil manufacturing output. Particularly high shares were recorded in the case of furniture (82 per cent of that industry's output), structural clay products (75 per cent), miscellaneous manufactures (51 per cent), leather products (46 per cent), garments (44 per cent), and footwear (42 per cent). See Hill, 1990a, Table 18.

[16] Thee (1993) provides a convenient summary of these programs.

[17] The exchange between McCawley and Tait (1979) and Dapice and Snodgrass (1979) is illustrative of some of the industrial employment issues being canvassed throughout the New Order period. For a comprehensive analysis of employment issues and trends since 1966, see Jones (1994) and Jones and Manning (1992).

[18] Both of the propositions advanced in this paragraph can be illustrated with reference to the now rather dated 1986 Industrial Census data. For example, in 1985 Jabotabek (Jakarta and the surrounding districts, extending also to the heavy industry locations around Cilegon) produced about 36 per cent of the nation's non-oil industrial output (among firms with at least 20 employees). The next major industrial centre, Surabaya and surrounds, generated just 11 per cent of the total, with Bandung (7 per cent) and Semarang (2 per cent) much smaller still. By contrast, there were eight provinces off-Java where the three largest plants generated over one-half of the entire provincial manufacturing output.

[19] The history of Indonesia's petroleum industry has yet to be written. The major source of information is the authoritative annual *Petroleum Sector Report*, published by the US Embassy in Jakarta. Some of these reports have been summarized and published in the BIES. Alex Hunter published several papers on the industry in the BIES in the late 1960s. Khong (1986) analyzed relations between the state oil company Pertamina and the oil MNCs from a political science perspective, while the Pertamina crisis of the mid-1970s resulted in several academic studies referred to in Chapter 6.

[20] For an informative review of Indonesia's non-oil mining industries, see van Leeuwen (1992). Some of the historical information in this and subsequent paragraphs is taken from this paper.

CHAPTER 9

[1] For general surveys of the service industry in East Asia, see Findlay (1990), Castle and Findlay (eds, 1988), and Tucker and Sundberg (1988).

[2] Indeed, as noted above, a legacy of the rampant smuggling of the 1950s and 1960s is that Singapore still withholds its merchandise trade statistics with Indonesia. Apart from the serious conceptual problems, Singapore's reluctance to release data on its commercial transactions with

Indonesia constitutes an additional obstacle in any attempt to estimate services trade within ASEAN.

[3] As an illustration of this phenomenon in Indonesia, in 1992 1.7 per cent of the country's workforce had a tertiary education (see Table 6.10), whereas 13.1 per cent of public servants had attained such a level.

[4] However, an important exception, as noted above in Chapter 4, and contrary to the experience of many army-backed regimes, has been the modest allocations to defence expenditure throughout the New Order period, rarely exceeding 2 per cent of GDP and less than most Asian developing countries. Even allowing for substantial "off-budget" activities, Indonesian defence expenditures would still be low.

[5] Although there has been a major transformation in marketing, the traditional small-scale trading (*pasar*) economy continues to display a good deal of resilience (Alexander and Booth, 1992, p. 296 ff), in part owing to segmented markets and clientele.

[6] For example, a report released in 1970 estimated that an investment of $140 million in railway infrastructure was required just to restore 1939 levels of service and efficiency (quoted by H.W. Arndt in *BIES* Survey, March 1971).

[7] Moreover, it is important to bear in mind that even with these extremely high growth rates, Indonesia's infrastructure is still quite basic in international comparisons. To give just one example from the commercial arena, in 1992 there were just two personal computers per 1,000 people in the country, compared with 33 in South Korea, 116 in Singapore, and 265 in the US (*The Australian*, 1 February 1994).

[8] Howard Dick has published extensively on various aspects of transportation in Indonesia. See Dick (1981, Parts I and II) on urban public transport, Dick (1987) on inter-island shipping, and Dick and Forbes (1992) for an overview of the period since the late 1960s.

[9] There is no comprehensive study of the *becak* industry, of how it has adapted to rising competition from motorized transport and increased government regulation. We also know little about the employment pattern of displaced *becak* drivers.

[10] Soesastro and Drysdale, writing in the December 1990 *BIES* Survey (pp. 27–9), report on the government's early initiatives in inviting the private sector to invest in infrastructure.

[11] An example of extremely slow approval procedures is the much-delayed Paitoon power generation project in East Java, one of the largest such projects in which private sector participation has been invited. Planning for the complex began in 1990, but through until early 1994 there was still no agreement over rates which the private consortium would be permitted to charge.

[12] The percentage increase in tourism numbers in the ASEAN countries over the 1982–91 period was Indonesia 334, Thailand 129, Malaysia 100, Singapore 84, and the Philippines 21. Conversely, however, Indonesia still lags in absolute numbers, in 1991 receiving some 2.6 million tourists, well below Singapore (5.4 million) and Thailand (5.1 million) (*Economics and Business Review Indonesia*, 14 August 1993).

[13] It is likely that a social cost-benefit analysis of tourism would reveal that the gains were even larger in the 1980s as compared with the 1970s. This is because many of the tourism-intensive inputs were subsidized in the earlier period. Fuel and energy prices were below international levels. There were sizeable government investments in low-profit hotel ventures, many receiving additional subsidies in the form of cheap credit. Domestic automobile production in all probability generated negative value added when measured at international prices. With the exception of the latter example, many of these subsidies had been scaled back by the mid-1980s.

[14] A major reason for the imposition of the tax was thought to be to deter the popular habit among high-income Indonesians of short shopping trips to Singapore. As domestic costs in Singapore have risen and Indonesia's trade barriers have fallen, Singapore is no longer such an

attractive proposition. But it is unlikely that the tax will be revoked quickly. It is simple and clean to administer, and progressive in its impact.

[15] For an overview of the industry's development and prospects see Booth (1990). Jayasuriya and Nehen (1989) provide a more detailed analysis of tourism in Bali. As noted in Chapter 11, tourism has been a key factor in the remarkable economic performance of Bali.

[16] A minor caveat attaches to the data in Figure 9.4. For convenience, the development banks have been included with the state banks, even though some of the former have private equity participation. However, this has little effect on the numbers or the trends, as development banks are only a small share of the total.

[17] As an illustration of its underdeveloped state, in 1992 life insurance premiums were estimated to be about A$3 per capita, equivalent in total to about 0.3 per cent of GDP. The corresponding figures for Australia in the same year were A$906 per capita and 3.7 per cent of GDP (*Australian Financial Review*, 19 January 1994).

[18] A small market was established in Surabaya, and there have been plans to open markets in other major cities. However, to all intents and purposes, Jakarta is and will remain Indonesia's stock market.

CHAPTER 10

[1] This "Development Trilogy" combines the goals of growth, stability and equality.

[2] In addition to World Bank (1990, 1993) see, for example, the *World Development Report 1990*, which reported that Indonesia experienced one of the sharpest reductions in poverty incidence among countries surveyed (see pp. 41–3).

[3] The Gini ratio is a measure of inequality (dispersion) which ranges from 0 (perfect equality) to 1 (perfect inequality). A ratio of 0.3 is regarded as "low" by international standards, while that in excess of 0.5 is "high".

[4] The first systematic analysis of the *Susenas* data was that of Sundrum (1973). Asra (1989) also examined the 1970s data, along with others cited in this section.

[5] One analysis, by an international authority on the subject, estimated that in the late 1960s the *average* daily calorie intake was 1,880 per person, little more than the minimum of 1,821 calories for a person engaged in physical work (see Clark, 1972). These figures are consistent with data to be presented shortly.

[6] See also Huppi and Ravallion (1991), World Bank (1990), and Thorbecke (1991, 1992). Booth (1992a, 1993) provides a synthesis and analysis of secondary data sources from the mid-1960s.

[7] For example, the government party, Golkar (*Golongan Karya*, Functional Group), has relied extensively on the BPS data in its recent election campaigns (even to the extent of including Gini coefficients in its background campaign material!).

[8] Important studies of this genre include Collier et al. (1973), Franke (1972), Hart (1986), the papers in Hart, Turton and White (eds, 1989) (especially White and Wiradi, 1989), Palmer (1977), Penny and Singarimbun (1973), and Timmer (1973). More recently, in 1991 an international conference at The Hague, chaired by Dutch Development Cooperation Minister Pronk, addressed this issue, the proceedings from which have been published as Dirkse, Huisken and Rutten (eds, 1993). The volume contains a selection of critical Dutch anthropological writings on this subject.

[9] The best general survey and analysis of a cautiously optimistic note from the 1980s is Manning (1988), who concluded (p.72) that " . . . there is little evidence of a general trend towards polarization among economic classes in the wake of the introduction of HYVs, or increasing immiserization of the rural poor as a consequence of labour displacement in agriculture".

[10] These figures are calculated from data presented in Hardjono (1993, p. 287).

[11] Two caveats to this conclusion need to be mentioned. First, the major literature on this topic relates to rural Java. There have been very few detailed studies off-Java, and those that have

(for example, Deuster (1982), who found no evidence of rising inequality in West Sumatra over the periods from 1972–73 to 1978–79) relate to somewhat atypical regions. It is quite likely that, given the presence of a sizeable plantation sector in some regions (for example, North Sumatra), the inequality of land distribution off-Java is both higher and rising. Secondly, the only secondary data on this subject relate to the now dated 1983 Agricultural Census, as the 1993 Census results had not been released at the time of writing.

[12] On the latter, see Firdausy and Tisdell (1992) for an application to Indonesia.

[13] Booth (1993) contains extensive discussion of alternative measures and their implications for the estimated numbers of people in poverty. She also points out (p. 77) that, in 1986, Indonesia's official poverty line was far lower than that of its ASEAN neighbours. Since poverty is a relative concept, it is not surprising that Indonesia's threshold is well below that of Malaysia and Singapore. But it is also much lower than that of the Philippines and Thailand—about one-half that of the former and some 75 per cent that of the latter.

[14] One widely used rice-based poverty line, developed by Professor Sajogyo of Bogor, assumes the urban threshold is 50 per cent higher than that of rural areas. This would seem excessive, especially for cities other than Jakarta, and in view of the widespread practice of circular migration.

[15] Morawetz (1977, p. 71), for example, advances such a proposition on the basis of his survey of the lessons of economic development from 1950 to 1975. Sundrum (1990, Ch. 16) provides a detailed survey and analysis of redistributive policies in developing countries.

[16] Conversely, as noted in the next chapter, promotion of the rice sector may have had the unintended consequence of exacerbating regional inequality, to the extent that the poorer Eastern provinces, in many of which rice is not the staple, have missed out on this source of growth.

[17] Oshima (1987) emphasizes both these points as being crucial to East Asia's good distributional outcomes, noting in particular that in the early stages of economic development intensive wet rice cultivation was rarely if ever associated with concentrated agricultural land holdings. Indonesia is the only major economy among the NIEs and ASEAN not included in this study, according to Oshima owing to deficiencies in its long-run economic statistics. Nevertheless, much of his analysis is highly relevant to Indonesia.

[18] These changes are illustrated in the rapidly declining share of rice in consumer expenditures in Jakarta (Timmer, 1993). In the early 1960s, the rice share was about one-third (and probably higher outside Jakarta). It had fallen to one-quarter by the mid-1970s, and one-tenth a decade later. By the early 1990s, it was just 5 per cent.

[19] This possibility arises because the FAO food equations data for Indonesia may not have taken sufficient account of above-average wastage rates and inferior quality rice. Both of these were serious problems during the peak of the intensification program in the late 1970s and early 1980s, although they are less serious now.

[20] Nevertheless, in the most detailed survey of wages over this earlier period, Papanek (1980b) demonstrated convincingly that real wages declined from the mid-1950s for at least a decade, but from the late 1960s began to recover quickly, most likely doubling in the early years of the New Order.

[21] These studies include Manning (1994), who provides the most complete picture, together with Jayasuriya and Manning (1990), Jones and Manning (1992), Naylor (1990), and two *BIES* Surveys, August 1988 (Sisira Jayasuriya and Chris Manning) and April 1992 (Chris Manning). I am particularly grateful to Chris Manning for his assistance with this section.

[22] It is not possible to verify the latter statement empirically, owing to the absence of comprehensive data on hours worked overtime. It is probable, however, that at least part of the increase in manufacturing wages is explained by this factor, especially for example the jump in textile wages after 1987 as export-oriented firms sought to increase hours worked to meet sales commitments abroad.

[23] This issue is explored in some detail by Naylor (1990), who includes a recalculation of the rural cost of living index after making appropriate adjustments for vegetable prices (most notably that of chilli!).

[24] Two minor exceptions to the latter proposition are that government employment is now almost exclusively reserved for *pribumi* employees (not many non-*pribumi* Indonesians wish to enter government service in any case!), and the very senior echelons of non-*pribumi* business conglomerates tend to be reserved for employees of similar ethnicity. However, the shortages of skilled personnel which emerged in the late 1980s are breaking down the second barrier.

[25] There are still amazingly few detailed studies of intra-industry wage differentials of the type undertaken by Manning (1979), so it is difficult to test this proposition for the 1980s and 1990s.

[26] According to Manning (1993b), the minimum wage in Jakarta, before the recent increases, was less than one-half of that of Bangkok, less than one-quarter of that in Malaysia, and also below that in Manila. However, it probably exceeded that in China, Vietnam, and the non-unionized segments of South Asia.

[27] For a comprehensive examination of educational progress and issues during the New Order, including reference to the major literature, see Jones (1994).

[28] For a detailed analysis of gender differentials in educational attainment, see Oey-Gardiner (1991).

[29] The understatement occurs partly because much of the education budget consists of teachers' salaries which, like civil service salaries in general, are lower in Indonesia than the other countries in the comparison. There may be further understatement to the extent that some of the country's education expenditure occurs within other government departments, such as Religious Affairs and Home Affairs, and owing to the complicated manner in which the budget is presented (see Ch. 4). The published version of the routine budget does not distinguish between departments and functional activities, while in the development budget, where education is separately identified, some items of educational expenditure (such as *Inpres* schemes and grants to lower tiers of government) may not be recorded as such.

[30] Examples include Behrman and Deolalikar (1993), Byron and Takahashi (1989), and Boediono, McMahon and Adams (eds, 1992), together with the references cited within these articles. Gannicott (1990) provides a survey of the economics of education literature on East Asia, while Ogawa, Jones and Williamson (eds, 1993) analyze human resource developments along the Asia-Pacific rim more generally.

[31] See for example Keyfitz and Oey-Gardiner (1989), the case studies in Hill (ed., 1991), and the relevant sections of Boediono, McMahon and Adams (eds, 1992).

[32] For an interesting case study of one such area, management education, in which the private sector has been the clear leader, see Habir (1991). This study also shows that the government bureaucracy had played very little role in this growth, and on occasions has hampered its development.

[33] This section draws in particular on Corner and Rahardjo (1993), Hull (1994), van de Walle (1992), and World Bank (1990).

CHAPTER 11

[1] One peculiar legacy of this period which persists to this day is that, as noted earlier, the Singapore government does not release statistics on that country's trade with Indonesia. The reverse, however, is not the case.

[2] Several of the economic surveys of provinces in the Outer Islands published in the *BIES* in the late 1960s and early 1970s capture the flavour of this economic isolation. References to these surveys can be found in the relevant chapters of Hill (ed., 1989).

[3] See Booth (1992b) for a discussion of regional issues in such a context.

[4] The caveats attached to BKPM investment need to be restated briefly here. The data exclude

very large investments in oil and gas, obviously concentrated mainly in the producing provinces (but with some exceptions, such as Cilacap, Central Java), and finance, much of it around Jakarta. Domestic investors are not required to obtain BKPM approval, and an unknown (but probably sizeable) proportion would not have obtained approval, especially since 1984 when most of the fiscal incentives were removed. In the cumulative figures there is no adjustment for inflation, with the result that provincial weights of recent years are disproportionately important. Nevertheless, there has been no major shift in provincial shares over the course of the New Order.

5 See Arndt and Sundrum (1975) for the first major treatment of the subject, at the time a pioneering analysis given the data deficiencies.

6 For extensive discussion of these issues, see Bidani and Ravallion (1992).

7 The only comprehensive set of estimates of which the author is aware are those of Islam and Khan (1986) for 1976.

8 See Azis (1988), Uppal and Budiono (1986), Kameo and Reitveld (1987), and Hill (1992b). These papers contain extensive discussion of the various approaches and indicators used in measuring regional inequality.

9 The only qualification to this assertion is, as noted above, that the Java-Bali provinces have benefited disproportionately from the rice boom, and they are no longer the serious poverty cases.

10 Intercountry comparisons of the power of central governments are fraught with difficulty, especially since fiscal indicators tell only part of the story. But for what the data are worth, in a comparison of 18 developing countries in the World Bank's *World Development Report 1988* (p. 155), subnational revenues were by far the smallest share of total government revenues in Indonesia.

11 These issues are discussed extensively in Azis (1989, 1992a, 1992b, 1992c), Booth (1986, 1988b), and Devas and Associates (1989). Earlier analyses, which focus on essentially similar issues, include van Leeuwen (1975) and Shaw (1980).

12 Recall from Chapter 4 that these grants are separate from and in addition to the special allocations made to the provinces of Irian Jaya and East Timor. By the late 1980s, these special grants had been terminated, although both provinces continue to receive generous fiscal treatment from Jakarta.

13 The problem is most serious in agriculture, since the government is less involved in the *specifics* of industrial development (although of course it intervenes extensively through the trade regime). Thinking on regional development priorities could be assisted by analytical approaches of the type undertaken by Ali (1987) on the rice sector, although the database underpinning this research is not strong and it would be important to avoid any strategy of "picking regional winners".

CHAPTER 12

1 In assessing the prominence of various pessimistic assessments, I am, of course, only referring to the views of critics essentially sympathetic to the regime, indeed many close to or even "inside" it. In addition to these groups, the regime continues to attract much more harsh assessments, mainly from groups located in universities or human rights organizations. These groups tend to be a good deal less sympathetic in their criticisms, and some have predicted the demise of the Soeharto regime. For a critique of some of these writings, and how their predictions compare with outcomes, see Emmerson (nd).

2 This section draws on sec. 4 of Hill (1993).

3 Two series of per capita GNP in constant prices are presented in Table 12.1, one based on actual market prices converted at international exchange rates, the other using purchasing power parity (PPP), that is based on common international prices for goods and services. The PPP series are more accurate for the purposes of comparisons both over time and across

countries. They are also more accurate in forecasting "catchup" periods, which are shorter than those projected in the table using actual exchange rates. The compression occurs because of relative price effects, namely the rise in the price of non-tradeables over the course of economic development, and was clearly evident in the dramatic catchup of the Asian NIEs over the past two decades. Such a rise manifests itself in either a nominal currency appreciation, such as occurred in Korea, Singapore and Taiwan during the 1980s, or through higher inflation with a fixed nominal exchange rate (that is a real effective appreciation), essentially the Hong Kong case over this period.

[4] It should be emphasized that the New Order's record in managing this sensitive issue has, by and large, been a most creditable one, especially given the historical backdrop and the series of unpleasant incidents in the 1960s. Yet there is an influential strand of thinking in the country which would prefer less Chinese business domination even at the expense of slower economic growth, to a more liberal economy with higher growth. One cannot always be confident that rational and cool voices will prevail on such an emotion-charged issue.

[5] For Thailand, this threat is not present to anything like the same degree, owing to the effective assimilation of ethnic Chinese into Thai society over several generations.

[6] It is an interesting comment on the rapid international transmission of jargon that, following the work of Yoshihara (1988), discussions of corruption, even in Bahasa Indonesia, are sometimes couched in terms of whether Indonesia is becoming more or less "ersatz".

[7] Important references include Amsden (1989), Johnson (1982), and Wade (1990).

[8] The scholarly assessment of McKendrick (1992) was referred to above. More recently, according to widely reported estimates in the World Bank's 1993 report on the economy, these firms have accounted for almost one-half of the total losses recently incurred in the state enterprise sector.

[9] The rise of the Habibie camp in the new Cabinet did receive strong public support in at least one instance, notably the new Minister for Education and Culture, a portfolio long regarded as in need of a major overhaul to make the country's education system more relevant to Indonesia's new industrial requirements.

[10] This abstracts from a number of possible problems, such as the negative externalities—for the economy as a whole in the form of a higher borrowing rate abroad—which could arise if a large number of private Indonesian borrowers defaulted on their international commitments.

[11] Of course one slipped through the net: in April 1992 the huge Chandra Asri petrochemicals project received approval from the Investment Coordinating Board. In this case, however, although the major backers were three very well-known Indonesian businessmen, who had already committed one of the state banks to a large stake in the project, the proposal mysteriously received approval as a 100 per cent foreign-owned concern, the announcement coinciding with the new policy of allowing full foreign ownership for major projects.

[12] It is instructive to note in this context that Indonesia's planned infrastructure expenditure over the 1990s is comparatively small by East Asian standards, even though its backlog is arguably the greatest. According to estimates by a leading commercial firm, Indonesia is likely to spend around 4.8 per cent of its GDP on infrastructure over the 1993-99 period. This is lower than that of all other East Asian developing economies—ASEAN plus the NIEs—except Thailand, for which the figure is projected to be marginally lower (4.6 per cent). It is also well below the group average, of 7 per cent. (See HG Asia, *Asian Infrastructure*, May 1994.)

[13] It is worth recalling that in the 1970s there were forecasts that oil exports would cease by around 1990. These figures were wrong for the reasons mentioned in this paragraph, in addition to the large increase in natural gas exports from the late 1970s.

[14] There are many such examples in Indonesia, as elsewhere. One which continues to attract frequent publicity concerns urban bus services. Many such buses are poorly maintained and are a major source of air pollution. Yet when there are proposals to address the problem, by phasing

out old buses and installing emission-control devices, both of which would result in higher passenger charges, there is strong public protest. The conclusion seems inescapable that, to put it starkly, at least a portion of the commuting population is prepared to tolerate dirty air in exchange for lower fares.

BIBLIOGRAPHY

(Note: *BIES* refers to the *Bulletin of Indonesian Economic Studies*)

Afiff, S., W.P. Falcon, and C.P. Timmer (1980), 'Elements of a Food and Nutrition Policy for Indonesia', in G.F. Papanek (ed.), *The Indonesian Economy*, Praeger, New York, pp. 406–27

Ahmed, S. (1991), 'Fiscal Policy for Managing Indonesia's Environment', *Working Paper*, WPS 786, World Bank, Washington, D.C.

Akita, T. (1988), 'Recent Economic Development', in S. Ichimura (ed.), *Indonesian Economic Development: Issues and Analysis*, Japanese International Cooperation Agency, Tokyo

Akita, T. and R.A. Lukman (1994), Interregional Inequalities in Indonesia: A Sectoral Decomposition Analysis for 1975–90, paper presented to the Fourth Convention of the East Asian Economic Association, Taipei, August

Alexander, J. and A. Booth (1992), 'The Service Sector', in A. Booth (ed.), *The Oil Boom and After: Indonesian Economic Policy and Performance in the Soeharto Era*, Oxford University Press, Singapore, pp. 283–319

Ali, I. (1987), 'Rice in Indonesia: Price Policy and Comparative Advantage', *BIES*, 23(3), pp. 80–99

Amsden, A. (1989), *Asia's Next Giant: South Korea and Late Industrialization*, Oxford University Press, New York

Anderson, B.R.O'G. (1983), 'Old State, New Society: Indonesia's New Order in Comparative Historical Perspective', *Journal of Asian Studies*, 42 (3), pp. 477–96

Anderson, K. (1992), 'Effects of the Environment and Welfare of Liberalising World Trade: The Cases of Coal and Food', in K. Anderson and R. Blackhurst (eds), *The Greening of World Trade Issues*, Harvester-Wheatsheaf, London

Anderson, K. and R. Blackhurst (eds) (1992), *The Greening of World Trade Issues*, Harvester-Wheatsheaf, London

Anderson, K., Y. Hayami and Associates (1986), *The Political Economy of Agricultural Protection: East Asia in International Perspective*, Allen & Unwin, for the Australia-Japan Reseach Centre, Sydney

Arndt, H.W. (1971), 'Banking in Hyperinflation and Stabilization', in B. Glassburner (ed.), *The Economy of Indonesia: Selected Readings*, Cornell University Press, Ithaca

Arndt, H.W. (1973), 'Regional Income Estimates', *BIES*, 9(3), pp. 87-102

Arndt, H.W. (1979), 'Monetary Policy Instruments in Indonesia', *BIES* 15(3), pp. 107–22

Arndt, H.W. (1980), 'Growth and Equity Objectives in Economic Thought about Indonesia', in R.G. Garnaut and P.T. McCawley (eds), *Indonesia: Dualism, Growth and Poverty*, Research School of Pacific Studies, Australian National University, Canberra

Arndt, H.W. (1984), *The Indonesian Economy: Collected Papers*, Chopmen Publishers, Singapore

Arndt, H.W. (1989), 'Trade in Services with Special Reference to ASEAN', *ASEAN Economic Bulletin*, 6(1), pp. 1-7

Arndt, H.W. and R.M. Sundrum (1975), 'Regional Price Disparities', *BIES*, 11(2), pp. 30-68

Arndt, H.W. and R.M. Sundrum (1984), 'Devaluation and Inflation: The 1978 Experience', *BIES*, 20(1), pp. 83-97

Asher, M.G. (1989), 'A Comparative Overview of ASEAN Fiscal Systems and Practices', in M.G. Asher (ed.), *Fiscal Systems and Practices in ASEAN: Trends, Impact and Evaluation*, Institute of Southeast Asian Studies, Singapore

Asher, M.G. and A. Booth (1992), 'Fiscal Policy', in A. Booth (ed.), *The Indonesian Economy During the Soeharto Era*, Oxford University Press, Kuala Lumpur, pp. 41-76

Asra, A. (1989), 'Inequality Trends in Indonesia, 1969-1981: A Re-examination', *BIES*, 25(2), pp. 100-10

Aswicahyono, H.H. and H. Hill (1993), 'Explaining Foreign Investment Shares in LDC. Industry: Incorporating the Policy Factor', *Economics Letters*, 41, pp. 167-70

Athukorala, P. (1993), 'International Labour Migration in the Asia-Pacific Region: Patterns, Policies and Economic Implications', *Asian-Pacific Economic Literature*, 7 (2), pp. 28-57

Azis, I.J. (1989), 'Key Issues in Indonesian Regional Development', in H. Hill (ed.), *Unity and Diversity: Regional Economic Development in Indonesia since 1970*, Oxford University Press, Singapore, pp. 55-74

Azis, I.J. (1990), 'Inpres' Role in the Reduction of Interregional Disparity', *Asian Economic Journal*, 4(2), pp.1-26

Azis, I.J. (1992a), 'Interregional Allocation of Resources: The Case of Indonesia', *Papers in Regional Science*, 71(4), pp. 393-404

Azis, I.J. (1992b), 'Regional Balance and the National Development Strategy', in S. Sediono and K. Igusa (eds), *Regional Development and Industrialization of Indonesia: Regional Economic Balance and Industrialization at Local Level*, Institute of Developing Economies, Tokyo, pp. 7-31

Azis, I.J. (1992c), 'Review of Regional Development: Equity and Foreign Exchange Accumulation', in T.J. Kim, G. Knaap, and I.J. Azis (eds), *Spatial Development in Indonesia: Review and Prospects*, Avebury, Aldershot, pp. 91-132

Azis, I.J. (1993), 'An Indonesian Economic Forecast Based on a Yearly Econometric Model', *BIES*, 29 (2), pp. 43-58

Azis, I.J. (1994), 'Indonesia', in J. Williamson (ed.), *The Political Economy of Policy Reform*, Institute for International Economics, Washington, D.C., pp. 385-416

Barker, R., R.W. Herdt, and B. Rose (1985), *The Rice Economy of Asia*, Resources for the Future, Washington, D.C.

Barlow, C. (1991), 'Developments in Plantation Agriculture and Smallholder Cash-crop Production', in J. Hardjono (ed.), *Indonesia: Resources, Ecology and Environment*, Oxford University Press, Singapore, pp. 85-103

Barlow, C. and S.K. Jayasuriya (1984), 'Problems of Investment for Technological Advance: The Case of Indonesian Rubber Smallholders', *Journal of Agricultural Economics*, 35(1), pp. 85-95

Barlow, C., S.K. Jayasuriya, and C.S. Tan (1994), *The World Rubber Industry*, Routledge, London

Barlow, C. and Muharminto (1982), 'The Rubber Smallholder Economy' *BIES*, 18(2), pp. 86-119

Barlow, C. and T. Tomich (1991), 'Indonesian Agricultural Development: The Awkward Case of Smallholder Tree Crops', *BIES*, 27(3), pp. 29-55

Barrichello, R.R. and F.R. Flatters (1991), 'Trade Policy Reform in Indonesia', in D.H. Perkins and M. Roemer (eds), *Reforming Economic Systems in Developing Countries*, Harvard Studies in International Development, Harvard Institute for International Development, Boston, pp. 271-91

Battacharya, A. and M. Pangestu (1993), *Indonesia: Development Transformation and Public Policy*, project on 'The Lessons of East Asia', World Bank, Washington, D.C.

Behrman, J. R. and A. B. Deolalikar (1993), 'Unobserved Household and Community Heterogeneity and the Labor Market Impact of Schooling: A Case Study of Indonesia', *Economic Development and Cultural Change*, 41 (3), pp. 461-88

Bennett, C.P.A. and R.A. Godoy (1992), 'The Quality of Smallholder Coffee in South Sumatra: The Production of Low-Quality Coffee as a Response to World Demand', *BIES*, 28(1), pp. 85-100

Bidani, B. and M. Ravallion (1993), 'A New Regional Poverty Profile for Indonesia', *BIES*, 29 (3), pp. 37-68

Binhadi and P. Meek (1992), 'Implementing Monetary Policy' in A. Booth (ed.) *The Oil Boom and After: Indonesian Economic Policy and Performance in the Soeharto Era*, Oxford University Press, Singapore, pp. 102-31

Birowo, A.T. and G.E. Hansen (1981), 'Agricultural and Rural Development: An Overview', in G.E. Hansen (ed.), *Agricultural and Rural Development*, Westview Press, Boulder, pp. 1-27

Boediono (1990), Fiscal Policy in Indonesia, Paper presented to the Second Convention of the East Asian Economic Association, Bandung

Boediono and T. Kaneko (1988), 'Price Changes', in S. Ichimura (ed.), *Indonesian Economic Development: Issues and Analysis*, Japanese International Cooperation Agency, Tokyo, pp. 283-305

Boediono, W.W. McMahon, and D. Adams (eds) (1992), *Education, Economic, and Social Development*, Second 25 Year Development Plan and Sixth 5 Year Development Plan, Background Papers and Goals, Department of Education and Culture, Jakarta

Bolnick, B.R. (1982), 'Concessional Credit for Small Scale Enterprise', *BIES*, 18(2), pp. 65-85

Bolnick, B.R. (1983), 'A Reply' [to McLeod, 1983], *BIES*, 19 (1), pp. 90-6

Bolnick, B. R. (1987), 'Financial Liberalization with Imperfect Markets: Indonesia during the 1970s', *Economic Development and Cultural Change*, 35 (3), pp. 581-97

Bolnick, B. R. and E. R. Nelson (1990), 'Evaluating the Economic Impact of a Special Credit Program: KIK/KMKP in Indonesia', *Journal of Development Studies*, 26(2), pp. 299-312

Booth, A. (1977), 'Irrigation in Indonesia, Parts I and II', *BIES*, 13(1), pp. 33-74; 13(2), pp. 45-77.

Booth, A. (1986), 'Efforts to Decentralize Fiscal Policy: Problems of Taxable Capacity, Tax Effort and Revenue Sharing', in C. McAndrews (ed.), *Central Government and Local Development in Indonesia*, Oxford University Press, Singapore, pp. 77-100

Booth, A. (1988a), *Agricultural Development in Indonesia*, Allen & Unwin, Sydney

Booth, A. (1988b), 'Central Government Funding of Regional Government Development Expenditures in Indonesia: Past Achievement and Future Prospects', *Prisma*, no.45, pp. 7-22

Booth, A. (1990), 'The Tourism Boom in Indonesia', *BIES*, 26(3), pp. 45-73

Booth, A. (1991), 'Regional Aspects of Indonesian Agricultural Growth, in J. Hardjono (ed.), *Indonesia: Resources, Ecology, and Environment*, Oxford University Press, Singapore, pp. 36-60

Booth, A. (ed.) (1992), *The Oil Boom and After: Indonesian Economic Policy and Performance in the Soeharto Era*, Oxford University Press, Singapore

Booth, A. (1992a), 'Income Distribution and Poverty', in A. Booth (ed.), *The Oil Boom and After: Indonesian Economic Policy and Performance in the Soeharto Era*, Oxford University Press, Singapore, pp. 323-62

Booth, A. (1992b), 'Can Indonesia Survive as a Unitary State?', *Indonesia Circle*, no. 58, pp. 32-47

Booth, A. (1993), 'Counting the Poor in Indonesia', *BIES*, 29(1), pp. 53-83

Booth, A. and P. McCawley (eds) (1981), *The Indonesian Economy During the Soeharto Era*, Oxford University Press, Kuala Lumpur

Booth, A. and P. McCawley (1981a), 'Fiscal Policy', in A. Booth and P. McCawley (eds.), *The Indonesian Economy During the Soeharto Era*, Oxford University Press, Kuala Lumpur, pp. 126-61

Booth, A. and P. McCawley (1981b), The Indonesian Economy Since the Mid-Sixties, in A. Booth and P. McCawley (eds.), *The Indonesian Economy During the Soeharto Era*, Oxford University Press, Kuala Lumpur, pp. 1-22

Booth, A. and P. McCawley (1981c), 'Conclusions: Looking to the Future', in A. Booth and P. McCawley (eds.), *The Indonesian Economy During the Soeharto Era*, Oxford University Press, Kuala Lumpur, pp. 315-22

Booth, A. and R. M. Sundrum (1981), 'Income Distribution', in A. Booth and P. McCawley (eds), *The Indonesian Economy During the Soeharto Era*, Oxford University Press, Kuala Lumpur, pp. 181-217

BPS, Biro Pusat Statistik, *National Accounts* Jakarta, various issues.

Bresnan, J. (1993), *Managing Indonesia: The Modern Political Economy*, Columbia University Press, New York

Byron, R.P. and H. Takahashi (1989), 'An Analysis of the Effects of Schooling, Experience and Sex on Earnings in the Government and Private Sectors of Urban Java', *BIES*, 25 (1), pp. 105–17

Castle, L. and C. Findlay (eds.) (1988), *Pacific Trade in Services*, Allen & Unwin, Sydney

Castles, L. (1965), 'Socialism and Private Business: The Latest Phase', *BIES*, No. 1, pp. 13–45

Chalmers, I. (1988), Economic Nationalism and the Third World State: The Political Economy of the Indonesian Automotive Industry, 1950-1984, PhD dissertation, Australian National University, Canberra

Chapman, R. (1992), 'Indonesian Trade Reform in Close-Up: The Steel and Footwear Experiences', *BIES*, 28(1), pp. 67–84

Clark, C. (1972), 'Calories and Proteins', *BIES*, 8(2), pp. 98–103

Clark, D. and M. Oey-Gardiner (1991), 'How Indonesian Lecturers Have Adjusted to Civil Service Compensation', *BIES*, 27(3), pp. 129–141

Cole, D.C. and B.F. Slade (1992), 'Financial Development in Indonesia', in A. Booth (ed.) *The Oil Boom and After: Indonesian Economic Policy and Performance in the Soeharto Era*, Oxford University Press, Singapore, pp. 77–101

Collier, W. and S.T. Werdaja (1972), 'Small Rubber Production and Marketing', *BIES*, 8(2), pp. 67–92

Collier, W., W.G. Wiradi, and Soentoro (1973), 'Recent Changes in Rice Harvesting Methods: Some Serious Social Implications', *BIES* 9(2), pp. 36–45

Collier, W. et al. (1974), 'Comment' [on Timmer, 1973], *BIES*, 10(1), pp. 106–20

Collier, W. R. et al. (1982), 'Acceleration of Rural Development in Java', *BIES*, 18(3), pp. 84–101

Corner, L. and Y. Rahardjo (1993), 'Indonesian Health Policy into the Twenty-First Century: the Role of Demand', *Economics Division Working Papers*, 9305, Research School of Pacific Studies, Australian National University, Canberra

Dapice, D.O. (1980a), 'An Overview of the Indonesian Economy', in G.F. Papanek (ed.), *The Indonesian Economy*, Praeger, New York, pp. 3–55

Dapice, D.O. (1980b), 'Trends in Income Distribution and Levels of Living, 1970-75' in G.F. Papanek (ed.), *The Indonesian Economy*, Praeger, New York, pp. 67–81

Dapice, D.O and D. Snodgrass (1979), 'Employment in Manufacturing 1970-77: A Comment', *BIES*, 15(3), pp. 127–31

Deuster, P. (1982), 'The Green Revolution in a Village of West Sumatra', *BIES*, 18 (1), pp. 86–95

Devarajan, S. and J.D. Lewis (1991), 'Structural Adjustment and Economic Reform in Indonesia: Model-Based Policies vs Rules of Thumb', in D.H. Perkins and M. Roemer (eds), *Reforming Economic Systems in Developing Countries*, Harvard Studies in International Development, Harvard Institute for International Development, Boston, pp. 159–87

Devas, N. and Associates (1989), *Financing Local Government in Indonesia*, Ohio University Center for International Studies, Monographs in International Studies, Athens

Dick, H. W. (1981), 'Urban Public Transport, Parts I and II', *BIES*, 17(1), pp. 66-82; 17(2), pp. 72-88

Dick, H.W. (1987), *The Indonesian Interisland Shipping Industry: An Analysis of Competition and Regulation*, Institute of Southeast Asian Studies, Singapore

Dick, H.W., J.J. Fox, and J.A.C. Mackie (eds.) (1993), *Balanced Development: East Java in the New Order*, Oxford University Press, Singapore

Dick, H.W. and D. Forbes (1992), 'Transport and Communications: A Quiet Revolution', in A. Booth (ed.), *The Oil Boom and After: Indonesian Economic Policy and Performance in the Soeharto Era*, Oxford University Press, Singapore, pp. 258-82

Dickie, R.B. and T.A. Layman (1988), *Foreign Investment and Government Policy in the Third World: Forging Common Interests in Indonesia and Beyond*, Macmillan Press, London

Dirkse, J.-P., F. Huisken, and M. Rutten (eds.) (1993), *Development and Social Welfare: Indonesia's Experience Under the New Order*, KITLV Press, Leiden

Donges, J.B., B. Stecher and F. Wolter (1974), *Industrial Development Policies for Indonesia*, Kieler Studien 126, J.C.B. Mohr, Tubingen

Drake, C. (1989), *National Integration in Indonesia: Patterns and Issues*, University of Hawaii Press, Honolulu

Drysdale, P. (1988), *International Economic Pluralism: Economic Policy in East Asia and the Pacific*, Allen & Unwin, Sydney

Drysdale, P. and R. Garnaut (1982), 'Trade Intensities and the Analysis of Bilateral Trade Flows in a Many-Country World: A Survey', *Hitotsubashi Journal of Economics*, 22(2), pp. 62-84

Drysdale, P. and R. Garnaut (1993), 'The Pacific: An Application of a General Theory of Economic Integration', in C.F. Bergsten and M. Noland (eds), *Pacific Dynamism and the International Economic System*, Institute for International Economics, Washington, D.C.

Edmundson, W,C. (1994), 'Do the Rich Get Richer, do the Poor Get Poorer?', *BIES*, 30 (2), pp. 133-148

Edwards, S. (1984), 'The Order of Liberalization of the External Sector in Developing Countries', *Essays in International Finance*, No. 156, Princeton University, Princeton

Ellis, F. (1990), 'The Rice Market and its Management in Indonesia', *IDS Bulletin*, 21(3), pp. 44-51

Emerson, C., R. Garnaut, and A. Clunies Ross (1984), 'Mining Taxation in Indonesia', *BIES*, 20(2), pp. 107-21

Emmerson, D.K. (1988), 'The Military and Development in Indonesia', in J.S. Djiwandono and Y.M. Cheong (eds), *Soldiers and Stability in Southeast Asia*, Institute of Southeast Asian Studies, Singapore, pp. 107-30

Emmerson, D.K. (n.d.), The Rabbit and the Crocodile: Expecting the End of the New Order in Indonesia, 1966-1991, University of Wisconsin, Madison

Esmara, H. (1975), 'Regional Income Disparities' *BIES*, 11(1), pp. 41-57

Falcon, W. et al. (1984), *The Cassava Economy of Java*, Stanford University Press, Stanford

Fane, G. and C. Phillips (1991), 'Effective Protection in Indonesia in 1987', *BIES*, 27(1), pp. 105-25

FAO, Food and Agriculture Organization (1993), *1992 Production Yearbook*, FAO, Rome.

Findlay, C. (1990), 'Trade in Services in the Asia-Pacific Region', *Asian-Pacific Economic Literature*, 4(2), pp. 3-20

Firdausy, C. and C. Tisdell (1992), 'Rural Poverty and its Measurement: A Comparative Study of Villages in Nusa Penida, Bali, Indonesia', *BIES*, 28(2), pp. 75-93

Fox, J.J. (1991), 'Managing the Ecology of Rice Production in Indonesia', in J. Hardjono (ed.), *Indonesia: Resources, Ecology, and Environment*, Oxford University Press, Singapore, pp. 61-84

Franke, R.W. (1972), The Green Revolution in a Javanese Village, PhD dissertation, Harvard University, Cambridge

Funkhouser, R. and P.W. MacAvoy (1979), 'A Sample of Observations on Comparative Prices in Public and Private Enterprises', *Journal of Public Economics*, 11, pp. 353-68

Gannicott, K. (1990), 'The Economics of Education in Asian-Pacific Developing Countries', *Asian-Pacific Economic Literature*, 4 (1), pp. 41-64

Garnaut, R.G. and P.T. McCawley (eds) (1980), *Indonesia: Dualism, Growth and Poverty*, Research School of Pacific Studies, Australian National University, Canberra

Gelb, A. and Associates (1988), *Oil Windfalls: Blessing or Curse?*, Oxford University Press, for the World Bank, New York.

Geertz, C. (1963), *Agricultural Involution*, University of California Press, Berkeley

Geertz, C. (1971), 'A Program for the Stimulation of the Social Sciences in Indonesia', Report to the Ford Foundation (Institute for Advanced Study, Princeton University, Princeton)

Gibson, J. (1966), 'Production Sharing: Parts I and II', *BIES*, 3, pp. 52-75; 4, pp. 75-100

Gillis, M. (1982), 'Allocative and X-Efficiency in State-Owned Mining Enterprises: Comparisons between Bolivia and Indonesia', *Journal of Comparative Economics*, 6, pp. 1-23

Gillis, M. (1984), 'Episodes in Indonesian Economic Growth', in A. C. Harberger (ed.), *World Economic Growth*, Institute for Contemporary Studies, San Francisco, pp. 231-64

Gillis, M. (1985), 'Micro and Macroeconomics of Tax Reform: Indonesia', *Journal of Development Economics*, 19, pp. 221-54

Gillis, M. (1988), 'Indonesia: Public Policies, Resource Management and the Tropical

Forest', in R. Repetto and M. Gillis (eds), *Public Policies and the Misuse of Forest Resources*, Cambridge University Press, Cambridge, pp. 43-113.

Gillis, M. (1989), 'Comprehensive Tax Reform: The Indonesian Experience, 1981-1988', in M. Gillis (ed.), *Tax Reform in Developing Countries*, Duke University Press, Duke, ch. 4

Glassburner, B. (1971), 'The Economy and Economic Policy: General and Historical', in B. Glassburner (ed.), *The Economy of Indonesia: Selected Readings*, Cornell University Press, Ithaca, pp. 1-5

Glassburner, B. (ed.) (1971), *The Economy of Indonesia: Selected Readings*, Cornell University Press, Ithaca

Glassburner, B. (1976), 'In the Wake of General Ibnu: Crisis in the Indonesian Oil Industry', *Asian Survey*, 16(12), pp. 1099-112

Glassburner, B. (1978), 'Political Economy and the Soeharto Regime', *BIES*, 14(3), pp. 24-51

Glassburner, B. (1979), 'Budgets and Fiscal Policy Under the Soeharto Regime in Indonesia', *Ekonomi dan Keuangan Indonesia*, 27(3), pp. 295-314

Godoy, R. and C. Bennett (1990), 'The Quality of Smallholder Cloves in Maluku: The Local Response to Domestic Demand for a High-Quality Product', *BIES*, 26(2), pp. 59-78

Gray, C. (1979), 'Civil Service Compensation in Indonesia', *BIES*, 15(1), pp. 85-113

Gray, C.W. (1991), 'Legal Processes and Economic Development: A Case Study of Indonesia', *World Development*, 19(7), pp. 763-77

Grenville, S. (1981), 'Monetary Policy and the Formal Financial Sector', in A. Booth and P. McCawley (eds), *The Indonesian Economy During the Soeharto Era*, Oxford University Press, Kuala Lumpur, pp. 102-25

Habir, A.D. (1990), 'State Enterprises: Reform and Policy Issues', in H. Hill and T. Hull (eds.), *Indonesia Assessment 1990*, Political and Social Change Monograph 11, Department of Political and Social Change, Australian National University, Canberra, pp. 90-107

Habir, A.D. (1991), 'The Development of Business Education in Indonesia', in H. Hill (ed), *Indonesia Asessment 1991*, Political and Social Change Monograph 13, Australian National University, Canberra, pp. 120-34

Habir, A.D. (1993), 'The Emerging Indonesian Managerial Elite: Professionals amid Patriarchs', in D. Singh (ed.), *Southeast Asian Affairs 1993*, Institute of Southeast Asian Affairs, Singapore, pp. 161-82

Hansen, G.E. (ed.) (1981), *Agricultural and Rural Development*, Westview Press, Boulder

Hardjono, J. (1991), 'Environment or Employment: Vegetable Cultivation in West Java', in J. Hardjono (ed.), *Indonesia: Resources, Ecology, and Environment*, Oxford University Press, Singapore, pp.133-53

Hardjono, J. (ed.) (1991), *Indonesia: Resources, Ecology, and Environment*, Oxford University Press, Singapore

Hardjono, J. (1993), 'From Farm to Factory: Transition in Rural Employment in Majalaya', in C.G. Manning and J. Hardjono (eds.), pp. 273–89

Hardjono, J. (1994), 'Resource Utilization and the Environment', in H. Hill (ed.), *Indonesia's New Order: The Dynamics of Socio-Economic Transformation*, Allen & Unwin, Sydney, pp. 179–215

Hart, G. (1986), *Power, Labor, and Livelihood: Processes of Change in Rural Java*, University of California Press, Berkeley

Hart, G., A. Turton, and B. White (eds.) (1989), *Agrarian Transformations: Local Processes and the State in Southeast Asia*, University of California Press, Berkeley

Hasibuan, N. (1993), *Ekonomi Industri: Persaingan, Monopoli, dan Regulasi* [Industrial Economics: Competition, Monopoly, and Regulation], LP3ES, Jakarta

Hayami, Y. and T. Kawagoe (1993), *The Agrarian Origins of Commerce and Industry: A Study of Peasant Marketing in Indonesia*, St Martin's Press, New York

Higgins, B. (1957), *Indonesia's Economic Stabilization and Development*, Institute of Pacific Relations, New York

Higgins, B. (1958), 'Hatta and Co-operatives: the Middle Way for Indonesia?' *The Annals of the American Academy of Political Science*, 318, pp. 45–7

Higgins, B. (1968), *Economic Development*, 2nd edn, W.W. Norton, New York

Hill, H. (1982), 'State Enterprises in a Competitive Industry: An Indonesian Case Study', *World Development*, 10(11), pp. 1015–23

Hill, H. (1983), 'Choice of Technique in the Indonesian Weaving Industry', *Economic Development and Cultural Change*, 31(2), pp. 337–53

Hill, H. (1988), *Foreign Investment and Industrialization in Indonesia*, Oxford University Press, Singapore

Hill, H. (ed.) (1989), *Unity and Diversity: Regional Economic Development in Indonesia since 1970*, Oxford University Press, Singapore

Hill, H. (1990a), 'Indonesia's Industrial Transformation: Parts I and II', *BIES*, 26(2), pp. 79–120; 26(3), pp. 75–110

Hill, H. (1990b), 'Foreign Investment and East Asian Economic Development', *Asian-Pacific Economic Literature*, 4(2), pp. 21–58

Hill, H. (1990c), 'Ownership in Indonesia: Who Owns What and Does it Matter?', in H. Hill and T. Hull (eds.), *Indonesia Assessment 1990*, Political and Social Change Monograph 11, Department of Political and Social Change, Australian National University, Canberra, pp. 52–65

Hill, H. (ed.) (1991), *Indonesia Assessment 1991*, Political and Social Change Monograph 14, Department of Political and Social Change, Australian National University, Canberra

Hill, H. (1992a), 'Manufacturing Industry', in A. Booth (ed.), *The Oil Boom and After: Indonesian Economic Policy and Performance in the Soeharto Era*, Oxford University Press, Singapore, pp. 204–57

Hill, H. (1992b), 'Regional Development in a 'Boom and Bust Petroleum Economy': Indonesia since 1970', *Economic Development and Cultural Change*, 40(2), pp. 351–79

Hill, H. (1992c), 'Survey of Recent Developments', *BIES*, 28 (2), pp. 3-41

Hill, H. (1992d), 'Indonesia's Textile and Garment Industries: Development in an Asian Perspective', *Occasional Paper No. 87*, Institute of Southeast Asian Studies, Singapore

Hill, H. (1993), 'Where is the Indonesian Economy Headed?', *Occasional Paper No. 3*, Centre of Southeast Asian Studies, Northern Territory University

Hill, H. (1994), 'The Economy', in H. Hill (ed.), *Indonesia's New Order: The Dynamics of Socio-Economic Transformation*, Allen & Unwin, Sydney, pp. 54-122

Hill, H. (ed.) (1994), *Indonesia's New Order: The Dynamics of Socio-Economic Transformation*, Allen & Unwin, Sydney

Hill, H. and T. Hull (eds.) (1990), *Indonesia Assessment 1990*, Political and Social Change Monograph 11, Department of Political and Social Change, Australian National University, Canberra

Hill, H. and K.P. Kalirajan (1993), 'Small Enterprise and Firm-level Technical Efficiency in the Indonesian Garment Industry', *Applied Economics*, 25, pp. 1137-44

Hill, H. and Pang E.F. (1988), 'The State and Industrial Restructuring: A Comparison of the Aerospace Industry in Indonesia and Singapore', *ASEAN Economic Bulletin*, 5(2), pp. 152-68.

Hull, T.H. (1994), 'Population Policy', in H. Hill (ed.), *Indonesia's New Order: The Dynamics of Socio-Economic Transformation*, Allen & Unwin, Sydney, pp. 123-44

Huppi, M. and M. Ravallion (1991), 'The Sectoral Structure of Poverty During an Adjustment Period: Evidence for Indonesia in the Mid-1980s', *World Development*, 19(12), pp. 1653-78

Ichimura, S. (ed.) (1988), *Indonesian Economic Development: Issues and Analysis*, Japanese International Cooperation Agency, Tokyo

Imada, P. and S. Naya (eds.) (1992), *AFTA: The Way Ahead*, Institute of Southeast Asian Studies, Singapore

IMF, International Monetary Fund (annual/monthly), *International Financial Statistics*, Washington, D.C.

ISEI (1990), *The Understanding of Economic Democracy*, Ikatan Sarjana Ekonomi Indonesia [The Indonesian Economists' Association], Jakarta

Islam, I. and H. Khan (1986), 'Spatial Patterns of Inequality and Poverty in Indonesia', *BIES*, 22(2), pp. 80-102

Jayasuriya, S.K. and C.G. Manning (1990), 'Agricultural Wage Growth and Rural Labour Market Adjustment: The Case of Java 1970-1988', *Working Papers in Trade and Development*, no. 90/2, Research School of Pacific Studies, Australian National University, Canberra

Jayasuriya, S.K. and I.K. Nehen (1989), 'Bali: Economic Growth and Tourism', in H. Hill (ed.), *Unity and Diversity: Regional Economic Development in Indonesia since 1970*, Oxford University Press, Singapore, pp. 331-48

Johnson, C. (1982), *MITI and the Japanese Miracle*, Stanford University Press, Stanford

Jones, E.L. (1988), *Growth Recurring: Economic Change in World History*, Clarendon Press, Oxford

Jones, G.W. (1976), 'Religion and Education in Indonesia', *Indonesia*, 22, pp. 19–56

Jones, G.W. (1994), 'Labour Force and Education', in H. Hill (ed.), *Indonesia's New Order: The Dynamics of Socio-Economic Transformation*, Allen & Unwin, Sydney, pp. 145–78

Jones, G. W. and C. Manning (1992), 'Labour Force and Employment During the 1980s', in A. Booth (ed.), *The Oil Boom and After: Indonesian Economic Policy and Performance in the Soeharto Era*, Oxford University Press, Singapore, pp. 363–410

Kameo, D. and P. Rietveld (1987), 'Regional Income Disparities in Indonesia: A Comment', *Ekonomi dan Keuangan Indonesia*, 35(4), pp. 451–9

Kelly, R. (1989), 'Property Taxation', in N. Devas and Associates, *Financing Local Government in Indonesia*, Ohio University Center for International Studies, Monographs in International Studies, Athens, pp. 109–34

Kelly, R. (1993), 'Property Tax Reform in Indonesia: Applying a Collection-Led Implementation Strategy', *BIES*, 29(1), pp. 85–104

Kerr, A. (1973), 'Regional Income Estimation in Indonesia: Historical Development', *Ekonomi dan Keuangan Indonesia*, 21(3), pp. 216–24

Keyfitz, N. (1965), 'Indonesian Population and the European Industrial Revolution', *Asian Survey*, 10, pp. 503-14

Keyfitz, N. and M. Oey-Gardiner (1989), *Indonesian Universities at the Crossroads*, Center for Policy and Implementation Studies, Jakarta

Khong, C.O. (1986), *The Politics of Oil in Indonesia: Foreign Company—Host Government Relations*, LSE Monographs in International Studies, Cambridge University Press, Cambridge

Kim, T.J., G. Knaap, and I.J. Azis (eds.), *Spatial Development in Indonesia: Review and Prospects*, Avebury, Aldershot

Kingston, J. (1993), 'Bolstering the New Order: Japan's ODA Relationship with Indonesia', in B. M. Koppel and R. M. Orr Jr (eds.), *Japan's Foreign Aid: Power and Policy in a New Era*, Westview Press, Boulder, pp. 41–62

Kristanto, Kustiah (1982), 'The Smallholder Cattle Economy in South Sulawesi', *BIES*, 18(1), pp. 61–85

Kuntjoro-Jakti, Dorodjatun and Prijono Tjiptoherijanto (1983), 'Indonesia-Japan Trade Relations', in Narongchai Akrasanee (ed.), *ASEAN-Japan Relations: Trade and Investment*, Institute of Southeast Asian Studies, Singapore, pp. 37–56

Kuntjoro-Jakti, Dorodjatun, et al. (1983), 'Japanese Investment in Indonesia', in S. Sekiguchi (ed), *ASEAN-Japan Relations: Investment*, Institute of Southeast Asian Studies, Singapore, pp. 27–60

Leake, J. (1980), 'The Livestock Industry', BIES, 16(1), pp. 65–74

Lee T.Y. (ed.) (1992), *Growth Triangle: The Johor-Singapore-Riau Experience*, Institute of Southeast Asian Studies, and Institute of Policy Studies, Singapore

Leinbach, T. R. (1986), 'Transport Development in Indonesia: Progress, Problems and

Policies Under the New Order', in C. McAndrews (ed.), *Central Government and Local Development in Indonesia*, Oxford University Press, Singapore, pp. 190-220

Lerche, D. (1980), 'Efficiency of Taxation in Indonesia', *BIES*, 16(1), pp. 34-51

Lindsay, H. (1989), 'The Indonesian Log Export Ban: An Estimation of Foregone Export Earnings', *BIES*, 25(2), pp. 111-23

Little, I.M.D. (1988), 'Small Manufacturing Enterprises and Employment in Developing Countries', *Asian Development Review*, 6(2), pp. 1-9

Little, I.M.D., R.N. Cooper, W.M. Corden, and S. Rajapatirana (1993), *Boom, Crisis, and Adjustment: The Macroeconomic Experience of Developing Countries*, Oxford University Press, for the World Bank, New York

McAndrews, C. (ed.) (1986), *Central Government and Local Development in Indonesia*, Oxford University Press, Singapore

McAndrews, C. (1994), 'The Indonesian Environmental Impact Agency: Its Role, Development and Future', *BIES*, 30(1), pp. 85-103

McCawley, P. (1971), 'The Indonesian Electric Supply Industry', PhD dissertation, Australian National University, Canberra

McCawley, P. (1978), 'Some Consequences of the Pertamina Crisis in Indonesia', *Journal of Southeast Asian Studies*, 9(1), pp. 1-27

McCawley, P. (1980), 'Indonesia's New Balance of Payment Problem: A Surplus to Get Rid of', *Ekonomi dan Keuangan Indonesia* 28(1), pp. 39-58

McCawley, P. (1981), 'The Growth of the Industrial Sector', in A. Booth and P. McCawley (eds.), *The Indonesian Economy During the Soeharto Era*, Oxford University Press, Kuala Lumpur, pp. 62-101

McCawley, P. (1990), 'Foreign Aid to Indonesia during the New Order', *Quarterly Aid Round-up*, Australian International Development Assistance Bureau, Canberra, no. 1, pp. 32-42

McCawley, P. and M. Tait (1979), 'New Data on Employment in Manufacturing, 1970-1977', *BIES*, 15(1), pp. 125-36

MacIntyre, A. J. (1991), *Business and Politics in Indonesia*, Allen & Unwin, Sydney

MacIntyre, A.J. (1992), 'Politics and the Reorientation of Economic Policy in Indonesia', in A.J. MacIntyre and K. Jayasuriya (eds.), *The Dynamics of Economic Policy Reform in South-East Asia and the South-West Pacific*, Oxford University Press, Singapore, pp. 138-57

MacIntyre, A. J. and K. Jayasuriya (eds.) (1992), *The Dynamics of Economic Policy Reform in South-East Asia and the South-West Pacific*, Oxford University Press, Singapore

McKendrick, D.G. (1989), 'Acquiring Technological Capabilities: Aircraft and Commercial Banking in Indonesia', PhD dissertation, University of California, Berkeley

McKendrick, D.G. (1992), 'Obstacles to "Catch Up": The Case of the Indonesian Aircraft Industry', *BIES*, 28(1), pp. 39-66

Mackie, J.A.C. (1961/62), 'Indonesia's Government Estates and their Masters', *Pacific Affairs*, 34(4), pp. 337-60

Mackie, J.A.C. (1970), 'The Report of the Commission of Four on Corruption', *BIES*, 6(3), pp. 87-101

Mackie, J.A.C. (1971), 'The Indonesian Economy, 1950-1963', in B. Glassburner (ed.), *The Economy of Indonesia: Selected Readings*, Cornell University Press, Ithaca, pp. 16-69 (first published 1964)

Mackie, J.A.C. (1980), 'Integrating and Centrifugal Factors in Indonesian Politics since 1945', in J.A.C. Mackie (ed.), *Indonesia: The Making of a Nation, Indonesia: Australian Perspectives* (vol.2), Research School of Pacific Studies, Australian National University, Canberra, pp. 669-84

Mackie, J.A.C. (1990), 'The Indonesian Conglomerates in Regional Perspective', in H. Hill and T. Hull (eds), *Indonesia Assessment 1990*, Political and Social Change Monograph 11, Australian National University, pp. 108-21

Mackie, J.A.C. (1992), 'Changing Patterns of Chinese Big Business in Southeast Asia', in R. McVey (ed.), *Southeast Asian Capitalists*, Cornell University, Ithaca, pp. 161-90

Mackie, J.A.C. (1993), 'Plantations and Cash Crops in East Java: Changing Patterns', in H.W. Dick, J.J. Fox, and J.A.C. Mackie (eds), *Balanced Development: East Java in the New Order*, Oxford University Press, Singapore, pp. 187-213

Mackie, J.A.C. and A. MacIntyre (1994), 'Politics', in H. Hill (ed.), *Indonesia's New Order: The Dynamics of Socio-Economic Transformation*, Allen & Unwin, Sydney, pp. 1-53

McKinnon, R.I. (1973), *Money and Capital in Economic Development*, The Brookings Institution, Washington, D.C.

McKinnon, R.I. (1991), *The Order of Economic Liberalization: Financial Control in the Transition to a Market Economy*, Johns Hopkins University Press, Baltimore

McLeod, R.H. (1980), *Finance and Entrepreneurship in the Small Business Sector in Indonesia*, PhD dissertation, Australian National University, Canberra

McLeod, R.H. (1983), 'A Comment' [on Bolnick, 1982], *BIES*, 19 (1), pp. 83-9

McLeod, R.H. (1984), 'Financial Institutions and Markets in Indonesia', in M. T. Skully (ed.), *Financial Institutions and Markets in Southeast Asia*, Macmillan, London, pp. 49-109

McLeod, R.H. (1992), 'Indonesia's New Banking Law', *BIES*, 28(3), pp. 107-22

McLeod, R.H. (1993a), 'Survey of Recent Developments', *BIES*, 29 (2), pp. 3-42

McLeod, R.H. (1993b), 'Analysis and Management of Indonesian Money Supply Growth', *BIES*, 29(2), pp. 97-128

McStocker, R. (1987), 'The Indonesian Coffee Industry', *BIES*, 23(1), pp. 40-69

Mangkusuwondo, S., D. Simandjuntak, and S. Surono (1988), 'Trade Policy Options for Indonesia', in M. Ariff and L.H. Tan (eds), *The Uruguay Round: ASEAN Trade Policy Options*, Institute of Southeast Asian Studies, Singapore, pp. 38-64

Manning, C.G. (1971), 'The Timber Boom with Special Reference to East Kalimantan', *BIES*, 7(3), pp. 30-60

Manning, C. G. (1979), Wage Differentials and Labour Market Segmentation in

Indonesian Manufacturing, PhD dissertation, Australian National University, Canberra

Manning, C.G. (1988), 'The Green Revolution, Employment, and Economic Change in Rural Java: A Reassessment of Trends under the New Order', *Occasional Paper* no. 84, Institute of Southeast Asian Studies, Singapore

Manning, C.G. (1993a), 'Structural Change and Industrial Relations during the Soeharto Era: An Approaching Crisis?', *BIES*, 29 (2), pp. 97-128

Manning, C.G. (1993b), 'Approaching the Turning Point? Labour Market Change under Indonesia's New Order', Paper presented to a conference at Murdoch University, Perth

Manning, C.G. (1994), 'What Has Happened to Wages in the New Order?', *BIES*, 30(3), pp. 73-114

Manning, C. G. and J. Hardjono (eds.) (1993), *Indonesia Assessment 1993—Labour: Sharing in the Benefits of Growth?*, Political and Social Change Monograph 20, Australian National University, Canberra

Manning, C.G. and M. Rumbiak (1989), 'Irian Jaya: Economic Change, Migrants, and Indigenous Welfare', in H. Hill (ed.), *Unity and Diversity: Regional Economic Development in Indonesia since 1970*, Oxford University Press, Singapore, pp. 77-106

Mardjana, I. K. (1993), Autonomy and Political Control in Indonesian Public Enterprises: A Principal–Agent Approach, unpublished PhD dissertation, Monash University, Clayton

Martin, W. and P.G. Warr (1993), 'Explaining the Relative Decline of Agriculture: A Supply-Side Analysis for Indonesia', *World Bank Economic Review*, 7 (1), pp. 381-401

Mears, L.A. (1978), 'Problems of Supply and Marketing of Food in Repelita III', *BIES*, 14(3), pp. 52-62

Mears, L.A. (1981), *The New Rice Economy of Indonesia*, Gadjah Mada University Press, Yogyakarta

Mears, L.A. and S. Afiff (1969), 'An Operational Rice Price Policy for Indonesia', *Ekonomi dan Keuangan Indonesia*, 17(1), pp. 3-13

Mears, L.A. and S. Moeljono (1981), 'Food Policy', in A. Booth and P. McCawley (eds.), *The Indonesian Economy During the Soeharto Era*, Oxford University Press, Kuala Lumpur, pp. 23-61

Miller, R.R. and M.A. Sumlinski (1994), 'Trends in Private Investment in Developing Countries 1994', *Discussion Paper no. 20*, International Finance Corporation, Washington, D.C.

Morawetz, D. (1977), *Twenty-five Years of Economic Development 1950 to 1975*, Johns Hopkins University Press, for the World Bank, Baltimore

Morrisson, C. and E. Thorbecke (1990), 'The Concept of Agricultural Surplus', *World Development*, 18(8), pp. 1081-95

Mubyarto (1977), 'The Sugar Industry: From Estate to Smallholder Cane Production?', *BIES*, 13(2), pp. 29-44

Mubyarto, (ed.) (1982), *Growth and Equity in Indonesian Agricultural Development*, Yayasan Agro Ekonomika, Jakarta

Muhaimin, Y.A. (1991), *Bisnis dan Politik: Kebijaksanaan Ekonomi Indonesia 1950-1980* [Business and Politics: Indonesian Economic Policy 1950-1980], LP3ES, Jakarta

Myrdal, G. (1968), *Asian Drama—An Inquiry into the Poverty of Nations*, Penguin, Harmondsworth

Napitupulu, B. (1968), 'Hunger in Indonesia', *BIES*, No. 9, pp. 60-70

Nasution, A. (1983), *Financial Institutions and Policies in Indonesia*, Institute of Southeast Asian Studies, Singapore

Nasution, A. (1989), 'Fiscal System and Practices in Indonesia', in M.G. Asher (ed.), *Fiscal Systems and Practices in ASEAN: Trends, Impact and Evaluation*, Institute of Southeast Asian Studies, Singapore, pp. 19-62

Naylor, R. (1990), 'Wage Trends in Rice Production in Java: 1976-1988', *BIES*, 26(2), pp. 133-56

Nehen, I.K. (1989), 'Insurance Industry and Employment in ASEAN', *ASEAN Economic Bulletin*, 6(1), pp. 46-58

Nelson, G.C. (1986), 'Labor Intensity, Employment Growth and Technical Change— An Example from Starch Processing in Indonesia', *Journal of Development Economics*, 24, pp. 111-17

Nelson, G.C. and M. Panggabean (1991), 'The Costs of Indonesian Sugar Policy: A Policy Analysis Matrix Approach', *American Journal of Agricultural Economics*, 73(3), pp. 703-12

Nibbering, J.W. (1991), 'Crisis and Resilience in Upland Land Use in Java', in J. Hardjono (ed.), *Indonesia: Resources, Ecology, and Environment*, Oxford University Press, Singapore, pp. 104-32

Odano, S., S. Sabilin, and S. Djiwandono, (1988), 'Financial Development', in S. Ichimura (ed.), *Indonesian Economic Development: Issues and Analysis*, Japanese International Cooperation Agency, Tokyo, pp. 167-89

Oey-Gardiner, M. (1991), 'Gender Differences in Schooling', *BIES*, 27 (1), pp. 57-79

Ogawa, N., G. W. Jones, and J. G. Williamson (eds.) (1993), *Human Resources in Development along the Asia-Pacific Rim*, Oxford University Press, Singapore

Oshima, H.T. (1987), *Economic Growth in Monsoon Asia: A Comparative Survey*, University of Tokyo Press, Tokyo

Paauw, D.S. (1963), 'From Colonial to Guided Economy', in R.T. McVey (ed.), *Indonesia*, Human Relations Area Files, New Haven, pp. 155-247

Pack, H. and J. R. Pack (1990), 'Is Foreign Aid Fungible? The Case of Indonesia', *Economic Journal*, 100, no. 399, pp. 188-194

Palmer, I. (1972), *Textiles in Indonesia: Problems of Import Substitution*, Praeger, New York

Palmer, I. (1977), *The New Rice in Indonesia*, United Nations Research Institute for Social Development, Geneva

Palmer, I. (1978), *The Indonesian Economy since 1965*, Frank Cass & Co., London

Pangestu, M. (1987), 'The Pattern of Direct Foreign Investment in ASEAN: The United States vs Japan', *ASEAN Economic Bulletin*, 3(3), pp. 301-28

Pangestu, M. (1991a), 'Managing Economic Policy Reforms in Indonesia', in S. Ostry (ed.), *Authority and Academic Scribblers: The Role of Research in East Asian Policy Reform*, International Center for Economic Growth, San Francisco, pp. 93-120

Pangestu, M. (1991b), 'Foreign Firms and Structural Change in the Indonesian Manufacturing Sector', in E.D. Ramstetter (ed.), *Direct Foreign Investment in Asia's Developing Economies and Structural Change in the Asia-Pacific Region*, Westview Press, Boulder, pp. 35-64

Pangestu, M. (1991c), 'Macroeconomic Management in the ASEAN Countries', in M. Ariff (ed.), *The Pacific Economy: Growth and External Stability*, Allen & Unwin, Sydney, pp. 121-54

Pangestu, M. (1992), 'An Indonesian Perspective', in Lee T.Y. (ed.), *Growth Triangle: The Johor-Singapore-Riau Experience*, Institute of Southeast Asian Studies, and Institute of Policy Studies, Singapore, pp. 75-115

Pangestu, M. (1994), AFTA and AFTA Plus: An Indonesian Perspective, Paper delivered to a conference 'AFTA and Beyond: An ASEAN Perspective', Bangkok

Pangestu, M. and Boediono (1986), 'Indonesia: The Structure and Causes of Manufacturing Sector Protection', in C. Findlay and R. Garnaut (eds), *The Political Economy of Manufacturing Protection: Experiences of ASEAN and Australia*, Allen & Unwin, Sydney, pp. 1-47

Pangestu, M. and A.D. Habir (1989), 'Trends and Prospects in Privatization and Deregulation in Indonesia', *ASEAN Economic Bulletin*, 5(3), pp. 224-41

Panglaykim, J. and H.W. Arndt (1966), 'Survey of Recent Developments', *BIES*, 4, pp. 1-35

Papanek, G.F. (ed.) (1980), *The Indonesian Economy*, Praeger, New York

Papanek, G.F. (1980a), 'Income Distribution and the Politics of Poverty', in G.P. Papanek (ed.), *The Indonesian Economy*, Praeger, New York, pp. 56-66

Papanek, G.F. (1980b), 'The Effects of Economic Growth and Inflation on Workers' Income', in G.F. Papanek (ed.), *The Indonesian Economy*, Praeger, New York, pp. 82-120

Papanek, G.F. (1985), 'Agricultural Income Distribution and Employment in the 1970s', *BIES*, 21(2), pp. 24-50

Papanek, G.F. (1993), 'Review Article [of Booth, ed., 1992]', *BIES*, 29 (2), pp. 129-40

Parker, S. (1985), 'A Study of Indonesian Trade Policy Between 1980 and 1984', unpublished paper, Jakarta

Patten, R.H. and J.K. Rosengard (1991), *Progress with Profits: the Development of Rural Banking in Indonesia*, International Center for Economic Growth, San Francisco

Patten, R., B. Dapice, and W. Falcon, (1980), 'An Experiment in Rural Employment Creation: The Early History of Indonesia's Kabupaten Development Program', in G.F. Papanek (ed.), *The Indonesian Economy*, Praeger, New York, pp. 155-82

Pearce, D., E. Barbier and A. Markandya (1990), *Sustainable Development: Economics and Environment in the Third World*, Edward Elgar, Aldershot

Pearson, S. et al. (1991), *Rice Policy in Indonesia*, Cornell University Press, Ithaca

Penny, D.H. (1969), 'Indonesia', in R. T. Shand (ed.), *Agricultural Development in Asia*, Australian National University Press, Canberra, pp. 251-79

Penny, D.H. and M. Singarimbun (1973), *Population and Poverty in Rural Java: Some Economic Arithmetic from Sriharjo*, Cornell International Agricultural Development Mimeograph 41, Cornell University, Ithaca

Perkins, D.H. and M. Roemer (eds) (1991), *Reforming Economic Systems in Developing Countries*, Harvard Studies in International Development, Harvard Institute for International Development, Boston

Pinto, B. (1987), 'Nigeria During and After the Oil Boom: A Policy Comparison with Indonesia', *World Bank Economic Review*, 1(3), pp. 419-45

Pitt, M.M. (1981), 'Alternative Trade Strategies and Employment in Indonesia', in A. O. Krueger et al. (eds.), *Trade and Employment in Developing Countries*, Vol. 1, University of Chicago Press, Chicago, pp. 181-237

Pitt, M.M. (1991), 'Indonesia', in D. Papageorgiou, M. Michaely and A. Chocksi (eds.), *Liberalizing Foreign Trade*, Vol. 5, Basil Blackwell, Cambridge, Mass., for the World Bank, pp. 1-196

Poot, H., A. Kuyvenhoven, and J. Jansen (1990), *Industrialization and Trade in Indonesia*, Gadjah Mada University Press, Yogyakarta

Poot, H. (1991), 'Interindustry Linkages in Indonesian Manufacturing', *BIES*, 27(2), pp. 61-89

Posthumus, G.A. (1971), *The Inter-Governmental Group on Indonesia*, Rotterdam University Press, Rotterdam

Potter, L. (1991), 'Environmental and Social Aspects of Timber Exploitation in Kalimantan, 1967-1989', in J. Hardjono (ed.), *Indonesia: Resources, Ecology, and Environment*, Oxford University Press, Singapore, pp. 177-211

Ram, R. (1985), 'Exports and Economic Growth: Some Additional Evidence', *Economic Development and Cultural Change*, 33 (2), pp. 415-25

Ravallion, M. (1988), 'INPRES and Equality: A Distributional Perspective on the Centre's Regional Disbursements', *BIES*, 24(3), pp. 53-71

Ravallion, M. and M. Huppi (1991), 'Measuring Changes in Poverty: A Methodological Case Study of Indonesia During an Adjustment Period', *World Bank Economic Review*, 5(1), pp. 57-82

Repetto, R. et al. (1989), *Wasting Assets: Natural Resources in the National Income Accounts*, World Resources Institute, Washington, D.C.

Rice, R.C. (1983), 'The Origins of Basic Economic Ideas and their Impact on 'New Order' Policies, *BIES*, 19(2), pp. 60-82

Richter, H.V. (1970), 'Problems of Assessing Unrecorded Trade', *BIES*, 6(1), pp. 45-60

Rix, A. (1993), 'Managing Japan's Aid: ASEAN', in B. M. Koppel and R. M. Orr Jr (eds),

Japan's Foreign Aid: Power and Policy in a New Era, Westview Press, Boulder, pp. 19–40

Robison, R. (1986), *Indonesia: The Rise of Capital*, Allen & Unwin, Sydney

Roche, F.C. (1994), 'The Technical and Price Efficiency of Fertilizer Use in Irrigated Rice Production', *BIES*, 30(1), pp. 59–83

Roeder, O.G. (1976), *The Smiling General—President Soeharto of Indonesia*, 2nd edn, Gunung Agung, Jakarta

Rosendale, P. (1976), 'The Equilibrium Exchange Rate: Some Considerations', *BIES*, 12(1), pp. 93–102

Rosendale, P. (1981), 'The Balance of Payments', in A. Booth and P. McCawley (eds.), *The Indonesian Economy During the Soeharto Era*, Oxford University Press, Kuala Lumpur, pp. 162–80

Ruttan, V.W. (1990), 'The Direction of Agricultural Development in Asia: Into the 21st Century, *Journal of Asian Economies*, 1(2), pp. 189–203

Ruzicka, I. (1979), 'Rent Appropriation in Indonesian Logging: East Kalimantan 1972/3-1976/7', *BIES*, 15(2), pp. 45–74

Sadli, M. (1972), 'Foreign Investment in Developing Countries: Indonesia', in P. Drysdale (ed.), *Direct Foreign Investment in Asia and the Pacific*, Australian National University Press, Canberra, pp. 201–25

Sadli, M. (1973), 'Indonesia's Experience with the Application of Technology and its Employment Effects', *Ekonomi dan Keuangan Indonesia*, 21(3), pp. 147–60

Sadli, M. (1988), 'Private Sector and Public Sector', in S. Ichimura (ed.), *Indonesian Economic Development: Issues and Analysis*, Japanese International Cooperation Agency, Tokyo, pp. 353–71

Sadli, M. (1989), 'Keynote Address', delivered to Conference on 'Indonesia's New Order: Past Present, Future', Australian National University, Canberra, December

Sato, Y. (1993), 'The Salim Group in Indonesia: The Development and Behaviour of the Largest Conglomerate in Southeast Asia', *Developing Economies*, 31 (4), pp. 408–41

Sawit, M.H. and I. Manwan (1991), 'The New Supra-Insus Rice Intensification Program: The Case of the North Coast of West Java and South Sulawesi', *BIES*, 27(1), pp. 81–103

Schwarz, A. (1994), *A Nation In Waiting: Indonesia in the 1990s*, Allen & Unwin, Sydney

Shaw, G.K. (1980), 'Intergovernmental Fiscal Relations', in G.F. Papanek (ed.), *The Indonesian Economy*, Praeger, New York, pp. 278–94

Shome, P. (1993), 'The Taxation of High Income Earners', *Papers on Policy Analysis and Assessment*, PPAA/93/19, International Monetary Fund, Washington, D.C.

Simkin, C.G.F. (1970), 'Indonesia's Unrecorded Trade', *BIES*, 6(1), pp. 17–44

Sinaga, R.S. (1978), 'Implications of Agricultural Mechanisation for Employment and Income Distribution', *BIES*, 14(2), pp. 102–11

Singarimbun, M. (1990), 'Perubahan-perubahan Sosial-Ekonomi di Miri Sriharjo' [Socio-Economic Change in Miri Sriharjo], in Mubyarto (ed.), *D.H. Penny—Kemiskinan:*

Peranan Sistem Pasar [D.H. Penny—Poverty: The Role of the Market System], Penerbit Universitas Indonesia, Jakarta, pp. 167–77

Singarimbun, M. (1993), 'The Opening of a Village Labour Market: Changes in Employment and Welfare in Sriharjo', in C.G. Manning and J. Hardjono (eds), *Indonesia Assessment 1993—Labour: Sharing in the Benefits of Growth?*, Political and Social Change Monograph 20, Australian National University, Canberra, pp. 261–72

Sjahrir (1987), *Kebijaksanaan Negara: Konsistensi dan Implementasi* [State Policy: Consistency and Implementation], LP3ES, Jakarta

Snodgrass, D.R. and R.H. Patten (1991), 'Reform of Rural Credit in Indonesia: Inducing Bureaucracies to Behave Competitively', in D.H. Perkins and M. Roemer (eds), *Reforming Economic Systems in Developing Countries*, Harvard Studies in International Development, Harvard Institute for International Development, Boston, pp. 341–63

Soehoed, A.R. (1967), 'Manufacturing in Indonesia', *BIES*, 8, pp. 65–84

Soehoed, A.R. (1988), 'Reflections on Industrialisation and Industrial Policy in Indonesia', *BIES*, 24(2), pp. 43–57

Soesastro, M.H. (1989), 'The Political Economy of Deregulation in Indonesia', *Asian Survey*, 29(9), pp. 853–68

Soesastro, M.H., D.S. Simandjuntak, and P.R. Silalahi (1988), *Financing Public Sector Development Expenditure in Selected Countries: Indonesia*, Economics Office, Asian Development Bank, Manila

Stoler, A. (1985), *Capitalism and Confrontation in Sumatra's Plantation Belt*, Yale University Press, New Haven

Sumantoro (1984), 'MNCs and the Host Country: The Indonesian Case', *Research Notes and Discussion Paper*, no. 45, Institute of Southeast Asian Studies, Singapore

Sumitro Djojohadikusumo (1986), 'Recollections of My Career', *BIES*, 22(3), pp. 27–39

Sundrum, R.M. (1973), 'Consumer Expenditure Patterns', *BIES*, 9(1), pp. 86–106

Sundrum, R.M. (1986), 'Indonesia's Rapid Economic Growth: 1968–81', *BIES* 22(3), pp. 40–69

Sundrum, R.M. (1988), 'Indonesia's Slow Economic Growth', *BIES*, 24(1), pp. 37–72

Sundrum, R.M. (1990), *Income Distribution in Less Developed Countries*, Routledge, London

Szirmai, A. (1994), 'Real Output and Labour Productivity in Indonesian Manufacturing, 1975–90', *BIES*, 30(2), pp. 49–90

Tabor, S.R. (1992), 'Agriculture in Transition', in A. Booth (ed.), *The Oil Boom and After: Indonesian Economic Policy and Performance in the Soeharto Era*, Oxford University Press, Singapore, pp. 161–203

Tamba, J. L. and H. Nishimura (1988), 'Agricultural Development', in S. Ichimura (ed.), *Indonesian Economic Development: Issues and Analysis*, Japanese International Cooperation Agency, Tokyo, pp. 62–78

Tan, T.K. (ed.) (1967), *Sukarno's Guided Indonesia*, Jacaranda Press, Brisbane

Thee K.W. (1984), 'Japanese Direct Investment in Indonesian Manufacturing', *BIES*, 20(2), pp. 90-106

Thee K.W. (1988), *Industrialisasi Indonesia: Analisis dan Catatan Kritis* [Industrialisation in Indonesia: Analysis and Critical Notes], Pustaka Sinar Harapan, Jakarta

Thee K.W. (1990), 'Indonesia: Technology Transfer in the Manufacturing Industry', in H. Soesastro and M. Pangestu (eds), *Technological Challenge in the Pacific*, Allen & Unwin, Sydney, pp. 200-32

Thee K.W. (1991), 'The Surge of Asian NIC Investment into Indonesia', *BIES*, 27(3), pp. 55-89

Thee K.W. (1993), 'Industrial Structure and Small and Medium Enterprise Development in Indonesia', *EDI Working Papers*, World Bank, Washington, D.C.

Thee K.W. and K. Yoshihara (1987), 'Foreign and Domestic Capital in Indonesian Industrialization', *Southeast Asian Studies*, 24(4), pp. 327-349

Thorbecke, E. (1991), 'Adjustment, Growth and Income Distribution in Indonesia', *World Development*, 19(11), pp. 1595-1614

Thorbecke, E. (1992), 'The Indonesian Adjustment Experience in an International Perspective', *Jurnal Ekonomi Indonesia*, 1(1), pp. 76-116

Timmer, C.P. (1973), 'Choice of Technique in Rice Milling in Java', *BIES*, 9(2), pp. 57-76

Timmer, C.P. (1974), 'Reply' [to Collier et al., 1974], *BIES*, 10(1), pp. 121-6

Timmer, C.P. (1975), 'The Political Economy of Rice in Asia: Indonesia', *Food Research Institute Studies*, 14(3), pp. 197-231

Timmer, C.P. (ed.) (1987), *The Corn Economy of Indonesia*, Cornell University Press, Ithaca

Timmer, C.P. (1989), 'Indonesia: Transition from Food Importer to Exporter', in T. Sicular (ed.), *Food Price Policy in Asia: A Comparative Study*, Cornell University Press, Ithaca, pp. 22-64.

Timmer, C.P. (1991), 'Food Price Stabilization: Rationale, Design, and Implementation', in D.H. Perkins and M. Roemer (eds.), *Reforming Economic Systems in Developing Countries*, Harvard Studies in International Development, Harvard Institute for International Development, Boston, pp. 219-48

Timmer, C.P. (1993), 'Rural Bias in the East and South-east Asian Rice Economy: Indonesia in Comparative Perspective', *Journal of Development Studies*, 29 (4), pp. 149-176.

Tjondronegoro, S.M.P., I. Soejono and J. Hardjono (1992), 'Rural Poverty in Indonesia: Trends, Issues and Policies', *Asian Development Review*, 10 (1), pp. 67-90

Tomich, T.P. (1991), 'Smallholder Rubber Development in Indonesia', in D.H. Perkins and M. Roemer (eds.), *Reforming Economic Systems in Developing Countries*, Harvard Studies in International Development, Harvard Institute for International Development, Boston, pp. 249-70

Tomich, T.P. (1992), 'Survey of Recent Developments', *BIES*, 28 (3), pp. 3-39.

Tomich, T.P., Hastuti, and C.P.A. Bennett, (1993), Policy Failure and Private Initiative in Upland Agriculture: Evidence from Smallholder Coffee in Highland Agriculture, Unpublished Paper.

Trewin, R. and Erwidodo, (1993), 'Agricultural Policy Options to Maintain Indonesian Rice Self-Sufficiency', Paper presented to the 37th Annual Conference of the Australian Agricultural Economics Society, Sydney, February

Tsurumi, Y. (1980), 'Japanese Investments in Indonesia: Ownership, Technology Transfer, and Political Conflict, in G.F. Papanek (ed.), *The Indonesian Economy*, Praeger, New York, pp. 295-323

Tucker, K. and M. Sundberg (1988), *International Trade in Services*, Routledge, London

Uppal, J.S. (1986), *Taxation in Indonesia*, Gadjah Mada University Press, Yogyakarta

Uppal, J.S. and Budiono Sri Handoko (1986), 'Regional Income Disparities in Indonesia', *Ekonomi dan Keuangan Indonesia*, 34(3), pp. 287-304

van de Walle, D. (1992), 'The Distribution of the Benefits from Social Services in Indonesia, 1978-87', *Policy Research Working Papers*, Country Economic Department, WPS 871, World Bank, Washington, D.C.

van Leeuwen, R. (1975), 'Central Government Subsidies for Regional Development', *BIES*, 11(1), pp. 66-75

van Leeuwin, T. M. (1992), Twenty Five Years of Mineral Exploration in Indonesia, Unpublished Paper, PT Rio Tinto Indonesia, Jakarta

Wade, R. (1990), *Governing the Market: Economic Theory and the Role of the Government in East Asian Industrialization*, Princeton University Press, Princeton

Warr, P.G. (1984), 'Exchange Rate Protection in Indonesia', *BIES*, 20(2), pp. 53-89

Warr, P.G. (1986), 'Indonesia's Other Dutch Disease: Economic Effects of the Petroleum Boom', in J.P. Neary and S. van Wijnbergen (eds.), *Natural Resources and the Macroeconomy*, Basil Blackwell, Oxford, pp. 288-320

Warr, P.G. (1992), 'Exchange Rate Policy, Petroleum Prices, and the Balance of Payments, in A. Booth (ed.), *The Oil Boom and After: Indonesian Economic Policy and Performance in the Soeharto Era*, Oxford University Press, Singapore, pp. 132-58

Webb, A.J. et al. (eds.) (1990), *Estimates of Producer and Consumer Subsidy Equivalents: Government Intervention in Agriculture 1982-87*, US Department of Agriculture, Statistical Bulletin 803, Washington, D.C.

Weinstein, F.B. (1976), 'Multinational Corporations and the Third World: The Case of Japan and Southeast Asia', *International Organization*, 30(3), pp. 373-404

Wells, L.T. Jr (1973), 'Economic Man and Engineering Man: Choice of Technology in a Low-Wage Country', *Public Policy*, 21(3), pp. 319-42

White, B. and G. Wiradi (1989), 'Agrarian and Nonagrarian Bases of Inequality in Nine Javanese Villages', in G. Hart, A. Turton, and B. White (eds.), *Agrarian Transformations: Local Processes and the State in Southeast Asia*, University of California Press, Berkeley, pp. 266-302

Wibisono, M. (1989), 'The Politics of Indonesian Textile Policy: The Interests of Government Agencies and the Private Sector', *BIES*, 25 (1), pp. 31-52

Wilson, F. (1981), *The Conquest of Copper Mountain*, Atheneum, New York

de Wit, Y.B. (1973), 'The Kabupaten Program', *BIES*, 9(1), pp. 65–85

Woo, W.T. (1991), 'Using Economic Methodology to Assess Models of Policy-Making in Indonesia', *ASEAN Economic Bulletin*, 7(3), pp. 307–21

Woo, W.T. and A. Nasution (1989), 'Indonesian Economic Policies and their Relation to External Debt Management, in J.D. Sachs and S.M. Collins (eds.), *Developing Country Debt and Economic Performance*, Vol. 3, University of Chicago Press, for the NBER, Chicago, pp. 17–149

Woo, W.T., B. Glassburner, and A. Nasution (1994), *Macroeconomic Policies, Crises, and Long-Term Growth in Indonesia, 1965-90*, World Bank Comparative Macroeconomic Studies, World Bank, Washington, D.C.

World Bank (1981), *Indonesia: Selected Issues of Industrial Development and Trade Strategy*, Annex 2—*The Foreign Trade Regime*, World Bank, Washington, D.C.

World Bank (1988), *Forest, Land and Water: Issues in Sustainable Development*, World Bank, Washington, D.C.

World Bank (1990), *Indonesia: Poverty Assessment and Strategy Report*, World Bank, Washington, D.C.

World Bank (1991), *Indonesia: Employment and Training: Foundations for Industrialization in the 1990s*, World Bank, Washington, D.C.

World Bank (1992), *Indonesia: Agricultural Transformation: Challenges and Opportunities*, 2 vols., World Bank, Washington, D.C.

World Bank (1993), *The East Asian Miracle: Economic Growth and Public Policy*, World Bank, Washington, D.C.

World Bank (1994), *Indonesia's Environment and Development: Challenges for the Future*, World Bank, Washington, D.C.

World Development, 19 (11), (1991), special issue on 'Adjustment with Growth and Equity'

Yoshihara, K. (1988), *The Rise of Ersatz Capitalism in Southeast Asia*, Oxford University Press, Singapore

ERRATA

The details concerning the source, notes, and units on the vertical axis of the Figures were unfortunately omitted. They are included in this errata.

Figure 2.1 Economic growth, 1965–92, p. 12
   Units: %
   Notes: 1991 and 1992 data are preliminary; data are based on a spliced constant 1983 prices series.
   Source: BPS, *National Accounts*, various years.

Figure 2.2 Estimates of GNP per capita, 1969–92, p. 13
   Units: 1987 prices
   Source: World Bank, *World Tables*, Washington, DC, various issues; and BPS, *National Accounts*.

Figure 2.3 Exports and GDP, 1967–92, p. 15
   Units: %
   Notes: Each series refers to exports as a percentage of GDP. GDP data have been converted to US dollars at the average exchange rate for each year. The 'non-oil' GDP series refers to GDP less mining.
   Source: BPS, *Ekspor*, and *National Accounts*, various issues.

Figure 2.4 Investment and efficiency, 1966–92, p.18
   a Gross domestic investment as a percentage of gross domestic product. Increases in stocks are included in GDI, which explains why the figures are higher than those sometimes cited.
   b Incremental capital output ratio. Calculated by dividing the rate of growth of GDP into GDI/GDP. The figures are three-year moving averages. No data are reported for 1982 since GDP growth was negative.

Figure 2.5 Structural change, 1966–92, p. 19
   Units: % of GDP
   Note: Output is measured at current prices.
   Source: As for Figure 2.1.

Figure 2.6 Structural change, excluding mining, 1966–92, p. 20
   Units: % of GDP
   Source: As for Figure 2.1.

Figure 2.7 The growth of GDP and GDY, 1970–91, p. 28
   Units: %
   Notes: Both series are based on constant 1987 prices. GDP and GDY refer to gross domestic product and gross domestic income, respectively. GDY equals GDP less the terms of trade adjustment. The latter is defined as the difference between the value of exports of goods and non-factor services deflated by the import price index, and the value in terms of constant (domestic) prices.
   Source: World Bank, *World Tables*, Washington, DC, various issues.

Figure 3.1 Inflation and interest rates, 1967–92, p. 31
> *Unit:* %
> *Note:* The real rate is the nominal rate for one-year time deposits of state banks, deflated by the CPI.
> *Source:* IMF, *International Financial Statistics*, various issues. Real interest rate data for 1968–89 are from Cole and Slade (1992, p. 85), and thereafter from BPS, *Indikator Ekonomi*, various issues.

Figure 3.2 The growth of money supply, 1967–92, p. 32
> *Unit:* %
> *Note:* M1 (narrow money) and M2 (broad money) growth rates have been deflated by the inflation rate, that is, they are real growth rates.
> *Source:* IMF, *International Financial Statistics*, various issues.

Figure 3.3 Money supply as a percentage of GDP, 1967–92, p. 33
> *Unit:* %
> *Notes and Source:* As for Figure 3.2.

Figure 3.4 The growth of commercial loans and GDP, 1974–92, p. 38
> *Unit:* %
> *Note:* Loans by commercial banks, as at December each year, deflated by the GDP deflator.
> *Source:* McLeod (1993a, p. 22).

Figure 3.5 Sources of changes in base money, 1969–91, p. 41
> *Unit:* %
> *Source:* McLeod (1993b, p. 107).

Figure 4.1 Real government expenditures, 1966–92, p. 44
> *Unit:* Rp billion in 1985 prices.
> *Notes:* Data are for financial years (1969 refers to 1969/70, etc.). Discretionary expenditure refers to total expenditure less debt service and repayment. Data have been adjusted to 1985 prices using the Indonesian consumer price index as reported in the IMF, *International Financial Statistics*, various issues.
> *Source: Nota Keuangan*, various issues.

Figure 4.2 The government budget as a percentage of GDP, 1969–92, p. 45
> *Unit:* %
> **a** Total expenditure less payment of debt principal and interest.
> *Source:* As for Figure 4.1.

Figure 4.3 The composition of government revenue, 1967–92, p. 46
> *Unit:* % of total
> *Source:* As for Figure 4.1.

Figure 4.4 Indicators of development expenditure, 1968–92, p. 48
> *Unit:* %
> *Notes:* DE and TE refer to development expenditure and total expenditure respectively. Years are financial years (1969 is 1969/70, etc.).
> *Source: Nota Keuangan*, various issues.

Figure 4.5 Program aid as a percentage of total aid, 1968–92, p. 48
Unit: %
Source: Nota Keuangan, various issues.

Figure 4.6 Non-oil domestic revenue, 1966–92, p. 49
Unit: Non-oil Domestic Revenue (NODR) as % of / Total NODR
a Real NODR, in 1985 prices.
Sources: Nota Keuangan, and BPS, *National Accounts*, various issues.

Figure 4.7 Government expenditure, 1966–92, p. 52
Unit: Rp billion
b Discretionary expenditure is defined as total expenditure less debt service and repayment.
Source: Nota Keuangan, various issues.

Figure 4.8 The composition of government expenditures, 1967–92, p. 53
Unit: % of total
DS—debt service, that is, interest and principal repayments.
Source: Nota Keuangan, various issues.

Figure 4.9 Defence expenditure in ASEAN, 1980–91, p. 58
Unit: % of GDP
Sources: IMF, *Government Finance Statistics*, Washington, DC, various issues; and World Bank, *World Development Report*, Washington, DC, various issues.

Figure 4.10 Macroeconomic balances, 1969–92, p. 62
Unit: % of GDP
Sources: IMF, *International Financial Statistics*, various issues, and author's estimates.

Figure 5.1 The terms of trade, oil prices, and competitiveness, 1971–92, p. 68
Unit: Indices, 1980=100
Notes and Sources: Oil prices refer to nominal prices of Minas crude ($ per barrel), deflated by the wholesale price index for industrial economies. The oil price and terms of trade data are from *Nota Keuangan*, various issues. The wholesale price data are from the IMF, *International Financial Statistics*. The 'competitiveness' data are from the Morgan Guaranty real effective exchange rate series, calculated as nominal effective exchange rates adjusted for inflation rates. All data are expressed as indices with 1980=100.

Figure 5.2 Indonesia's exchange rate management in comparative perspective, 1981–92, p. 75
Unit: Indices, 1980−82=100
Note: The data refer to nominal effective exchange rates, adjusted for relative inflation rates domestically in comparison with those of major trading partners. The numbers are indices with base period 1980−82=100.
Source: Morgan Guaranty.

Figure 5.3 Foreign and domestic investment, 1968-92, p. 76
   Unit: $ million
   Notes: The data are in 1985 prices. Real data have been calculated using the US producer price for finished goods, capital equipment as a deflator; they are expressed in 1985 prices. Domestic approvals data have been converted at each year's exchange rate. BKPM data exclude the oil and gas and financial services sectors; they refer to total planned and approved investments, and include foreign and domestic equity and loan contributions.
   Sources: IMF, *International Financial Statistics* for realised foreign investment, exchange rates and deflators; BKPM for approved foreign and domestic investment.

Figure 5.4 The relative importance of foreign investment, 1969-92, p. 77
   Unit: % of GDP
   DFI—direct foreign investment.
   GCF—gross capital formation.
   Source: IMF, *International Financial Statistics*, various issues.

Figure 5.5 Resource flows by source, 1969-91, p. 80
   Unit: $ million
   Note: ODA and OOF refer to Official Development Assistance and Other Official Flows, respectively. 'Total Official' flows are the sum of these two. Private flows include direct investment, portfolio investment, and export credits. All data are net. There are considerable discrepancies between Organization for Economic Cooperation and Development and International Monetary Fund estimates of direct investment.
   Source: Organization for Economic Cooperation and Development, *Geographical Distribution of Financial Flows to Developing Countries*, Paris, various issues.

Figure 5.6 Commodity composition of exports, 1966-92, p. 82
   Unit: % of total
   Note: The following definitions are used (SITC codes):
   Agriculture: 0, 1, 2 (excl. 27 and 28), 4
   Fuels, Minerals, Metals: 27, 28, 3, 68
   Manufactures: 5, 6 (excl. 68), 7, 8
   Source: BPS, *Ekspor*, various issues.

Figure 5.7 Export growth, 1967-92, p. 82
   Unit: %
   Notes: The SITC classifications of the three groups are given in Figure 5.6. The manufactures total is very small before the early 1980s, and so the growth rates mean very little. The figures refer to real annual percentage increases. The deflator used is the US wholesale price index for each group, as reported in IMF, *International Financial Statistics*, various issues.
   Source: International Economic Data Bank, Australian National University, based on United Nations trade data tapes.

Figure 5.8 RCA indices, exports, 1966–92, p. 83

Notes: The RCA (revealed comparative advantage) index is defined as follows:

$$\frac{Xij}{Xi} \bigg/ \frac{Xwj}{Xw}$$

where Xij = country i's exports of commodity j

Xi = country i's total exports

Xwj = world exports of commodity j

Xw = world exports.

The following SITC codes are used: Agriculture; Fuels, Metals, Minerals—see Figure 5.6., Manufactures—see Table 8.3.

Source: As for Figure 5.7.

Figure 5.9 The regional composition of Indonesia's trade, 1966–92, p. 85

Unit: % of total

Notes: DEA, developing East Asia, includes ASEAN, China, Hong Kong, South Korea and Taiwan. EC, European Community, refers to the current 12 members.

Source: As for Figure 5.7.

Figure 5.10 The regional composition of Indonesia's exports, 1966–92, p. 85

Units: % of total

Notes and Sources: As for Figure 5.7.

Figure 5.11 The regional composition of Indonesia's manufactured exports, 1975–92, p. 86

Unit: % of total

Notes and Sources: As for Figure 5.7.

Figure 5.12 The regional composition of Indonesia's agricultural exports, 1966–92, p. 86

Unit: % of total

Notes and Sources: As for Figure 5.7.

Figure 5.13 The regional composition of Indonesia's energy and metals exports, 1966–92, p. 87

Unit: % of total

Notes and Sources: As for Figure 5.7.

Figure 5.14 Major aid donors, 1969–91, p. 91

Unit: % of total

Note: Data refer to net ODA (Official Development Assistance) flows. ODA includes the major concessional aid flows.

b The EC figure includes both individual donor programs and the (generally very small) multilateral EC flows.

c In most years Australia is the largest source, but in some years there have been sizeable flows from Canada, non-EC European countries, and the Middle East.

d Principally the UN and its agencies, the World Bank, and the Asian Development Bank.

Source: Organization for Economic Cooperation and Development, *Geographical Distribution of Financial Flows to Developing Countries*, Paris, various issues.

Figure 6.1 Public investment shares, 1981–92, p. 109
　　Unit: Public investment as a percentage of private investment.
　　Source: Miller and Sumlinski (1994, pp. 15–16).

Figure 7.1 The growth of agricultural output, 1966–92, pp. 125–6
　　Unit: %
　　Notes and Sources: As for Figure 2.1.

Figure 7.2 Indices of per capita agricultural production, 1965–92, p. 128
　　Unit: 1979–81=100
　　Source: Food and Agriculture Organization, *Production Yearbook*, Rome, various
issues.

Figure 7.3 Production of food crops, 1969–92, p. 130
　　Unit: '000 tons
　　Note: Before 1987, data do not include East Timor.
　　Sources: BPS, *Statistik Indonesia*, and *Indikator Ekonomi*, various issues.

Figure 7.4 Yields of major food crops, 1969–92, p. 131
　　Unit: '00 kilogram/hectare
　　Notes and Sources: As for Figure 7.3.

Figure 7.5 Rice: intensification and fertilizer use, 1969–92, p. 133
　　a Includes all intensification programs, 'special' and 'general', and various initiatives
within these categories, such as Bimas, Inmas, and Insus.
　　b Includes the three principal fertilizers, N, P2O, and K2O. The data refer to fertilizer
used for the entire food crop sector, whereas the land area includes only rice.
　　Source: Lampiran Pidato Kenegaraan, various issues.

Figure 7.6 Rice: price ratios, 1969–92, p. 134
　　a Ratio of Bangkok (5% broken) price, allowing 15–25% CIF Jakarta, to an average
of the domestic floor and ceiling prices.
　　b Ratio of the floor price to the official fertilizer price.
　　Source: Data kindly supplied by Dr Erwidodo and Dr Ray Trewin, from various unpublished sources.

Figure 7.7a Estate production of major cash crops, 1968–92, p. 138
　　Unit: '000 tons
　　a Includes smallholder output processed by estates.
　　Sources: BPS, *Statistik Indonesia*, and *Indikator Ekonomi*, various issues.

Figure 7.7b Smallholder production of major cash crops, 1969–91, p. 139
　　Unit: '000 tons
　　Source: As for Table 7.1.

Figure 7.8a Estate yields of major cash crops, 1969–92, p. 140
　　Unit: kilogram/hectare
　　Source: As for Table 7.1.

Figure 7.8b Smallholder yields of major cash crops, 1970–91, p. 141
   Unit: kilogram/hectare
   Source: As for Table 7.1.

Figure 7.9 Production of forest products, 1973–91, p. 146
   Unit: '000 cubic metres
   Source: As for Table 7.1.

Figure 8.1 The growth of industrial output, 1966–92, p. 153
   Unit: %
   Notes and Sources: As for Figure 2.1.

Figure 8.2 Labour productivity in manufacturing, 1975–91, p. 160
   Unit: Rp '000, 1975 prices
   Note: The data have been deflated using the wholesale price series for the relevant
   manufacturing activity.
   Source: BPS, *Statistik Industri*, various issues.

Figure 8.3 The growth of manufactured exports, 1981–92, p. 162
   Unit: %
   Note: The figures are real growth rates, using the US producer price (industrial goods)
   series as the deflator.
   Source: BPS, *Ekspor*, various issues.

Figure 8.4 Mining production, 1969–92, p. 173
   Note: 1992 data are preliminary. The production of gold and silver by private firms
   is included from 1984. Therefore, the post-1984 series is not comparable with the
   previous years.
   Sources: Lampiran Pidato Kenegaraan, and BPS, *Indikator Ekonomi*, various issues.

Figure 9.1 The growth of services output, 1966–92, p. 180
   Unit: %
   Notes and Sources: As for Figure 2.1.

Figure 9.2 The growth of physical infrastructure, 1969–92, pp. 182–3
   DWT—deadweight ton
   Mwh—megawatt hour
   Source: Lampiran Pidato Kenegaraan, various issues.

Figure 9.3 The growth of tourism, 1969–92, p. 187
   b In constant 1985 prices.
   Source: Lampiran Pidato Kenegaraan, various issues.

Figure 9.4 Bank deposits by ownership, 1972–93, p. 189
   Unit: % of total
   Note: End of year, except for 1993 which is end-October.
   b Includes development banks, which are a minor proportion of the total (3.3% in
   1993) and are not strictly state-owned.
   Source: Nota Keuangan, various issues.

Figure 9.5 The Jakarta stock exchange, 1985–93, p. 190

   Note: End of year, except for 1993 which is end-June.

   Source: Bapepam, and Jakarta Stock Exchange.

Figure 10.1 Trends in real wages, 1972–90, p. 203

   Unit: Indices, 1983=100

   Notes and Sources: **Manufacturing:** The total refers to average yearly earnings per worker in firms with at least 20 employees, for all non-oil manufacturing. 'Textiles' includes textiles, clothing, footwear and leather processing. The source is BPS, *Statistik Industri*, various issues. **Rice:** Average daily wage rates for hoeing in West, Central and East Java, from BPS data. **Estates:** Earnings of permanent workers in all activities, from BPS data. **Construction:** Average monthly wages of construction labourers in Jakarta, from unpublished data of the Department of Public Works. **Civil Servants:** Basic salary of a primary-education civil servant, from unpublished data of the Department of Finance. All data have been deflated by the Indonesian CPI, except for hoeing wages, which are deflated by rice prices. I am indebted to Chris Manning for providing the rice, estates, construction, and civil servants wage data, which were reported in an earlier version of Manning (1994). The growth rates are calculated on the basis of three-year moving averages. '1972' and '1990' refer respectively to the earliest and latest three-year periods for which data are available; '1984' refers to 1983–85.

Figure 10.2 Education enrolment, 1971–90, p. 208

   Unit: % of each age attending school

   Source: The original source is BPS, *Sensus Penduduk*, 1971, 1980, 1990. I am indebted to Gavin Jones and Pat Quiggan for providing these data.

Figure 11.1 Regional economic growth, 1983–90, p. 233

   Source: BPS, Regional Accounts.